PENGUIN

THE ROBBERS · WALLENSTEIN

FRIEDRICH SCHILLER, poet, critic, historian and the principal dramatist of German Classicism, was born at Marbach, near Stuggart, in 1759. The dominating theme of his work is a passionate concern with personal and political freedom. He began his dramatic career as a belated member of the German 'Storm and Stress' movement, the first major outburst of European Romanticism. But after his violent and rebellious early plays, he turned in *Don Carlos* (1786) to historical tragedy in the grand manner. Though the theme of freedom continues to run through his finest classical works, the *Wallenstein* trilogy and *Maria Stuart* (1800), the lesson of the French Revoution was not lost on the erstwhile revolutionary and his mature dramas are principally concerned with attempts to achieve ideal spiritual freedom and to overcome the constraints imposed by fate, by the weakness of human character, by the impersonal forces of physical and historical necessity. In this the influence of Kantian philosophy is evident. But in his last completed play, *Wilhelm Tell*, both personal and political freedom are finally triumphant. From 1789 Schiller held a chair of history at Jena, and in the following years developed a close relationship with Goethe in neighbouring Weimar. He died in Weimar in 1805.

F. J. LAMPORT, now retired, taught German at Oxford for many years. He has published a number of studies of classical German literature, especially drama. The present translation of *Wallenstein* was the basis of the adaptation performed by the Royal Shakespeare Theatre Company in 1993.

FRIEDRICH SCHILLER

THE ROBBERS

WALLENSTEIN

TRANSLATED
WITH AN INTRODUCTION BY
F. J. LAMPORT

PENGUIN BOOKS

PENGUIN BOOKS

Published by the Penguin Group
Penguin Books Ltd, 80 Strand, London WC2R 0RL, England
Penguin Putnam Inc., 375 Hudson Street, New York, New York 10014, USA
Penguin Books Australia Ltd, 250 Camberwell Road, Camberwell, Victoria 3124, Australia
Penguin Books Canada Ltd, 10 Alcorn Avenue, Toronto, Ontario, Canada M4V 3B2
Penguin Books India (P) Ltd, 11 Community Centre, Panchsheel Park, New Delhi – 110 017, India
Penguin Books (NZ) Ltd, Cnr Rosedale and Airborne Roads, Albany, Auckland, New Zealand
Penguin Books (South Africa) (Pty) Ltd, 24 Sturdee Avenue, Rosebank 2196, South Africa

Penguin Books Ltd, Registered Offices: 80 Strand, London WC2R 0RL, England

www.penguin.com

This translation first published 1979

039

Copyright © F. J. Lamport 1979
All rights reserved

Printed and bound in Great Britain by Clays Ltd, Elcograf S.p.A.
Set in Monotype Bembo

ISBN-13: 978-0-14-044368-4

www.greenpenguin.co.uk

CONTENTS

INTRODUCTION

THIS volume contains the first tragedy Schiller produced, written in 1780, and the dramatic trilogy which opened the series of his mature classical masterpieces nineteen years later. Naturally enough, they are very different works, worlds apart in most of their external features. Yet both bear their author's characteristic stamp in their grand rhetoric and powerful dramatic situations, in their blend of idealism and realism – of the sense of the boundless potential of the human spirit, and of the cruel frustrations to which it is submitted in the harsh business of life – and above all in their central theme. For both are concerned with freedom: with man's attempt to spread his wings and fly, to be the arbiter of his own destiny, even to change the world in accordance with his own designs.

Friedrich Schiller was born in 1759, the son of a junior officer in the service of Duke Karl Eugen of Württemberg, one of the more notoriously extravagant and tyrannical of the eighteenth-century German despots. When the boy was fourteen, he was taken from his parents and consigned, against their wishes and his own, to the military academy which the Duke, in furtherance of his grand designs, had founded in Stuttgart for the production of efficient servants of the state. The curriculum of the academy was advanced for its day, and some of the teachers were able, enlightened and sympathetic men, from whom the young Schiller learnt a great deal; but the general atmosphere was one of stifling, rigid military discipline, with the Duke himself exercising close personal supervision. Small wonder that Schiller felt with the keenness of his own experience the truth of Rousseau's message that man was born free, but everywhere was in chains. Written in the academy, *The Robbers* is accordingly a play of dreams of rebel-

lion, of gestures of heroic defiance. But it also shows with
surprising percipience the tragedy which must ensue when
such dreams are lived, such gestures acted out in reality. Karl
Moor identifies the injustice he has suffered with the wrongs
of humanity at large, and sets out to put the world to rights;
but in so doing he becomes, as he is forced to recognize, as
great a monster as his brother Franz, the author of his original
wrong. And Franz himself is not merely a melodramatic villain
(though he certainly is that), but, as Schiller noted, a *speculative*
villain, an experimental philosopher of evil; moreover, he too
is a rebel. Karl rebels against man-made institutions, the law,
the state and society; on the face of it, Franz represents those
institutions – but he is a rebel against deeper ties of blood
and human affection and against nature itself, and is as
conscious of his rebellious role as Karl is of his. Each is ultimately in his rebellion driven to despair (it is a key word of the
play), and each is destroyed, or destroys himself; though Karl
by his recognition and repentance manages to retain his human
dignity, while Franz dies like a rat (the animal imagery forms
another linking pattern running throughout the work). The
conflict between the two brothers is less important than the
parallel between them: their destinies unfold side by side,
mirror images of each other; most remarkably, they never
meet on stage. Schiller himself evidently thought this was odd,
for in his revision of the play for the Mannheim theatre, Franz
does not kill himself but is brought back by Schweitzer to be
judged by Karl. But the first version is much more logical:
Karl *cannot*, morally, judge his brother; and in the revised final
scene neither he nor, it seems, Schiller really knows what to do
with him. He is handed over to the robbers, who consign him
to the dungeon from which the old Count Moor had been
rescued; but this is feeble, compared to the way in which
Schiller had originally made the two brothers confront their
distinct, though parallel fates. The motif of hostile brothers
was a contemporary favourite, but Schiller's unusual treatment

of it highlights his originality. In fact, scarcely any of the elements which go to make up *The Robbers* was his own invention, but of them he has made something utterly new. In his preface, disclaiming any ambition to see the work performed (though it is in fact superbly theatrical, and is, deservedly, revived on the German stage at least as often as any of his other plays), Schiller calls the work 'a novel in dramatic form'; and indeed, not only does it defy all the received rules, the unities and the proprieties of eighteenth-century drama, but it has much in common with what we have learnt to call 'epic theatre'. Its plot, as such, is conventional, melodramatic, and full of inconsistencies and improbabilities; but this does not matter, for the mechanics of the action merely serve as a thread to link a series of powerful scenes whose real structural coherence is to be found in parallel and contrast, in repetition and variation, of character and situation, of theme and image. Within the robber band Karl has another powerful foil in Spiegelberg, a curious mixture of bogus Messiah, universal confidence-trickster, and the kind of hectoring N.C.O. at whose hands (and tongue) Cadet Schiller had no doubt suffered. But again, though he and Karl are ostensibly rivals, there is virtually no direct conflict between them. The other bandits are not really distinguished as individuals. The least successful scenes in the play are, as Schiller himself admitted, those with Amalia. She is an excessively sentimental and 'literary' character, and her death is unconvincing – it is clear only that she has somehow to be got rid of. But if one can accept the frank melodrama in the spirit in which it is meant, scenes like those between Karl and Amalia in Act IV can still have a powerful emotional impact.

The style of the play is wild and unfettered, spanning a wide range from passages of lofty rhetoric, adorned with Biblical and Shakespearian echoes, to others of rough colloquial crudity spiced with obscenities (fairly shocking by the standards of the day), student slang, and a fair sprinkling of those untranslatable

German meteorological oaths (I am in general a believer in literal translation, but 'Thunder, lightning, hail and storm!' will clearly never do). Karl's passionate outbursts are mocked in Franz's discursive schemings and the vulgar boastings of Spiegelberg. The more emotional scenes strain the expressive possibilities of prose to the limit, and here Schiller inserts songs or lyrical interludes which sum up a character, a situation or a mood; one of the Shakespearian devices so often imitated by German dramatists of this generation. Violence of language is also paralleled in violence of stage direction: old Count Moor tears his face and hair, Franz writhes in his armchair, Karl runs against a tree. (Schiller, we are told, ruined a performance of Goethe's *Clavigo* at the academy in 1780, reducing the spectators to laughter by his convulsively exaggerated gestures in the title role.) This kind of thing is overdone; and it must also be admitted that Schiller's changes of register are sometimes awkward and unconvincing. But the violence and the excesses are only the overflowings of the vigour and passion which are the play's propelling force. As Carlyle wrote, 'It is in vain that we rebel against the inconsistencies and crudities of the work: its faults are redeemed by the living energy that pervades it.'

The play was published in 1781 and performed, drastically cut and revised, in Mannheim in January 1782, Schiller having gone absent without leave from Stuttgart to be present at the first night. It was a tremendous success; it earned Schiller the Duke's displeasure, but he was soon emboldened to leave Württemberg for good and establish himself as a playwright in Mannheim. A number of editions appeared, one bearing the motto *In tirannos*. The play and its author were indeed widely regarded as subversive, even revolutionary. In a number of places performance was actually forbidden on these grounds, although the stage version had already been back-dated from the eighteenth* to the sixteenth century in setting lest the

---

* The action takes place about the middle of the century: the battle of Prague, in which Karl in II.ii is reported killed, was fought in 1757.

attack on tyranny should seem too topical. Schiller's fame spread to Italy, to Britain, to revolutionary France: on the strength of a French translation or rather adaptation of his play, Schiller was on 26 August 1792 proclaimed an honorary citizen of the French republic. And although by this time Schiller was a declared opponent of the Revolution, and even in the play itself had depicted the inevitable failure of rebellion, and the voluntary submission of his principal hero to the forces of law and the established order, the gesture was not inappropriate: for *The Robbers* is the supreme tragedy of liberty and fraternity.

The *Wallenstein* trilogy was completed in 1799. In those intervening years, Schiller had completed three more plays before turning in 1786 to the study of aesthetics, philosophy and history and producing a series of notable essays in those fields. He had made the acquaintance of Goethe, the giant of German literature, ten years older than himself; after an initial coldness – Goethe had disapproved of the wild young poet of *The Robbers* – they became friends and collaborators, determined to create a 'classical' German literature which would put their native language on a cultural level with the other European tongues. And he had lived through some of the most momentous events of European history, events which could not fail to arouse the passionate interest of a writer whose principal theme was freedom. Up to the writing of *Don Carlos* and the *Ode to Joy* in the mid-eighties Schiller remains an enthusiastic champion of liberty and the brotherhood of man, though he never loses sight of the perils with which such high ideals are attended. The first stages of the French Revolution he welcomed, as did so many of his contemporaries, as a victory over tyranny and a confirmation of the eighteenth-century belief in enlightenment and progress; but subsequent events, above all the Terror of 1792, shocked him profoundly, as a relapse into barbarism, a tyranny worse than that it had replaced, a refutation of the meaning of history. Europe in the nineties seemed to be reverting to the chaos of the Thirty

Years' War of the previous century (1618–48), which on ostensibly ideological grounds (it was supposedly a war between Catholics and Protestants) had inflicted senseless destruction on huge tracts of Europe, Germany in particular. The parallels scarcely needed to be emphasized. Even the figure of Wallenstein had his contemporary equivalents: the soldier of fortune, carried along on the tide of history; the 'great man' at the heart of events, who seems to control them, believes himself that he does, but is perhaps really at the mercy of other, lesser men, of chance, of the blind causality of events themselves. It has even been suggested that Schiller had Napoleon Bonaparte in mind. Though Bonaparte's star was rising rapidly at the time of completion of the trilogy (he became First Consul in 1799), this seems very unlikely; but Schiller's Wallenstein is at least as much a study of a man betrayed by his delusions of historical destiny and his belief in his own power as is Tolstoy's Napoleon in *War and Peace*.

All Schiller's later plays are concerned with the problematic nature of historical greatness, but none more than this; and to illustrate this theme, Schiller could not have picked a better protagonist. Albrecht von Wallenstein (or Waldstein) was a minor, impecunious Bohemian nobleman who during the first half of the Thirty Years' War rose, largely by adroit speculation in land and war profits, to become one of the richest and most powerful men in Europe; by 1625 he was a Duke, and his estate of Friedland in Northern Bohemia, with its capital at Gitschin (Jičin), was like a little kingdom, virtually independent of Bohemia and of the Holy Roman Emperor Ferdinand. He became commander-in-chief of the Imperial (Catholic) forces, was removed from the post in 1630 largely on account of the jealousy of the old-established princes of the Empire, notably Maximilian of Bavaria, but within eighteen months was reappointed; in 1633 he was negotiating with the Protestants to bring the war to an end – but the negotiations came to nothing; in 1634 he was assassinated on the grounds of his alleged intention to defect to the Protestant side, and the war dragged on for another fourteen years. Wallenstein was a legend in his own lifetime. He held court with a magnificence fully commensurate with his wealth and power; as he was so rich, he would have none less than Kepler to cast his horoscope (Kepler forecast disaster for 1634); his eccentricities, such as his hypersensitivity to noise, were eagerly embroidered by the popular imagination; to complete the myth, his body was allegedly found to be quite undecomposed two years after his death – though in the last year or so of his life he was almost falling to pieces with some form of gout. More important, nobody knew and nobody has ever known what his true motives were; even to our own day historians disagree as to whether he is to be accounted amongst the heroes or the villains of the past – whether he genuinely desired peace (and if so, whether he could have achieved it) or merely sought his own aggrandizement. This profound historical enigma is the subject of Schiller's play; though of course as an artist he is, as he tells us in his Prologue, not concerned to *solve* it, but merely to exhibit it in the light of his imagination. Moreover, Schiller's Wallenstein is not merely an enigma to the historian, and the object of radically different interpretations by his friends and enemies in the play; he is an enigma to himself.

It is here that Schiller's portrayal of the historical character takes on more general philosophical and moral aspects: Wallenstein is presented to us as a man who has perceived, but cannot solve, the paradox of human freedom. Man's experience of choice, of decision and action, tells him that he is a free agent; but his observation of the world about him shows him chains of cause and effect and the workings of immutable laws, embracing himself, his own actions and their consequences. He is free to act, but once he has acted he has committed himself and is free no longer. Wallenstein seeks to preserve his freedom of choice even in a situation which demands that the choice – open rebellion, or submission to the Emperor – be actually made; as a result, he hesitates until it is too late, when the choice has been taken away from him by the decisions of others. He seeks reassurance from the stars; contrary to history, Schiller makes him take up astrology only after the shock of his first dismissal, as a prop or substitute for his shaken self-reliance, and like many consulters of horoscopes, he ignores the signs when they are unfavourable. Despite repeated warnings, he never realizes the falsity of his position; despite the example of young Max Piccolomini, he will not realize that one must make one's choice and accept the consequences, even unto death; he retains his capacity for self-deception to the end – his very last words, laden though they are with tragic irony for the spectator, should be read brusquely, even brutally, without a hint of conscious pathos. Yet in his death we undoubtedly feel the sense of tragic waste: we see in him a figure of tremendous, though unrealized, potential; a greater man by far than either of his principal antagonists, the political realist Octavio Piccolomini, who may be on the right side* but whose actions are morally disastrous, or the idealist Max, who preserves his moral integrity only by a death which is not so much a deed of heroism as a gesture of despair. At the end of *The Robbers*, the moral order was restored through tragic sacrifice; but *Wallenstein* ends grimly, with the victory of Nothingness, as Hegel put it, of death over life. Even Octavio ultimately achieves nothing by his machinations but the destruction of a man who was once his friend, the alienation and death of his only son, and the loss of his own self-respect – the princely title he has earned can only be a perpetual reproach to him.

* Schiller was a Protestant, and his own *History of the Thirty Years' War* has a definite Protestant bias; the play also clearly requires us to take seriously (as Max does) the suggestion that Wallenstein is seeking to end the war, the Emperor to prolong it. But ultimately, within the play at any rate, the Emperor is Wallenstein's legitimate overlord and disloyalty to him a fatal moral transgression.

The world depicted is one in which goodness, truth and beauty cannot survive.

The conflict between the three characters Wallenstein, Max and Octavio is the heart of the drama. (The character of Octavio is historical, but Max is a fictitious personage introduced by Schiller for his dramatic purposes.) And whereas in *The Robbers* there was little direct conflict and no direct confrontation between the principal antagonists, here the conflict is acted out in a series of major scenes of argument and decision (though it is obviously of the essence of Octavio's manoeuvrings against Wallenstein that they are carried on behind his back). Once again, though, these scenes form a pattern of repetition and variation, linked and extended by the play's imagery. Particularly noteworthy are the images of crooked and straight, with their obvious (which is not to say simple) moral connotations, and the theme of the urgency of time, which runs through the play from the very first line of *The Piccolomini*, where Butler welcomes Isolani, 'better late than never', to the end of *Wallenstein's Death*, where the same Butler brutally tells Gordon that Octavio has arrived 'too late' to countermand his fatal order. Around the central core, the subsidiary characters are deftly sketched in: the various officers, each a distinct individual but none claiming too much of our attention; minor figures such as the grotesque Seni or the garrulous cellarer; an important, sharply-contrasted group of female characters, whose debates and conflicts echo those of the male protagonists.

Formally this is a much more rigorous work than *The Robbers*. Schiller had decisively turned his back on the deliberately chaotic, avant-garde style of his early work: his aim in *Wallenstein* was, he declared, to combine the best of Sophocles, Shakespeare, and French classical drama. In this he was successful to a high degree: the play has tautness and concentrated action combined with breadth of portrayal, classical discipline combined with variety of character, scene and tone. But as he worked, it became evident that this rich mass of dramatic and thematic material could not be confined within the normal limits of a five-act drama. The conflict between the two Piccolomini, father and son, became almost a drama in its own right, and could fill an evening by itself. (Just as this conflict is really only one part or aspect of the larger, three-way conflict, however, so the division between the phases of the action is to some extent arbitrary: as first performed, *The Piccolomini* included what were subsequently printed as the first two acts of *Wallenstein's Death*.) And Schiller also realized that he needed to depict Wallenstein's power and reputation amongst the common soldiery, the base on which his political power rested. Shakespeare would have provided a subsidiary action with its own group of 'low' characters – its Falstaffs and Bardolphs and Pistols – threaded through the course of the whole drama. Schiller however chooses to separate this element from the main body of the tragedy in the form of an independent dramatic prelude, *Wallenstein's Camp*. The *Camp* is one of Schiller's most remarkable and original creations. It shows us, in the words of the Prologue, Wallenstein's shadow: the various characters prefigure elements in Wallenstein himself, or in other protagonists of the main drama, reduced as it were to silhouette. It illustrates the growth of legend about the historical figure, and explores the mysterious relationship between the great names and the great events recorded in the history books and the lives and doings of anonymous, ordinary people; it shows us something of what the war meant in everyday terms to the common people over whose fields and houses and bodies it was fought. Many of the themes of the main action – 'those objects men hold most sublime', as the Prologue defines them – are anticipated here: power, freedom, loyalty, the choice of life and death. All this is done effortlessly, with no pretensions to classicity, in a series of lively sketches, a kind of historical revue: once again we are in the realm of 'epic theatre'.

Though he had written two more plays in prose after *The Robbers*, Schiller soon came to feel the need for a more harmonious and generally elevated dramatic medium. A number of German eighteenth-century dramatists had experimented with blank verse – again in imitation of English drama and specifically of Shakespeare – and Schiller chose this metre for *Don Carlos* (1786) and for all his subsequent plays. He may employ occasional rhymes and metrical variations, or interpolate lyrical strophic forms, but he never again uses prose (except in quotation marks, as in the generals' oath to Wallenstein). It is perhaps fair to say that compared with Shakespeare's (or even Goethe's or Kleist's), Schiller's dramatic verse is rhetorical rather than poetic: that is, situations, emotions and ideas are expressed *through* the words rather than perceived and grasped *in* them. But it is still an impressive instrument, capable of powerful, memorable formulations and a wide range of tone: the musings of Wallenstein and the brutality of his murderers, the enthusiasm of Max and the political arguments of Octavio. *Wallenstein's Camp* is written throughout in quite a different metre. In keeping with its historical colour and revue-like character, Schiller chose for it, alone amongst his dramatic works, the same traditional German rhymed doggerel verse that Goethe had adopted for his *Faust*. But even in the *Camp* Schiller retains the classical French convention of counting a new 'scene' for each new entrance or exit. Only in *The Robbers* did he use 'scene' in the English sense of a break in the action with a change of setting.

As has been mentioned, Schiller drastically revised *The Robbers* for stage performance, so that two widely differing basic texts were current in his lifetime; whole sheets of the first printed edition were changed in the press; there are innumerable variants, and no single version can claim to be definitive.

The text translated here (complete, I believe, for the first time) is the fullest, that of the first printed edition. No such problems arise in the case of *Wallenstein*. Coleridge's translation of 1800 was made from a manuscript copy which retained the original division between *The Piccolomini* and *Wallenstein's Death*, rather than that subsequently adopted for printed publication. Coleridge omitted the *Camp* from his version, among other reasons 'from the incongruity of those lax verses with the present taste of the English Public'. I have included not only the *Camp* but also the blank verse Prologue designed for the first performance (of the *Camp* by itself) on 12 October 1798, which also marked the reopening of the Weimar court theatre: in part it is simply an occasional piece, but it is also a statement of Schiller's artistic intentions and an introduction to some of the main work's major themes, notably its historical aspect.

There were other things in the trilogy besides the *Camp* of which Coleridge was critical. To one passage he appends the note, 'There are few, who will not have taste enough to laugh at the concluding lines of this soliloquy; and still fewer, I would fain hope, who would not have been more disposed to shudder, had I given a *faithful* translation.' Perhaps the reader of the present version will be able to guess which is the speech in question: I have not made it my business to censor or improve on Schiller, but I hope the reader will not too often feel disposed either to laugh or to shudder except as Schiller intended. With a few exceptions I have kept German names throughout. In *The Robbers* to do otherwise would have produced to my mind quite inappropriate associations. (Charles and Francis? Charlie and Frank?) I have also decided to retain the traditional rendering of the title, even if it is only a transliteration of the German *Die Räuber*, for I do not think there is a fully adequate English equivalent. In *Wallenstein* there is the question of German versus Czech forms for Bohemian place and personal names. The historian will tend to use the Czech forms, but Schiller naturally used German and I have followed him. This is partly for manageability – 'Terzky' fits English tongues and English verse better than 'Trčka' – but also because the characters and events are, after all, Schiller's and not the historian's. Like any dramatist, Schiller has altered, compressed, omitted, invented for his own purposes. The facts are in the history books for those who seek them. The name 'Piccolomini' is stressed on the third syllable, 'Sesina' (which is Czech, not Italian) on the first.

THE ROBBERS

A PLAY

What drugs cure not, *iron* will cure;
what iron cures not, *fire* will cure.

(HIPPOCRATES)

CHARACTERS

COUNT MAXIMILIAN VON MOOR

KARL
FRANZ ⎫ his sons

AMALIA VON EDELREICH, his niece

SPIEGELBERG
SCHWEITZER
GRIMM
RATZMANN ⎫ libertines and bandits
SCHUFTERLE
ROLLER
SCHWARZ

KOSINSKY

HERRMANN, bastard son of a nobleman

DANIEL, Count Moor's servant

PASTOR MOSER

A PRIEST

ROBBERS, and others

The scene of the action is Germany;
the duration about two years.

ACT ONE

SCENE I

A room in OLD MOOR'*s castle in Franconia.*

[FRANZ VON MOOR, OLD MOOR.]

FRANZ: But are you sure you are well, father? You look so pale.

OLD MOOR: Quite well, my boy; what did you have to tell me?

FRANZ: The post has arrived; a letter from our informant in Leipzig –

OLD MOOR [*eagerly*]: News of my son Karl?

FRANZ: H'm, h'm! – Yes, indeed. But I am afraid – I don't know – whether I should – your health – Father, are you really quite well?

OLD MOOR: As fit as a fiddle! Is it about my son, his letter? – why are you so anxious? That is twice you have asked me.

FRANZ: If you are not well – if you have the slightest suspicion that you are not well, then let me – I will tell you at some more appropriate moment. [*Half aside*] This is no news for a delicate constitution.

OLD MOOR: God in Heaven, what can it be?

FRANZ: Let me first turn aside and shed a tear of pity for my lost brother – I ought to hold my peace for ever, for he is your son; I ought to conceal his disgrace for ever, for he is my brother. But to obey you is my first, sad duty; and so forgive me.

OLD MOOR: Oh, Karl, Karl! If only you knew how your wild

ways torture your old father's heart; if only you knew, how
a single piece of good news of you would add ten years to
my life – would make me young again; while now, ah,
every word brings me a step nearer the grave!

FRANZ: If that is so, old man, then goodbye – this very day we
should all be tearing our hair over your coffin.

OLD MOOR: Wait! It is only one single short step more – let
him have his will. [*Sitting down*] The sins of the fathers are
visited upon the third and the fourth generations – let it be
accomplished.

FRANZ [*taking the letter from his pocket*]: You know our informant. Look! I would give the finger of my right hand to
be able to say he was a liar, a black and venomous liar – Be
prepared! Forgive me if I do not give you the letter to read
for yourself – you shall not at once hear everything.

OLD MOOR: Everything, everything – my son, you will spare
me the need for crutches.

FRANZ [*reading*]: 'Leipzig, May 1st. – If it were not that the
most solemn promise binds me not to conceal the slightest
piece of information I can come by regarding the fate of
your brother, then, my dear friend, never should my innocent pen have exercised such tyranny over you. From a
hundred of your letters I can tell how news of this kind must
pierce a brother's heart like a dagger; it is as if I could see the
worthless wretch –'

   [OLD MOOR *covers his face.*]

Father, look! it is only the mildest parts I am reading – 'see
the wretch already costing you a thousand bitter tears' – ah,
they flowed, they poured streaming down my cheeks in
pity – 'it is as if I could see your good old father, deathly
pale already' – Dear God! and so you are, already, before
you have heard anything at all?

OLD MOOR: Go on! Go on!

FRANZ: – 'deathly pale already, reeling in his chair, and cursing the day those childish lips first framed the name "father".

I could not find out everything, and of the little that I know
it is only a little that I tell. Your brother, it seems, has run
the whole gamut of infamy; I at any rate know nothing
worse than the things he has done, though his imagination
may well surpass the bounds of mine. Last night at midnight
he made a grand resolution – since he had run up debts of
forty thousand ducats' – a pretty sum, father – 'and as he
had robbed a rich banker's daughter here in town of her
honour, and fatally wounded her fiancé, a fine young fellow
of good birth, in a duel – to flee with seven others whom he
had depraved like himself and escape the arm of the law' –
father! In heaven's name, father! What is the matter?

OLD MOOR: It is enough! Stop, my son!

FRANZ: I will spare you – 'he has been declared a wanted man,
his victims are crying out for satisfaction, a price has been
put on his head – the name of Moor' – no! my miserable
lips shall never be my father's murderers! [*Tearing up the
letter*] Do not believe it, father! Do not believe one syllable
he writes!

OLD MOOR [*weeping bitterly*]: My name! my honourable
name!

FRANZ [*throwing his arms round his neck*]: Shameful, thrice
shameful Karl! Did I not suspect it, when he was still a boy,
and was always following after girls, chasing up hill and
down dale with street-urchins and ruffians, shunning the
sight of the church as a miscreant shuns the gaol, and tossing
the pennies he had wheedled from you to the first beggar he
met, while we sat at home improving our minds with
prayer and with reading pious sermons? Did I not suspect it,
when he would rather read the adventures of Julius Caesar
and Alexander the Great and other such benighted heathens
than the story of the penitent Tobias? A hundred times I
prophesied to you – for my love for him always kept the
limits set by a son's duty to his father – the boy will yet bring
shame and misery upon us all! Oh, that he did not bear the

name of Moor! that my heart did not beat so warmly for him! The sinful love for him, that I cannot suppress, will one day bear witness against me before the judgement seat of God.

OLD MOOR: Ah – my hopes, my golden dreams!

FRANZ: I know; that is what I was saying. The fiery spirit that burns in the lad, so you always said, that makes him yearn so keenly for every kind of beauty and grandeur; the frankness that mirrors his soul in his eyes, the tender feeling that melts him to tears of sympathy at any sight of suffering, the manly courage that sends him climbing hundred-year-old oak trees and leaping ditches and fences and foaming rivers; the youthful ambition, the implacable constancy; all these shining virtues that took root in his father's favourite son, one day will make him a friend's true friend, a model citizen, a hero, a great, great man – and now, father, look! the fiery spirit has grown, has burgeoned, has brought forth glorious fruit. See how this frankness has so neatly turned to insolence, see how this tenderness coos for any coquette, so readily yields to the seduction of a Phryne! See how this fiery genius has burnt up the oil of its life in six short years, to the last drop, so that to his very face people can say 'Voilà, c'est l'amour qui a fait ça!' No, just look at this bold imagination, just look at the plans it makes and carries out, so that the heroic deeds of a Cartouche or a Howard* pale into insignificance beside them! And only let these magnificent beginnings grow to full maturity – for after all, who can expect perfection at such a tender age? Perhaps, father, you will live to see the glorious day when he is the commander of an army, ensconced in the stillness of the forests, ready to ease the weary wanderer's journey by taking half his burden from him – perhaps before you are laid to rest you will be able to visit his monument, that he will have erected

*Notorious seventeenth- and eighteenth-century highwaymen (*Translator's note*).

for him between heaven and earth – perhaps, oh father, father, father – find yourself another name, or shopkeepers and street-urchins will point their fingers at you, for they will have seen your fine son's portrait at Leipzig fair!

OLD MOOR: And you too, my Franz, you too? Oh, my children! How they pierce my heart!

FRANZ: You see, I have my wits about me too; but my wit is the bite of scorpions. – And then that everyday dullard, that cold, wooden Franz, and all the other names that the contrast between the two of us so often prompted, when he sat on your lap or pinched your cheek – one day he will die within the walls of his own estate, and rot and be forgotten, while the fame of this virtuoso flies from pole to pole – ah! gracious Heaven, see him join his hands in gratitude to you, that dry, cold, wooden Franz – that he is so unlike him!

OLD MOOR: Forgive me, my son; do not be angry with a father whose expectations have been dashed. The God who sends me tears through Karl will wipe them away, my Franz, by your hand.

FRANZ: Yes, father, my hand shall wipe them away. Your Franz will make it his life's work to lengthen your days. Your life shall be the oracle that I will consult above all else in all my doings; the glass in which I shall see all things; no duty shall be too sacred for me to break it in the service of your precious life. Will you believe me?

OLD MOOR: You bear a heavy burden of duty, my son – God bless you for what you have been and for what you shall be to me!

FRANZ: But tell me, now – If you did not have to call this son your own, would you be a happy man?

OLD MOOR: Oh, still! – when the midwife brought him to me, I lifted him up to Heaven and cried: am I not a happy man?

FRANZ: So you said. And now, have you found it so? You envy the wretchedest of your peasants, that he is not the father of this son – Sorrow will be yours as long as you have this son. That grief will grow with Karl. That sorrow will undermine your days.

OLD MOOR: Oh! it has made me like a man of fourscore years.

FRANZ: Why, then – if you were to disown this son of yours?

OLD MOOR [*starting up*]: Franz! Franz! What are you saying?

FRANZ: Is it not your love for him that brings you all this grief? Without that love, he exists for you no longer. Without this criminal love, this sinful love, he is dead for you – he was never born to you. Not flesh and blood, the heart makes father and son. Love him no more, and this degenerate is no longer your son, were he cut from the flesh of your own body. He was the apple of your eye, but it is written, if thine eye offend thee, pluck it out; it is better for thee to enter into the kingdom of God with one eye, than having two eyes to be cast into hell fire. Better to enter childless into the kingdom of God, than that father and son should be cast into hell fire. It is the word of God!

OLD MOOR: You would have me curse my son?

FRANZ: Not so, not so! It is not your son that I would have you curse. What is he that you call your son? he whom you gave his life, while he spares no effort to shorten yours?

OLD MOOR: Oh, it is true, it is all too true! it is a judgement upon me! The Lord wills it so!

FRANZ: See how the child of your bosom treats its father. Through your father's sympathy he strangles you, murders you through your love, has importuned your father's heart itself to strike the final blow. When once you are no more, he is master of your estates and king of his passions. The dam is broken, and the torrent of his desires can rage freely on. Imagine yourself in his place! How often he must wish them under the earth, his father, his brother, who stand pitiless in the way of his excesses? But is that love for love? Is that filial gratitude for a father's tenderness? When he sacrifices ten years of your life to a moment's lust? when he gambles the good name of his fathers, unspotted for seven centuries, on the pleasure of a fleeting minute? Is that he whom you call your son? Answer! Do you call that a son?

OLD MOOR: An unloving child! oh! but still my child! still my child!

FRANZ: A precious, darling child, whose sole pursuit it is, not to know it has a father. Oh, if only you would learn to see it as it is! if only the scales would fall from your eyes! But your indulgence can only confirm him in his depravity, your support give it legitimacy. Yes, indeed, you will turn aside the curse from his head; upon you, father, upon you will the curse of damnation fall.

OLD MOOR: It is just! it is only just! Mine, mine is all the fault!

FRANZ: How many thousands who have drained the cup of pleasure to the dregs have been brought by suffering to see the error of their ways! And does not the bodily pain which accompanies every excess bear the fingerprint of the divine will? Should man by cruel mercifulness turn it aside? Shall a father let go to eternal damnation what is entrusted to him? – Think, father, if you deliver him up to his misery for a little while, will he not have to mend his ways and learn to be a better man? or else he will remain a scoundrel, even in that great school of misery, and then – woe to the father who flouted the decrees of a higher wisdom by his tenderness! – What then, father?

OLD MOOR: I will write and say that my hand is turned from him.

FRANZ: What you do is just and wise.

OLD MOOR: That he shall not show his face before me.

FRANZ: It will work to his salvation.

OLD MOOR [*tenderly*]: Until he mend his ways!

FRANZ: Very well, very well! But if then he should come with the mask of the hypocrite, should gain your pity by his tears and your forgiveness by his flattery, and the next day should mock your weakness in the arms of his whores? No, father! He will come of his own accord, when his conscience tells him he is free.

OLD MOOR: Then I will write this moment and tell him so.

FRANZ: Stop! just one more word, father! Your indignation, I fear, might dictate too harsh words for your pen, words that would rend his heart – and then, – do you not think he might even take it as a token of forgiveness, that you deign to write to him with your own hand? It will be better to let me write for you.

OLD MOOR: Do so, my son. – Ah! it would have broken my heart! Tell him –

FRANZ [quickly]: Shall I, then?

OLD MOOR: Tell him that a thousand tears of blood – tell him that a thousand sleepless nights – But do not drive my son to despair.

FRANZ: Should you not go to bed, father? It was hard for you to bear.

OLD MOOR: Tell him that his father's bosom – I tell you, do not drive my son to despair. [Exit, sadly.]

FRANZ [watching him go, and laughing]: Console yourself, old man, you will never clasp him to that bosom, the way to it is firmly barricaded to him, as heaven is to hell. – He was torn from your arms before you knew that you could will it so – I should be a poor hand at it, if I could not manage to prise a son from his father's heart, and if he were bound to it with fetters of brass – I have drawn a magic circle of curses about you, that he will not be able to cross – Good luck, Franz! The favourite is gone; things are looking brighter. I must pick up all these pieces of paper, someone might easily recognize my hand – [collecting the torn pieces of the letter]. And the old man's grief will soon put an end to him; and she – I must drive her precious Karl from her thoughts too, even if he is half her life to her. I have every right to be resentful of

nature; and by my honour, I will make my rights known!
Why was I not the first to creep out of our mother's womb?
Why not the only one? Why did nature burden me with
this ugliness? why me? Just as if she had been bankrupt when
I was born. Why should I have this Laplander's nose? Why
should I have these blackamoor's lips, these Hottentot's eyes?
I truly think she made a heap of the most hideous parts of
every human kind as the ingredients for me. Death and
damnation! Who gave her the power to make him like that,
and to keep it from me? Could anyone pay court to her
before she made him? Or offend her, before he existed? Why
was she so partial about her own creation? No, no! I do her
an injustice. After all, she gave us the gift of ingenuity too
when she set us naked and miserable upon the shores of this
great ocean of the world: swim who can, and let sink who
is too clumsy! She gave me nothing; what I can make of
myself is my affair. Each man has the same right to the
greatest and the least; claim destroys claim, impulse destroys
impulse, force destroys force. Might is right, and the limits
of our strength our only law. It is true, there are certain conventions men have made, to rule the pulses that turn the
world. Honourable reputation! A valuable coin indeed, one
to drive a fine bargain with for the man who knows how to
use it. Conscience – yes, indeed! an excellent scarecrow, to
keep the sparrows from the cherry-trees! and a well-written
cheque to help the bankrupt too at the last moment. Yes
indeed, most admirable devices to keep fools respectful and
to hold down the mob, so that clever people can live in
better comfort. It must be admitted, most ingenious devices!
They remind me of the hedges my peasants plant so cunningly around their fields, so that the rabbits cannot jump
over – no, not on your life, not one single rabbit! – But
their lord and master sets spur to his horse, and gallops away
where the crops were standing. Poor little rabbit! It's a sad
part to play, to be a rabbit in this world! But your lord and

master needs his rabbits! So, away we go! Fear nothing, and you are as powerful as if all fear you. It is the fashion nowadays to lace one's breeches so that one can wear them tight or loose as one pleases. We will have ourselves a conscience made in the latest style, so that we can let it out nicely as we grow. How can we help it? Go to the tailor! I have heard a great deal of idle talk about something called love of one's kin, enough to turn a sound man's head. – He is your brother! which, being interpreted, is: he was baked in the same oven that you were; so let him be sacred to you! – Just consider this extraordinary conclusion, this ridiculous argument from the proximity of bodies to the harmony of minds; from the identity of domicile to the identity of feeling; from the uniformity of diet to the uniformity of inclination. But there is more to it – he is your father! He gave you life, you are his flesh and blood; so let him be sacred to you! Another cunning conclusion! I should like to know *why* he made me? Not out of love for me, surely, since there was no *me* to love? Did he know me before he made me? Or did he think of me while he was making me? Or did he wish for me as he was making me? Did he know what I should be like? I hope not, or I should want to punish him for making me regardless! Can I feel any gratitude to him for my being a man? No more than I could grudge it him if he had made me a woman. Can I acknowledge any love that does not rest on respect for my person? Could respect for my person exist, when my person could only come into being through that for which it must be the condition? And what is so sacred about it all? The act itself through which I was created? As if that were anything but the animal gratification of animal desires? Or the result of that act, when that is nothing but brute necessity, that one would gladly be rid of if one could, if it were not at the cost of flesh and blood. Am I to speak well of him for loving me? That is vanity, the professional sin of all artists, who fancy their own work, however ugly it may be. – There it is then, the witchcraft that they veil in clouds of holy incense to abuse our fearful natures. Am I too to let myself be led along by it, like a little boy? Very well, then! courage, and to work! I will crush everything that stands in the way of my becoming master. And master I must be, to force my way to goals that I shall never gain through kindness. [*Exit.*]

SCENE 2

A tavern on the borders of Saxony.

[KARL VON MOOR *deep in a book*, SPIEGELBERG *drinking at the table.*]

MOOR [*laying the book aside*]: I hate this age of scribblers, when I can pick up my Plutarch and read of great men.

SPIEGELBERG [*puts a glass before him. Drinking*]: Josephus is the man you should read.

MOOR: The bright spark of Promethean fire is burnt out. All we have now is a flash of witch-meal – stage lightning, not flame enough to light a pipe of tobacco. Here we scratch about like rats at Hercules' club, and addle our miserable brains with speculation over what he had between his legs. A French cleric proclaims that Alexander was a coward, a consumptive professor with a bottle of smelling-salts under his nose gives lectures on energy. Fellows who faint when they have had a girl write commentaries on the tactics of Hannibal – boys still wet behind the ears crib their proses from Livy on the battle of Cannae, and snivel over Scipio's victories because they have to construe them.

SPIEGELBERG: You go on in the grand style.

MOOR: A fine reward for your valour on the battlefield, to live on in the grammar-school, and be dragged around immortal in a schoolboy's satchel. A worthy repayment for the blood you shed, to be wrapped round buns by a Nuremberg confectioner, or if your luck's in, to be hoisted on stilts by a French tragedian, and pulled about like puppets on a string! Haha!

SPIEGELBERG [*drinking*]: I tell you, you should read Josephus.

MOOR: Pah! An age of eunuchs, fit for nothing but chewing over the deeds of bygone days, mutilating the heroes of old with their learned interpretations and mocking them with their tragedies. The strength of their loins is dried up, and the dregs of a beer-barrel must help to propagate mankind.

SPIEGELBERG: Tea, brother, tea!

MOOR: There they go, smother healthy nature with their ridiculous conventions. Haven't the courage to drain a glass, because they would have to wish 'Good health!' Fawn on the man who polishes His Highness's boots, and make life a misery for the wretch they have no need to fear. Praise each other to the skies for the sake of a dinner, and would gladly poison each other when they lose a bedstead at an auction. Damn the Sadducee who doesn't show himself enough in church, and reckon up their filthy lucre at the altar; fall on their knees so that they can show off their coat-tails the better; don't take their eye off the preacher, so as not to miss the cut of his wig. – Fall in a faint if they see a goose bleeding, and clap their hands when their rival goes bankrupt – No, however much I pleaded – 'Just one more day!' – no! to gaol with him, the dog! – Pleas! Oaths! Tears! [*Stamping his foot*] Hell and damnation!

SPIEGELBERG: And all for a few thousand miserable ducats –

MOOR: No, I'll not think of it. I am supposed to lace my body in a corset, and strait-jacket my will with laws. The law has cramped the flight of eagles to a snail's pace. The law never yet made a great man, but freedom will breed a giant, a colossus. They ensconce themselves in a tyrant's belly,

humour every whim of his digestion, and draw in their
breath when his guts rumble. – Oh, if only Arminius's spirit
still glowed in the ashes! – Give me an army of fellows like
me to command, and I'll turn Germany into a republic that
will make Rome and Sparta look like nunneries. [*Tosses his
sword onto the table and stands up.*]

SPIEGELBERG [*jumping up*]: Bravo! bravissimo! just what I
wanted to talk to you about! Look, Moor, I'll tell you something I've been thinking about for a long time, you're just
the man for it – drink up, have another – suppose we all
turned Jews, and started talking about the Kingdom again?

MOOR [*laughing out loud*]: Ha! I see, I see! You want to put
foreskins out of fashion, because the barber has had yours
already?

SPIEGELBERG: You clown! It is true, I do happen, strangely
enough, to be circumcised in advance. But look, isn't it a
brave and cunning plan? We'll send out a manifesto to all
the corners of the world and summon everyone who won't
eat pork to Palestine. I shall have authentic documents to
prove that Herod the Tetrarch was my great-great-grand-
father, and so on. Man, what a jubilation, when they find
their feet again, and can build Jerusalem anew. Then clear
the Turks out of Asia while the iron is still hot, cut down the
cedars of Lebanon, build ships, and flog ribbons and old tat
to all the nations. And then –

MOOR [*smiling, and taking him by the hand*]: Now, friend! No
more pranks of that kind.

SPIEGELBERG [*taken aback*]: Bah, you're not going to play the
prodigal son now, are you? A fellow like you, who has
written enough on faces with his sword to fill three attor-
neys' books in a leap year? Do you want me to tell the tale
of the dog's funeral? What? I shall have to remind you of
your own doings; that will put a spark into you again, if
nothing else can stir you up. Do you remember? Those fellows on the Council had had your mastiff's leg shot off, and

to pay them back, you proclaimed a fast in the whole town.
People grumbled about it. But you lost no time, bought up
all the meat in Leipzig, so that in eight hours there wasn't a
bone left to gnaw in the whole place, and the price of fish
began to rise. The town council and the worthies were plot-
ting revenge. Seventeen hundred of us lads out on the
streets, and you leading us, and butchers and tailors and
grocers following, and publicans and barbers and all the
tradesmen, and swore they would wreck the town if anyone
touched a hair of our heads. So they drew a blank, and went
off with their tails between their legs. You sent for a whole
panel of doctors, and offered three ducats to the one who
would write a prescription for the dog. We thought the
gentlemen would think it beneath their dignity and say no,
and had already agreed we were going to force them to do
it. But that wasn't necessary, they fought for the three
ducats, even when it was knocked down to threepence, they
wrote a dozen prescriptions in the hour, that soon finished
the brute off.

MOOR: Miserable creatures!

SPIEGELBERG: The funeral was arranged with all pomp and
ceremony, there were odes in honour of the departed dog,
and we went out at night, nearly a thousand of us, a lantern
in one hand and sword in the other, and so on through the
town with bells and music till we had buried the dog. Then
we stuffed ourselves with food till it was broad daylight, and
you thanked the gentlemen for their heartfelt sympathy, and
sold all the meat at half price. *Mort de ma vie!* They respected
us then, like a garrison in a conquered fortress –

MOOR: And you are not ashamed to boast of such a thing?
Haven't even shame enough to be ashamed of playing such
tricks?

SPIEGELBERG: Go along with you! I don't recognize Moor
any longer. Don't you remember how you have railed a
thousand times against the old skinflint, and said: let him

pinch and scrape, so that you could swill to your heart's content! Don't you remember? eh? don't you remember? Oh, you Godforsaken coxcomb, that was spoken like a man, like a man of breeding, but now –

MOOR: Curse you for reminding me of it! Curse myself for saying it! But it was only in the heat of the wine, and my heart knew not the vain things my tongue spoke.

SPIEGELBERG [*shaking his head*]: No, no, no! it cannot be! No, brother, you can never be in earnest. My dear fellow, is it hardship that makes you so downcast? Come, let me tell you one of my exploits when I was a lad. There beside my house was a ditch, eight feet wide at least, and we lads used to have contests, trying to jump across it. But it was no good. Flop! there you lay, and they hissed you and laughed at you, and threw snowballs at you, one after the other. Next door to our house a ranger kept his dog on a chain, a bad-tempered brute that used to bite, it would catch the girls by the skirt in no time if they didn't look out and went a shade too close. It was the best thing I knew to tease that dog whenever I could, and I would laugh till I was half dead to see the creature glowering so and longing to take a jump at me, if it could only get free. What happened? Another time I was giving it my usual treatment, and threw a stone and hit it so hard in the ribs, that it broke the chain, it was so furious, and was at me, and I was off and away like greased lightning. But hell's bells! there was the damned ditch in my way. What then? The dog at my heels, mad with rage, so never say die, a quick run up and – over I go. That jump saved my skin; the brute would have torn me to pieces.

MOOR: But why are you telling me this?

SPIEGELBERG: Why, to make you see – that necessity brings out the best in us! That's why I shan't be afraid if it comes to the worst. Danger fortifies our courage; our strength grows in adversity. Fate must intend to make a great man of me, since it crosses me so often.

MOOR [*irritated*]: What should we need courage for, that we have not dared already?

SPIEGELBERG: What? So you will let your talents moulder? Hide your light under a bushel? Do you really think your tomfooleries in Leipzig exhaust the range of human wit? Just wait till we have seen the wide world! Paris and London! – where you earn a box on the ears for calling anyone an honest man. It's a sight for sore eyes, to see business done on the grand scale! – I'll make you stare! I'll make your eyes pop! How to forge a signature – how to load dice – how to pick a lock – how to see the insides of a safe – just wait, and Spiegelberg will show you! The first gallows we come to, for the milksop who will rather go hungry than get his fingers dirty.

MOOR [*absently*]: What? You have done all that, and more, I suppose?

SPIEGELBERG: I do believe you don't trust me. Just wait, let me really get warmed up; you shall have the surprise of your life, your brain will turn somersaults in your head, when my wits are delivered of their progeny. [*Standing up, heatedly*] Why, I see it all now! Great thoughts are taking shape in my soul! Mighty plans are fermenting in my ingenious mind! Curse me for sleeping! [*striking his forehead*] for letting my energies lie fettered, my prospects barred and thwarted; I am awake, I feel what I am – what I must and shall be!

MOOR: You are a fool. The wine has gone to your head.

SPIEGELBERG [*in greater excitement*]: Spiegelberg, they will say, are you a magician, Spiegelberg? What a pity you did not become a general, Spiegelberg, the King will say, you would have beaten the Austrians into a cocked hat. Yes, I can hear the doctors complaining, it is wicked that he didn't take up medicine, he would have discovered a new powder for the goitre.* Ah! and that he didn't study economics, the

---

*Changed by Schiller in the press from 'a cure for the clap' (*Translator's note*).

Sullys* will sigh in their treasuries, he would have conjured louis d'or from stones. And Spiegelberg will be the name, in east and west, and into the mud with you, cowards and toads, as Spiegelberg spreads his wings and flies high into the temple of fame.

MOOR: Good fortune to you! Climb up on pillars of shame to the summits of glory. In the shady groves of my father's home, in my Amalia's arms a nobler pleasure waits for me. A week ago and more I wrote to my father begging his forgiveness. I did not conceal the slightest detail from him, and where there is honesty, there too is compassion and a helping hand. Let us say good-bye, Moritz. We shall see no more of each other after today. The post has arrived. My father's forgiveness is already within the walls of this town.

[*Enter* SCHWEITZER, GRIMM, ROLLER, SCHUFTERLE, RATZMANN.]

ROLLER: Do you know they are looking for us already?

GRIMM: That we are not safe from arrest at any minute?

MOOR: I am not surprised. Let it be as it will! Didn't you see Schwarz? Didn't he say anything about a letter he had for me?

ROLLER: He has been looking for you for a long time, I think it's something of the kind.

MOOR: Where is he, where, where? [*Making as if to hurry away.*]

ROLLER: Don't go! We told him to come here. You are shaking?

MOOR: I am not shaking. Why should I be shaking? Comrades! that letter – rejoice with me! I am the happiest man on earth, why should I tremble?

[*Enter* SCHWARZ.]

MOOR [*rushing to meet him*]: Brother! brother! the letter, the letter!

*French seventeenth-century minister and financial reformer (*Translator's note*).

SCHWARZ [*giving him the letter, which he hurriedly opens*]: What is it? You are as white as a sheet!

MOOR: My brother's hand!

SCHWARZ: What is the matter with Spiegelberg?

GRIMM: The fellow is crazy. He looks as though he has caught St Vitus's dance.

SCHUFTERLE: He must be out of his mind. I think he is composing verses.

RATZMANN: Spiegelberg! Hey, Spiegelberg! – The brute won't listen.

GRIMM [*shaking him*]: Man, are you dreaming, or – ?

SPIEGELBERG [*who has all the while been miming a mountebank's act in the corner of the room, jumping up wildly*]: *La bourse ou la vie!* [*He seizes* SCHWEITZER *by the throat;* SCHWEITZER *calmly pushes him back against the wall.* MOOR *drops the letter on the ground and runs out. All start back.*]

ROLLER [*after him*]: Moor! Where are you going, Moor? What are you doing?

GRIMM: What's the matter, what's the matter? He's as pale as a corpse!

SCHWEITZER: Fine news that must be! Let's see!

ROLLER [*picks up the letter, and reads*]: 'Unfortunate brother!' That's a jolly way to begin. 'I am obliged to tell you in brief that your hopes are in vain; Father asks me to tell you that you are to go wherever your disgraceful deeds may take you. He also says that you are to entertain no hope of ever weeping your way to forgiveness at his feet, unless you are prepared to live on bread and water in the deepest of his dungeons, till your hairs are grown like eagles' feathers, and your nails like birds' claws. These are his very words. He commands me to write no more. Farewell for ever! I pity you – Franz von Moor.'

SCHWEITZER: A sweet, charming brother! Indeed, Franz is the creature's name?

SPIEGELBERG [*creeping up quietly*]: Bread and water, do I hear?

That's a fine life! But I have made other plans for you!
Didn't I say I should have to think for you all one day?

SCHWEITZER: What does he say, the donkey? He think for
us all, the sheep's-head?

SPIEGELBERG: Cowards, cripples, lame dogs is what you are,
all of you, if you have not the courage for a great venture!

ROLLER: Well, that's true, so we should be; but is it going to
get us out of this damned fix, your great venture? Is it?

SPIEGELBERG [*laughing contemptuously*]: You poor fool! Get
you out of this fix? Ha, ha! Out of this fix? Is that all your
thimbleful of brain can think of? Is that enough to see your
horses home? Don't call me Spiegelberg, if that was all I had
in mind. Heroes, I tell you, lords, princes, gods it will make
of you!

RATZMANN: That's enough to be getting on with, to be sure!
But it will be a breakneck job, it will cost us our heads at
least.

SPIEGELBERG: It will cost nothing but courage, for I will
supply what wits are needed. Courage, I say, Schweitzer!
Courage, Roller, Grimm, Ratzmann, Schufterle! Courage!

SCHWEITZER: Courage? Is that all? I've enough courage to
go barefoot through hell.

SCHUFTERLE: Courage enough to scrap with the devil at the
gallows' foot for a poor sinner's soul.

SPIEGELBERG: That's what I like to hear! If you have courage,
let one amongst you say he still has anything to lose, and not
everything to gain!

SCHWARTZ: Indeed, there would be plenty to lose, if I were
to lose what I still have to gain!

RATZMANN: Yes, in hell's name! and plenty to gain, if I were
to gain what I can't lose!

SCHUFTERLE: If I were to lose everything I have on me that's
borrowed, then by tomorrow I should have nothing left to
lose.

SPIEGELBERG: Very well, then! [*He takes his place in the midst of them, and adopts an imperious tone.*] If there is still one drop of heroic German blood running in your veins – then come! We will hide in the forests of Bohemia, raise a robber band, and – why are you staring at me? Has your little bit of courage melted away already?

ROLLER: I don't suppose you are the first rogue to overlook the gallows – and yet – what else is there we can do?

SPIEGELBERG: What else? Nothing else! There is no choice in the matter! Do you want to sit starving in the debtors' prison till the last trump blows? Do you want to scratch with spade and hoe for a scrap of stale bread? Do you want to beg for alms, singing ballads at people's windows? Do you want to take the King's shilling – if they would trust the looks of you, that's the first question – and do your stint in Purgatory while you are still on earth, at the mercy of some splenetic tyrant of a corporal? Or be drummed out to run the gauntlet, or tramp the galleys and drag the whole arsenal of Vulcan's smithy behind you? That is what else there is, that is all the choice you have!

ROLLER: It's not such a bad idea of Spiegelberg's. I have been making plans too, but it is the same kind of thing. How would it be, I thought, if you all sat down and cooked up an anthology or an almanac or something like that, or wrote reviews for a shilling or two? It's all the rage nowadays.

SCHUFTERLE: I'll be hanged if your plans aren't very much like mine. I was thinking to myself, what if you were to turn evangelical, and hold weekly classes in spiritual improvement?

GRIMM: That's it! and if that was no good, turn atheist, blaspheme against the four gospels, have our book burnt by the hangman, and we should do a roaring trade.

RATZMANN: Or we could set up to cure the pox – I know a doctor who built himself a house on a foundation of mercury, so the motto over the door says.

SCHWEITZER [*stands up and gives* SPIEGELBERG *his hand*]:

Moritz, you are a great man – or a blind pig has found an acorn.

SCHWARZ: Excellent plans! most reputable professions! How great minds think alike! All that's left now is to turn into women and become bawds, or even sell our own virginity on the streets.

SPIEGELBERG: Nonsense, nonsense! And what is to stop you being most of these things in one person? My plan will still do the best for you, and make you famous and immortal too! Look, you poor things! As far ahead as that you must think! Think of the fame that will live after you, the sweet feeling that you will never be forgotten –

ROLLER: And at the top of the list of honest people! You are a master orator, Spiegelberg, when it comes to turning an honest man into a villain. – But doesn't anyone know where Moor is?

SPIEGELBERG: Honest, do you say? What, do you think it will make you any less of an honest man than you are today? What do you call being honest? Relieving rich skinflints of a third of their worries, that only disturb their golden slumbers; bringing idle money into circulation, restoring the fair distribution of wealth, in a word bringing back the golden age; taking away some of the good Lord's burdens, so that he can be rid of them without war, pestilence, famine and doctors – that's what I call being an honest man, that's what I call being a worthy instrument in the hand of Providence; and with every joint you roast to be able to flatter yourself with the thought that it's your own cunning, your own lion's courage, your own long vigils that have earned it; to be respected by great and small –

ROLLER: And in the end to be hoisted up to heaven in the flesh, and come wind come weather, in spite of old father ....ne and his greedy appetite, to swing there with sun and moon and all the stars in the firmament, while the birds sing a heavenly concert at the feast and the long-tailed angels sit

in sacred council? What? And while monarchs and poten-
tates make a feast for moths and worms, to have the honour
of being visited by Jove's royal bird? Moritz, Moritz,
Moritz! Beware, beware the three-legged beast!

SPIEGELBERG: And that frightens you, coward? Why, there's
many a virtuoso rotting on the gibbet who might have re-
formed the world, and won't such a one be spoken of for
hundreds and thousands of years, while many a king and
many an elector might be left out of history altogether, if it
weren't that the historians were afraid to leave a gap in the
line of succession, and if it weren't that it made their books a
few pages thicker and brought in more cash from the publisher. And if the passer-by does see you floating back and
forth in the wind, why, he'll think to himself, that must
have been no ordinary fellow, and he'll sigh that the world
has gone to the dogs.

SCHWEITZER [slapping him on the back]: Superb, Spiegelberg!
Superb! Why the devil do you stand there hesitating?

SCHWARZ: And even if it meant degradation – What more
can there be? One can always have a pinch of powder with
one, to speed one across the Acheron if it should come to
that, so that one will never hear the cock crow again. No,
friend Moritz! it's a good proposal. That's my catechism too.

SCHUFTERLE: Hell! And mine as well. Spiegelberg, I'm your
man!

RATZMANN: Like another Orpheus, you have sung my howling brute of a conscience to sleep. Take me as I am!

GRIMM: *Si omnes consentiunt ego non dissentio.* With no comma,
mind.* They are holding an auction in my head: evangelist,
quack-doctor, reviewer and rogue. I'm to be had for the
best offer. Here, Moritz, my hand!

ROLLER: And you too, Schweitzer? [Offering SPIEGELBERG
his right hand] Then the devil can take my soul.

*'If all give their assent, I do not withhold mine.' A comma after *non*
gives the sense 'I do not, I withhold mine' (Translator's note).

SPIEGELBERG: But your name shall be written in the stars! What does it matter where your soul goes? When troops of couriers gallop ahead to announce our descent, so that the devils put on their Sunday best, rub the soot of millennia out of their eyes, and horned heads in their thousands poke from the smoky chimneys of their sulphur-ovens to see our arrival? Comrades! [*Jumping up*] Away! Comrades! Is there anything in the world so glorious, so thrilling? Come, comrades, and away!

ROLLER: Gently now, gently! where are you going? the beast must have its head, children!

SPIEGELBERG [*venomously*]: What words of hesitation are these? Wasn't the head there before a single limb stirred? follow me, comrades!

ROLLER: Steady on, I say. Even liberty must have its master. Without a head, Rome and Sparta were destroyed.

SPIEGELBERG [*ingratiatingly*]: Yes – wait, Roller is right. And the head must be a brilliant one. Do you understand? A shrewd political head it must be. Yes, if I think of what you were an hour ago, and what you are now – are by virtue of a single lucky idea – Yes, of course, of course you must have a chief – and the man who thought up that idea, tell me, mustn't he have a brilliant, political head?

ROLLER: If we could only hope – if we could only dream – but I am afraid he will not do it.

SPIEGELBERG: Why not? Speak your mind, friend! Heavy though the task may be of steering the struggling ship against the gale, heavy though the weight of a crown may weigh – speak without fear, Roller! Perhaps he will do it after all.

ROLLER: And the whole thing falls to pieces if he will not. Without Moor we're a body without a soul.

SPIEGELBERG [*turning away from him in disgust*]: Blockhead!
[*Enter* MOOR *in wild agitation. He paces violently up and down the room, talking to himself.*]

MOOR: Men, men! False breed of hypocrites and crocodiles!

Their eyes water, but their hearts are of iron! Kisses on their lips, but swords in their bosom! Lions and leopards feed their young, ravens take their chicks to feast on corpses, and *he, he* – Wickedness I have learnt to endure. I can smile when my arch-enemy is drinking my heart's blood; but when blood kinship turns traitor, when a father's love becomes a raging fury; oh, then catch fire, manly resignation, be as a ravening tiger, gentle lamb, and let every fibre stiffen to hatred and destruction!

ROLLER: Listen, Moor! What do you think? A robber's life is better than bread and water in the deepest dungeon after all, isn't it?

MOOR: Why was this spirit not formed into a tiger, that fastens its savage jaws in human flesh? Is this a father's devotion? Is this love for love? Would that I were a bear, and could raise the bears of the north against this race of murderers – repentance, and no forgiveness! Oh, would that I might poison the ocean, that they might drink death from every spring! Trust, submission that none could turn away, and no pity!

ROLLER: Moor, listen to what I am saying!

MOOR: It is unbelievable, it is a dream, a delusion – such moving pleas, such keen representation of my misery and my melting repentance – a brute beast would have wept in compassion! Stones would have shed tears, and yet – it would be thought a wicked slur on all mankind, if I were to say so – and yet, and yet – oh, would that I could blow the trumpet of rebellion throughout the realm of nature, to stir up earth, sky and sea to battle against this brood of hyenas!

GRIMM: Listen, will you! You are so mad you do not hear.

MOOR: Get away from me! Are you not a man? Are you not born of woman? Out of my sight, you creature with man's face! – I loved him so unspeakably! no son loved so, my life I would a thousand times – [*foaming, stamping on the ground*] ha! he who should put a sword into my hand, to deal a

deadly blow to this generation of vipers! he who should say
to me: if I can pierce the heart of its life, crush it, strangle it –
that man shall be my friend, my angel, my god – I will
worship him!

ROLLER: We want to be those friends of yours, let us tell you!

SCHWARZ: Come with us into the forests of Bohemia! We
are going to raise a band of robbers, and you –

  [MOOR *stares at him.*]

SCHWEITZER: You are to be our captain! you must be our
captain!

SPIEGELBERG [*hurling himself into a chair in fury*]: Slaves and
cowards!

MOOR: Who gave you that idea? Listen, fellow! [*Seizing*
SCHWARZ *fiercely*] It did not come from your man's soul!
Who prompted you? Yes, by the thousand arms of death!
we shall, we must! a thought fit for gods! Robbers and
murderers! As sure as my soul breathes, I am your captain!

ALL [*shouting aloud*]: Long live our captain!

SPIEGELBERG [*jumping up, aside*]: Until I see him off!

MOOR: See, the scales have fallen from my eyes! What a fool
I was, to seek to return to the cage! My spirit thirsts for
deeds, my lungs for freedom – murderers, robbers! at that
word I trampled the law beneath my feet – men showed me
no humanity, when to humanity I appealed; so let me forget
sympathy and human feeling! I have no father now, I have
no love now, and blood and death shall teach me to forget
that ever I held anything dear! Oh, my amusement shall be
the terror of the earth – it is agreed, I shall be your captain!
and good fortune to the champion among you who lights
the fiercest fires, who does the foulest murders, for I say to
you, he shall have a kingly reward! Gather round me every
one, and swear loyalty and obedience till death! Swear by
this man's right hand of mine!

ALL [*reaching him their hands*]: We swear loyalty and obedience
to you till death!

MOOR: Now, and by this man's right hand of mine! I swear to you to remain your captain in loyalty and constancy till death! If any show cowardice or hesitation or retreat, this arm shall strike him down on the spot; the same fate meet me from any and every one of you, if I offend against my oath! Are you agreed?

[SPIEGELBERG *paces furiously up and down.*]

ALL [*throwing their hats in the air*]: We are agreed!

MOOR: Very well then, let us go! Fear not death or danger, for an inflexible fate rules over us all. We must endure our going hence, be it on soft pillows of down, be it in the hurly-burly of battle, or be it on the gallows and the wheel! One or the other must be our lot! [*Exeunt.*]

SPIEGELBERG [*watching them go, after a pause*]: There is one missing in your list. Poison you have forgotten. [*Exit.*]

SCENE 3

OLD MOOR's *castle*. AMALIA's *rooms*.

[FRANZ, AMALIA.]

FRANZ: You look away, Amalia? Am I less worthy than he whom my father has cursed?

AMALIA: Away! – oh, merciful, loving father, who will cast his son to the wolves and the wild beasts! while he at home is refreshed with sweet, precious wine, and cossets his feeble limbs in pillows of eiderdown, while his great and glorious son may perish! Shame on you, inhuman creatures! shame on you, you monsters, you abomination of mankind! His only son!

FRANZ: I thought that he had two.

AMALIA: Yes, it is sons like you that he deserves. On his

deathbed he will stretch out his withered hands in vain to
seek his Karl, and start back in horror when he catches the
icy hand of his Franz – oh, it is sweet, it is a sweet and noble
thing, to earn your father's curse! Speak, Franz, good soul,
good brother, what must one do if one would earn his curse?

FRANZ: My poor love, your fantasy is leading you astray.

AMALIA: Oh, I beg you – do you pity your brother? No, inhuman creature, you hate him! and you hate me too?

FRANZ: I love you as I love myself, Amalia.

AMALIA: If you love me, can you refuse me one request?

FRANZ: Not one, not one! if it is not more than my life.

AMALIA: Oh, if that is true! One request, that you will fulfil
so easily, so gladly – [*Proudly*] Hate me! I cannot but blush
crimson with shame, if I think of Karl and realize that you
do not hate me. You promise me? Now go, and leave me –
let me be alone!

FRANZ: My sweet dreamer! how I adore your gentle loving
heart. [*Touching her breast*] Here, here Karl reigned like a god
in his temple, Karl stood before you while you were awake,
Karl ruled your dreams, all creation seemed to you to
be dissolved in him, to reflect him, to echo him and him
alone.

AMALIA [*moved*]: Yes, it is true, I admit it. In spite of you,
barbarians, I confess it to all the world – I love him!

FRANZ: Inhuman, cruel! To reward such love like this! To
forget the one –

AMALIA [*starting up*]: What, to forget me?

FRANZ: Did you not put a ring upon his finger? a diamond
ring, as a pledge of your constancy? But after all, how can a
young man withstand a courtesan's charms? Who can blame
him when he had nothing left to give away? And did she not
pay him with interest for it, with her embraces, with her
caresses?

AMALIA [*indignantly*]: A courtesan, my ring?

FRANZ: Pah! it is shameful. But if that was all! A ring,

however precious, any Jew can replace, if it comes to that – perhaps he did not like the setting, perhaps he changed it for a better one.

AMALIA [*angrily*]: But *my* ring, *my* ring, I say?

FRANZ: The very same, Amalia – ah, such a jewel, on my finger – and from Amalia! – death itself could not have torn it from me – is it not so, Amalia? it is not the size of the diamond, it is not the skill of the cutting – it is love that makes it precious – dearest child, you are weeping? Cursed be he who makes these heavenly eyes shed their precious drops – oh, and if only you knew everything, if only you could see him, as he is now! –

AMALIA: Monster! What do you mean, as he is now?

FRANZ: Be still, sweet creature, do not ask me! [*As if to himself, but aloud*] If only there were some veil that could hide it, that filthy vice, so that it could creep out of sight of the world! But no! it shows in all its vileness, in the yellow leaden ring round the eye; the deathly pallor of the sunken cheeks betrays it, and the hideous protruding bones – the stifled, strangled voice mutters of it – the tottering, decrepit frame proclaims it aloud in all its horror – it gnaws the very marrow of the bones, and saps the bold youth's strength – there, there! the suppurating juices start forth from forehead and cheeks and lips and cover the whole body with their loathsome sores, and fester in the dark hollows of bestial disgrace – pah! it revolts me. Nose, ears, eyes shudder at it – you saw him, Amalia, that wretch who coughed out his soul in our infirmary, the modest eye of shame seemed to turn aside from the sight of him – alas for him, you cried! Think of it, summon up that vision once more before your mind's eye, and it is Karl that you see! – His kisses are a pestilence, his lips would poison yours!

AMALIA [*striking him*]: Shameless slanderer!

FRANZ: Does it fill you with horror, the thought of such a Karl? Does even my pale sketch disgust you? Go, gape at him himself, your handsome, angelic, divine Karl! Go, breathe in the perfume of his breath, let the sweet vapours that his throat streams forth envelop you; one breath from his lips, and you would feel the same black swoon of death upon you as if you smelt a rotting corpse, or saw the carrion of a battlefield.

[AMALIA *turns her face away*.]

FRANZ: What surging tide of love! What bliss in his embrace! – But is it not unjust to damn a man for the sickness of his body? Even the most miserable cripple of an Aesop may hide a great and noble soul, as the mud hides the ruby. [*Smiling maliciously*] Even scabbed lips may breathe of love – But yet, if vice has sapped the strength of his character as well, if virtue has fled with chastity, as the perfume fades from the withered rose – if with the body the spirit too is crippled –

AMALIA [*starting up, joyfully*]: Ah, Karl! Now I see you truly again! you are still your own true self! It was all a lie! Do you not know, wicked creature, that these things can never touch my Karl?

[FRANZ *stands for a while deep in thought, then turns suddenly as if to go*.]

Where are you hurrying to, would you fly from your own shame?

FRANZ [*hiding his face*]: Let me go, let me go! let my tears flow – tyrant of a father! to cast the best of your sons into such misery – to expose him to shame on every side – let me go, Amalia! I will fall on my knees at his feet, I will implore him to let me, me bear the curse that he spoke – to disinherit me – me – to – my life, my blood – everything –

AMALIA [*throwing her arms round his neck*]: Oh, my Karl's brother, dearest, most precious Franz!

FRANZ: Oh, Amalia! how I love you for your unshakeable constancy to my brother – forgive me, for presuming to put your love to so harsh a test! How perfectly you vindicate my hopes! With these your tears, these your sighs, this your heavenly displeasure – for me, me too – our souls were always as one.

AMALIA: No, that they never were!

FRANZ: Oh, they were as one, in such sweet harmony, I always thought that we should have been twins! and if it were not for the unhappy difference in outward looks between us, which I admit is not to his advantage, then ten times the one might have been taken for the other. Yes, you are, I said to myself so often, you are Karl himself, his echo, his living image!

AMALIA [shaking her head]: No, no! by the chaste light of Heaven! not one drop of his blood, not one spark of his spirit!

FRANZ: So alike in all our tastes: the rose was his favourite flower – what flower did I ever rate above the rose? He loved music more than words can tell, and I! you stars are my witnesses, how often you have heard me at the keyboard in the silence of the night, when all around me lay buried in shadows and sleep – how can you doubt it still, Amalia, when our love coincided in the same point of perfection, and if love is one, how can its children deny their ancestry?

[AMALIA stares at him in amazement.]

FRANZ: It was a clear, still evening, the last night before he set off for Leipzig, when he took me with him to the arbour where you so often sat together, dreaming of love – we sat there long in silence – at last he took my hand and spoke softly and with tears in his eyes: I am leaving Amalia, I do not know – I feel that it may be for ever – do not you leave her, brother! be her friend – her Karl – if Karl should – not – return – ! [He falls on his knees before her and kisses her hand passionately.] No, he will not return, never, never, and I have promised him with a sacred oath!

AMALIA [drawing back sharply]: Traitor, I have found you out! In this same arbour he made me swear, never to love another – if he should not – see, how blasphemously, how vilely you – out of my sight!

FRANZ: You mistake me, Amalia, you are quite mistaken in me!

AMALIA: Oh, I am not mistaken in you, I know you from this moment – and you would be his equal? And you say it was to you he wept for my sake? To you? He would sooner have written my name upon the pillory! Go, this instant!

FRANZ: You do me an injustice!

AMALIA; Go, I say! You have robbed me of a precious hour, let your life be so much the shorter.

FRANZ: You hate me.

AMALIA: I despise you, go!

FRANZ [*stamping his foot*]: Wait! I will make you tremble before me! To sacrifice me to a beggar? [*Exit, angrily.*]

AMALIA: Go, base creature! – now I am with Karl again – a beggar, did he say? Why then, the world is turned upside-down, beggars are kings and kings are beggars! I would not change the rags he wears for the purple of the anointed – the look with which he begs for alms must be a noble and a kingly look – a look to wither the pomp and splendour, the triumphs of the great and rich! Into the dust with you, idle jewels! [*Tearing the pearls from her throat.*] Be condemned, you great and rich, to wear your gold and silver and your precious stones, to glut yourselves at feasts and banquets, to stretch your limbs on the soft couch of ease! Karl! Karl! You see that I am worthy of you. [*Exit.*]

ACT TWO

SCENE I

[FRANZ VON MOOR, *brooding in his room.*]

FRANZ: It takes too long for my liking – the doctor says he is on the mend – an old man's life is an eternity! And now my path would be clear and smooth before me, but for this miserable lump of tough flesh that bars the way to my treasures like the magic subterranean dog in the fairytale. But must my plans submit to the iron yoke of mechanical laws? Is my high-flying spirit to be bound to the snail's pace of material necessity? – Blow out a light that in any case is only stretching the last drop of oil – that is all there is to it; and yet I would rather not have done it myself, on account of what people will say. I would not have him killed, but put down. I should like to do it like a skilled doctor – only the other way about: not to put a spoke in Nature's wheel, but to help her in her own designs. And if we can prolong the conditions of life as we can, why should we not be able to abbreviate them? Doctors and philosophers have taught me how finely the motions of the mind are attuned to those of the machine that houses it. Convulsive attacks are accompanied by dissonant vibrations in the machine; passions disturb the vital force; the overburdened spirit weighs down its vehicle. What then? If one could discover how to smooth death this untrodden path into the citadel of life? to destroy the body through the soul? – ha! a masterpiece! The man who could do that – ? A work of genius! Think, Moor! An art that deserved you for its discoverer! After all, poisoning has now been raised almost to the rank of a full-blown

science, and experiments have forced nature to make known
her limitations, so that the beats of the heart can now be
reckoned out years in advance and one can say to the pulse:
thus far, and no further!* Is not this a field where one might
try one's wings? And how must I set about it, now, to disturb the sweet peace and harmony of body and soul? What
species of sensation shall I have to choose? Which will be the
deadliest enemies of the flower of life? Anger? – a ravening
wolf that devours its prey too quickly. Carking care? – a
worm that gnaws too slowly. Sorrow? – a snake that creeps
too sluggishly. Fear? – when hope will always check its
growth? What? Has man no other executioners? Is the
arsenal of death so soon exhausted? [*Brooding*] What? Well?
No! – Ah! [*Starting up*] Terror! What can terror not accomplish? What can reason or religion do to stay the monster's
icy embrace? – And yet? – If he could withstand that
assault? If he could? – Oh, then come to my aid, grief, and
you, repentance, Fury of hell, burrowing serpent that chew
again what you have once devoured, and feed again upon
your own filth; eternal destroyers and eternal breeders of
your poison; and you, howling self-reproach, who make
desolate your own house, and wound your own mother's
heart – And come you too to my aid, you beneficent Graces
yourselves, soft smiling Past, and Future with your cornu-
copia overflowing with blossoms, show him in your glass
the joys of heaven, and then let your fleeting foot escape his
greedy arm – Blow upon blow, storm upon storm I will
bring down upon this fragile life, till at last there comes, to
crown the troop of furies – despair! Triumph! triumph!
The plan is made – Tight and cunning as could be – safe –
foolproof; for [*mockingly*] there will be no trace of a wound

---

*A woman in Paris is said to have achieved such success in systematic
experiments with doses of poison that she could give the date of death in
advance with some measure of reliability. Shame on our doctors, that
this woman excels them in prognosis! (*Schiller's note*).

nor corrosive poison for the anatomist's knife to reveal. [*Resolutely*] Very well, then!

[*Enter* HERRMANN.]

Ha! *Deus ex machina!* Herrmann!

HERRMANN: At your service, young master!

FRANZ[*giving him his hand*]: I am not ungrateful for it.

HERRMANN: I have proofs of that.

FRANZ: You shall have more very soon – very soon, Herrmann! – I have something to tell you, Herrmann.

HERRMANN: I am all ears.

FRANZ: I know you, you are a resolute fellow – a soldier's heart – a man of courage. – My father did you a great injustice, Herrmann!

HERRMANN: The devil take me if ever I forget it!

FRANZ: Spoken like a man! Revenge is sweet, and a man deserves it. I like you, Herrmann. Take this purse, Herrmann. It would be heavier, if only I were lord here.

HERRMANN: That is my only wish, young master. I thank you.

FRANZ: Truly, Herrmann? do you truly wish that I was lord? – But my father is as strong as a lion, and I am the younger son.

HERRMANN: I wish you were the elder son, and I wish your father were as strong as a consumptive girl.

FRANZ: Oh, how the elder son would reward you then! how he would raise you from this ignoble dust, that suits so ill your spirit and nobility, raise you up into the light! – Then you should be covered with gold, just as you are, and rattle through the streets with four horses, indeed you should! – but I am forgetting what I wanted to say to you. Have you forgotten the Lady Amalia, Herrmann?

HERRMANN: Damnation! why do you remind me of that?

FRANZ: My brother whisked her away from you.

HERRMANN: He'll pay for it!

FRANZ: She turned you down. I believe he even threw you down the stairs.

HERRMANN: I'll hurl him into hell for it.

FRANZ: He said people were whispering that you were got between the roast beef and the horse-radish, and your father could never look at you without beating his breast and sighing: God have mercy on me, miserable sinner!

HERRMANN [*furiously*]: By the burning fiery furnace! be silent!

FRANZ: He told you to auction your patent of nobility, and have your breeches patched with it.

HERRMANN: By all the devils! I'll tear out his eyes with my nails!

FRANZ: What? you are angry? what can make you angry with him? What can you do to him? How can a rat hurt a lion? Your anger will only make his triumph sweeter. You can do nothing but grit your teeth, and vent your rage on a piece of stale bread.

HERRMANN [*stamping on the floor*]: I'll grind him to dust.

FRANZ [*clapping him on the shoulder*]: Pah, Herrmann! You are a gentleman. You must not be content to bear these insults. You must not let the lady go, no, you must not do that for all the world, Herrmann! Hell and damnation! I would stop at nothing if I were in your shoes.

HERRMANN: I will not rest till I have him, and have him under the ground.

FRANZ: Not so wild, Herrmann! Come closer – you shall have Amalia!

HERRMANN: I must, come Satan himself! I must!

FRANZ: You shall have her, I tell you, and I shall help you to her. Come closer, I say! – perhaps you did not know that Karl is as good as disinherited?

HERRMANN [*coming closer*]: Incredible! It is the first I have heard of it.

FRANZ: Keep calm, and listen! I will tell you more about it another time – yes, I say, as good as banished, eleven months ago. But the old man is already regretting his hasty step –

and after all [*laughing*], I believe it was not his own doing. And my Lady Amalia besieges him every day with her reproaches and her lamentations. Sooner or later he will send to the four corners of the earth to look for him and then good night, Herrmann! if he finds him. You can swallow your pride and hold the carriage door for him, when he drives to the church with her for their wedding.

HERRMANN: I'll throttle him before the altar!

FRANZ: Father will soon hand affairs over to him, and retire to live in peace on his estates. Then the proud hothead will have the reins in his hands, then he will laugh at those who hated him and envied him – and I, Herrmann, I who would have made you a great man, a man to be looked up to, will be bowing my knee at his door –

HERRMANN [*heatedly*]: No! as true as my name is Herrmann, you shall not! not if a spark of wit still glimmers in my brain! you shall not!

FRANZ: Will you be able to stop it? you too, my dear Herrmann, will be feeling his whip, he will spit in your face if you meet him in the street, and woe betide you then if you shrug your shoulder or curl your lip – there, that is what will come of your suit to the lady, of your prospects, of your designs.

HERRMANN: Tell me, what am I to do?

FRANZ: Listen, then, Herrmann! so that you may see what a good friend I am to you, how nearly your fate touches my heart – go, put on different clothes, disguise yourself so that no one will know you, and have yourself announced to the old man – say that you have come straight from Bohemia, that you were with my brother at the battle of Prague, that you saw him breathe his last on the battlefield –

HERRMANN: Will they believe me?

FRANZ: Aha, let me take care of that! Take this packet. Here you will find everything set out for you to do. And documents that would convince doubt itself – look to it now, be on your way, and don't be seen! through the back door into the courtyard, jump over the garden wall – leave the climax of this tragicomedy to me!

HERRMANN: And that will be: long live our new lord and master, Franciscus von Moor!

FRANZ [*stroking his cheek*]: Clever, are you not? – for do you see, in this way we shall achieve all our goals at once, and quickly. Amalia will give up all hope of him. The old man will blame himself for his son's death, and – he is sickly – a rickety building does not need an earthquake to bring it crashing down – he will not survive the news. Then I shall be his only son – Amalia will have lost all support, and will be the plaything of my will, you can imagine – in short, everything will be as we would have it – but you must not take back your word!

HERRMANN: What are you saying? [*Jubilant*] Sooner may the bullet turn in its flight and tear the marksman's own bowels – count on me! Leave everything to me – Adieu!

FRANZ [*calling after him*]: The harvest is yours, my dear Herrmann! – When the ox has carted the corn to the barn, he has to make do with hay. A stablemaid for you, and no Amalia! [*Exit.*]

SCENE 2

OLD MOOR's *bedroom.*

[OLD MOOR, *asleep in an armchair.* AMALIA.]

AMALIA [*creeping softly in*]: Softly, softly, he is asleep! [*Standing before him as he sleeps*] How handsome, how venerable! – venerable like the portrait of a saint – no, I cannot be angry with you! Dear white head, with you I cannot be angry! Rest asleep, wake joyfully – I alone will go my way in suffering.

OLD MOOR [*dreaming*]: My son! my son! my son!

AMALIA [*taking his hand*]: Hark, hark! his son is in his dreams.

OLD MOOR: Is it you? is it really you? ah, how wretchedly you look! Do not turn that sorrowful gaze upon me! I am wretched enough!

AMALIA [*waking him quickly*]: Look about you, sweet old man! You only dreamt. Have courage!

OLD MOOR [*half awake*]: He was not here? Did I not hold his hands in mine? Cruel Franz! will you tear him even from my dreams?

AMALIA: Do you hear, Amalia?

OLD MOOR [*more cheerfully*]: Where is he? where? Where am I? You here, Amalia?

AMALIA: How is it with you? You were asleep, your rest has refreshed you.

OLD MOOR: I was dreaming of my son. Why could I not dream on? I might have heard his lips speak forgiveness.

AMALIA: Angels bear no grudge – he has forgiven you. [*Taking his hand sorrowfully*] Father of my Karl! I forgive you.

OLD MOOR: No, my daughter! His father stands condemned by the deathly pallor of your face. Unhappy girl! I robbed you of the joys of your youth – oh, do not curse me!

AMALIA [*kissing his hand tenderly*]: You?

OLD MOOR: Do you know this portrait, my daughter?

AMALIA: Karl's!

OLD MOOR: So he looked, when he was in his sixteenth year. Now he is different – Oh, my breast is aflame, – this gentleness is wrath, this smile despair – Is it not so, Amalia? It was his birthday when you painted him, in the jasmine arbour? – Oh, my daughter! Your love brought me such joy.

AMALIA [*not taking her eyes off the portrait*]: No, no! it is not he. In Heaven's name, that is not Karl. Here, here – [*pointing *to her heart and her forehead*] The whole, so different. These dull colours cannot reflect the divine spirit that shone in his fiery eye. Away with it! this is a mere man. I was but a bungler.

OLD MOOR: This warm look of devotion – if he had stood before my bed, in the midst of death I had lived! Never, never should I have died!

AMALIA: Never, never should you have died! A leap it would have been, as one springs from one thought to another and a finer – this look would have lighted your path beyond the grave. This look would have borne you on beyond the stars!

OLD MOOR: It is sad, it is hard to endure! I am dying, and my son Karl is not here – I shall be carried to my grave, and he will not be at my grave to weep – how sweet it is to be lulled into the sleep of death by a son's prayer – it is like a lullaby.

AMALIA [*rapturously*]: Yes, sweet, sweet as heaven it is, to be lulled into the sleep of death by a lover's song – perhaps we may dream on still in the grave – one long eternal never-ending dream of Karl until the bell tolls for the day of resurrection [*leaping to her feet in ecstasy*] – and from that moment on, in his arms for ever. [*Pause. She goes to the keyboard, and plays.*]

> Hector, wilt thou bid farewell for ever,
> Now Achilles with his murd'rous quiver
> Fearful vengeance for Patroclus swears?
> Who will teach thy tender son to fight,
> To cast his spear, and fear the Gods of right,
> When thy corpse grim Xanthus downward bears?

OLD MOOR: A beautiful song, my daughter. You must play it for me before I die.

AMALIA: It is the farewell of Andromache and Hector – Karl and I have often sung it to the lute together. [*Continuing*]

> Dearest wife, go, fetch the fateful lance,
> Let me go to tread war's horrid dance,
> On my back the weight of Ilium;

The Gods shield Astyanax with their hand!
Hector falls, to save his fatherland,
We shall greet each other in Elysium.

[*Enter* DANIEL.]

DANIEL: There is a man waiting for you outside. He asks to be allowed to see you, he says he has an important piece of news for you.

OLD MOOR: Only one thing in the world is important to me, you know what that is, Amalia – is it a man fallen on ill-luck, who has need of help from me? He shall not go sighing on his way.

AMALIA: If it is a beggar, make haste and send him up.

[*Exit* DANIEL.]

OLD MOOR: Amalia, Amalia! have pity on me!

AMALIA [*continuing to play*]:

Never shall I hear thy weapons sing,
In thy hall thy arms lie mouldering;
Priam's race of heroes is passed by!
Thou art gone where never daylight gleams,
Where Cocytus through the desert streams,
In dread Lethe's flood thy love will die.

All my thoughts, ambition's crown
Shall dread Lethe's flood in blackness drown,
But never yet my love!
Hark now! at the walls, the wild one raving –
Gird my sword about me, cease thy grieving!
Lethe shall not drown thy Hector's love!

[*Enter* FRANZ, HERRMANN *in disguise,* DANIEL.]

FRANZ: Here is the man. Terrible news, he says, awaits you. Can you bear to hear it?

OLD MOOR: It can be only one thing. Come here, friend, and do not spare me! Give him a cup of wine.

HERRMANN [*disguising his voice*]: My lord! do not punish a poor man, if against his own will he should pierce your heart. I am a stranger in this land, but you I know well, you are Karl von Moor's father.

OLD MOOR: How do you know?

HERRMANN: I knew your son –

AMALIA [*starting up*]: He is alive? alive? You know him? where is he, where, where? [*Making as if to run out.*]

OLD MOOR: You can tell me what has happened to my son?

HERRMANN: He was a student in Leipzig. From there he went on his wanderings, I do not know how far. He wandered all over Germany, bareheaded, as he told me, and without shoes, and begged his bread at men's doors. Five months later, the hateful war broke out between Prussia and Austria, and as he had nothing left to hope for in this world, King Frederick's victorious drum summoned him to Bohemia. Let me die, he said, to the great Schwerin, let me die the death of a hero, as I have no father more!

OLD MOOR [*burying his face in the pillows*]: Oh, peace, oh peace!

HERRMANN: A week later came the great fight at Prague – I can tell you, your son stood his ground like a true warrior. He did miracles before the army's eyes. Five times they had to relieve the regiment beside him, he stood firm. Grenades fell to left and to right of him, your son stood firm. A bullet shattered his right hand, your son took the standard in his left, and stood firm –

AMALIA [*ecstatically*]: Hector, Hector! Stood firm, you hear it, stood firm –

HERRMANN: I found him on the evening of the battle, lying there with the bullets whistling round, with his left hand trying to stem the flow of blood, his right he had buried in the ground. Brother! he cried out when he saw me, there was a rumour in the ranks that the general was killed an hour ago – killed! I cried, and you? – Why then, he cried, and took his left hand away, let every true soldier follow his general with me! Soon after he breathed out his mighty soul, to follow where the hero led.

FRANZ [*attacking* HERRMANN *savagely*]: May death seal your accursed lips! Have you come here to deal our father his death-blow? – Father! Amalia! Father!

HERRMANN: It was my dying comrade's last wish. Take my sword, he groaned, take it, give it to my old father, it is stained with his son's blood, he is revenged, let him rejoice. Tell him it was his curse that drove me to battle, war and death, tell him I am fallen in despair! His last gasp was – Amalia!

AMALIA [*as if roused from a sleep of death*]: His last gasp, Amalia!

OLD MOOR [*crying out horribly, tearing his hair*]: My curse that drove him to death! fallen in despair!

FRANZ [*pacing about the room*]: Oh, father, what have you done? My Karl, my brother!

HERRMANN: Here is the sword, and here too is a portrait that he took from his bosom! It is this lady, to the life! Give this to my brother Franz, he said – I do not know what he meant by it.

FRANZ [*as if amazed*]: To me? Amalia's portrait? To me, Karl, Amalia? Me?

AMALIA [*attacking* HERRMANN *furiously*]: Vile deceiver, who has paid you, who has bribed you? [*Seizing him.*]

HERRMANN: No one, my lady. See for yourself if it is not your portrait – you must have given it to him yourself.

FRANZ: Dear God, Amalia, it is yours! It is truly yours!

AMALIA [*returning the portrait*]: Mine, mine! Oh, heaven and earth!

OLD MOOR [*crying out, clawing at his face*]: Woe, woe! my curse that drove him to death! fallen in despair!

FRANZ: And he could think of me in the last terrible hour of his departing, of me! Soul of an angel – as death's black banner already swept over him – of me!

OLD MOOR [*babbling*]: My curse that drove him, to death, fallen, my son, in despair!

HERRMANN: This grief is more than I can bear. Farewell, old

lord! [*Softly to* FRANZ] Why did you have to go so far,
young master? [*Exit, quickly.*]

AMALIA[*jumping up, running after him*]: Stay, stay! What were
his last words?

HERRMANN[*calling over his shoulder*]: His last gasp was Amalia.
[*Exit.*]

AMALIA: His last gasp was Amalia! – No, you are not deceiving us! So it is true – true – he is dead – dead! [*Swaying to
and fro, and finally falling to the ground.*] Dead – Karl is dead –

FRANZ: What do I see? What is this on the sword? words
written in the blood – Amalia!

AMALIA: His words?

FRANZ: Do I see aright, or am I dreaming? Look there, letters
of blood: Franz, do not desert my Amalia! Look, look! and
on the other side: Amalia, all-powerful death releases you
from your oath – Do you see, do you see? He wrote it as his
fingers stiffened, wrote it in his heart's warm blood, wrote it
upon the solemn brink of eternity! his fleeting spirit stayed
a moment, that Franz and Amalia might be joined.

AMALIA: God in Heaven! it is his hand. – He never loved me!
[*Hurrying off.*]

FRANZ [*stamping on the floor*]: Desperation! all my art is foiled
by such obstinacy!

OLD MOOR: Woe, woe! Do not leave me, my daughter! –
Franz, Franz! give me back my son!

FRANZ: Who was it that cursed him? Who was it that drove
his son to battle and death and despair? – Oh! he was an
angel! a jewel in heaven's crown! Curses upon them that
slew him! Curses, curses upon you yourself! –

OLD MOOR[*striking breast and forehead with his clenched fist*]: He
was an angel, a jewel in heaven's crown! Curses, curses,
destruction and curses upon myself! I am the father that slew
his mighty son! Me, me he loved unto death! To avenge me
he hurled himself into battle and death! Monster, monster!
[*Venting his rage upon himself.*]

FRANZ: He is gone, it is too late for remorse! [*Laughing scornfully*] It is easier to murder than to bring to life. You will never raise him from his grave again.

OLD MOOR: Never, never, never raise him from his grave again! Gone, gone, lost for ever! – And it was you who talked me into cursing him, you – you – Give me back my son!

FRANZ: Do not tempt my wrath! I will leave you to die!

OLD MOOR: Vampire! vampire! give me my son again! [*Springing up from his chair and attempting to seize* FRANZ *by the throat;* FRANZ *hurls him back.*]

FRANZ: Feeble old bag of bones! You dare – die! despair!

OLD MOOR: A thousand curses ring about your ears! You stole my son from my very arms. [*Twisting and turning in his chair in despair.*] Woe, woe! To despair, but not to die! They flee, they leave me to die – my good angels flee from me, all that is holy flees the cold grey murderer – Woe! woe! is there no one to hold my head, is there no one to free my struggling soul from its prison? No sons! no daughters! no friends! – only men – is there none, alone – abandoned – woe! woe! – To despair, but not to die!

[*Enter* AMALIA, *her eyes red with weeping.*]

OLD MOOR: Amalia! Messenger of heaven! Have you come to free my soul?

AMALIA [*in a gentler tone*]: You have lost a glorious son.

OLD MOOR: Murdered him, you mean to say. Laden with this accusation shall I step before God's judgement-seat!

AMALIA: Not so, old man who grieve so greatly! Our heavenly Father summoned him. We should have been too happy in this world. – There, there beyond the stars – We shall see him again.

OLD MOOR: See him again, see him again! Oh, it shall be as a sword to smite my soul – if I a saint find him among the ranks of the saints – in the midst of heaven I shall be encompassed with the terrors of hell! In the sight of the Eternal, bowed down as I recall: it was I that slew my son!

AMALIA: Oh, he will smile the recollection and the pain from your soul, be of good cheer, dear father, even as I am! Has he not already sung the name Amalia to the angel's harp, for the heavenly hosts to hear, and the hosts of heaven whispered it after him? His last gasp was – Amalia; will he not cry out in his jubilation: Amalia! before all?

OLD MOOR: Heavenly comfort drops from your lips! He will smile, you say? forgive me? You must stay at my side, my Karl's true love, when I am dying.

AMALIA: To die is to fly to his arms! Oh, happy! I envy you. Why are these bones not brittle? Why are the hairs of this head not grey? Alas, for the strength of youth! Welcome, feeble old age! to bring me nearer to heaven and my Karl.

[Enter FRANZ.]

OLD MOOR: Come to me! my son! Forgive me if I was too harsh with you before! I forgive you everything. I would so gladly breathe my last in peace.

FRANZ: Have you done with weeping for your son? – as far as I can see, you have only the one.

OLD MOOR: Jacob's sons were twelve, but for the one he wept tears of blood.

FRANZ: Humph!

OLD MOOR: Go and fetch the Bible, my daughter, and read me the story of Jacob and Joseph! It moved me always so to hear it, and then I was not yet a Jacob.

AMALIA: What part shall I read you? [She takes the Bible and turns the pages.]

OLD MOOR: Read me the grief of him in his bereavement, when he could not find him among his children – and waited in vain for him, in the circle of the eleven – and his lamentation, as he heard his Joseph was taken from him for ever –

AMALIA [*reads*]: 'And they took Joseph's coat, and killed a kid
  of the goats, and dipped the coat in the blood; and they rent
  the coat of many colours, and they brought it to their
  father; and said, This have we found: know now whether it
  be thy son's coat or no?'

  [FRANZ *hurries suddenly away*.]

  'And he knew it, and said, It is my son's coat; an evil beast
  hath devoured him; Joseph is without doubt rent in pieces.'

OLD MOOR[*falls back upon the pillow*]: Rent in pieces! An evil
  beast hath devoured him!

AMALIA [*reading on*]: 'And Jacob rent his clothes, and put
  sackcloth upon his loins, and mourned for his son many
  days. And all his sons and all his daughters rose up to comfort him; but he refused to be comforted; and he said, For I
  will go down into the grave unto my son mourning. – '

OLD MOOR: Stop, stop! I am not well!

AMALIA [*rushing to his side, dropping the book*]: Heaven protect
  us! What is this?

OLD MOOR: It is death! Black – swimming – before – my
  eyes – I beg you – call the pastor – that I may – take the
  sacrament – Where is – my son Franz?

AMALIA: He is fled! God have mercy upon us!

OLD MOOR: Fled – fled from the bedside of the dying? – And
  this all – all – two sons, full of hope – the Lord gave – the
  Lord hath – taken away – blessed be the name of —

AMALIA [*crying out suddenly*]: Dead! All dead! [*Exit, in despair.*]

  [*Enter* FRANZ, *skipping for joy*.]

FRANZ: Dead! they cry, dead! Now I am your lord and
  master. A hue and cry in all the castle: dead! – But what,
  perhaps he is only asleep? to be sure! a sleep that surely is
  that will never hear a good-morning again – sleep and death
  are but twins. Let us just confuse the names! Welcome, brave
  sleep! We will call you death. [*Closing his father's eyes.*] Who
  will come now, and dare to summon me before the courts?

or say to my face: you are a villain! Away then with this burdensome mask of gentleness and virtue! Now you shall see Franz naked as he is, and cringe in terror! My father sugared his commands, made his territories one happy family, sat smiling at the gate, and called everyone brother and sister. – My brows shall beetle over you like storm-clouds, my imperious name hover like a threatening comet over these mountain-tops, my forehead shall be your barometer! He stroked and fondled the necks that would not bow, but rose in spite against him. I am not one for stroking and fondling. I will set my pointed spurs into your flesh, and see what a keen whip will do. – In my lands the day will come when potatoes and small beer make a holiday feast, and woe betide any I meet with full and rosy cheeks! Ashen-white of poverty and slavish fear is my favourite colour: that is the livery I will have you wear! [*Exit.*]

SCENE 3

The forest of Bohemia.

[SPIEGELBERG, RATZMANN, ROBBERS.]

RATZMANN: Are you there? Is it really you? Ah, Moritz, Moritz, brother of my heart; I could hug you to pulp! Welcome to the forest of Bohemia! Why, you've grown big and strong. Hell's bells, buckets of blood! New men too, a whole gang you've brought! That's what I call recruiting!

SPIEGELBERG: Isn't it, brother, isn't it? And fine fellows too! – Do you not think the hand of God is upon me, poor hungry wretch that I was, with my staff I passed over this Jordan, and now there are seventy-eight of us; mostly bankrupt shopkeepers, bachelors who've failed their disputations, clerks from the Swabian provinces, what a body of men! charming fellows, who would steal each other's fly-buttons, and won't sleep beside each other without their guns loaded – who keep their pistols primed, and have a reputation for a hundred miles around, you'd never believe it. You'll not find a newspaper without a little item about Spiegelberg the master-mind – it's the only reason I take them – descriptions of me from head to toe, you'd think you could see me with your own eyes – they've not left out the buttons on my jacket. But we have been leading them a terrible dance. One day I went to a printer's, told him I had seen the notorious Spiegelberg, and dictated to a scribbler that was sitting there the spitting likeness of some miserable quack doctor in the town; the thing gets around, the fellow is arrested, shown the instruments, and the fool is so fright-ened that damn me if he doesn't confess that he is your notorious Spiegelberg! Hell's teeth! I was near jumping up to go and complain to the magistrates about the scurvy creature abusing my name – anyhow, three months later there he swings. I had to take a strong pinch of snuff, I can tell you, when I strolled by the gibbet and saw pseudo-Spiegelberg up there in all his glory – and while Spiegelberg dangles, Spiegelberg slips quietly out of the noose, and cocks a snook at wise-owl Justice behind her back – it's enough to make you weep!

RATZMANN [*laughing*]: You're still the same as ever.

SPIEGELBERG: I am indeed, as you see, body and soul. Fool! – I must tell you the trick I played at St Cecilia's convent. I reached the convent on my wanderings one evening as it was getting dark, and as I hadn't fired a single shot that day – you know I hate the thought of *diem perdidi* like poison, so it was high time to brighten up the night with some escapade, even if it meant singeing the devil's ears! We wait quietly until late at night. Everything is as quiet as a mouse. The lights go out. We reckon the nuns will be between the sheets. Now I take my comrade Grimm with me, tell the others to wait outside the gate until they hear my whistle – take care of the convent porter, get his keys off him, creep in where the girls are sleeping, whisk their clothes away, and pile them all up outside the gate. On we go, one cell after the other, take all the sisters' clothes in turn, last of all the abbess's – then I whistle, and my fellows outside kick up a commotion as if it was the Day of Judgement, and into the sisters' cells, roaring like wild beasts! – ha, ha, ha! you should have seen the sport we had, the poor creatures fumbling around in the dark for their petticoats, and weeping and wailing, when they found the devil had taken them! and us upon them like a whirlwind, and them rolling themselves up in their blankets, so surprised and scared they were, or creeping under the stove like cats, and some of them wetting themselves with fright, poor things, you could have learnt to swim in there, and the hue and cry and lamentation, and last of all the old hag of an abbess, dressed like Eve before the Fall – brother, you know there is no creature in all this world I hate more than a spider and an old woman, and just imagine now that wizened, hairy old dragon dancing about in front of me, conjuring me by her maiden's honour – the devil! I was already putting my fists up to knock her last few teeth all the way through her guts – make up your mind! either out with the silver, the treasure-chest and all those dear little shiny sovereigns, or – my fellows knew what I meant – I tell you, I cleaned out that convent of more than a thousand's-worth, and had the fun too, and my fellows left them a memento to carry around for the next nine months.

RATZMANN: Damnation, why wasn't I there?

SPIEGELBERG: You see? Go on, tell me, isn't that a life of luxury? and it keeps you fit and strong, and the corpus is all in one piece, and growing every hour like a bishop's belly – I don't know, there must be something magnetic about me, that attracts all the rogues and vagabonds on God's earth like iron and steel.

RATZMANN: A fine magnet you are! But hang me, I should like to know what witchcraft you use!

SPIEGELBERG: Witchcraft? No need of witchcraft – you must just have your wits about you! A certain practical expertise, that doesn't grow on trees, I admit – what I always say is, you see: you can make an honest man out of any old stick, but for a villain, you need grey matter – and you want a certain national talent too, a kind of, so to speak, villain's climate – and I'll tell you what, go to Switzerland: the Grisons, that's the Mecca of rogues today.

RATZMANN: Ah, brother! Italy, they tell me, is a good place altogether.

SPIEGELBERG: Oh yes, yes! everyone must have his due, Italy has had its share of good men, and if Germany goes on as it is going today, and they abolish the Bible completely, as there is every appearance, then Germany may produce something worthwhile too, in time – but altogether, let me tell you, climate makes very little difference, genius will thrive in any soil, and the rest, brother – well, you know, a crab won't turn into a pineapple even in the Garden of Eden – but, as I was explaining to you – where was I?

RATZMANN: You were coming to the tricks of the trade.

SPIEGELBERG: Yes, the tricks of the trade! Well then, the first thing you must do, when you come to any town, is to find out from the police, the jailor and the poor-house keeper who it is they see most of, who comes to present his compliments most often, and these are the customers you must look for – then, you establish yourself in the coffee-houses, the brothels, and the inns, keep your eyes open, sound people out, see who complains the loudest about their miserable five per cent these days, or about the pestilential increase in law and order, who curses the government most, or holds forth about the fashion for physiognomy and that kind of thing! Then you know where you are, brother! Honesty wobbles like a hollow tooth; just get out your pincers – Or, better and quicker: you go and drop a purse full of money in the street where everyone can see it, hide yourself somewhere by, and see who picks it up; then after a bit you come chasing after, looking around, and crying out, and ask him, just as it might be in passing, did the gentleman not find a purse of money? If he says yes, well, then the devil was watching; but if he denies it? You will excuse me, sir – I really cannot remember – I am sorry, [*jumping up*] victory, brother, victory! Put out your light, cunning Diogenes! – you have found the man you wanted.

RATZMANN: You are an expert practitioner.

SPIEGELBERG: God! as if I had ever doubted it. – Now you have got your man on the hook, you must be careful how you go about landing him! Look, my lad, this is how I have always done it. As soon as I was on the trail, I stuck to my candidate like a burr, drank and swore friendship with him, and *nota bene*! you must pay for every round! It will cost you a tidy penny, but you must not mind that – on you go, introduce him to gaming and doubtful company, get him involved in a fight, and mischief of one kind and another, till he is bankrupt of strength and resistance and money and conscience and good name; and by the by, I must tell you, you will get nowhere unless you destroy both body and soul – believe me, brother! I must have drawn the conclusion fifty times in my extensive operations, that once the honest man is chivvied from his nest, the devil is master – it's as easy a step – oh, as easy a step as from a whore to a pious old maid. – But hark! was that a shot?

RATZMANN: It was the thunder, go on!

SPIEGELBERG: A still quicker, better way is this, you rob your man of house and home, till he hasn't a shirt left to his back, then he'll come to you of his own accord – don't ask me the tricks, brother, just ask that red-faced fellow over there – the pox! I got him tangled up a treat – I showed him forty ducats, said they were his if he would take a pressing of his master's keys in wax for me – imagine! the stupid brute does it, devil take me if he doesn't bring me the keys and ask for his money – My good fellow, says I, let me tell you that I shall take these keys straight to the superintendent of police and book you a place on the gibbet! – Strike me dead! you should have seen the fellow: his eyes popped and he shivered like a wet poodle – 'In heaven's name! will the gentleman not be reasonable? I will – I will –' 'What then, man? Will you tuck up your pigtail and go to the devil with me?' – 'Oh yes, with pleasure, anything you say' – ha, ha, ha! poor simpleton, mice like cheese, don't they? – Have a good laugh at him, Ratzmann! ha, ha!

RATZMANN: Yes, yes, I must admit. I will inscribe your lesson in golden characters on the tablets of my memory. Satan must know his man, choosing you for his scout.

SPIEGELBERG: Don't you think so, brother? And I reckon if I catch ten more for him he will let me go free – a publisher gives his agent one free copy in ten, why should the devil be such a Jew? – Ratzmann! I can smell powder.

RATZMANN: Confound it! I have smelt it for a long time. Mark my words, something will be up not far from here! – Yes, yes, I tell you, Moritz – the Captain will be glad to see you and your recruits – he has enlisted some fine fellows, too.

SPIEGELBERG: But mine! mine! Pah –

RATZMANN: Yes, they look light-fingered enough – but I tell you, our Captain's reputation has led honest men into temptation too.

SPIEGELBERG: I hope not!

RATZMANN: *Sans* jest! and they're not ashamed to serve under him. He doesn't murder for plunder as we do – he didn't seem to care about the money, as long as he could keep his pistols primed, and even his third of the booty that is his by right, he would give away to orphans, or to promising lads from poor homes so that they could study. But if there is a squire to be fleeced, one that drives his peasants like cattle, or if we get hold of some gold-braided scoundrel that twists the laws to his own advantage, and makes justice wink with silver, or any fine fellow of that kind – man! then he's in his element, and the devil's in him, as if every nerve of his body was a fury.

SPIEGELBERG: H'm, h'm!

RATZMANN: Not so long ago we were in an inn, and got wind that a rich count was on his way from Regensburg, who had just won a case worth a million, thanks to a crafty lawyer – he was sitting at the table playing backgammon – how many of us are there? he asked me, and jumped to his feet, I saw him biting his lip, as he only does when he is in a real rage – five at the most! I said – it's enough! he said, threw the money for the landlady on the table, left the wine untouched that he had ordered – we set off on our way. The whole time he didn't speak a word, went aside by himself, only asked us from time to time whether we could not hear anything yet, and told us to put our ears to the ground. At last, there comes the count riding along, his carriage weighed down with baggage, the lawyer sitting inside with him, one man riding ahead, two servants alongside – then you should have seen the man, bounding up to the carriage ahead of us, with two pistols in his hand! and his voice, as he shouted Stop! The coachman didn't want to stop, but he had to take a dive from the box, the count shot out of the carriage door, but it was useless, the riders fled – your money, scum! he cried, in a voice like thunder – he lay like a bullock under the axe – and are you the villain who makes a whore of justice? The lawyer shook so that you could hear his teeth chattering – then there was a dagger in his belly, sticking up like a stake in a vineyard – I have done my part! he cried, and turned away from us in his proud fashion – plundering is your business. And with that he disappeared into the woods –

SPIEGELBERG: H'm, h'm! – brother, what I told you just now was between ourselves, he needn't know about it. Do you understand?

RATZMANN: Yes, yes, I understand!

SPIEGELBERG: You know what he is like? He has his whims. You understand me.

RATZMANN: Very well, I understand.

[*Enter* SCHWARZ, *at full speed.*]

SCHWARZ: Quick, quick! where are the others? By all the sacraments! you standing there, and talking? Don't you know – don't you know, then? – and Roller –

RATZMANN: What then, what then?

SCHWARZ: Roller has been hanged, and four others too.

RATZMANN: Roller? The plague! but when – how do you know?

SCHWARZ: Three weeks and more he was inside, and we heard nothing, three times they have had him up, and we heard nothing, they tortured him to find out where the captain was – he gave nothing away, stout lad, yesterday they tried him and this morning he was sent express to the devil.

RATZMANN: Damnation! Does the captain know?

SCHWARZ: He only heard about it yesterday. He was foaming like a wild boar. You know Roller was always his favourite, and now, torture – he had ropes and ladders brought to the prison, but it was no use – he dressed up as a friar himself and got in there, and wanted to take Roller's place, but Roller turned it down flat, now he has sworn an oath that made our blood freeze, that he will light him a funeral pyre such as no king ever had, one that will burn them black and blue. I wouldn't like to be in that town. He has had it in for them for a long time, because they are such miserable bigots, and you know, when he says: I will do it! it's as much as if you or I had already done it.

RATZMANN: That's true! I know the captain. If he had given
the devil his word that he would go to hell, he would never
say a prayer, even though he could save himself with half an
Our Father! But oh! poor Roller! poor Roller!

SPIEGELBERG: *Memento mori!* But it makes no difference to
me. [*Singing.*]

> As I go past the gallows tree,
> I turn my head and blink my eye,
> And think, as you swing there so free,
> Who's the fool now, you or I?

RATZMANN[*jumping up*]: Hark! a shot.

[*Shooting and noises off.*]

SPIEGELBERG: Another!

RATZMANN: And another! the captain!

VOICES [*singing offstage*]:

> In Nuremberg you'll never hang,
> Unless they catch you first.

> [*Da capo.*]

SCHWEITZER, ROLLER [*offstage*]: Hey, hallo! halloo, ho!

RATZMANN: Roller, Roller! Ten devils take me!

SCHWEITZER, ROLLER [*offstage*]: Ratzmann! Schwarz!
Spiegelberg! Ratzmann!

RATZMANN: Roller! Schweitzer! Death, devils, hell and
damnation! [*Running to meet them.*]

[*Enter* ROBBER MOOR *on horseback;* SCHWEITZER, ROL-
LER, GRIMM, SCHUFTERLE, *and a troop of* ROBBERS,
covered with dust and dirt.]

MOOR[*jumping down from his horse*]: Freedom, freedom! – you
are home and dry, Roller! Schweitzer, take my horse and
wash him down with wine. [*Throwing himself on the ground*]
That was warm work!

RATZMANN [*to* ROLLER]: By Pluto's fiery furnace! are you
resurrected from the wheel?

SCHWARZ: Are you his ghost? or am I a fool? or is it really
you?

ROLLER [*recovering his breath*]: It is. Flesh and blood, entire. Where do you think I've come from?

SCHWARZ: Ask the Sibyl! the judge had put on his black cap for you.

ROLLER: That he had, and that's not all. I've come express from the gallows. Just let me get my breath back. Schweitzer here will tell you. Get me a glass of brandy! – you here again too, Moritz? I thought I should be seeing you in another place – get me a glass of brandy, will you? my bones are falling apart – oh, captain! where's the captain?

SCHWARZ: Straight away, straight away! – but tell us, say! how did you get away? how have we got you again? My head is spinning. From the gallows, you say?

ROLLER [*drinking a bottle of brandy*]: Ah, that's good, that warms your heart! Straight from the gallows, I tell you! There you stand gasping, and can't imagine it – I was only three steps from the blessed ladder that was going to take me up to Abraham's bosom – so near, so near! sold to the dissecting-theatre already, head to foot, inside and out! you could have had my life for a pinch of snuff, but I owe the captain breath, life and liberty.

SCHWEITZER: It's a tale worth telling. The day before, we had heard from our spies that Roller was in a pretty pickle, and if the skies didn't fall in time, then the next morning at break of day – that would be today – he would have to go the way of all flesh. – Up! says the captain, what won't we do for a friend. We'll save him, or if we can't save him, then at least we'll light him a funeral pyre such as no king ever had, one that will burn them black and blue. The whole band turned out. We sent a messenger express to him, with a note of what we were going to do, to drop it in his soup.

ROLLER: I never believed they would succeed.

SCHWEITZER: We bided our time till all the alley-ways were empty. All the town had gone out to see the show, on horseback and on foot and in carriages all jostling together, you could hear the din and the penitential psalm a long way off. Now, says the captain, set alight, set alight! Our fellows flew like arrows, set fire to the town in thirty-three places at once, threw down burning firebrands near the powder-magazine, in the churches and the barns – by God, before a quarter of an hour was up, the north-east wind came and served us a treat – he must have had his grudge against the town too! – and helped the fire on its way to the topmost gables. And us meanwhile up and down the streets like furies – fire, fire! all through the town – shrieks and howls and rampage – the firebells start to ring, then up goes the powder-magazine in the air, as if the earth was split in two, and heaven burst, and hell sunk ten thousand fathoms deeper.

ROLLER: And now my escort looked over their shoulders – there lay the town like Sodom and Gomorrha, the whole horizon was fire and smoke and brimstone, forty hills echoing the hellish blast all around, everyone falls to the ground in panic – I seize the opportunity, and whish! like the wind – they had untied me, we were as close to it as that – with my company staring back petrified like Lot's wife, away! through the crowds, and off! Sixty yards on and I throw off my clothes, jump into the river, swim under the water till I thought I was out of their sight. The captain ready and waiting with clothes and horses – and so I escaped. Moor, Moor! I only hope you land in such a stew, so that I can repay you in the same coin!

RATZMANN: A brute of a wish, that you deserve to be hanged for – but what a trick to pull off!

ROLLER: It was rescue in my darkest hour, you'll never know what it was like. You should have been there, with the rope round your neck, marching wide awake to the grave like me, and all their accursed rituals and hangman's ceremonies, and every tottering, frightened step nearer and nearer to the loathsome contrivance where I was going to be installed, rising in the hideous glow of the morning sun, and the hangman's assistants lurking, and the horrible music – I can still hear it ringing in my ears – and the hungry ravens croaking, thirty of them perched there on my half-rotten predecessor, and all that, all that – and the foretaste of the eternal bliss that was waiting for me too! Brother, brother! and all of a sudden, the password to freedom – a bang as if heaven had burst its hoops – listen, you vermin! I tell you, if you were to jump from the glowing furnace into icy water, you would not feel such a difference as I did when I reached the opposite bank.

SPIEGELBERG [*laughing*]: Poor bastard! Now it's out of your system. [*Drinks to him.*] Here's to your happy resurrection!

ROLLER [*throwing his glass away*]: No, by all the treasures of Mammon! I shouldn't care to live through that again. Dying is more than a harlequinade, and the fear of death is worse than dying itself.

SPIEGELBERG: And the powder-magazine blown up – you see now, Ratzmann? That was why the air smelt of sulphur for miles around, as if Moloch's privy had been tipped out beneath the firmament – it was a master-stroke, captain! I envy you for it.

SCHWEITZER: If the town makes a holiday out of seeing my comrade done away with like a baited pig, why the devil should we have any qualms at setting off the town for the sake of our comrade? And on top of that, our fellows had the chance of plundering scot free. Tell us, what did you get?

ONE OF THE BAND: I crept into St Stephen's in the confusion and cut the gold trimmings off the altar-cloth – the good Lord is a rich man, I said, and can spin gold out of old rope.

SCHWEITZER: Well done! – What is the use of that stuff in a church? They dedicate it to the Creator, who laughs at their trumpery – and his creatures go hungry – And you, Spangeler – where did you cast your nets?

ANOTHER: Bügel and I raided a chandler's, and have brought enough gear for fifty of us.

A THIRD: Two golden fob-watches I've spirited away, and a dozen silver spoons too.

SCHWEITZER: Good, good! And we have given them enough to keep them busy for a fortnight. If they want to put the fire out, they will have to ruin the town with water. – Schufterle, didn't you hear how many dead there were?

SCHUFTERLE: Eighty-three, they say. The magazine alone blew sixty to smithereens.

MOOR [very gravely]: Roller, your life is dearly bought.

SCHUFTERLE: Pah! what do you mean? Now if it had been men; but it was only babes in arms still dirtying their linen, wrinkled grandmothers chasing the flies from them, shrivelled old stay-at-homes who couldn't find their way to the door – hypochondriacs whining for the doctor, while he had gone out to follow the mob at his own solemn pace – Everyone with a sound pair of legs had run to see the spectacle, and only the dregs of the town was left behind to mind the houses.

MOOR: Oh, the poor, miserable creatures! Children, you say, the old and the sick? –

SCHUFTERLE: Yes, the devil take them! and women in childbed, and pregnant ones afraid of aborting under the gallows, and young wives who thought the hangman's tricks might give them a shock, and brand the child in their womb with a gallows-mark – poor poets who had no shoes to put on because their only pair was at the menders', and riff-raff of that kind, not worth the trouble of talking about. I happened to be going past a row of cottages there, and heard a howling and peeped in, and when I took a good look, what was it? A baby, lying there as right as rain under the table, and the table just about to catch fire – Poor little brute! I said, you're freezing! and threw it into the flames –

MOOR: Did you, Schufterle? And may those flames burn in

your breast till the day eternity grows grey! - Away, monster! Never let me see you in my band again! What, are you murmuring? Are you hesitating? Who can hesitate when I command? Away with him, I say - there are others among you who are ripe for my wrath. I know you, Spiegelberg. But I shall come amongst you, and terrible shall be my judgement upon you.

[*Exeunt* ROBBERS, *trembling, leaving* MOOR *alone, pacing violently up and down.*]

MOOR: Hear them not, avenger in Heaven! How can I prevent it? How can you prevent it, when your pestilence, your famine, your floods devour the just man with the wicked? Who can command the flame, and bid it spare the hallowed crops when it shall destroy the hornets' nest? Oh shame upon the murder of children! of women! of the sick! How this deed bows my head! It has poisoned my finest works - see the boy standing there, flushed with disgrace and mocked before the eyes of Heaven, he who ventured to play with Jove's thunderbolt, and hurled down pygmies when his task was to shatter titans - go, go! you are not the man to wield the highest tribunal's avenging sword, the first stroke was too much for your strength - here I renounce the impertinent plan, go to hide myself in some crevice of the earth, where the daylight shrinks before my shame. [*As if to flee.*]

[*Enter* ROBBERS, *in haste.*]

A ROBBER: Look out, captain! The forest is alive! Whole troops of Bohemian cavalry are on the rampage - Hell's constable must have put them up to it.

MORE ROBBERS: Captain, captain! They have trailed us here - thousands of them are cordoning off the woods around us!

MORE ROBBERS: Help, help! They have caught us, we shall be hanged and quartered! Thousands and thousands of hussars and dragoons and scouts are riding up the hillside, and have cut off our bolt-holes.

[*Exit* MOOR. *Enter* SCHWEITZER, GRIMM, ROLLER,

SCHWARZ, SCHUFTERLE, SPIEGELBERG, RATZMANN,
and the ROBBER BAND.]

SCHWEITZER: Have we shaken them out of their beds?
Cheer up, Roller! That's what I have been waiting for for a
long time, a set-to with some of these cookhouse champions
– where is the captain? Is the whole band together? We have
powder enough, haven't we?

RATZMANN: Powder and plenty to spare. But there are no
more than eighty of us – we're scarcely one to twenty.

SCHWEITZER: All the better! and if it was fifty of them to
my finger-nail! Didn't they sit tight till we'd set fire to the
straw under their arses? Brothers! brothers! there's nothing
to worry about! They gamble their lives for ten kreutzers,
aren't we fighting for our necks and our freedom? We shall
be upon them like the Flood and rain down on their heads
like thunder-bolts – Where in the Devil's name is the
captain?

SPIEGELBERG: He has left us in our hour of need. Can't we
get away?

SCHWEITZER: Get away?

SPIEGELBERG: Oh, why didn't I stay in Jerusalem!

SCHWEITZER: Why, then I hope you drown in a sewer, you
miserable rat! When it's naked nuns you've enough to say
for yourself, but when you see a pair of fists – Coward, let
us see now what you are made of, or we'll sew you into a
sow's skin and set the dogs on you!

RATZMANN: The captain, the captain!
    [Enter MOOR.]

MOOR [slowly, aside]: I have let them encircle us completely,
now these fellows will have to fight in desperation. [Aloud]
Now, lads! Now is the time! We are lost, or we must fight
like wild boars at bay.

SCHWEITZER: Ha! I'll rip their bellies with my tusks till their
tripes come bursting out by the yard! Lead on, captain! We
will follow you into the jaws of death!

MOOR: Load all weapons. There is no shortage of powder?

SCHWEITZER [*bounding up*]: No, powder enough to blow the earth sky-high!

RATZMANN: Every man has five pairs of pistols loaded, every man three rifles as well.

MOOR: Good, good! And now some of you must climb the trees, or hide among the thickets, and fire at them from the rear –

SCHWEITZER: That is your place, Spiegelberg!

MOOR: The rest of us, like furies, will fall upon their flank.

SCHWEITZER: That's the place for me!

MOOR: At the same time everyone must let them hear him whistle, and move around in the woods, so that our numbers will seem more formidable; and we must let all the dogs loose, and set them amongst their ranks, to separate and spread them out and drive them into your fire. We three, Roller, Schweitzer and I will fight in the thick of it.

SCHWEITZER: Masterly, superb! We will beat them so that they do not know where the blows are coming from. I can shoot a cherry out of a man's mouth – just let them come!

[SCHUFTERLE *tugs at* SCHWEITZER's *sleeve*; SCHWEITZER *goes on one side with the captain and speaks quietly with him.*]

MOOR: Silence!

SCHWEITZER: I beg you –

MOOR: Away! Let him thank his disgrace, it has saved his life. He shall not die when I and my Schweitzer die, and my Roller. Take his clothes from him, I will say he was a passer-by and I robbed him – Calm yourself, Schweitzer! I swear he will yet be hanged one day.

[*Enter a* PRIEST.]

PRIEST [*aside, taken aback*]: Is this the dragon's lair? – By your leave, gentlemen! I am a servant of the Church, and out there are seventeen hundred men, set to guard every hair of my head.

SCHWEITZER: Bravo, bravo! a fine speech to keep one's belly warm.

MOOR: Silence, comrade! – Speak, father, and be brief! What business have you with us?

PRIEST: I am sent by the authorities, whose word is life and death – you thieves – you murderous incendiaries – you scoundrels – poisonous brood of vipers, that creep in darkness, and sting where no man sees – plague upon the face of mankind – generation of hell – feast for ravens and vermin – colony for the gallows and the wheel –

SCHWEITZER: Dog! enough of your abuse, or – [*Thrusting a rifle-butt into his face.*]

MOOR: Shame on you, Schweitzer! You have spoilt his peroration – he has learnt his sermon so perfectly by heart – go on, sir! – 'for the gallows and the wheel...'?

PRIEST: And you, glorious captain! Duke of cutpurses! King of villains! Great Mogul of all the scoundrels under the sun! Image of that first loathsome rabble-rouser, who stirred up a thousand legions of innocent angels to fiery rebellion, and dragged them down with him to the pit of damnation – the accusing cries of abandoned mothers howl at your heels, blood is the water you drink, men weigh on your murderous dagger no more than a bubble of air. –

MOOR: Very true, very true! Go on!

PRIEST: What? Very true, very true? Is that your answer?

MOOR: What, sir? That was not quite what you expected? Go on, go on! What more did you have to say?

PRIEST [*heatedly*]: Terrible man! get thee behind me! Does not the murdered Count's blood stick to your accursed fingers? Have not you with thieving hands violated the Lord's sanctuary, and villainously seized the consecrated vessels of the sacrament? What? Did not you hurl brands of fire into our God-fearing city, and blow up its magazine over the heads of pious Christians? [*Clasping his hands together*] Hideous, hideous sins, that stink to high heaven, and

call the Last Judgement to arms, that it may break upon you!
Ripe for retribution, ready for the last trumpet!

MOOR: Masterly, so far! but to the matter! What is it that the
right worshipful gentlemen would have you tell me?

PRIEST: That which you are not worthy to hear! – Look
about you, incendiary and murderer! As far as your eye can
see, you are pinned in by our cavalry – there is no room for
you to escape now – as sure as cherries will grow upon these
oaks, and these pine-trees bear peaches, so surely will you
turn your back upon these oaks and pines unharmed.

MOOR: Do you hear, Schweitzer? – But go on!

PRIEST: Hear then, how graciously, how patiently justice has
borne with your iniquities. If you will crawl upon your
knees to the cross, and beg for grace and mercy, then see,
severity itself will yield to pity, justice will be as a loving
mother – she will turn a blind eye to the half of your
crimes, and – consider! – you will only be broken on the
wheel.

SCHWEITZER: Do you hear, captain! Shall I go and squeeze
this worn-out sheepdog by the throat till he sweats blood
from every pore? –

ROLLER: Captain! Death, devils and hell! Captain! – see how
he chews his lip between his teeth! shall I turn the fellow
upside-down beneath the firmament like a ninepin?

SCHWEITZER: Me, me! Let me kneel, let me beg at your
feet! Let me have the pleasure of grinding him to powder!
   [PRIEST cries out.]

MOOR: Leave him alone! Let no one dare to touch him! [To
the PRIEST, drawing his sword] Look, father! here stand
seventy-nine men, whose captain I am, and none of them
will fly at a command, or dance to the music of your can-
nons; and out there stand seventeen hundred who have
grown grey beneath their muskets – but hear me! thus says
Moor, captain of murderers and incendiaries. It is true, I
killed the Count, I plundered the Dominican church and set

it alight, I cast firebrands into your city of bigots, I blew up the powder-magazine over the heads of pious Christians – but that is not all. [*Stretching out his right hand*] Look at these four precious rings that I wear, one on each finger – go and tell the worshipful gentlemen with their powers of life and death, tell them point by point, what you are about to see and hear. – This ruby I took from the finger of a minister whom I laid low at his prince's feet when he was hunting. He was a man of the common people, who had made his way by flattery to his master's highest favour – his neighbour's fall was the footstool of his exaltation – orphan's tears bore him aloft. This diamond I took from a minister of finance, who sold offices and honours to the highest bidder, and turned the sorrowing patriot away from his door. This agate I wear in honour of one of your cloth, whom I strangled with my own hands after he had lamented in the pulpit, before his congregation, that the Inquisition had declined so. – I could tell you many more stories of my rings, if it were not that I already regretted the few words I have wasted upon you –

PRIEST: O Pharaoh, Pharaoh!

MOOR: Do you hear? Did you mark him groan? Does he not stand there as if he would call down fire from Heaven upon the Korahites with prayer? judging with a shrug of his shoulders, damning with a Christian sigh! Can a man be so blind? He who has Argus' hundred eyes to spy out his brother's spots, can he be so blind to his own? – Gentleness and tolerance they thunder from their clouds, and offer the God of love human sacrifices like a fiery-armed Moloch – they preach the love of their neighbour, and they curse the blind octogenarian at their door – they fulminate against covetousness, and they have slaughtered Peru for the sake of golden brooches and harnessed the pagans like beasts of burden to drag their wagons – they rack their brains in wonder that nature could have brought forth a Judas

Iscariot, and he is not the meanest of them who would betray God's Holy Trinity for ten pieces of silver! Oh, you Pharisees, you forgers of the truth, you apes and mockers of God! You are not ashamed to kneel before cross and altar, to flay your backs with scourges and to mortify your flesh with fasting, and you think these miserable mountebank's tricks will deceive Him whom you fools yet call all-knowing – just as one mocks the great most bitterly by flattering them that they hate flatterers; you boast of your honesty and upright life, and the God who looks into your hearts would be seized with rage against the creator, if it were not He himself who created the monster of the Nile. – Take him out of my sight.

PRIEST: That the wicked can be so proud!

MOOR: Not enough! – now I will speak with pride. Go and tell the right worshipful gentlemen that dice for life and death – I am no thief that conspires with midnight and with sleep, and plays the great man when he mounts the ladder – what I have done, doubtless I shall read one day in the ledgers of Heaven, but with their miserable hirelings I will waste my words no more. Tell them my trade is retribution – vengeance is my calling. [*Turning his back on him.*]

PRIEST: So you do not seek grace and mercy? Very well, I have nothing more to say to you. [*Turning to the band*] You then, listen to what I have to tell you in the name of justice! – If you will now lay hands on this condemned criminal, bind him and deliver him up, then see! you shall be spared punishment for the horrors you have committed – the memory of them shall be wiped out – Holy Mother Church will receive you once again into her loving bosom like sheep that have strayed, and to each one of you the way to rank and honour shall be open. [*Smiling triumphantly*] What then! What do you say to that, your Majesty? – Hurry then! Bind him, and you are free!

MOOR: Do you hear? Do you hear him? Why do you hesi-

tate? Do you not know what to do? Justice offers you freedom, and you are in truth her prisoners. – She grants you
your lives, and those are no empty words, for you are in
truth condemned men. – She promises you rank and honour,
and what can be your lot, even if you were to be victorious,
other than shame and curses and persecution. – She speaks
to you with Heaven's voice of reconciliation, and you are in
truth damned. There is not a hair upon your heads, not upon
one of you, that is not destined for hell. Will you still consider? Are you still in doubt? Is it so hard to choose between
heaven and hell? Will you not help them, father!

PRIEST [aside]: Is the fellow mad? – What, do you think perhaps it is a trap to catch you all alive? Read for yourselves,
here is the general pardon, signed and sealed. [Handing
SCHWEITZER a paper] Can you still be in doubt?

MOOR: Look, look! What more can you ask? Signed with his
own hand – mercy beyond bounds – or are you afraid they
will break their word, have you heard that no faith is kept
with traitors? – Oh, have no fear! Politics could make them
keep their word, even if they had given it to Satan himself.
Who would ever believe them again? Would they ever be
able to play the trick again? – I would swear that they mean
it! They know it is I who have stirred you up and embit-
tered you, you they think are innocent. Your crimes they
interpret as the errors of hasty youth. It is I alone whom
they seek, I alone who must pay the penalty. Is it not so,
father?

PRIEST: What is the devil called that speaks out of him? – Yes,
yes, it is so – the fellow has me spinning.

MOOR: What, still no reply? Surely you do not think you can
break out by force of arms? Look about you, look about
you! surely you cannot think that! such confidence would
be but childish folly. – Or do you flatter yourselves, thinking
to die the death of heroes, because you saw how I rejoiced at
the thought of battle? – Oh, do not believe it! You are not

Moor. – You are nothing but a gang of thieves! Miserable instruments of my greater designs, like the rope contemptible in the hangman's hand! Thieves cannot die the death of heroes. Life is the thief's profit, after it come terrors. – Thieves have the right to be afraid of death. – Hear how their trumpets sound! See how their threatening sabres flash! What? Still undecided? are you mad? are you out of your minds? – It is unforgiveable! I will not owe my life to you, I despise your sacrifice!

PRIEST [*in astonishment*]: He will drive me mad, I must fly from this place! Whoever heard such things as this?

MOOR: Or are you afraid that I will kill myself, and by my suicide invalidate the treaty that counted only while I was alive? No, children! that is an idle fear. Here I throw away my dagger, here my pistols and my phial of poison that I had in readiness – so wretched I am, I have lost even the power of my own life. – What, still undecided? Or do you think I will resist, if you attempt to bind me? Look! see me lash my right hand to this oak-tree's branch, I am defenceless, a child can conquer me – Who will be the first to abandon his captain in his hour of need?

ROLLER [*in furious excitement*]: And if nine circles of hell surrounded us! [*Brandishing his sword*] Every man who is not a dog, save your captain!

SCHWEITZER [*tearing up the pardon, and throwing the pieces in the* PRIEST's *face*]: Pardon, in our bullets! Away, vermin! tell the magistrates who sent you that in Moor's band you could not find a single traitor. – Save, save the captain!

ALL [*shouting*]: Save, save, save the captain!

MOOR [*tearing himself free, joyfully*]: Now we are free – Comrades! I feel an army in my fist – death or liberty! – at least they shall take none of us alive!

[*The trumpets sound the attack. Noise and tumult. Exeunt, with drawn swords.*]

ACT THREE

SCENE I

[AMALIA *in her garden, playing upon the lute.*]

AMALIA:

    Fair as angels, full of heaven's delight,
    Fairer far than other youths was he,
    His gaze as Maytime sunbeams tender-bright,
    Mirrored in the heavenly azure sea.

    His embrace – o raging ecstasies!
    Fiery hearts around each other furled,
    Our lips and ears entranced – before our eyes
    The night – and our two spirits heavenward whirled.

    And his kiss – o taste of paradise!
    As two burning flames will grasp and cling,
    As two harps will join their melodies
    And their heavenly harmonies will sing,

    Plunging, racing, soaring, spirits bound,
    Lip and cheek a-tremble and ablaze,
    Soul joined with soul and heaven and earth around
    The lovers lost and melted in the haze.

    – He is gone! alas, it is in vain
    The timid sigh recalls him to our grasp!
    He is gone – and life is now but pain,
    All joy expiring in a dying gasp.
[*Enter* FRANZ.]

FRANZ: Here again, wilful dreamer? You crept away from our merry feast, and spoilt our guests' pleasure.

AMALIA: I am sorry for these innocent delights! When the dirge must still be ringing in your ears that sang your father to his grave –

FRANZ: Would you mourn for ever? Let the dead sleep, and make the living happy! I have come –

AMALIA: And when will you be gone again?

FRANZ: Oh, Amalia! Let me not see these black, proud looks! You grieve me. I have come to tell you –

AMALIA: I suppose I must hear that Franz von Moor has succeeded to the title.

FRANZ: Yes, I came to hear what you would say – Maximilian has been laid to rest with his forefathers. I am your lord and master. But Amalia, I would be so in every respect. – You remember what you have been to our family, Moor treated you as his daughter, his love for you lives on even after his death – can you ever forget that?

AMALIA: Never, never. Who could be so thoughtless as to drown those memories in feasting!

FRANZ: My father's love for you must be repaid to his sons, and Karl is dead – you wonder? you are giddy? Yes, truly, the thought of it is so grand, so flattering, that it must even numb a woman's pride. Franz tramples upon the hopes of the noblest young ladies in the land, Franz comes and offers his heart and his hand to a poor orphan who would be helpless without him, and with it all his gold and all his castles and forests. Franz, whom men envy and fear, comes of his own free will to declare himself Amalia's slave –

AMALIA: Why does not the lightning split the blaspheming tongue that speaks such shameful words? You, you murdered my love, and Amalia should call you husband! you –

FRANZ: Not so hasty, your most gracious highness! – It is true, Franz cannot mop and mow like a cooing Celadon before you – true, he has not learnt to moan his lover's plaint

to the echo of the rocks and caves like a languishing Arcadian
swain – Franz speaks, and if he hears no answer, he will –
command.

AMALIA: Command? You, reptile, command? command me?
– and if I throw your command back in your face with
scorn?

FRANZ: You will not do that. I know a way that will nicely
tame your blind obstinate pride – a convent cell!

AMALIA: Bravo! excellent! in a convent cell, spared your
basilisk's look for ever, and with time enough to think of
Karl, to cling to his memory. Welcome with your convent!
Let your cell enfold me!

FRANZ: Ha! is it so! – beware! Now you have taught me the
art of tormenting you – the sight of me shall scourge this
everlasting fancy of Karl from your head like a fury with
locks of fire, the bogey-man Franz shall lurk behind your
lover's image like the dog in the fairy-tale, that lay on the
underground treasure – by your hair I will drag you into the
chapel with my sword in my hand, force the oath of
matrimony out of your soul, take your virgin bed by storm,
and conquer your proud innocence with my greater pride.

AMALIA [striking him across the face]: Take this for your dowry!

FRANZ [provoked]: Ha! ten times and ten times more you shall
be paid back for that! Not my wife – you shall not have the
honour – no, I will have you for my mistress, and honest
peasant women will point their fingers at you if you dare to
cross the street. Yes, gnash your teeth – spit fire and venom
from your eyes – I like a woman to be angry, it makes you
more beautiful, more desirable. Come – your struggling will
be sauce to my triumph and spice to my pleasure when I
force my embraces on you – Come with me to my room – I
am burning with desire – now, this minute you shall go with
me! [Attempting to drag her off.]

AMALIA [falling upon him]: Forgive me, Franz! [As he is about
to embrace her, she snatches his sword from his side and steps

quickly back.] Look, villain, what I can do to you now! I am a woman, but a woman in desperation – once dare to lay your lustful hands upon my body – this steel shall pierce your loathsome breast, and my uncle's spirit will guide my hand! Away, this minute! [*Drives him away.*] Ah! how good, how good – now I can breathe – I felt I was strong as a fiery steed, fierce as the tigress pursuing the triumphant robber of her cubs – A convent, he said! Thanks, for this happy discovery! Now love betrayed has found its resting-place – a convent – the Redeemer's cross is the resting-place for love betrayed. [*About to go.*]

[*Enter* HERRMANN, *timidly.*]

HERRMANN: Lady Amalia! Lady Amalia!

AMALIA: Wretch, why do you disturb me?

HERRMANN: I must shed this weight from my soul before it drags me down to hell – [*Falling at her feet*] Forgive me! forgive me! I have wronged you grievously, Lady Amalia!

AMALIA: Stand up! Leave me! I do not want to hear!

HERRMANN [*detaining her*]: No! Stay! In God's name! In God's eternal name, you shall hear it all!

AMALIA: Not another sound – I forgive you – go home in peace! [*Hurrying away.*]

HERRMANN: Then hear me this one word – it will give you peace again!

AMALIA [*comes back and looks at him in amazement*]: What, friend! – who, what on earth or in heaven can give me peace again?

HERRMANN: One single word from my lips – listen to me!

AMALIA [*seizing his hand with pity*]: Good fellow – can a word from your lips draw back the bolts of eternity?

HERRMANN [*standing up*]: Karl is alive!

AMALIA [*crying out*]: Miserable wretch!

HERRMANN: It is so – And one word more – Your uncle –

AMALIA [*rushing at him*]: You are lying –

HERRMANN: Your uncle –

AMALIA: Karl is alive!

HERRMANN: And your uncle –

AMALIA: Karl is alive?

HERRMANN: Your uncle too – Do not betray me. [*Rushes off.*]

AMALIA [*standing as if petrified, then starting up wildly and rushing after him*]: Karl is alive!

SCENE 2

A country scene, near the Danube.

[*The* ROBBERS, *camped on rising ground beneath trees. The horses are grazing downhill.*]

MOOR: Here I must lie and rest [*throwing himself on the ground*]. My limbs are shattered and my tongue is dried up like a potsherd.

    [SCHWEITZER *creeps off unnoticed.*]

I would bid you fetch me a handful of water from the river, but you are all weary unto death.

SCHWARZ: And the wine in our wineskins is no more.

MOOR: See how fair the corn stands! The trees almost breaking beneath their fruits. The vine full of promise.

GRIMM: It will be a fine harvest.

MOOR: You think so? Then one man is repaid for the sweat of his brow. One! – And yet the night may bring hail, and all be beaten to the ground.

SCHWARZ: It may well be. All can be beaten to the ground, a few hours before the reapers are come.

MOOR: It is as I say All will be beaten to nothingness. Why should man succeed where he imitates the ant, when he is thwarted where he is like the gods? Or is this the limit destined for his endeavour?

SCHWARZ: I do not know.

MOOR: Well said, and, it were better still that you should never seek to know! – Brother – I have seen men, their insect worries, and their giant designs; their godlike schemes and their mouse's scurryings, their wondrous chasing after happiness; this one trusting the leap of his horse – another, his donkey's nose – another, his own legs; this many-coloured lottery of life, where so many stake their innocence, their hopes of heaven, to draw the winning number, and – blanks, blanks every one – there was no lucky number there. Brothers, a spectacle to draw tears from your eyes, just as it stirs your stomach to laughter!

SCHWARZ: How gloriously the sun goes down!

MOOR [*lost in the sight*]: A hero's death! – Meet for worship!

GRIMM: Are you so moved?

MOOR: When I was a boy, my dearest wish was – to live like that, to die like that – [*Biting back his anguish*] A foolish boy's wish!

GRIMM: I should think so!

MOOR [*pulling his hat down over his eyes*]: There was a time – Leave me alone, comrades!

SCHWARZ: Moor, Moor! What, in the devil's name –? See how pale he has turned!

GRIMM: Why, confound it! what's the matter? is he sick?

MOOR: There was a time when I could not sleep at night if I had not said my prayers –

GRIMM: Have you lost your wits? Would you take lessons from when you were a boy?

MOOR [*laying his head on* GRIMM's *breast*]: Brother! brother!

GRIMM: What? look! are you a child?

MOOR: Oh, if I were – if only I were again!

GRIMM: Fie, shame!

SCHWARZ: Take courage! Look at the beauty of the landscape, see how fine the evening is!

MOOR: Yes, friends, this world is so fair.

SCHWARZ: Why, well spoken!

MOOR: This earth is so glorious.

GRIMM: Yes, yes – that is what I like to hear.

MOOR [*sinking back*]: And I so hideous in this fair world – and I, a monster on this glorious earth.

GRIMM: Oh, in God's name!

MOOR: My innocence! my innocence! – See! all went out to sun themselves in the peaceful beams of spring – Why I, I alone to drain hell from the joys of heaven? All so happy, all kin through the spirit of peace! the whole world one family, a father there above – a father, but not mine – I alone cast out, I alone set apart from the ranks of the blessed – not for me the sweet name of child – not for me the lover's melting glance – never, never more the bosom friend's embrace. [*Starting back wildly*] Set about with murderers, in the midst of hissing vipers – fettered to vice with bands of iron – rocked giddily over the abyss of destruction on the frail reed of vice – I, I alone cast out, a howling Abaddon amidst the fair world's happy blossoms!

SCHWARZ [*to the others*]: Incredible! I have never seen him like this.

MOOR [*sorrowfully*]: Oh, that I might enter again into my mother's womb! Oh, that I might be born a beggar! No! I would ask for no more, oh ye heavens – than that I might be as one of these who earn their daily bread! Oh, I would labour till the blood sprang from my brow – to buy the sweet joy of a single afternoon's rest – the bliss of a single tear.

GRIMM [*to the others*]: Patience! the fit will soon have left him.

MOOR: There was a time when they would flow so freely – oh, you days when I was at peace! You, my father's castle – you green dreaming valleys! Oh, Elysium of my childhood! – Will you never return? never cool my burning breast with your sweet murmurings? Mourn with me, Nature – Never, never will they return, never cool my burning breast with their sweet murmurings – Gone! gone! gone beyond recall! –

[*Enter* SCHWEITZER, *with water in his hat.*]

SCHWEITZER: Drink your belly full, captain – here's water in plenty, and cold as ice.

SCHWARZ: You're bleeding – what have you been doing?

SCHWEITZER: Fool, it might have cost me two broken legs – and a broken neck. There I was going along one of those sandbanks by the river, whoosh! the stuff slips away from under my feet and down I go, a good ten-foot drop – and when I'd picked myself up and got my wits back, there was the clearest water you could ask for, running between the stones. Enough of a caper for this time, I thought, this is what the captain wants.

MOOR [*giving him back his hat, and wiping his face for him*]: Let me – we do not often see the scars the cavalrymen left on your forehead, back there in Bohemia – your water was good, Schweitzer – these scars suit you well.

SCHWEITZER: Pah! there's room for thirty more!

MOOR: Yes, children – it was a warm afternoon's work – and only one man lost – my Roller died a fine death. There would be a monument on his grave, if he had not died for my sake. This will have to serve [*wiping his eyes*]. How many was it of our enemies that we killed?

SCHWEITZER: A hundred and sixty hussars – ninety-three dragoons, forty or so riflemen – three hundred in all.

MOOR: Three hundred against one! – Each one of you has a claim on this head. [*Baring his head*] Here I raise my dagger – as truly as my soul draws breath I swear – swear I will never forsake you.

SCHWEITZER: Do not swear! One day, you do not know! your good luck may return, and you will regret it.

MOOR: By my Roller's bones! I swear I will never forsake you!

[*Enter* KOSINSKY.]

KOSINSKY [*aside*]: Hereabouts they told me I should find him – hallo! what faces are these? Is it – might they – they are, they are! I will speak to them.

SCHWARZ: Look out! Who goes there?

KOSINSKY: Gentlemen, forgive me! I do not know, is this the right way?

MOOR: And who might we be, if it is?

KOSINSKY: Men!

SCHWEITZER: Haven't we proved it, captain?

KOSINSKY: Men I am seeking, who can look death in the face and let danger play about them like a charmed snake, who value freedom more than life and honour, whose very name, sweet sound to the poor and the oppressed, strikes terror in the valiant and turns the tyrant pale.

SCHWEITZER [*to the captain*]: I like this lad. Listen, friend! We are the ones you are looking for.

KOSINSKY: I think you are, and I hope we shall soon be brothers. – Then you can show me the way to the man I want, your captain I mean, the great Count Moor.

SCHWEITZER [*giving him his hand, warmly*]: You're a lad after my own heart!

MOOR [*coming closer*]: And do you know their captain?

KOSINSKY: You are he – these features – who could look upon them, and seek another? [*Gazing at him for a long time.*] I have always wished that I could see the man with destruction in his eye, there as he sat upon the ruins of Carthage – now I need wish it no longer.

SCHWEITZER: This is a fine fellow!

MOOR: And what brings you to me?

KOSINSKY: Oh, captain! my more than cruel destiny – I have been shipwrecked in the rough seas of this world, have seen my life's hopes sink beneath the ocean, and nothing left to me but the memory of what I had lost, a torment that would drive me insane if I had not sought to stifle it in distractions.

MOOR: Another with a grievance against God! – Go on.

KOSINSKY: I joined the army. Still my ill-luck pursued me –
I went on a journey to the East Indies, my ship ran aground
on the rocks – nothing but frustrated plans! At last, I heard
tell everywhere of your deeds – of your murder and arson,
as they called them – and I have travelled thirty leagues
firmly resolved to serve with you, if you will accept my services – I beg you, noble captain, do not turn me away!

SCHWEITZER [*with a bound*]: Hurrah, hurrah! Roller again, a
thousand times over! A real assassin for our band!

MOOR: What is your name?

KOSINSKY: Kosinsky.

MOOR: What, Kosinsky? And do you realize that you are a
rash and foolish boy, taking the great step of your life as
thoughtlessly as a careless girl – This is no skittle-alley, as
you may think.

KOSINSKY: I know what you mean – I am twenty-four years
old, but I have seen swords flash, and heard bullets whistle
by me.

MOOR: Indeed, young sir? – and have you only learnt to
fence so that you can strike down poor travellers for a few
shillings, or run women through from behind? Go, go! you
have run away from your governess because she threatened
to whip you. –

SCHWEITZER: What the devil, captain! what are you thinking of? you'll not send this Hercules away? Doesn't he look
the man to chase the Marshal of Saxony over the Ganges
with a kitchen ladle?

MOOR: Because your rags and tatters of schemes have come
to nothing, you come here to be a villain, a cut-throat? –
Murder, boy, do you know what the word means? You
could chop off poppy-heads and go to sleep with a clear
conscience, but to bear murder on your soul –

KOSINSKY: I will answer for every murder you bid me commit.

MOOR: What? are you so clever? Do you think to catch a man

with your flatteries? How do you know that I never have bad dreams, or that I will not turn pale on my deathbed? What have you done, to make you think of answering for it?

KOSINSKY: Little indeed – but I have come to you, Count Moor!

MOOR: Has your tutor been telling you tales of Robin Hood? – They should clap such careless creatures in irons, and send them to the galleys – exciting your childish imagination, and infecting you with delusions of greatness? Do you itch for fame and honour? would you buy immortality with murder and arson? Be warned, ambitious youth! Murderers earn no laurels! Bandits win no triumphs with their victories – only curses, danger, death and shame – do you not see the gibbet on the hill-top there?

SPIEGELBERG [*pacing up and down in irritation*]: Senseless! hideously, unforgivably stupid! that's not the way! that's not how I used to do it!

KOSINSKY: What should I fear, if I do not fear death?

MOOR: Splendid! incomparable! You learnt your lessons like a good boy, I see you know your Seneca by heart. – But my friend, fine phrases like that will not talk away the sufferings of your flesh, will never blunt the darts of your pain. Consider well, my son! [*Taking him by the hand*] Let me advise you as a father – see how deep is the abyss, before you jump into it! If there is still one single joy known to you in this world – there could be moments, when you – wake up – and then – find it was too late. Here you step beyond the bounds of humanity – you must either be more than a man, or you are a devil – Once more, my son! if one single spark of hope gleams anywhere within your life, then leave this terrible alliance which only despair can make – unless a higher wisdom founded it – we can easily be mistaken – Believe me, a man can think it strength of mind, and yet at the last it is despair – Believe me, me! and go back, as quickly as you can.

KOSINSKY: No, there is no turning back for me. If my pleas
cannot move you, then hear the story of my misfortune.
After that you will thrust the dagger into my hand yourself;
you will – sit round me here on the ground, and listen carefully!

MOOR: I will listen.

KOSINSKY: Let me tell you, then, that I come of a noble
family in Bohemia, and through my father's early death
inherited a sizeable estate. My lands were like a paradise –
for they contained an angel – a girl with all the charms that
the bloom of youth can endow, and chaste as the light of
heaven. – But why do I tell you this? it can only fall on deaf
ears – you have never loved, have never been loved –

SCHWEITZER: Be still! our captain is as red as fire.

MOOR: Stop! I will hear it another time – tomorrow, soon, or
– when I have seen blood.

KOSINSKY: Blood, blood – let me go on! My tale will fill
your soul with blood. She was from Germany, a com-
moner's daughter – but the sight of her would melt any
nobleman's prejudice. As shy and modest as could be, she
accepted the ring from my hand, and within a few days I
was to lead my Amalia to the altar.

[MOOR *leaps to his feet.*]

Amidst the dizziness of the joys that awaited me, in the
middle of my wedding preparations, I was summoned to
court by an express messenger. I presented myself. I was
shown letters that I was supposed to have written, full of
treasonable utterances. I was inflamed at this wickedness –
my sword was taken from me, I was thrown senseless into
prison –

SCHWEITZER: And meanwhile – go on! I think I can tell
what was brewing.

KOSINSKY: I lay there for a month, and did not know what
was happening to me. I was afraid for my Amalia, who
would be suffering the pains of death every minute on my

account. At last the chief minister of the court appeared, congratulated me with honeyed words on the establishment of my innocence, read me the proclamation of my release, gave me back my sword. Now in triumph to my castle, to fly to my Amalia's arms – she was gone. At midnight they said she had been taken away, no one knew where, and had not been seen since. It flashed across my mind like lightning – away! to the city, I sound them out at court – all eyes were on me, no one would tell me anything – at last I catch sight of her through a secret grating in the palace – she threw me a note.

SCHWEITZER: Didn't I say so?

KOSINSKY: Death, hell and devils! there it was! they had offered her the choice of seeing me die or of becoming the Prince's mistress. Forced to decide between her honour and her love – she chose the second, and [*laughing*] I was saved!

SCHWEITZER: What did you do?

KOSINSKY: I stood there, thunderstruck. Blood! was my first thought, blood! my last. I run home foaming with rage, pick myself a three-edged sword, and off like a fury to the minister's house, for he, he alone was the infernal pander. I must have been seen in the street, for when I got there all the rooms were locked. I hunted, I asked for him: he was with the prince, I was told. I hurry there straight away, they denied that they had seen anything of him. I go back, break down the doors, find him, was on the point – but then five or six of his men sprang out of hiding and robbed me of my sword.

SCHWEITZER [*stamping on the ground*]: And he got off scot free, and all your efforts were in vain?

KOSINSKY: I was arrested, charged, tried for my life, banished – do you hear? – as a mark of special consideration, banished from the country with ignominy, my estates confiscated and given to the minister, my Amalia is still in the tiger's clutches, sighing and mourning her life away, while my vengeance must go hungry, and bow beneath the yoke of despotism.

SCHWEITZER [*standing up, whetting his sword*]: Here is grist for our mill, captain! Here is a fire to be lit!

MOOR [*who has been pacing up and down in violent agitation, starting suddenly, to the* ROBBERS]: I must see her! – away! strike camp! – you shall stay with us, Kosinsky – pack up quickly!

THE ROBBERS: Where? What?

MOOR: Where? who can ask, where? [*Violently, to* SCHWEITZER] Traitor, would you hold me back? But by every hope of heaven! –

SCHWEITZER: I, a traitor? – lead us to hell and I will follow you!

MOOR [*embracing him*]: Brother of my heart! you shall follow me – she weeps, she mourns her life away. Up! away! all! to Franconia! Within the week we must be there! [*Exeunt.*]

ACT FOUR

SCENE I

A country scene, by OLD MOOR's *castle.*

[ROBBER MOOR, KOSINSKY *in the distance.*]

MOOR: Go before and announce me. You remember everything you have to say?

KOSINSKY: You are Count Brand, from Mecklenburg, and I am your groom – have no fear, I shall play my part well enough, good-bye! [*Exit.*]

MOOR: Soil of my fatherland, I salute you! [*He kisses the ground.*] Sky of my fatherland! Sun of my fatherland! meadows and hills and rivers and forests! I salute you, from my heart I salute you all! – how sweet the breezes blow from the

mountains of my home! with what joyous balm you greet
the poor outcast! Elysium! a world of poetry! Stop, Moor!
your feet tread the floor of a holy temple. [*Coming closer*] See
there, the swallows' nests in the castle courtyard – the little
gate that leads to the garden! – and the corner by the pali-
sade, where so often you would lie listening and mock your
pursuer – and there below, the valley with its meadows,
where as Alexander the hero you led your Macedonians into
the battle of Arbela, and the hill hard by, where you repulsed
the Persian satraps – and your victorious banner fluttered on
high! [*Smiling*] Those golden years of boyhood's May come
to life again in an outcast's soul – Oh, you were so happy, so
full of pure unclouded joy – and now – there lie the ruins of
your schemes! Here you were one day to wander, a great
man, dignified and renowned – here to live your boyhood
once more in Amalia's blossoming children – here! here, the
idol of your people – but the Enemy scowled at your plans!
[*Starting up*] Why did I come here? To hear like a prisoner
the clanking chain wake me with a start from dreams of
freedom – no, let me return to my exile and misery! – the
prisoner had forgotten the light, but the dream of freedom
flashed past him like the lightning in the night that it leaves
darker behind – Farewell, you valleys of my fatherland!
once you saw Karl the boy, and Karl the boy was a happy
and fortunate boy – now you have seen the man, and he was
in despair. [*He turns and goes quickly to the furthest part of the
scene, where he suddenly stops, stands still and gazes across at the
castle with an expression of grief.*] Not to see her, not one
glance? – And but a single wall between myself and Amalia
– No! I must see her – and him – and let me be annihilated!
[*Turning round*] Father! father! your son is coming – away,
black, reeking blood! away, fearful, hollow, convulsive
stare of death! This single hour I beg of you – Amalia!
father! your Karl is coming! [*He goes quickly towards the
castle.*] – Torment me when the daybreak comes, do not

leave me when the night has fallen – torment me with
dreams of horror! but do not poison this my one last joy!
[*At the gate*] What feelings are these? what is it, Moor? Be a
man! – Pangs of death – Horror and foreboding – [*He goes
in.*]

SCENE 2

A gallery in the Castle.

[*Enter* ROBBER MOOR *and* AMALIA.]

AMALIA: And do you believe that you can recognize his likeness amongst these pictures?

MOOR: Oh yes, quite certainly. His image was always fresh in
my memory. [*Going round looking at the pictures*.] This is not
he.

AMALIA: Rightly guessed! This is the first Count, the founder
of the line, who was ennobled by Barbarossa when he served
under him against the corsairs.

MOOR [*in front of the pictures*]: Nor is *this* he, nor *this* – nor *that*
one there – he is not among them.

AMALIA: Why, look more closely! – I thought you said you
knew him –

MOOR: I should not know my own father better! He lacks
that cast of gentleness about the lips, that would distinguish
him among thousands – it is not he.

AMALIA: You amaze me. What? Not seen him for eighteen
years, and yet –

MOOR [*quickly, his face suddenly flushed*]: This is he! [*He stands
as if thunderstruck.*]

AMALIA: A fine figure of a man!

MOOR [*gazing wrapt at the portrait*]: Father, father, forgive me!
– Yes, a fine figure of a man! – [*Wiping his eyes*] A godlike
figure of a man!

AMALIA: It seems you are deeply moved to think of him.

MOOR: Oh, a fine figure of a man! and he is gone?

AMALIA: Gone! as all our purest joys must go – [*gently taking his hand*] Dear Count, there is no happiness upon this earth.

MOOR: True, very true – and can it be that you have already found out that sad truth? You cannot be twenty-three years old.

AMALIA: And I have found it out. Everything that lives, lives but to die a sorrowful death; nothing we care for, nothing we make our own, but one day we must grieve at its loss.

MOOR: And what can you have lost already?

AMALIA: Nothing. Everything. Nothing. – Shall we not go further, my lord?

MOOR: In such haste? – Whose is that portrait on the right? I seem to read ill-luck in his features.

AMALIA: The portrait on the left is the Count's son, the present holder of the title – will you not come?

MOOR: But the portrait on the right?

AMALIA: Will you not see the garden?

MOOR: But the portrait on the right? – you are weeping, my Amalia?

[*Exit* AMALIA *in haste.*]

MOOR: She loves me, she loves me! – her whole being began to stir, the telltale drops flowed down her cheeks. She loves me! – Wretch, was this what you deserved? Am I not standing here like a condemned man before the fatal block? Is that the couch where at her bosom I dissolved in rapture? Are these my father's halls? [*Catching the eye of his father's portrait, as if transfixed*] You, you – Flames of fire from your eye – Curses, curses and rejection! – Where am I? Night before my eyes – the terrors of God – I, I have killed him. [*He rushes off.*]

[*Enter* FRANZ VON MOOR, *deep in thought.*]

FRANZ: Away with this vision! away, miserable coward! why

are you afraid, and of whom? does it not seem, these few
hours that the Count has trodden these floors, as if a spy of
hell were creeping at my back – I ought to know him!
There is something grand, something familiar in his wild
sunburnt face, something that makes me tremble – and
Amalia is not indifferent to him! Does she not linger upon
the fellow with greedy, pining glances, of a kind of which
she is otherwise so niggardly? – Did I not see her let fall a
few furtive tears into his wine, that he gulped down behind
my back as hastily as if he would have swallowed the glass
as well? Yes, I saw it, saw it in the mirror with my own two
eyes. Ho there, Franz! beware! there lurks some monster
pregnant with ruin! [*He stands studying* KARL's *portrait.*] His
long goose-neck – his black, fiery-flashing eyes – h'm, h'm!
– his dark overhanging bushy eyebrows! [*With a sudden
seizure*] Cunning, malicious hell! is it you who prompt me
with this suspicion? It is *Karl*! Yes! all his features spring to
life once more – It is he! despite his disguise – it is he! Death
and damnation! [*Pacing violently up and down.*] Was it for
this that I sacrificed my nights – levelled rocks and filled in
yawning chasms – rebelled against every instinct of humanity, all for this giddy vagrant to come blundering through
my cunningest coils – Gently, gently! All that remains is
child's play – Have I not already waded up to the ears in
mortal sin? – it would be folly to swim back when the shore
lies so far behind me – There can be no thought of turning
back – heavenly grace itself would be reduced to beggary, and
God's infinite mercy bankrupted, if all that I have incurred
should be paid – Forward then, like a man! [*He rings the bell.*]
Let him be coupled with his father's ghost and come, I care
nothing for the dead. – Daniel! hey, Daniel! – What do you
say, have they not already stirred him up against me too! He
looks like a man with a secret.

[*Enter* DANIEL.]

DANIEL: You wish, my lord?

FRANZ: Nothing. Go, fill this cup with wine, but hurry!
   [*Exit* DANIEL.]
   Just wait, old man! I will catch you out, I will look you in
   the eye, I will fix you so that your startled conscience will
   pale beneath your mask! – He shall die! – A poor workman
   he, who leaves a job half-finished, and stands back idly
   watching for what will happen next.
   [*Enter* DANIEL *with wine.*]

FRANZ: Put it down here! Look me straight in the eye! How
   your knees are shaking! How you tremble! Confess, old
   man! What have you done?

DANIEL: Nothing, your lordship, as true as God's alive, and
   my poor soul!

FRANZ: Drink this wine! drain it! – What? You hesitate? –
   Out with it, quickly! What did you put in this wine?

DANIEL: So help me God! – What? I – in the wine?

FRANZ: Poison you put in the wine! Are you not as white as a
   sheet? Confess, confess! Who gave it to you? The Count,
   wasn't it, the Count gave it to you?

DANIEL: The Count? Mary and Jesus! the Count didn't give
   me anything.

FRANZ [*seizing him violently*]: I will throttle you till you are
   blue in the face, you grizzled old liar! Nothing! And what
   were you doing with your heads together like that? You
   and he and Amalia? And what have you been whispering
   together? Out with it all! What were the secrets, what were
   the secrets he confided to you?

DANIEL: That God knows who knows everything. He didn't
   confide any secrets to me.

FRANZ: Will you deny it? What plots have you been hatching
   to get *me* out of the way? It's true, isn't it? You're going to
   strangle me in my sleep? Cut my throat when you are shav-
   ing me? Put poison in my wine or my chocolate? Out with
   it, out with it! – Send me to eternal rest with my soup? Out
   with it, I say! I know everything!

DANIEL: Then may God help me in my hour of need, but it's nothing but the truth I'm telling you!

FRANZ: This time I will forgive you. But isn't it true he put money in your purse? He shook your hand more firmly than the custom is? Firmly, as if he were greeting an old friend?

DANIEL: Never, my lord.

FRANZ: He said to you, for example, that he thought he knew you of old? – that you ought almost to recognize him? That the time would come when the scales would fall from your eyes – that – what? Do you tell me he never said such things?

DANIEL: Not a word of them.

FRANZ: That circumstances prevented him – that one often had to wear a mask, to get within range of one's enemy – that he would take revenge, take the most terrible revenge?

DANIEL: Not a breath of any such thing.

FRANZ: What? Nothing at all? Think carefully – that he knew your former master well – knew him exceptionally well – that he loved him – loved him uncommonly – loved him like a son –

DANIEL: Something of the kind I do remember I heard him say.

FRANZ [turning pale]: He did, he did, indeed? What, let me hear! He said he was my brother?

DANIEL [taken aback]: What, your lordship? No, he didn't say that. But when the young lady took him through the gallery – I was just dusting the frames of the pictures – suddenly he stood still before the late master's portrait, as if he was thunderstruck. Her ladyship pointed to it, and said: a fine figure of a man! Yes, a fine figure of a man! he answered her, and wiped his eye as he did so.

FRANZ: Listen, Daniel! You know I have always been a good master to you, I have fed you and clothed you, I have spared you tasks that were too hard for you in your old age –

DANIEL: And may God reward you for it! – and I have always served you well.

FRANZ: That was what I was going to say. You have never refused me anything all the days of your life, for you know too well that you owe me obedience in all that I command.

DANIEL: In everything and with all my heart, as long as it's not against God and my conscience.

FRANZ: Nonsense, nonsense! Are you not ashamed? An old man, still believing in Christmas fairy-tales! Away with you, Daniel! that was a foolish thought. I am your master. God and conscience may punish me, if there are such things as God and conscience.

DANIEL [clasping his hands together]: Merciful heavens!

FRANZ: By the obedience you owe me! Do you understand? By the obedience you owe me, I tell you, by tomorrow the Count must no longer be in the land of the living.

DANIEL: Help, holy God! Why not?

FRANZ: By the blind obedience you owe me! – and I tell you, I shall depend on you.

DANIEL: On me! Help me, holy Mother of God! On me? What wrong has an old man like me done?

FRANZ: There is no time to think about it, your fate is in my hand. Would you sigh out the rest of your days in my deepest dungeon, where hunger will drive you to gnaw the flesh from your own bones, and burning thirst to drink your own water? Or would you rather eat your bread in peace, and live a quiet old age?

DANIEL: What, master? Peace, and a quiet old age – and a murderer?

FRANZ: Answer my question!

DANIEL: My grey hairs, my grey hairs!

FRANZ: Yes or no!

DANIEL: No! – God grant me mercy!

FRANZ [about to go]: Good, you shall have need of it.

[DANIEL holds him back and falls on his knees before him.]

DANIEL: Mercy, my lord, have mercy!

FRANZ: Yes or no!

DANIEL: Your lordship, I am seventy-one years old today, and honoured my father and mother, and never knowingly cheated anyone of a penny all the days of my life, and have stood by my faith like a true and honest man, and have served in your house for four and forty years, and look to die in peace and with a clear conscience, oh my lord, my lord! [*Embracing his knees violently.*] And you would rob me of my last comfort at my end, and have the sting of conscience stifle my last prayer, and have me pass over as an abomination in the sight of God and men – No, no, my dear good dear gracious lord and master, you wouldn't do that, you couldn't want to do that to an old man of seventy-one.

FRANZ: Yes or no! What is this babbling?

DANIEL: I will be an even better servant from this day on, I will work my poor old fingers to the bone in your service like a common labourer, I will get up earlier, I will go to bed later – Oh, and I will say a prayer for you too in the morning and in the evening, and God will not refuse to hear an old man's prayer.

FRANZ: To obey is better than sacrifice. Did you ever hear of the hangman putting on airs when he had a sentence to carry out?

DANIEL: Oh, no, no, I know! but to slaughter innocence – to –

FRANZ: Am I accountable to you? may the axe ask the executioner, why strike here and not there? – but see how patient I am – I shall reward you for the loyalty you have sworn to me.

DANIEL: But I hoped to stay a Christian man when I swore loyalty to you.

FRANZ: No contradictions! look, I will give you one more whole day to consider! Think on it again. Happiness and misery – do you hear, do you understand? The greatest happiness – and the depths of misery! I shall do miracles of torture.

DANIEL [*after a little reflection*]: I will do it, tomorrow I will do it. [*Exit.*]

FRANZ: Temptation is strong, and *he* was not born to be a martyr for his faith. – Your health then, sir count! It looks very much as though tomorrow morning you will be eating your hangman's breakfast! – Everything depends on how one looks at these things; and the man who does not look according to his own advantage is a fool. The father perhaps has drunk another bottle of wine, and – feels the itch; and the result is – one man more, and the man was surely the last thing to be thought of in the whole Herculean labour. Now it so happens that I feel the itch; and the result is – one man less, and surely there is more intelligence and intention in the loss than there ever was in the increase – Is not the existence of the most of mankind largely the result of a hot July afternoon, or the tempting sight of bed-linen, of the horizontal position of some sleeping kitchen nymph, or the putting out of a light? And if a man's birth is the work of an animal desire, of a mere chance, who is to think that the negation of his birth is any very important matter? A curse on the folly of our nursemaids and governesses, who corrupt our fantasy with horrific fairy-tales, and impress our soft brains with hideous images of judgements and punishments, so that involuntary shudders will seize a grown man's limbs with the chill of dread, – bar the way to our boldest resolutions, bind our awakening reason in fetters of superstitious darkness – Murder! a whole Hell full of furies swoops about the very word – Nature forgot to make another man – they didn't tie the umbilical cord – the father's guts were running on his wedding night – and the whole shadow-play is gone. There was *something* and there is *nothing* – is that not just the same as: there was nothing and

there is nothing and about nothing there is not a word to be
said – man is born of filth, and wades a little while in filth,
and makes filth, and rots down again in filth, till at the last
he is no more than the muck that sticks to the soles of his
great-grandson's shoes. That's the end of the song – the
filthy circle of human destiny, and so it goes – a pleasant
journey, brother dear! Our gouty, splenetic moralist of a
conscience may chase wrinkled hags out of brothels, and
torture old usurers on their death-beds – it will never get a
hearing with me. [*Exit.*]

SCENE 3

Another room in the castle.

[*Enter* ROBBER MOOR *from one side,* DANIEL *from the other.*]

MOOR [*hurriedly*]: Where is the lady?

DANIEL: Your lordship! Will you permit an old man to make
one request of you?

MOOR: It is granted. What do you want?

DANIEL: Nothing, and everything, only a little, and yet so
much – let me kiss your hand!

MOOR: That you shall not, good old man! [*Embracing him*]
Would that I might call you father!

DANIEL: Your hand, your hand! I beg you.

MOOR: You shall not.

DANIEL: I must! [*He seizes* KARL's *hand, looks at it quickly, and
falls on his knees before him.*] My beloved, my precious
Karl!

MOOR [*startled, but coldly and with self-control*]: What are you
saying, my good man? I do not understand you.

DANIEL: Yes, deny it, disguise yourself! Very well, very well!
You are still my own dear good young master – Merciful
God! I an old man, and live to see – fool that I was, straight

away I should have – oh, father in heaven! So you have come back, and the old master is under the ground, and there you are again – what a donkey I was, blind I must have been, [*beating his forehead*] not to know you the very – well, well, well! Who would have dreamt it – all that I prayed for – Christ Jesus! here he is, as large as life, in these old rooms again!

MOOR: What is this talk? Have you got up in a raging fever, or is it a part in some comedy you are rehearsing?

DANIEL: Oh for shame, for shame! It's not right to play such tricks on your old servant – This scar! Look, you remember! – Great God, how you frightened me! I was always so fond of you, and the pain you could have caused me – you were sitting on my lap – you remember? There in the round room – what, my chick? you've forgotten that, haven't you – and the cuckoo-clock that you liked to hear so much – think of it! the cuckoo-clock's gone, smashed to smithereens – old Susie knocked it flying, when she was cleaning the room – yes, that's right, there you were sitting on my lap, and called out horsey! and I ran off to fetch your horsey for you – oh sweet Jesus! why did I have to run off so, old donkey that I am – and how it ran hot and cold down my back – hear the crying and shouting out there in the passage-way, come running in, and there is the blood all bright, and you on the floor, with – holy mother of God! I felt as if a bucket of icy water was poured over me – but that's what happens with children, if you don't watch them all the time. Great God, if it had gone in your eye – And it was your right hand, too. As long as I live, I said, never again will I let a child get hold of a knife or a pair of scissors or anything sharp like that, I said – thanks be, my lord and lady away – yes indeed, I shall let that be a warning to me, all the days of my life, I said – My godfathers! I could have lost my position, I could, may the Lord forgive you, you godless child! but praise be! it all healed up well, but for that wicked scar.

MOOR: I do not understand a word of what you are saying.

DANIEL: Oh yes, those were the days, weren't they? Many's the cake and biscuit and sweetmeat I've tucked into your hand, you were always my favourite, and do you remember what you said, down there in the stable, when I put you on the old master's sorrel horse, and let you gallop all round the great meadow? Daniel, you said, just wait till I'm a great man, Daniel, and you shall be my bailiff, and ride with me in my coach – Yes, I said and laughed, if the good Lord give life and health, and if you're not ashamed of an old man, I said, then I shall ask you to let me have the cottage there in the village that's been standing empty for so long, and lay in a cask of wine, and play mine host in my old age. – Yes, go on, laugh! Forgotten all about it, hadn't you, young master – don't want to know an old man, behave like a stranger, so grand – and still you're my precious young gentleman – a bit of a wild one you were, to be sure – don't take it amiss! Young blood will have its day – and it can all turn out well in the end.

MOOR [*throwing his arms around his neck*]: Yes, Daniel! I'll not conceal it any longer! I am your Karl, your long-lost Karl! And what about my Amalia?

DANIEL [*beginning to weep*]: Oh, that I should live to see this happy day, old sinner that I am! – and the master – God rest his soul! – wept for nothing! Down, down, old white head and weary old bones, go to your grave rejoicing! My lord and master is alive, I have seen him with my own eyes!

MOOR: And he will keep the promises he made – take this, you honest greybeard, for the sorrel horse in the stable. [*Thrusts a heavy purse of money into his hand.*] No, I had not forgotten you, old man.

DANIEL: Stop, what are you doing? Too much! You didn't mean it!

MOOR: Yes, I meant it, Daniel! [DANIEL *is about to fall on his knees.*] Stand up, tell me, what about my Amalia?

DANIEL: God reward you! God reward you! Oh, good Lord!
— Your Amalia, oh, it will be the end of her, she will die of joy!

MOOR [*eagerly*]: She has not forgotten me?

DANIEL: Forgotten? What talk is that? Forgotten you? — you should have been there, you should have seen her when she heard the news that you were dead, the news his lordship gave out —

MOOR: What did you say? my brother —

DANIEL: Yes, your brother, his lordship, your brother — I will tell you about it another day, when there is time — and the ticking-off she gave him, every time he came, day after day, paying her his compliments and wanting to make her his lady. Oh, I must go, I must go, I must tell her, bring her the news. [*Going.*]

MOOR: Stop, stop! she must not know, no one must know, nor my brother either —

DANIEL: Your brother? No, not he, heaven forbid that he should know, he of all people! — If he doesn't already know more than he ought to — Oh, let me tell you, there are wicked people, wicked brothers, wicked masters — but for all my master's gold I wouldn't be a wicked servant — his lordship thought you were dead.

MOOR: H'm! What are you muttering?

DANIEL [*more softly*]: And to be sure, with you coming alive again so uninvited — Your brother was the late master's only heir —

MOOR: Old man! What are you mumbling between your teeth, as if some monstrous secret was on the tip of your tongue, not wanting to come out — and yet it should come out! Speak more clearly!

DANIEL: But I will rather gnaw the flesh from my old bones for hunger, and drink my own water for thirst, than earn a life of plenty by doing murder. [*He hurries off.*]

MOOR [*starting up, after a pause of horror*]: Betrayed, betrayed! it flashes upon my soul like lightning! — *A villain's trickery!*

Heaven and hell! not you, my father! *A villain's trickery!* A robber, a murderer, through a villain's trickery! Slandered by him! my letters forged, intercepted – full of love his heart – oh, monstrous fool that I have been – full of love his father's heart – oh, knavery, knavery! It would have cost me a single step, it would have cost me a single tear – oh, fool, fool, fool, blind fool that I have been! [*Running against the wall.*] I could have been happy – oh villainy, villainy! my life's happiness vilely, vilely betrayed. [*Raging up and down.*] A murderer, a robber through a villain's trickery! – He was not even angry. Not the thought of a curse in his heart – oh, fiend! unbelievable, creeping, loathsome fiend!

[*Enter* KOSINSKY.]

KOSINSKY: Captain, where are you? What is it? You want to stay here longer, I see?

MOOR: Up! Saddle the horses! Before sunset we must be over the borders.

KOSINSKY: You are joking.

MOOR [*imperiously*]: Hurry, hurry! Do not hesitate, leave everything here! and let no man catch sight of you.

[*Exit* KOSINSKY.]

I must flee from within these walls. The slightest delay could drive me to frenzy, and he is my father's son – oh my brother, my brother! You have made me the most miserable outcast upon earth, I have done nothing to offend you, it was not a brotherly deed – Reap the fruits of your wickedness in peace; my presence shall no longer sour your enjoyment – but truly, it was not a brotherly deed. Let it be ever veiled in darkness, and let not death disturb it!

[*Enter* KOSINSKY.]

KOSINSKY: The horses are saddled, you may mount as soon as you will.

MOOR: Such haste, such haste! Why do you harry me so? Am I not to see her again?

KOSINSKY: I will unharness again straightway if you bid me; you made me run, head over heels.

MOOR: Once more! one more farewell! I must drain this poisoned bliss to the last drop, and then – stop, Kosinsky! Ten minutes more – behind, by the courtyard gate, – and we will gallop away!

SCENE 4

The garden.

[AMALIA.]

AMALIA: *You are weeping, my Amalia?* – and his voice as he said it! his voice! I felt as if nature were reborn – all the happy springtimes of love awakened again in his voice! The nightingale sang as it did then – the blossoms breathed perfume as they did then – and I lay in ecstasy upon his breast – Ah, false, faithless heart! how you seek to flatter your treachery! No, no, away, flee from my soul, deceitful image! – my own, my only one, I have not broken my oath! Flee from my soul, treacherous, godless desires! in the heart where Karl reigns there is no place for mortal man – But why, my soul, why do you seek this stranger against my will? Why does he stand so close beside the image of my own, my only one? why is he his constant companion? You are weeping, *my* Amalia? Ah, I will flee him, flee him! Never shall my eye behold this stranger more!

[MOOR *opens the garden gate.*]

AMALIA [*with a shudder*]: Hark, hark! did I not hear the gate? [*She sees* MOOR, *and springs to her feet.*] He? – where? – what? – here I stand rooted and cannot flee – do not forsake me, God in Heaven! – No, you shall not rob me of my Karl! My soul has not room for two divinities, and I am a mortal maid! [*Taking out* KARL's *portrait.*] O you my Karl, be my angel to guard me against this stranger, this intruder on my love! You, you, let me gaze at you unceasing – no more these blasphemous glances at the other – [*She sits in silence, her gaze fixed upon the portrait.*]

MOOR: You here, my lady? – and in sorrow? – and a tear upon this picture? –

[AMALIA *does not answer.*]

And who is the fortunate man for whose sake an angel's eye will glisten? may I see the idol of your – [*Trying to see the portrait.*]

AMALIA: No, yes, no!

MOOR [*starting back*]: Ah! – and does he deserve such adoration? – does he deserve it?

AMALIA: If you had known him!

MOOR: I should have envied him.

AMALIA: Worshipped him, you mean!

MOOR: Ah!

AMALIA: Oh, you would have loved him so – there was so much, in his face – in his eyes – in the tone of his voice – so much like you – so much that I love –

[MOOR *stands with downcast eyes.*]

AMALIA: Here, where you are standing, he stood a thousand times – and beside him she who at his side forgot all heaven and earth – here his eyes feasted on the glorious scene about him – Nature seemed to feel his generous, approving gaze, and to grow yet more beautiful in the approbation of her masterpiece – here he would make heavenly music, and hold an airy audience captive – here from this bush he would pluck roses, would pluck roses for me – here he lay upon my bosom, here his burning lips touched mine, and the flowers were glad to be crushed beneath the feet of lovers –

MOOR: He is no more?

AMALIA: He sails upon stormy seas – Amalia's love sails with him – he treads the pathless sandy desert – Amalia's love makes the burning sand grow green beneath him, and the thorny bushes blossom – the noonday sun scorches his bare head, the arctic snows blister his feet, hailstorms beat about his brow, and Amalia's love soothes him in the tempest – oceans and mountains and horizons between the lovers, but their souls escape the dusty prison, and are united in the paradise of love – You seem sorrowful, count?

MOOR: These words of love stir my love too to life.

AMALIA [*turning pale*]: What do I hear? You love another? – Alas for me, what have I said?

MOOR: She believed me dead, and was true to him she thought dead – she learnt that I was alive, and would sacrifice for me the diadem of a saint. She knows that I roam an outcast, a wanderer in the desert, and her love flies through exile and desert to be with me. And her name is Amalia like yours, my lady.

AMALIA: How I envy your Amalia!

MOOR: Oh, she is an unhappy lady, she gives her love to one who is lost, and never in all eternity will she be rewarded.

AMALIA: No, no, she will be rewarded in heaven. Are we not told that there is a better world, where the sorrowful shall rejoice, and lovers recognize each other again?

MOOR: Yes, a world where all veils are rent, and love sees itself again, in terror – Eternity is its name – my Amalia is an unhappy lady.

AMALIA: Unhappy, and she loves you?

MOOR: Unhappy because she loves me! Why, what if I were a murderer? What, my lady? What if your lover could count a man killed for each one of your kisses? Alas for my Amalia! she is an unhappy lady.

AMALIA [*joyfully, springing to her feet*]: Ah! and I, I am happy! My only one is like the light of heaven itself, and heaven is grace and mercy! He could not bear to hurt the merest insect – his soul is as far from thoughts of blood as the pole of day from midnight.

[MOOR *turns quickly away between the bushes, gazing fixedly into the distance.*]

AMALIA [*takes her lute, plays and sings*]:

Hector, wilt thou bid farewell for ever,
Now Achilles with his murd'rous quiver
Fearful vengeance for Patroclus swears?
Who will teach thy tender son to fight,
To cast his spear, and fear the Gods of right,
When thy corpse grim Xanthus downward bears?

MOOR [*takes the lute silently from her, and plays*]:

Dearest wife, go, fetch the fateful lance,
Let me go – to tread – war's horrid dance –

[*He throws down the lute, and rushes off.*]

SCENE 5

A nearby forest: night. In the centre, an old ruined castle.

[*The* ROBBERS *encamped on the ground, singing.*]

CHORUS:

Thieving, whoring, killing, fighting,
So we live from day to day,
For every one the hangman's waiting,
Let's be merry while we may.

We lead a life of liberty,
A life of merry joys,
Our lodging is the forest free,
In gale and tempest us you'll see,
The moon's our sun, my boys!
To Mercury we say our prayer,
The god of thieves, and light as air.

Today we'll be the farmer's guest,
Tomorrow the priest's so fat,
And for the next, we think it best
To let the Lord take care of that!

And every time the tale is told
Of drinking and of toasting,
We're fellows stout enough and bold
To join the enemy of old,
Who sits in hell a-roasting!

The stricken father's cries and groans,
The anguished mother's fearful moans,
The lonely bride's despairing tears,
Are joy and music to our ears!

Ha! see them twitch when their heads we lop,
Like oxen they bellow, like flies they drop,
That's a pleasure to our sight,
That's what gives our ears delight!

And when at last the tide has turned,
Then let the hangman take us,
It is but our reward we've earned,
We'll be gone before they make us.
A drop of Bacchus' juice to speed us as we go,
And up, my lads, away! and swifter than you know!

SCHWEITZER: It will soon be night, and the captain not yet back!

RATZMANN: And promised he'd be here with us again on the stroke of eight.

SCHWEITZER: If anything has happened to him – comrades! we'll burn the place down and kill every man, woman and child.

SPIEGELBERG [*taking* RATZMANN *on one side*]: A word in your ear, Ratzmann.

SCHWARZ [*to* GRIMM]: Shouldn't we be sending out scouts?

GRIMM: Let him be! He will come back with a prize to shame us all.

SCHWEITZER: No, I swear by hell you're wrong there! He didn't look like a man planning a trick of that kind when he left us. Have you forgotten what he told us as he led us over the heath? 'Let one of you steal as much as a turnip from the field, if I find out then his head will fall on the spot – as sure as my name is Moor.' – He has forbidden us to rob!

RATZMANN [*softly, to* SPIEGELBERG]: What are you driving at? Speak plainer.

SPIEGELBERG: Hush! – I don't know what sort of a price you or I put on our freedom, straining away like oxen at a wagon, and holding forth all the time about our independence – I don't like it.

SCHWEITZER [*to* GRIMM]: What do you think that windbag is brewing now?

RATZMANN [*softly to* SPIEGELBERG]: Do you mean the captain?

SPIEGELBERG: Hush, I say! He has his informers among us all the time – Captain, did you say? Who made him our captain? Didn't he usurp a title that by rights belongs to me? – What? is that why we gamble our lives – is that why we let fortune vent her spleen on us, to count ourselves lucky at the last to be the bondsmen of a slave? Bondsmen, when we might be princes? By God, Ratzmann – I never liked it.

SCHWEITZER [*to the others*]: Yes, you're a hero – good for squashing frogs with a stone. – Why, the sound of him blowing his nose would knock you flying –

SPIEGELBERG [*to* RATZMANN]: Yes – and for years now I've been thinking: things will have to change. Ratzmann – if you're the man I've always taken you for – Ratzmann – he's disappeared – half given up for lost – Ratzmann – I do believe his hour of doom has struck – what? Not a flush, not a flicker when you hear the bells of freedom ring? Have you not the spirit to take the hint?

RATZMANN: Ah, Satan! what snares are you laying for my soul?

SPIEGELBERG: Have I caught you? – Good! then follow me! I kept note of which way he crept – come! Two pistols rarely miss, and then – we shall have struck the first blow! [*He is about to drag* RATZMANN *away with him.*]

SCHWEITZER [*drawing his knife in fury*]: Ha! Vermin! Just in time you remind me of the forests of Bohemia! Were not you the coward whose teeth began to chatter when they cried 'The enemy is here!' That day on my soul I swore – away with you, assassin. [*Stabs* SPIEGELBERG *to death.*]

ROBBERS [*in agitation*]: Murder! murder! Schweitzer! Spiegelberg! Separate them!

SCHWEITZER [*throwing his knife down on the body*]: There! and that is the end of you! Calm now, comrades – take no notice of him – the vermin, he was always jealous of the captain, and he hadn't a scar on his body – never mind, lads! – ah, the scoundrel! would he stab a man in the back? he, a man, in the back? Is that why we have felt the sweat glowing on our cheeks, to slink out of the world like rats? Vermin! Is that why we made our beds amidst fire and smoke, to be put down like curs at the last?

GRIMM: But the devil – comrade – what was it between you? The captain will be furious.

SCHWEITZER: Let me take care of that. And you, you scoundrel [*to* RATZMANN] – you were his right-hand man! Out of my sight with you – Schufterle tried that trick too, but now he is hanging there in Switzerland, as the captain prophesied he would.

[*A shot is heard.*]

SCHWARZ [*jumping up*]: Hark! a pistol-shot!

[*Another shot is heard.*]

Another! Hurrah! The captain!

GRIMM: Patience! He must fire a third shot.

[*Another shot is heard.*]

SCHWARZ: It is, it is! Look out for yourself, Schweitzer – let us answer him!

[*They fire.*]

[*Enter* MOOR *and* KOSINSKY.]

SCHWEITZER [*going to meet them*]: Welcome, captain! – I have been a little hasty while you were away. [*Leading him to the body*] You shall be judge between the two of us – he wanted to stab you in the back.

ROBBERS [*in amazement*]: What? The captain?

MOOR [*gazing for a while at the body, then bursting out furiously*]: O inscrutable hand of avenging Nemesis! – was it not he who sang me the siren song? – Let this knife be consecrated to that dark spirit of retribution! – it was not you who did this, Schweitzer.

SCHWEITZER: By God! it was I who did it, and by the devil I swear it is not the worst thing I have done in my life. [*Exit, with an ill grace.*]

MOOR [*reflectively*]: I understand – guiding hand of Heaven – I understand – the leaves are falling from the trees – and for me too it is autumn. – Take this from my sight.

[SPIEGELBERG'*s body is removed.*]

GRIMM: Give us the word, captain – what are we to do now?

MOOR: Soon – soon all shall be accomplished. – Give me my lute. – I have lost myself since I went in there – My lute, I say – I must nurse myself back to strength – Leave me.

ROBBERS: It is midnight, captain.

MOOR: But those were only tears at a play – I must hear the Roman's song, to wake my sleeping spirit once more – My lute – Midnight, you said?

SCHWARZ: If not past already. Sleep weighs on us like lead. Three days since we closed an eye.

MOOR: What, does the balm of sleep fall even on the eyes of knaves? Why then should I not feel it? I have never been a

coward or a base fellow – Lie down and sleep – Tomorrow
at daybreak we go on.

ROBBERS: Good night, captain! [*They lie down on the ground
and go to sleep.*]

[*Profound silence.*]

MOOR [*takes up the lute and plays*]:

BRUTUS

Be ye welcome, fields of peace and calm,
Where the last of Romans seeks his rest.
From Philippi with its wild alarm
I come, with shame and anguish in my breast.
Cassius, where art thou? Rome is gone,
My band of brothers lying in their gore,
To death's dark gate my steps are hurried on,
The world no place for Brutus more.

CAESAR

Who is that with steps so fierce and bold
Comes to meet me from the rocks ahead?
Can it be the truth my eyes have told?
That must be a Roman's tread.
Son of Tiber – whence has come thy way?
Stands the city on her seven hills?
Often I have mourned the grievous day
That she lacks a Caesar for her ills.

BRUTUS

Ah, thou with wounds from three-and-twenty hands?
Who summoned thee from death to light?
Reel in horror, back where Hell-gate stands!
Triumph not, proud mourner, in thy spite!
Upon Philippi's brazen altar smokes
The final sacrifice of freedom's blood;
While Rome upon the bier of Brutus chokes.
Brutus to Minos goes – Sink in thy flood!

CAESAR

O fatal blow that Brutus' sword should deal!
Thou also, Brutus, thou?
My son – thy father – son, didst thou not feel,
The earth entire to thee should homage vow?
Go – thou as the noblest Roman art renowned,
Since in thy father's breast thou plunged thy sword.
Go – howl it till the gate of Hell resound.
Brutus the noblest Roman is renowned
Since in his father's breast he plunged his sword!
Go – for now thou knowest by what hand
I was kept on Lethe's strand;
Come, dark ferryman, leave this land!

BRUTUS

Father, stay! – Upon the earth so wide
I have never known but one
Fit to stand at mighty Caesar's side:
It was he whom you called son.
Only Caesar could have sought Rome's doom,
Only Brutus Caesar would not fight.
Where Brutus lives, for Caesar is no room,
Go leftward, let me pass upon the right.

[*He lays down the lute and paces up and down, deep in thought.*]

Who would be my surety? – All is so dark – labyrinths of confusion – no way out – no star to guide – if it were *over* with this last drawn breath – *over* like a shallow puppet-play – But why this burning hunger for happiness? Why this ideal of unattained perfection? This looking to another world for what we have failed to achieve in this – when one miserable touch of this miserable object [*holding his pistol to his forehead*] will make a wise man no better than a fool – a brave man no better than a coward – a noble man no better than a rogue? There is such divine harmony in the world of inanimate nature, why such discord in the world of reason? – No! no! there is something more, for I have not yet known happiness.

Do you think that I shall tremble? Spirits of my slaughtered victims! I will not tremble. [*Trembling violently.*] The terror of your dying moans – the blackness of your strangled faces – the hideous gaping of your wounds are but links in an unending chain of fate, and depend at the last on my idle moments, on the whims of my tutors and nursemaids, on my father's temperament and my mother's blood – [*Shuddering*] Why did my Perillus make a brazen bull of me, to roast mankind in my glowing belly? [*He aims the pistol.*]

Time and eternity – linked together by a single moment! – O thou fearful key that will lock the prison of life behind me, and unbar before me the dwelling of eternal night – tell me – tell me – where, oh where wilt thou lead me? – Strange, undiscovered country! – See, mankind grows weak before such visions, the tensile force of finitude is relaxed, and fancy, wilful ape of our senses, spins strange shadows to deceive our credulous mind – No, no! A man must not stumble – Be what thou wilt, nameless *Beyond* – if but my own self to me is true – Be what thou wilt, let me only take *myself* with me – Externals are but the varnish upon a man – I am my heaven and my hell. If Thou wouldst leave me nothing but some smoking desert banished from Thy sight, where lonely night and everlasting desolation all I must behold? – Then I would people the silent emptiness with my imagination, and should have all eternity to pick apart the tangled threads of universal misery. – Or wilt Thou lead me born and reborn again, through ever-changing scenes of misery step by step – to utter destruction? Can I not snap the threads of life that are woven for me there beyond, as easily as this present one? – You can make of me – nothing; of this freedom you cannot rob me. [*He loads the pistol. Suddenly he pauses.*] And am I to die out of fear of a life of suffering? Am I to grant misery this victory over me? – No! I will endure it! [*Throwing the pistol away*] Let suffering yield before my pride! It shall be accomplished!

[*The darkness deepens.*

Enter HERRMANN *through the forest.*]

HERRMANN: Hark, hark! fearful the owl's cry – twelve has struck in the village beyond – all is well, all is well – villainy sleeps – no spies listening in this wilderness. [*He comes to the ruined castle and knocks.*] Come out, man of sorrows, dungeon-dweller! Your meal is ready.

MOOR [*drawing back quietly*]: What can this mean?

A VOICE [*from the tower*]: Who knocks? Ho, Herrmann, my raven, is it you?

HERRMANN: I, Herrmann, your raven. Climb up to the grating and eat.

[*Owls hoot.*]

A dreary song they sing, the companions of your sleep – Is it good, old man?

THE VOICE: I was much hungered. – Thanks be to thee, sender of ravens, for this bread in the wilderness! – And what news of my dear child, Herrmann?

HERRMANN: Silence – hark – a sound like snoring! can you not hear it?

VOICE: What? can you hear something?

HERRMANN: The wind sighing in the crannies of your prison – a lullaby to make your teeth chatter and your nails turn blue – But hark again – I keep thinking that I hear men snoring – You have company, old man! – Oh, oh!

VOICE: Can you see anything?

HERRMANN: Fare you well – fare you well – a fearful place is this – Down into your hole – above, on high your help and your avenger – accursed son! [*Fleeing.*]

MOOR [*emerging, with horror*]: Stand!

HERRMANN [*cries out*]: Ah!

MOOR: Stand, I say!

HERRMANN: Mercy! mercy! mercy! now all is betrayed!

MOOR: Stand! Speak! Who are you? What business have you here? Speak!

HERRMANN: Have pity, have pity on me, gracious master – hear one word before you kill me.

MOOR [*drawing his sword*]: What am I to hear?

HERRMANN: I know you forbade me on pain of death – I could not help – I could do nothing else – a God in Heaven – your own father there – I took pity – Strike me down!

MOOR: Here is some mystery – out with it! Speak! I will hear everything.

THE VOICE [*from the ruin*]: Alas, alas! Is it you, Herrmann, speaking there? Who is it you are speaking to?

MOOR: Someone down there too – what is happening here? [*Running up to the castle.*] Is it some captive men have cast aside – I will release his chains. – Voice! again! Where is the door?

HERRMANN: O have mercy, my lord – do not press further, my lord – for pity's sake, go by on the other side! [*Blocking his way.*]

MOOR: A fourfold lock! Away! – It must out – Now for the first time, tricks of the thief's trade, come to my assistance. [*He takes housebreaking instruments and forces the lock of the grating. From below an* OLD MAN *emerges, emaciated like a skeleton.*]

OLD MAN: Have pity on a miserable wretch! Have pity!

MOOR [*starting back in terror*]: That is my father's voice!

OLD MOOR: Thanks be to you, O God! The hour of my deliverance is come.

MOOR: Spirit of Count Moor! What has disturbed you in your grave? Did you take a sin with you into the other world, that has barred you entry to the gates of Paradise? I will have masses read that shall speed the wandering spirit to its home. Did you take the gold of widows and orphans and bury it in the earth, to drive you howling from your resting-place at this midnight hour – then I will tear the buried treasure from the enchanted dragon's claws, and if he should vomit a thousand crimson flames upon me, and bare his pointed teeth against my sword – or have you come at my request, to answer the riddles of eternity? Speak, speak! I am no man to pale with fear.

OLD MOOR: I am not a spirit – Touch me, I live, oh, a life of misery and wretchedness!

MOOR: What? Were you not buried?

OLD MOOR: I was buried – that is to say, a dead dog is lying in the vault of my fathers; and I – for three months and more I have lain languishing in this dark underground chamber, with not a glimmer of light, with not a breath of warm air, with not a friend to visit me, with the croak of wild ravens about me, and the hoot of owls at midnight.

MOOR: Heaven and earth! Who could do such a thing?

OLD MOOR: Do not curse him! – It was my son Franz who did it.

MOOR: Franz? Franz? – oh, everlasting chaos!

OLD MOOR: If you are a man, and have the heart of a man, o my unknown deliverer, then hear, hear a father's sorrow, the sorrow his sons have brought upon him – for three months I have cried it to these unhearing rocky walls, but there was only a hollow echo to mock my lamentations. And so, if you are a man, and have the heart of a man –

MOOR: A challenge to bring the wild beasts from their lairs!

OLD MOOR: There I lay upon my sickbed, and had scarcely begun to recover my strength after my grave illness, when they brought a man to me who told me my firstborn was dead on the field of battle, and with him brought a sword stained with his blood, and his last farewell, and that it was my curse that had driven him to battle and death and despair.

MOOR [turning away with a violent movement]: It is revealed!

OLD MOOR: Hear me further! I fell into a swoon at the message. They must have thought I was dead, for when I came to my senses again, I was lying in my coffin, and wrapped in my shroud like a dead man. I scratched at the lid of the coffin, and it was opened. It was the dead of night, my son Franz stood before me. – What? he cried, in a terrible voice, will you live for ever? – and straightway the lid was slammed shut again. The thunder of those words had robbed me of my senses; when I awoke once more I felt the coffin being lifted up and taken in a carriage, half an hour's journey. At last it was opened – I found myself at the entrance to this dungeon, my son before me, and the man who had brought me Karl's sword with his blood – ten times I clasped his knees, and pleaded and implored him – his father's pleadings did not touch his heart – down with him, the bag of bones! his lips thundered, he has lived for long enough, and down I was thrust without pity, and my son Franz locked the door behind me.

MOOR: It is not possible, not possible! You must have been mistaken.

OLD MOOR: I may have been mistaken. Hear me further, but do not be angry! So I lay for a day and a night, and no man thought of me in my need. Nor did any man set foot in this wilderness, for the story goes that in these ruins the ghosts of my forefathers drag their rattling chains, and make deathly moan at midnight. At last I heard the door open again, this man brought me bread and water, and told me that I had been condemned to die of hunger, and that his life would be in danger if it were known that he was feeding me. And so I have clung feebly to life these many days, but the unrelenting cold – the foul air of my own filth – the boundless grief – my strength ebbed from me, my body withered, a thousand times with tears in my eyes I pleaded with God for death, but the measure of my punishment cannot yet be accomplished – or some joy must yet await me, that I have been so miraculously preserved. But my sufferings are earned – my Karl, my Karl! – and there was not a grey hair upon his head.

MOOR: It is enough. Up, you blocks, you lumps of ice! you dull unfeeling sleepers! Up! will none of you awake? [*He fires a pistol-shot over the sleeping robbers' heads.*]

THE ROBBERS [*aroused*]: Ho! hallo! hallo! What is it?

MOOR: Did not this tale stir you in your slumbers? sleep everlasting had roused to wakefulness! Look, look! the laws of creation are made a game of dice, the bonds of nature are rent asunder, the ancient strife is let loose, the son has struck his father dead.

THE ROBBERS: What is the Captain saying?

MOOR: No, not struck him dead! the words are too kind! A thousand times the son has racked his father, flayed him, spitted him, broken him upon the wheel! no, these are words of men – has done what makes sin blush, what makes the cannibal shudder, what no devil in aeons could conceive. – His own son, his father – oh see, see, he has fallen in a swoon – his son, his own father, here in this dungeon he – cold – nakedness – hunger – thirst – oh look, oh see – he is my own father, it is the truth.

THE ROBBERS [*running and gathering round the old man*]: Your father? your father?

SCHWEITZER [*approaches reverently and falls down before him*]: Father of my captain! I kiss your feet! my dagger is yours to command.

MOOR: Vengeance, vengeance, vengeance shall be yours! venerable old man, so offended, so profaned! Thus from this moment I rend for ever the band of brotherhood. [*Rending his garment from top to bottom.*] Thus I curse every drop of brother's blood before the face of heaven! Hear me, moon and stars! Hear me, midnight heavens! who look down upon this deed of shame! Hear me, thrice-terrible God, You who reign above the moon, and sit in judgement and retribution

above the stars, and flame with fire above the night! Here I
kneel – here I stretch forth my three fingers in the horror of
the night – here I swear, and may nature spew me forth from
her creation like a venomous beast if I break this oath, swear
never to greet the light of day again, until the blood of my
father's murderer, spilt before these stones, shall smoke
beneath the sun. [*Standing up.*]

THE ROBBERS: The very devil! Call us villains! No, in Belial's
name! we never did the like of this!

MOOR: Yes! and by the fearful groans of all who ever died
beneath your daggers, of those my flames consumed and
those my falling tower crushed – no thought of murder or
of robbery shall find its place within your breasts, till all
your garments are stained scarlet with the reprobate's blood
– did you ever dream that you were the arm of a greater
majesty? the tangled knot of our destinies is unravelled!
Today, today an invisible power has conferred nobility upon
our handiwork! Bow down in adoration before him who
decreed you this sublime fate, who led you to this place, who
deemed you worthy to be the terrible angels of his dark
judgement! Uncover your heads! Kneel in the dust, that you
may stand up sanctified!
    [*They kneel.*]

SCHWEITZER: Your command, captain! what are we to do?

MOOR: Stand up, Schweitzer! and touch these hallowed locks!
[*He leads him to his father, and makes him hold a lock of his hair.*]
Do you remember how you split the skull of that Bohemian
cavalryman, just as he was raising his sabre over my head,
and I had sunk to my knees, breathless and exhausted from
my work? I promised you then that you should have a kingly
reward, but till this moment I could not pay my debt. –

SCHWEITZER: You swore it, it is true, but let me not claim
that debt from you in all eternity!

MOOR: No, I will pay it now. Schweitzer, no mortal man till
this day was so honoured – Be my father's avenger!

SCHWEITZER [*standing up*]: My great captain! Today you make me proud for the first time! Your command! where, when, how shall he be struck down?

MOOR: Minutes are precious, you must hurry now – choose the worthiest men of our band, and lead them straight to the count's castle! Snatch him from his bed if he is asleep or lying in the arms of pleasure, drag him from table if he is gorged, tear him from the crucifix if you find him on his knees in prayer! But I tell you, and make no mistake of this! I do not want him dead! scratch his skin, or harm one hair of his head, and I will tear your flesh in pieces, and cast it to the hungry vultures for food! Alive and whole I must have him, and if you bring him to me alive and whole, you shall have a million for your reward, I will steal it from a king at the risk of my own life, and you shall go as free as the air – if you understand me, hurry!

SCHWEITZER: Enough, captain – Here is my hand on it: either you shall see the two of us return, or neither. Schweitzer's angel of death is approaching! [*Exit, with a troop of robbers.*]

MOOR: You others, disperse in the woods – I shall remain.

ACT FIVE

SCENE I

A long vista of rooms – a dark night.

[*Enter* DANIEL *with a lantern and a bundle.*]

DANIEL: Good-bye, dear old home – so much joy and happiness I've seen here, when the good old master was still alive – tears on your mouldering bones! to ask such a thing of an old and faithful servant – it was a refuge for every orphan, and a haven for all with no one to care for them, and this son has made it a den of murderers – Good-bye, old floor! how many times Daniel has swept you – good-bye, old stove, it's hard for Daniel to take his leave after all these years – everything so familiar – it will be painful, faithful old Eliezer – But may God in his mercy protect me from the snares and wiles of the Evil One – Empty-handed I came – empty-handed I go – but my soul is saved.

[*As he is about to go,* FRANZ *rushes in, in his dressing-gown.*]

DANIEL: God be with me! The master! [*Blowing out his lantern.*]

FRANZ: Betrayed! betrayed! Spirits spewed from their graves – roused from eternal sleep the kingdom of death cries to my face *Murderer! murderer!* – Who's there?

DANIEL [*nervously*]: Holy Mother of God! is it you, my lord, screaming through the passages so horribly that everyone starts from their sleep?

FRANZ: Sleep? who bade you sleep? Off with you, and bring a light!

[*Exit* DANIEL. *Enter another* SERVANT.]

No one is to sleep tonight. Do you hear? Everyone must be up, and armed – all weapons loaded – Did you see them, there, along the gallery?

SERVANT: Who, your lordship?

FRANZ: Who, you fool, who? So coldly, so emptily you ask who? Why, it took hold of me like a fit! Who, you mule, who? Spirits and devils! How far on is the night?

SERVANT: The watchman has just called two o'clock.

FRANZ: What? will this night last till the day of judgement? Did you not hear a tumult close at hand? No shouts of triumph? No galloping horses' hooves? Where is Ka – I mean the Count?

SERVANT: I don't know, master!

FRANZ: You don't know? You are one of them as well? I will

kick your heart out from between your ribs! you with your
accursed *I don't know!* Be off, and fetch the pastor!

SERVANT: My lord!

FRANZ: Do you grumble? do you hesitate?

[*Exit* SERVANT, *hurriedly*.]

What? rogues and beggars conspired against me too?
Heaven, hell, all conspired against me?

DANIEL [*coming with a light*]: Master –

FRANZ: No! I shall not tremble! It was nothing but a dream.
The dead are not yet risen – who says that I am pale and
trembling? I feel quite well, quite calm.

DANIEL: You are as pale as death, and your voice is quaking
with fear.

FRANZ: I have a fever. Tell the pastor when he comes that I
have a fever. I will have myself bled tomorrow, tell the
pastor.

DANIEL: Shall I bring you some drops of balsam and sugar?

FRANZ: Some drops of balsam and sugar! the pastor will not
be here for a little while. My voice is weak and quaking, yes,
balsam and sugar!

DANIEL: Give me the keys, so that I can go and open the cup-
board –

FRANZ: No, no, no! Stay! or I shall go with you. You see, I
cannot bear to be alone! how easily I might – you see – faint,
if I am alone. No, let me be, let me be! It will pass, you must
stay.

DANIEL: Oh, you are sick, in earnest.

FRANZ: Yes, of course, of course! that is all. – And sickness
turns the brain, and hatches strange fantastic dreams – but
dreams mean nothing, Daniel, do they? Dreams come from
the belly, and dreams mean nothing – why, just now I had a
merry dream – [*He collapses in a faint.*]

DANIEL: In the name of Jesus, what is this? George! Conrad!
Sebastian! Martin! don't just lie there! [*Shaking him.*] Oh,

Joseph and Mary Magdalen! can you not be sensible? They will say I murdered him, God have pity on me!

FRANZ [*in confusion*]: Away – away! Why do you shake me like that, you hideous death's-head? – the dead are not yet risen –

DANIEL: Oh, everlasting mercy! He is out of his mind.

FRANZ [*raising himself feebly*]: Where am I? – you, Daniel? What have I been saying? Take no notice! I was lying, whatever it was – come, help me up! – it was nothing but a fit of giddiness – because – I did not sleep properly.

DANIEL: If only Johann was here! I will call for help, I will send for a doctor.

FRANZ: Stay! sit here beside me on this sofa – there – you are a sensible man, a good man. Let me tell you about it!

DANIEL: Not now, another time! I will put you to bed, rest will be better for you.

FRANZ: No, I beg you, let me tell you about it, and laugh me to scorn! – See, I dreamt I had feasted like a king, and my heart was merry within me, and I lay drunken amidst the lawns of the castle gardens, and suddenly – it was the middle of the day – suddenly – but I tell you, laugh me to scorn!

DANIEL: Suddenly?

FRANZ: Suddenly a fearful thunderclap struck my slumbering ear, shuddering I leapt up, and behold, I thought I saw the whole horizon stand ablaze with fiery flames, and mountains and cities and forests melted like wax in a furnace, and a howling whirlwind swept away the sea and the earth and the sky – and a voice rang out as of a brazen trumpet: Earth, give up thy dead, give up thy dead, O sea! and the bare ground was in labour, and began to cast up skulls and ribs and jaws and all manner of bones that joined together and made bodies of men, and they gathered in a great stream, more than the eye could see, a living torrent! Then I looked up, and behold, I stood at the foot of Sinai, the mountain of thunder, and a throng above me and below, and on the summit of the mountain upon three smoking thrones three men before whose glance all creatures fled –

DANIEL: That is the very image of the Day of Judgement.

FRANZ: Yes! the fantasies of a madman! Then there came forth one who was like the starry night, and he had in his hand a signet of iron, and he held it between the place of sunrise and of sunset and spoke: Everlasting, holy, just and incorruptible! There is but one truth and there is but one virtue! Woe, woe, woe to the creature that still dwells in doubt! – Then there came forth another, who had in his hand a looking-glass, and he held it between the place of sunrise and of sunset and spoke: This glass is truth; masks and hypocrisy shall be no more – then I was afraid and all the people, for we saw the faces of serpents and tigers and leopards in the terrible glass reflected – Then there came forth a third, who had in his hand a balance of brass, and he held it between the place of sunrise and sunset and spoke: come forth, ye generation of Adam – for I shall weigh your thoughts in the balance of my wrath! and your works with the weight of my anger!

DANIEL: God have mercy on me!

FRANZ: All stood as white as death, and each breast beat with fearful expectation. Then it was as if I heard my name named first in the thunder of the mountain, and the marrow of my bones froze, and my teeth chattered aloud. Then straightway the balance began to ring, and the rocks to thunder, and the hours went by, one by one, by the scale that hung on the left, and each one after the other cast in a deadly sin –

DANIEL: Oh, may God forgive you!

FRANZ: But He did not! – and the scale was piled high like a mountain, but the other filled with the blood of atonement kept it up still in the air – at the last there came an old man, bent double with grief, his own arm gnawed in his hunger, all eyes were cast down in awe before him, I knew that man, he cut a lock from the silvery hairs of his head, and cast it upon the scale of sins, and lo! it sank, sank suddenly into the pit, and the scale of atonement flew up aloft! – Then I heard a voice that spoke from the fiery rocks: forgiveness, forgiveness for every sinner upon earth and in the pit! thou only art cast out! [*Pause, profound silence.*] Well, why do you not laugh?

DANIEL: How can I laugh, when you make my flesh creep? Dreams come from God.

FRANZ: Pah, nonsense! do not say that! Tell me that I am a fool, a crazy senseless fool! Say so, good Daniel, I beg you, make mock of me!

DANIEL: Dreams come from God. I will pray for you.

FRANZ: It is a lie, I say – go this instant, hurry, run, see where the pastor is, tell him to make haste, haste, but I tell you, it is a lie.

DANIEL: God be merciful to you! [*Exit.*]

FRANZ: Peasant's wisdom, peasant's fears! – No one has yet discovered whether the past is not past, or whether there is an eye watching beyond the stars – h'm! Who prompted me to such thoughts? Is there an Avenger there beyond the stars? – No, no! Yes, yes! I hear a fearful hissing about me: there is a Judge beyond the stars! To go this very night to face the Avenger beyond the stars! No, I say! – a miserable corner where your cowardice seeks to hide – empty, desolate it is beyond the stars, and none to hear you – but if there should be something more? No, no, there is not! I command it not to be! – but if it were? Woe to you if all has been accounted! if it should be counted up before you this very night! – why do my bones shiver? – To die! – why does the word catch my throat so? To answer for myself to the Avenger beyond the stars – and if He is just, the widows and the orphans, the tortured and the oppressed cry out to Him, and if He is just? – Why did they suffer? for what did you triumph over them?

[*Enter* PASTOR MOSER.]

MOSER: You sent for me, my lord. I am astonished. The first time in my life! Do you have it in mind to make mock of religion, or are you beginning to tremble at its message?

FRANZ: To mock or to tremble, according to how you answer me. – Listen, Moser, I will show you that you are a fool, or that you are making a fool of the whole world, and you shall answer me. Do you hear? By your life you shall answer me.

MOSER: It is One greater than I to whom you issue your summons; one day He will surely give you your answer.

FRANZ: Now I will have it, now! this instant, so that I do not commit a shameful folly and call on the peasants' idol in my desperation, so often I have shouted and laughed to you as the wine flowed: There is no God! – Now I am talking to you in earnest, I tell you, there is none! and you are to muster all the arguments you have at your command, but I shall blow them away with the breath of my lips.

MOSER: But if you could so easily blow away the thunder that will fall on your proud soul with a weight like ten thousand tons! that all-seeing God whom you, fool and villain, would banish from the midst of His creation, has no need of justification from the lips of common dust. For His greatness is as surely seen in your tyrannies, as in any smile of triumphant virtue.

FRANZ: Very good, priest! I like you like this.

MOSER: I stand here in the name of a greater master, and speak with one a mere worm like myself, and have no business to be liked. Indeed I should have to be able to work miracles to wring confession from your obstinate wickedness – but if your convictions are so firm, why did you send for me? Tell me this – why did you send for me, at this hour of midnight?

FRANZ: Because I am bored, and can find no pleasure at the chessboard. I want to amuse myself with a little priest-baiting. You will not unman my courage with your empty terrors. I know very well that those who have come off badly in this life put their trust in eternity; but they will find themselves horribly cheated. I have always read that our being is but a motion of the blood, and when the last drop of blood has ebbed, with it go mind and spirit too. They suffer all the infirmities of our body, will not they also cease when it is destroyed? go up in vapour as it rots? Let a drop of water find its way into your brain, and your life makes a sudden pause, and that pause is like the end of being, and its continuation is death. Our sensibility is the vibration of certain cords – and a broken instrument will sound no more. If I have my seven palaces demolished, if I smash this Venus to pieces, then symmetry and beauty have ceased to exist. Look! there is your immortal soul for you!

MOSER: That is your philosophy of despair. But your own heart, that beats with anxious dread against your ribs even as you utter your proofs, gives the lie to them. These spiders' webs of systems can be torn to pieces with the single word: you must die! – I challenge you, that shall be the proof, if you still stand firm in death, if your principles do not desert you even then, then the victory is yours; but if in the hour of death you feel but the slightest qualm, then woe unto you! you have been deceived.

FRANZ [*in confusion*]: If in the hour of death I feel a qualm –?

MOSER: Oh, I have seen many such wretches, who until that moment had defied the truth like giants, but in death their delusions fluttered away. I will stand by your bedside when you are dying – I should so like to see a tyrant die – I will stand there, and look you straight in the eye when the doctor takes your cold, damp hand, and can scarcely feel the limping, dwindling pulse, and with that fearful shrug of his shoulders looks up and says: mortal assistance is in vain! Then beware, oh then beware, that you do not look like a Nero or a Richard Crookback!

FRANZ: No, no!

MOSER: Even this No will then be turned into a howl of Yes –
a tribunal within, that your sceptical speculations will not be
able to silence, will then awake, and sit in judgement upon
you. But it will be an awakening as of one buried alive in
the bowels of the churchyard, it will be a reluctant stirring –
like that of the suicide who repents after the fatal stroke, it
will be a flash of lightning that illuminates the midnight of
your life, it will be a revelation, and if you still stand firm,
then you will have won!

FRANZ [pacing up and down in agitation]: Priest's gossip, priest's
gossip!

MOSER: Now for the first time the sword of eternity will cut
through your soul, and now for the first time it will be too
late. – The thought of God will arouse a fearful neighbour,
that is called the Judge. Moor, the lives of thousands hang
upon your finger-tips, and of each of those thousands nine
hundred and ninety-nine you have made a misery. You
would have been a Nero in the days of ancient Rome, in
Peru a Pizarro. And now do you suppose that God will
allow one man to dwell in His creation like a raging demon,
and turn His works to nothing? Do you suppose that those
nine hundred and ninety-nine were only there to be destroyed, puppets only for your devilish play? Oh, do not
believe it! Every minute of theirs that you have murdered,
every joy that you have poisoned, every perfection that you
have kept from them, shall be demanded of you then, and if
you can answer, Moor, then you will have won.

FRANZ: No more! not a word more! am I to be at the mercy
of your liverish fancies?

MOSER: See, the destinies of men are held in a balance, fearful
but beautiful to behold. Where the scale of this life falls, the
scale of that will rise, where this rises, that will sink to the
ground. But that which here was but temporal affliction will
there be made eternal triumph, that which here was mortal
triumph, will there be made everlasting despair.

FRANZ [*rushing at him furiously*]: May the thunder strike you dumb, lying spirit! I will tear out your accursed tongue by the roots!

MOSER: Do you feel the weight of truth so soon? But I have said nothing of proof as yet. Let me come to the proofs –

FRANZ: Be silent, go to Hell with your proofs! the soul is annihilated, I tell you, I will hear no more of it!

MOSER: So the spirits of the pit do whimper, but He in Heaven shakes His head. Do you think you can escape the arm of His retribution in the empty realm of nothingness? ascend up into heaven, and He is there! make your bed in hell, and He is there! say to the night: hide me! and to the darkness: cover me! but the darkness shall be made bright round about you, and the midnight shall be day about the damned – but your immortal spirit will refuse to hear the word, and shall be victorious over the blind thought.

FRANZ: But I will not be immortal, – let those who will, live for ever, I will not seek to hinder it! But I will compel him to annihilate me, I will provoke him to rage, that in his rage he will annihilate me. Tell me, what is the greatest sin, the sin that stirs him to the greatest wrath?

MOSER: I know but two. But they are not such as men commit, nor even dream of.

FRANZ: These two! –

MOSER [*with a weight of meaning*]: Parricide the one is called, fratricide the other – But why do you suddenly turn so pale?

FRANZ: What did you say, old man? Are you in league with Heaven or with Hell? Who told you that?

MOSER: Woe unto him who has both upon his conscience! Better it were for him that he had never been born! But be at ease, you have neither father nor brother more!

FRANZ: Aha! – what, you know of none greater? Think again – death, heaven, eternity, damnation hang upon your lips – none greater than these?

MOSER: None greater than these.

FRANZ [*collapsing into a chair*]: Annihilation! annihilation!

MOSER: Rejoice, rejoice and be glad! – for all your abomina-
tions, you are still a saint compared with the parricide. The
curse that will light upon you, compared with that awaiting
him, is a song of love – the retribution –

FRANZ [*leaping up*]: Away! may a thousand catacombs swallow you up, screech-owl! who sent for you? go, I say, or I
will run you through and through!

MOSER: Can priest's gossip put a philosopher in such a rage?
Blow it away with the breath of your lips! [*Exit.*]

[FRANZ *writhes on his chair in fearful convulsions.*
Profound silence.
Enter a SERVANT, *in haste.*]

SERVANT: Amalia has flown, the Count has suddenly disappeared.

[*Enter* DANIEL, *terrified.*]

DANIEL: Your lordship, a troop of fiery horsemen galloping
down the hill, crying murder, murder – the whole village is
aroused.

FRANZ: Go and have all the bells rung at once, get everyone
to church – on their knees, everyone – They must pray for
me – all the prisoners shall be freed – at liberty – the poor
shall have their goods restored, everything twice, thrice over,
I will – I will – go, go, call the confessor to bless my sins
away, are you not gone yet?

[*The tumult becomes more audible.*]

DANIEL: God have mercy on me, sinner that I am! How am I
to make sense of this? You've always refused to hear a word
of the comfort of prayer, thrown Bible and prayerbook at
my head so often when you caught me praying –

FRANZ: No more of that – To die! You see? Die? It will be
too late.

[SCHWEITZER *is heard making a furious noise.*]

Pray, I tell you, pray!

DANIEL: I always told you – you can be so scornful of the

comfort of prayer – but look out, look out! when your hour of need is come, when the waters rise about your soul, you will give all the treasures of this world for a whisper of Christian prayer – Do you see? You cursed at me, but now do you see?

FRANZ [*embracing him wildly*]: Forgive me! Daniel, dear, good, precious, golden Daniel, forgive me! I will clothe you from head to foot – will you not pray – I will make you a bridegroom – I will – will you not pray – I beseech you – in the devil's name! will you not pray!

[*Tumult in the street outside, cries, knocking.*]

SCHWEITZER [*in the street*]: Take them by storm! Kill them! Break the doors down! I can see a light! he must be there.

FRANZ [*on his knees*]: Hear me pray, o God in Heaven! – It is the first time – and shall never happen again – Hear me, God in Heaven!

DANIEL: Mercy, what are you saying? That is a godless prayer!

PEOPLE [*rushing in*]: Robbers! murderers! who is it making such a din at midnight?

SCHWEITZER [*still outside*]: Push them aside, comrade – it's the devil come to fetch your master – where are Schwarz and his band? – Surround the castle, Grimm – Storm the walls!

GRIMM: Brands and torches here – it's us up or him down – I will set his rooms alight.

FRANZ [*praying*]: Lord God, I have been no common murderer – Lord God, I have never stooped to trifles –

DANIEL: God have mercy on us, his prayer itself's a sin.

[*Stones and flaming brands fly through the air. The windows are broken. The castle is set on fire.*]

FRANZ: I cannot pray – here, here! [*Beating his breast and forehead*] All dry, all withered [*Standing up*]. No, nor will I pray – Heaven shall not have this victory, hell will not make this mock of me –

DANIEL: Mary and Jesus! help – save us – the whole castle is in flames!

FRANZ: Here, take this sword. Quickly. Thrust it into my ribs from behind, so that these villains cannot come and abuse me.

[*The fire gains ground.*]

DANIEL: God forbid, God forbid! I don't want to send any-one to Heaven before his time, still less to – [*He runs away.*]

FRANZ [*staring wide-eyed after him. After a pause*]: To Hell, were you going to say? In truth, I can smell something like – [*In a frenzy.*] Are those its twitterings? do I hear you hissing, ser-pents of the pit? – They are forcing their way up – attacking the doors – why am I so afraid of this sharp steel? – the doors give way – crash down – no way out – Ha! you then, take pity on me! [*He tears the golden cord from his hat and strangles himself. Enter* SCHWEITZER *with his men.*]

SCHWEITZER: Murdering scum, where are you? – Did you see how they ran? – has he so few friends? Where has he crept to, the vermin?

GRIMM [*coming upon the body*]: Stop! what's this in the way? Bring a light here –

SCHWARZ: He's stolen a march on us. Put up your swords, here he is, laid out like a dead cat.

SCHWEITZER: Dead? What? dead? Without me, dead? It's a lie, I tell you – see how quickly he will jump up! – [*Shaking him.*] Hey, you there! There's a father to be murdered.

GRIMM: Spare yourself the trouble. He's as dead as a rat.

SCHWEITZER [*leaving the body*]: Yes! That's the end of him – He is as dead as a rat. – Go back and tell the Captain: He is as dead as a rat – he will not see me again. [*Shoots himself.*]

SCENE 2

The setting as in the last scene of the preceding Act.

[OLD MOOR *seated upon a stone* – ROBBER MOOR *opposite him* – ROBBERS *scattered in the woods.*]

ROBBER MOOR: He is not yet back? [*He strikes a stone with his dagger, making sparks.*]

OLD MOOR: Forgiveness be his punishment – my vengeance redoubled love.

ROBBER MOOR: No, by the anger of my soul. It shall not be. I will not have it so. Such a deed of shame he shall drag behind him into eternity! – Why else should I have killed him?

OLD MOOR [*bursting into tears*]: O my child!

ROBBER MOOR: What? – you weep for him? here by this dungeon?

OLD MOOR: Mercy! O have mercy! [*Wringing his hands violently.*] At this moment – at this moment my child is judged!

ROBBER MOOR [*in fright*]: Which?

OLD MOOR: Ah! what do you mean by that?

ROBBER MOOR: Nothing. Nothing.

OLD MOOR: Have you come to laugh in mockery at my grief?

ROBBER MOOR: Oh, my treacherous conscience! – Take no notice of what I say!

OLD MOOR: Yes, I had a son whom I tormented, and so a son must torment me in turn, it is the finger of God – o my Karl! my Karl! if you hover about me in the raiment of peace, forgive me! O forgive me!

ROBBER MOOR [*quickly*]: He forgives you. [*Checking himself*] If he is worthy to be called your son – he must forgive you.

OLD MOOR: Ah, he was too glorious for me – But I will go to meet him with my tears, with my sleepless nights and my torturing dreams, I will embrace his knees and cry – will cry aloud: I have sinned in the sight of Heaven and before you. I am not worthy to be called your father.

ROBBER MOOR [*deeply moved*]: He was dear to you, your other son?

OLD MOOR: Heaven is my witness! Why did I let myself be deceived by the wiles of a wicked son? Praised as a father I went among the fathers of men. Fair about me blossomed my children full of promise. But – O, unhappy the hour! – the evil spirit entered into the heart of my youngest, I believed the serpent – lost my children, both of them. [*Covering his face*.]

ROBBER MOOR [*going away some distance from him*]: Lost for ever.

OLD MOOR: Oh, I feel it so deeply, what Amalia said, the spirit of vengeance spoke through her lips. In vain your dying hands you will stretch out to touch your son, in vain you will think you grasp the warm hand of your Karl, who will never come to stand at your bedside –

[ROBBER MOOR *holds out his hand to him, with averted gaze*.]

OLD MOOR: Would that this were my Karl's hand! But he lies far away in his narrow dwelling, is already sleeping his iron sleep, cannot hear the voice of my grief – woe to me! To die in the arms of a stranger – no son more – no son more to close my eyes –

ROBBER MOOR [*in the most violent agitation*]: Now it must be – now – leave me [*to the* ROBBERS]. And yet – Can I give him back his son again? – I can no longer give him back his son – No! I will not do it.

OLD MOOR: What, my friend? What were you saying to yourself?

ROBBER MOOR: Your son – Yes, old man – [*stammering*] Your son – is – lost for ever.

OLD MOOR: For ever?

ROBBER MOOR [*looking up to heaven in anguish*]: O but this

once – let not my soul be weakened – but this once sustain me!

OLD MOOR: For ever, you say?

ROBBER MOOR: Ask no more. For ever, I said.

OLD MOOR: Stranger! Stranger! Why did you drag me out of my dungeon?

ROBBER MOOR: And what then? – What if I were to snatch his blessing – snatch it like a thief, and creep away with that godlike prize – a father's blessing, they say, can never be lost.

OLD MOOR: And my Franz lost too?

ROBBER MOOR [*prostrating himself before him*]: It was I who broke the locks of your dungeon – Give me your blessing.

OLD MOOR [*with grief*]: That you had to destroy the son, to save the father! – See, the Divinity is unwearying in its mercy, and we poor worms let the sun go down on our wrath. [*Laying his hand on the* ROBBER'S *head.*] Be happy, according as you are merciful.

ROBBER MOOR [*standing up, tenderly*]: Oh – where is my manhood? My sinews grow slack, the dagger slips from my hand.

OLD MOOR: How good and how pleasant for brethren to dwell together in unity, as the dew of Hermon, and as the dew that descended on the mountains of Zion – Learn to deserve such bliss, young man, and the angels of heaven will bask in the glory that shines about you. Let your wisdom be the wisdom of grey hairs, but your heart – let your heart be the heart of an innocent child.

ROBBER MOOR: Oh, a foretaste of such bliss. Kiss me, godlike old man!

OLD MOOR [*kissing him*]: Imagine that it is a father's kiss, and I will imagine I am kissing my son – can you also weep?

ROBBER MOOR: I thought it was a father's kiss! – Alas for me if they should bring him now!

[*Enter* SCHWEITZER'S *companions in silent mourning procession, with lowered heads and faces covered.*]

ROBBER MOOR: Heavens! [*Drawing back anxiously, and trying*

to hide. The procession passes him. He looks away from them. Profound silence. They stop.]

GRIMM [*in a subdued voice*]: Captain!

[ROBBER MOOR *does not answer, and draws further back.*]

SCHWARZ: Beloved Captain!

[ROBBER MOOR *draws still further back.*]

GRIMM: We are innocent, captain.

ROBBER MOOR [*without looking at them*]: Who are you?

GRIMM: You will not look at us. We are your true and faithful band.

ROBBER MOOR: Woe to you if you have been true to me!

GRIMM: The last farewell of your trusty servant Schweitzer – he will come no more, your trusty servant Schweitzer.

ROBBER MOOR [*springing to his feet*]: Then you did not find him?

SCHWARZ: Found him dead.

ROBBER MOOR [*leaping up with joy*]: Thanks be to Thee, guider of all things – Embrace me, my children – Mercy is the password from now on – So, even that might be overcome – all, all overcome!

[*Enter more* ROBBERS, *and* AMALIA.]

ROBBERS: Hurrah, hurrah! A catch, a magnificent catch!

AMALIA [*with hair flowing free*]: The dead, they cry, are resurrected at the sound of his voice – my uncle alive – in these woods – where is he? Karl! Uncle! Ah! [*Rushing over to the old man.*]

OLD MOOR: Amalia! My daughter! Amalia! [*Holding her tightly in his arms.*]

ROBBER MOOR [*starting back*]: Who conjures up this vision before my eyes?

AMALIA [*tears herself away from the old man, runs to* KARL *and embraces him with rapture*]: He is mine, o you stars! he is mine!

ROBBER MOOR [*tearing himself loose, to the* ROBBERS]: Strike camp, all of you! The fiend has betrayed me!

AMALIA: Oh, my bridegroom, you are raving! Ah, for rapture! Why am I so unfeeling, in this whirl of joy so cold?

OLD MOOR [*drawing himself upright*]: Bridegroom? Daughter! daughter! A bridegroom?

AMALIA: His for ever! Mine for ever and for ever and for ever! – o you heavenly powers, take from me this joy unto death, or I shall faint beneath its burden!

ROBBER MOOR: Tear her from my neck! Kill her! Kill him! me, yourselves! Everything! The whole world falls in ruins! [*Trying to escape.*]

AMALIA: Where are you going? what is it? Love, eternity! Rapture unending, and you would flee?

ROBBER MOOR: Away, away! Unhappiest of brides! See for yourself, ask for yourself and hear! Unhappiest of fathers! Let me flee this place for ever!

AMALIA: Take me, in God's name, take me in your arms! It is as night before my eyes – He is running away!

ROBBER MOOR: Too late! In vain! Your curse, father – ask me no more! I am, I have – your curse – your curse, as I thought! – Who lured me to this place? [*Drawing his sword and rushing at the* ROBBERS.] Which of you lured me to this place, you creatures of the pit? Swoon then, Amalia! – Die, father! Die through me a third time! – These your rescuers are robbers and murderers! Your Karl is their captain!

[OLD MOOR *expires.*

AMALIA *is silent, and stands like a statue. The whole band pauses in silent horror.*]

ROBBER MOOR [*running against an oak-tree*]: The souls of those I strangled in the ecstasy of love – those I shattered in their blessed sleep – those – ha! Do you hear the powder-magazine exploding over the beds of those women in labour? Do you see the flames licking at the cradles of their nurselings? – our nuptial torch, our wedding music – oh, he does not forget, he knows how to join the links – so, not for me the joy of love! so, for me love a torment! it is retribution!

AMALIA: It is true! Great Lord in Heaven, it is true! What have I done, innocent lamb that I was! I loved him!

ROBBER MOOR: This is more than a man can bear. Have I not heard death whistling towards me from more than a thousand musket-barrels, and without yielding a foot, and am I now to learn to quake like a woman? to quake before a woman? – No, no woman shall shake my manhood – Blood! blood! It is only something caught from a woman – give me blood to swill, and it will pass. [*Trying to escape.*]

AMALIA [*falling into his arms*]: Murderer! Devil! Angel – I cannot leave you.

ROBBER MOOR [*hurling her away from him*]: Away, you serpent, you would mock a madman with your scorn, but I defy the tyrant destiny – what, you are weeping? Oh you wicked, wanton stars! She is pretending to weep, pretending there is a soul that weeps for me.

[AMALIA *throws her arms about his neck.*]

Ah, what is this? She does not spit at me, she does not thrust me from her – Amalia! Have you forgotten? do you know who it is you are embracing, Amalia?

AMALIA: My only one, I shall never leave you!

ROBBER MOOR [*in ecstatic joy*]: She forgives me, she loves me! I am pure as the heavenly aether, she loves me! Tears of gratitude to you, merciful God in Heaven! [*He falls on his knees, convulsed with weeping.*] Peace has returned to my soul, the raging torment is past, Hell is no more – See, O see, the children of light weep upon the neck of the weeping devil – [*standing up, to the* ROBBERS] Why do you not weep too? weep, weep, for you are so blessed. Oh, Amalia! Amalia! Amalia! [*He hangs upon her lips, they remain silently embraced.*]

A ROBBER [*approaching angrily*]: Stop, traitor! – Let go this arm straightway, or I shall tell you a word that will make your ears ring and your teeth chatter with horror! [*He parts them with his sword.*]

AN OLD ROBBER: Remember the forests of Bohemia! Do you

hear, do you hesitate – then remember the forests of Bohemia! Faithless man, where are your oaths? Do you forget
wounds so quickly? When we set fortune, honour and life
itself at a venture for you? When we stood round you like
ramparts, bore like shields the blows that were aimed at your
life – did you not then raise your hand and swear an iron
oath *never to forsake us*, as we had never forsaken you? – Have
you no honour? have you no faith? Will you abandon us for
a whining whore?

A THIRD ROBBER: Shame on your perjury! the spirit of Roller
that died for you, Roller whom you summoned from the
dead to be your witness, will blush for your cowardice, and
rise armoured from his grave to punish you.

THE ROBBERS [*all together, tearing open their clothes*]: Look,
look here! Do you recognize these scars? you belong to us!
We bought you for our bondsman with our heart's blood,
you belong to us, and if the archangel Michael should fight
with Moloch for you! – march with us, one sacrifice for
another! Amalia for the band!

ROBBER MOOR [*letting go of her hand*]: It is finished! – I sought
to mend my ways and turn again to my father, but Heaven
spoke, and said it should not be. [*Coldly*] Fool, and why did
I seek it? Can so great a sinner still mend his ways? So great
a sinner cannot mend his ways, that I should have known
long ago. – Be calm, I beg you, be calm! it is as it should be –
when he sought me, I would not, now when I seek him he
will not – what could be more just than that? – Do not roll
your eyes like that – he has no need of me. Has he not
creatures in abundance, he can so easily let one go, and that
one am I. Come, comrades!

AMALIA [*dragging him back*]: Stop, stop! One stroke, one fatal
stroke! Forsaken anew! Draw your sword, and have pity on
me!

ROBBER MOOR: Pity is flown to the wild beasts, – I will not
kill you!

AMALIA [*clasping his knees*]: Oh, in the name of God, in the name of all mercies! I ask no more for love, I know that our stars above flee one another in enmity – death is my only wish. – Forsaken, forsaken! Think of it in all its horror, forsaken! I cannot bear it. You can see, a woman cannot bear it. Death is my only wish! See, my hand is trembling! I have not the heart to strike. I am afraid of the flashing steel – for you it is so easy, you are a master in the art of slaughter, draw your sword, and I shall be happy!

ROBBER MOOR: Would you alone be happy? Away with you, I kill no woman.

AMALIA: Ah, assassin! you can only kill those who are happy, those who are tired of life you pass by. [*Crawling to the* ROBBERS.] Then you must take pity on me, you hangman's apprentices! – There is such bloodthirsty pity in your looks, that is comfort for the wretched – your master is a vain faint-hearted braggart.

ROBBER MOOR: Woman, what are you saying?

[*The* ROBBERS *turn away from her.*]

AMALIA: No friend? not a friend among these either? [*Standing up*] Then let Dido teach me to die!

[*She is going, one of the* ROBBERS *takes aim.*]

ROBBER MOOR: Stop! Would you dare – Moor's love shall die by Moor's hand alone! [*He kills her.*]

ROBBERS: Captain, captain! What have you done, are you mad?

ROBBER MOOR [*with gaze fixed on the body*]: She is hit! This last convulsion, and it is over – Now, see! what more can you demand? You sacrificed to me a life that you could no longer call your own, a life of horror and disgrace – I have slaughtered an angel for you. Look, look, I say! Are you satisfied now?

GRIMM: You have paid your debts with interest. You have done more than any man would do for his honour. And now come with us!

ROBBER MOOR: You say that? The life of a saint for the lives
of rogues, it is an unequal bargain, is it not? – Oh, I tell you,
if every one of you were to walk the scaffold, and to have
your flesh torn from your bones, piece by piece with red-hot
pincers, that your torments should last eleven summer days
long, it would not make good these tears. [*With bitter
laughter*] The scars, the forests of Bohemia! Yes, yes! of
course, that had to be repaid.

SCHWARZ: Be calm, captain! Come with us, this is no sight
for you. Lead us on!

ROBBER MOOR: Stop – one word before we go on – Listen,
you all too zealous executioners of my barbaric command –
From this moment I cease to be your captain – With shame
and loathing I lay down this bloodstained baton under whose
sway you thought yourselves entitled to sin, and to affront
the light of heaven with works of darkness – Draw aside to
left and right – We shall never make common cause in all
eternity.

ROBBERS: Ha! have you lost your courage? Where are your
high-flying plans? Were they but soap-bubbles, that burst at
a woman's breath?

ROBBER MOOR: Oh, fool that I was, to suppose that I could
make the world a fairer place through terror, and uphold
the cause of justice through lawlessness. I called it revenge
and right – I took it upon myself, O Providence, to smooth
the jagged edges of your sword and make good your
partiality – but – oh, childish vanity – here I stand at the limit
of a life of horror, and see now with weeping and gnashing
of teeth, that *two men such as I would destroy the whole moral
order of creation.* Mercy – mercy for the youth who sought to
anticipate Thy judgement – Thine alone is vengeance. Thou
hast no need of man's hand. And now, truly, it is no longer
in my power to make up for the past – what is ruined, is
ruined – what I have overthrown will never rise again. But
still something remains that can reconcile me to the laws

against which I have offended, and restore the order which I have violated. They must have a sacrifice – a sacrifice that will make manifest their invulnerable majesty to all mankind – and I myself shall be the victim. For them I must surely die.

ROBBERS: Take his sword from him – He is going to kill himself.

ROBBER MOOR: You fools! Damned to eternal blindness! Do you suppose a mortal sin can cancel out mortal sins, do you suppose the harmony of creation will be restored by such blasphemous discord? [*Throwing his weapons contemptuously at their feet.*] He shall have me alive. I shall go and give myself up into the hands of the law.

ROBBERS: Tie him up, chain him! He is raving mad.

ROBBER MOOR: Not that I doubt they would find me soon enough, if the powers above so will it. But they might surprise me in my sleep, or catch me as I fled, or surround me by force and with swords, and then I should have lost my one remaining merit, of dying for justice of my own free will. Why should I still seek like a common thief to keep hidden a life that in the eyes of Heaven has long been forfeit?

ROBBERS: Let him go! These are fantasies of greatness. He will stake his life on empty admiration.

ROBBER MOOR: I might be admired for it. [*After some reflection*] I remember speaking to a poor wretch as I came here – a day-labourer, with eleven children living – They are offering a thousand louis-d'ors' reward for handing over the great robber alive – I can help that man. [*Exit.*]

WALLENSTEIN

A DRAMATIC POEM

PROLOGUE

Spoken on the occasion of the reopening of the
Weimar Court Theatre in October 1798

The play of masks, both serious and gay,
To which you lent so often willing ears
And eyes, and gently yielded up your souls,
Unites us in this selfsame room once more;
And see! in youth renewed it stands, the arts
Serenely for their temple have adorned it.
A spirit lofty and harmonious
Addresses us amidst these noble columns,
And in our minds arouses festive thoughts.

And yet this is the same familiar stage,
The cradle of so many youthful powers,
Scene where so many talents did unfold,
And we ourselves the same that learnt our craft
Before your eyes, with eager warmth and zeal.
A noble master stood upon these boards,
A genius and creator, who could bear
You by his art upon its heights serene.
O may these rooms in new nobility
Draw to our midst the noblest and the best,
And may the hope that we so long have cherished
Now be fulfilled, and stand achieved in splendour.
A great example stirs to emulation
And teaches higher laws that we should judge by.
So let this gathering, let this new stage
Be witnesses of talent now perfected.
And where indeed should it essay its powers,
Recapture and renew its fame of old,
But here before a chosen gathering,

Sensible to the magic touch of art
And delicate of feeling, quick to capture
The fleeting apparition of the spirit?

For swiftly flits the actor's wondrous art
Before our senses, leaving not a trace,
While mark of sculptor's chisel and the song
Of poets live a thousand years and more.
Here, when the artist dies, his spell dies with him,
And as the echoes fade within our ear,
The moment's swift creation is dissolved,
No lasting monument preserves its fame.
That art is hard, inconstant its reward,
The future winds no garlands for the actor;
So he must seize the present greedily,
Fulfil the moment that is his alone,
Win recognition from the world he lives in,
And in the best and noblest minds erect
Himself a living monument, that here
And now he may enjoy his fame immortal.
For he who satisfies the best of his
Own age, has lived for every age to come.

The fresh, new dawn Thalia's art begins
Upon this stage today, has also made
The poet bold to leave well-trodden paths,
And carry you beyond the confines of
Domestic life, on to a wider stage,
That will not be unworthy of the high,
Momentous times in which we live and strive.
Only an object of sublimity
Can stir the deepest depths within man's soul;
In narrow confines men grow narrow too,
But greater when their goals are higher set.
And as our century so gravely ends,

When truth, it seems, would take the shape of art,
When we behold a struggle of great natures
For a momentous goal before our eyes,
And for those objects men hold most sublime
They fight, for power and for liberty –
So art upon its shadow-stage as well
May strive for higher flights, indeed it must,
Or yield in shame before the stage of life.

Crumbling before us in these days we see
The old, assured, familiar form, that once
A welcome peace, one hundred and fifty years
Ago, gave Europe's kingdoms, precious fruit
Of thirty years of war and suffering.
Now once again permit the poet's fancy
To bring those dark days back before your eyes;
Then look with reassurance on the present,
And to the distant future rich in hope.
Into the middle of that war the poet
Will now transport you. Sixteen years of waste,
Of plunder and of misery have sped.
A dull fermenting mass the world still lies,
No distant hope of peace can yet be glimpsed.
The Empire is a raging battlefield,
Its towns a desolation, Magdeburg
In ruins, trade and industry abandoned;
Only the soldier counts, the honest citizen
Is scorned, and insolence may go unpunished,
And savage hordes encamp, made rough and wild
By years of war, upon the ravaged earth.

Against this sombre background of the times
We see a bold and reckless enterprise
Take shape, a character of boundless daring.
You know him – the creator of bold armies,

The idol of the camp, the scourge of kingdoms,
The prop and terror of his Emperor,
The child and nurseling of adventurous fortune,
Who, borne aloft by favourable times,
Climbed swiftly to the highest peaks of honour,
And striving onwards, never satisfied,
Fell victim to ambition unconfined.
Partisan hatreds and affections shroud
His character, as history portrays it;
But art shall bring him closer, as a man,
Both to your eyes, and to your feeling hearts.
For art, that shapes and limits all, will lead
All monstrous aberrations back to nature,
See man encompassed by the press of life
And lay the greater share of blame and guilt
Upon ill-fortune written in the stars.

It is not he himself who will appear
Upon these boards today. But in the hosts
Of gallant men his mighty word commands,
His spirit moves, you may perceive his shadow,
Until the timid Muse at last may dare
To bring his living shape before your eyes;
For it was his own power seduced his heart,
His camp must help us understand his crime.

And so forgive the poet, if he does
Not sweep you all at once with rapid stride
To the catastrophe, but only brings
A row of captive scenes before your eyes,
In which those great events unfold themselves.
So let our play today win back again
Your ears and hearts to unaccustomed tones;
Let it transport you to that time of old,
On to that unfamiliar stage of war

Which soon our hero with his mighty deeds
Will fill.

      And if today the gentle muse,
The goddess of the dance and melody,
Should with due modesty insist upon
Her ancient native right, the play of rhyme,
Then do not scold her, but be thankful rather
That she should thus transform the sombre hues
Of truth into the realm of art serene,
Create illusion, then in honesty
Reveal the trick she plays, and not pretend
That what she brings us is the stuff of truth.
Life is in earnest, art serene and free.

WALLENSTEIN'S CAMP

CHARACTERS

SERGEANT-MAJOR ⎫ from a regiment of
TRUMPETER ⎭ Terzky's carabineers
BOMBARDIER
SHARPSHOOTERS
TWO TROOPERS from Holk's light cavalry
DRAGOONS from Butler's regiment
ARQUEBUSIERS from Tiefenbach's regiment
CUIRASSIER from a Walloon regiment
CUIRASSIER from a Lombard regiment
CROATS
ULANS
RECRUIT
CITIZEN
PEASANT
PEASANT BOY
CAPUCHIN FRIAR
CAMP SCHOOLMASTER
CANTEEN-WOMAN
SERVING-GIRL
SOLDIER'S CHILDREN
BANDSMEN

Scene: Before the town of Pilsen in Bohemia.

SCENE I

A canteen-tent with a huckster's stall in front of it.
SOLDIERS *in all kinds of uniforms and with all kinds of*
badges are crowded together, and all the tables are
occupied. CROATS *and* ULANS *are cooking over an open*
coal fire. CANTEEN-WOMAN *is pouring out wine,*
SOLDIERS' CHILDREN *are playing dice on a drum,*
singing is heard from the tent.

[*A* PEASANT *and his son.*]

PEASANT BOY: No good will come of this, I say.
  Father, from the soldiers let's stay away!
  I tell you, they are a wild rough sort,
  I only hope they won't make us their sport!
PEASANT: What nonsense! They're not going to eat us,
  Even though they may seem rough when they greet us.
  You see? There are more new troops again,
  Freshly arrived from Saale and Main,
  Their pockets are full of treasure bright,
  All for us, if we play it aright.
  A captain – murdered he was, I fear –
  Left me these lucky dice you see here.
  It was to try them out I came,
  To see if they deserve their name.
  Just take care not to look too clever;
  These fellows are all as foolish as ever,
  They love to hear themselves praised and flattered,
  All that they've won is quickly scattered.
  If they come and take what's ours by the sack,

Then a pinch at a time we must get it back;
If they use their swords to hack and pry,
Then we shall have to be cunning and sly.
   [*Singing and jubilation is heard from the tent.*]
God bless my soul, just hear how they crow!
And it all goes on the peasant's slate.
Eight months this swarm has been on us now,
Turning us out of house and gate,
Not a feather or claw of a fowl's to be seen,
For miles around on field or green,
So we for hunger and wretchedness
Are left with our own bare bones to gnaw.
I tell you, our troubles and woes were no less
In the days when the Saxons were burning our straw.
And these call themselves Imperial troops!

BOY: Here come some more to fill their cups,
   But they look as though we'll get nothing from them!

PEASANT: They're from Bohemia, local men,
   Terzky's carabineers they are called,
   For many months they've been installed.
   Of all the soldiers they are the worst,
   Stick out their chests and would always be first.
   Reckon that they are too fine a class
   To sit with a peasant and share a glass.
   But look at the Sharpshooters over there,
   On the left sitting by the fire.
   Tiroleans, if I'm not mistaken.
   Come along, Emmerich, there's our bacon,
   They're merry, talkative fellows, you'll find,
   Well set up and their purses well lined.
   [*They go towards the tents.*]

SCENE 2

[*Enter* SERGEANT-MAJOR, TRUMPETER, ULAN.]

TRUMPETER: What does that peasant want? Off, you scum!

PEASANT: Oh, please sir, can't you spare a crumb?
  All day we've had nothing to eat or drink.

TRUMPETER: It's of nothing but their bellies they think.

ULAN [*with a glass*]:
  No breakfast, you dog? Come and drink with me!
    [*He leads the* PEASANT *towards the tent; the others come
    forward.*]

SERGEANT-MAJOR [*to the* TRUMPETER]:
  Is it just pure liberality,
  Do you think, that they've paid us double today,
  Just so that we can be merry and gay?

TRUMPETER: The Duchess arrives today, you know,
  With the princess her daughter –

SERGEANT-MAJOR: That's just for show.
  All these troops from foreign lands,
  That have gathered here where Pilsen stands,
  We have to win over behind our lines
  With tasty titbits and tasty wines,
  So that they think it was worth the journey
  And pledge themselves to us more firmly.

TRUMPETER: Yes, something is afoot, it seems!

SERGEANT-MAJOR: The generals and commanders all –

TRUMPETER: I don't believe I trust their schemes.

SERGEANT-MAJOR: So many of them who obeyed the call –

TRUMPETER: They are not only here for play.

SERGEANT-MAJOR: And all the rumour and report –

TRUMPETER: Yes! Yes!

SERGEANT-MAJOR: And Old Periwig from the Court,

Who's been in the camp since yesterday,
With his golden chain, a-wandering round,
He's up to something, I'll be bound.

TRUMPETER: Another of those bloodhounds, look,
They send from Vienna to sniff out the Duke.

SERGEANT-MAJOR: They don't trust us, and that's no lie,
They're afraid of the look in Friedland's eye.
It's far too high for their liking he's flown,
They'd dearly love to bring him down.

TRUMPETER: But we will sustain him, never fear!
If only the others held him so dear!

SERGEANT-MAJOR: Our own regiment and the other four
here,
Commanded by Terzky, his brother-in-law,
The stoutest troops that ever you saw,
Are loyal and devoted to him to the death –
It was he himself who gave us breath,
All the captains himself did enrol;
They are his to the last man, body and soul.

SCENE 3

[*Enter* CROAT *with a necklace,* SHARPSHOOTER
following him.]

SHARPSHOOTER: Croat, that necklace you've stolen there!
It's of no use to you. I'll buy it, see!
I'll give you this pair of pistols to wear.

CROAT: No, no, sharpshooter! You're swindling me.

SHARPSHOOTER: Well, this blue bonnet too, if you'll agree,
That by good fortune I've just won.
Look how grandly this feather curls!

CROAT [*letting the sun play on the necklace*]:

But these are the finest garnets and pearls.
See how it sparkles in the sun!

SHARPSHOOTER [takes the necklace]:
I'll let my water-bottle go – [examining the necklace]
I only want it for the show.

TRUMPETER: Look at him cheating that Croat there!
Yes, I'll keep quiet, if you'll give me a share.

CROAT [has tried on the bonnet]:
I like your bonnet, it suits me well –

SHARPSHOOTER [with a sign to the TRUMPETER]:
Done! These gentlemen witness the deal.

SCENE 4

[Enter BOMBARDIER]

BOMBARDIER [going up to the SERGEANT-MAJOR]:
Well now, brother carabineer!
How long must we sit here warming our hands
With the enemy ravaging all these lands?

SERGEANT-MAJOR: Master bombardier, why do you haste
and fret?
The roads are hardly passable yet.

BOMBARDIER: Not I. I am very comfortable here;
But there's come a report, if I'm not mistaken,
That the city of Regensburg has been taken.

TRUMPETER: Then soon we'll be getting our marching
orders!

SERGEANT-MAJOR: What, to protect the Bavarian's borders,
Whose passion against the Duke is so hot?
We'll not rush to be his supporters.

BOMBARDIER: Indeed? You seem to know a lot.

SCENE 5

[*Enter two* TROOPERS. *Then* CANTEEN-WOMAN,
CAMP BOYS *and* SCHOOLMASTER, SERVING-GIRL.]

FIRST TROOPER: Halloo, hallee!
  Here's a merry company.
TRUMPETER: Do you know who they are, those fellows in
    green?
  How they swagger and like to be seen!
SERGEANT-MAJOR: Yes, they're Holk's men; the silver they
    wear
  Wasn't picked up at the Leipzig fair.
CANTEEN-WOMAN [*bringing wine*]:
  Welcome, sirs!
FIRST TROOPER: Why, it can't be shammed,
  It's Gussie from Blasewitz, or I'll be damned!
CANTEEN-WOMAN: It is! And you, monsieur – I know!
  Lanky Peter from Itzehoe!
  Who gambled away his father's horses
  One merry night with our regiment
  When up to Glückstadt we were sent –
FIRST TROOPER: And laid down his pen to join the forces.
CANTEEN-WOMAN: Why then, we two are friends of old!
FIRST TROOPER: And meet again on the Bohemian wold!
CANTEEN-WOMAN: Here today, tomorrow gone –
  That's the way the rough broom of war
  Rousts us out and sweeps us on;
  Since we last met, I've travelled far.
FIRST TROOPER: I'll believe you! That's how it feels.
CANTEEN-WOMAN: To Temesoara and back again
  I followed with the baggage-train
  When we were harrying Mansfeld's heels.

When Friedland laid siege to Stralsund, to his cost,
I was there too – and my business was lost.
I was with the relief of Mantua,
Came away with the Duke of Feria,
And with a Spanish regiment
On the way back I stopped at Ghent,
Now in Bohemia my luck I'm trying,
Chasing old debtors that I've left lying;
With the Prince's help, I hope they'll come clean –
And that tent over there is my canteen.

FIRST TROOPER: Well, here you'll find everyone once
more!
But what have you done with that Scottish boor?
In those days you were very thick.

CANTEEN-WOMAN: The villain! He played me a scoundrelly
trick,
No words are too strong for the way he behaved,
He ran off with every penny I'd saved,
Left me with nothing but his brat!

BOY [comes running up to her]:
Mother, don't talk of my dad like that!

FIRST TROOPER: Another mouth for the Emperor to feed.
If the army would keep alive, it must breed!

CAMP SCHOOLMASTER [enters]:
Come along, you boys! There are lessons to learn!

FIRST TROOPER: They're afraid of the school, where there's
no room to turn!

SERVING GIRL [comes from the tent]:
They want to go, cousin.

CANTEEN-WOMAN: I'm coming, quickly!

FIRST TROOPER: Hello, who's that saucy little piece?

CANTEEN-WOMAN: My sister's child, from Germany.

FIRST TROOPER: Oho, I see, your charming niece?
[Exit CANTEEN-WOMAN.]

SECOND TROOPER [holding on to the girl]:

Won't you stay with us for a while, my pet?

SERVING-GIRL: There are customers waiting, I can't stop
    yet.

    [*She frees herself and goes off.*]

FIRST TROOPER: That's not a bad little girl, I declare!

    And as for her aunt – the devil be praised!

    All the lads in our regiment were crazed

    And fought for her favours, that was an affair!

    What people in this world we meet,

    And how time onward speeds so fleet –

    Who knows what more life for me will bear?

    [*To the* SERGEANT-MAJOR *and the* TRUMPETER]

    Well, gentlemen, I drink to you!

    Let's sit together here a while.

SCENE 6

[*Two* TROOPERS, SERGEANT-MAJOR, TRUMPETER.]

SERGEANT-MAJOR: Thank you, and here's to your health
    too.

    Bohemia welcomes with a smile!

FIRST TROOPER: You're well off here. In enemy country

    We often had to live hard and vile.

TRUMPETER: We'd never have thought it, you look like
    gentry.

SERGEANT-MAJOR: Oh yes, in the lands by the Saale and in
    Meissen

    They're glad to see *you* gone beyond the horizon.

SECOND TROOPER: What do you mean by that? You're a
    nice one!

    The Croats, now, they were a different kind,

    We only had what they left behind.

TRUMPETER: That's a fine lace collar – such delicate stitches –
    My word, and look at the cut of your breeches!
    Your clean white linen, the plumes in your hat!
    Not many who wouldn't be taken by that!
    These fellows have all the good fortune, you know,
    While you and I have nothing to show.
SERGEANT-MAJOR: But we are Friedland's own regiment,
    And so we are honoured, respected, and famed.
FIRST TROOPER: You pay us others no compliment,
    Who also after himself are named.
SERGEANT-MAJOR: Yes, you belong too to the general
    flock.
FIRST TROOPER: I suppose you think you're a special stock?
    The only difference that I can see
    Is in our coats – and mine suits me.
SERGEANT-MAJOR: Trooper, I can see it's not pleasant
    To live out in the wilds like a peasant;
    Good manners and a proper tone
    Are learnt from the general's person alone.
FIRST TROOPER: Well, over your head the lesson has flown.
    The way he clears his throat and spits
    You copy well, the picture fits;
    But his genius – you know, what's up there –
    Doesn't show itself on the barrack square.
SECOND TROOPER: By the elements! Everywhere you'll be
    told,
    Friedland's wild hunt is the name we are called,
    And we do not disgrace it, wherever we go,
    We take no account of friend or of foe,
    Across the fields, through the golden corn –
    They know the sound of Holk's hunting-horn!
    Here in a moment, gone in another,
    Swift as the deluge our forces we gather –
    Swift as the flames of fire that break
    Into houses at night, when none is awake –

No resistance can save, no fight and no plaint,
All order crumbles and all restraint –
The maiden struggles – for war knows no quarter –
In the sinewy arms of the trooper who's caught her –
Ask and be told, what I say is no boast,
From Bavaria's heights to the North Sea coast,
Everywhere we have left our trail,
Generations will tell the tale
For a hundred years and a hundred more
Of Holk and his men and their deeds in this war.

SERGEANT-MAJOR: Ah, there we have it! Riot and plunder.
Does that make a soldier? No, by thunder!
Discipline makes him, style and address,
Smartness, importance, a look of finesse.

FIRST TROOPER: It's freedom that makes him! Can anyone
    doubt it?
I'll mince no more words with you about it. –
Did I run away from my desk in the school
Only to find the same labour and rule,
The narrow study, the toil and the cramp
Awaiting me here in the soldier's camp?
I want to live well, not have too much to do,
Every day of my life see something new,
Cheerfully seize the moment, in sum,
Not brood on the past, nor on things to come –
That's why I've sold Ferdinand my skin:
In the face of care I can merrily grin.
Lead me where cannon roar and thud,
Across the Rhine in its raging flood,
Let a third of the company shed their life's blood;
I'll not be squeamish, or make a dance.
But otherwise, if you don't object,
Spare me your fuss and circumstance.

SERGEANT-MAJOR: Why, is there nothing more you expect?
Then that jerkin should help you to all you desire.

FIRST TROOPER: What a torture that was, like the rack and
    the fire,
  When I served Gustavus, that miserable Swede!
  His camp was more like a chapel, indeed,
  Prayers every morning, straight after reveille,
  Each night at Lights Out, and before every sally;
  If we got a bit merry, like any good Germans,
  He was up on his horse and preaching us sermons.

SERGEANT-MAJOR: Yes, yes, he was a God-fearing man.

FIRST TROOPER: If you brought in a woman, that wouldn't
    do:
  It was straight to church, and swear to be true!
  I couldn't stand it, I tell you, I ran.

SERGEANT-MAJOR: It's changed there too since the new
    reign began.

FIRST TROOPER: So I crossed to the Catholic side,
  For Magdeburg they were preparing to ride.
  That was a different kettle of fish,
  Everything there was just as you'd wish,
  Gaming and booze and girls by the dozen!
  I tell you, that was a first-class dish,
  For Tilly knew all about commanding.
  On himself he was strict and demanding,
  But the soldiers he would never cozen,
  And if he didn't have to foot the bill,
  His motto was: Live and let live! with a will.
  But destiny he couldn't master –
  The battle of Leipzig was a disaster,
  And after that our fortunes stuck,
  Whatever we did, we met bad luck;
  Wherever we came and knocked at the door,
  No one would open any more.
  We had to scrounge from place to place,
  It seemed our name had become a disgrace. –
  And so I took the Saxon's shilling,

To see if that would make fortune more willing.

SERGEANT-MAJOR: Why then, you did the best that you
    could!

The sack of Bohemia –

FIRST TROOPER: That was no good.
    Strict discipline we had to keep,
    The harvest of war was not ours to reap,
    The Emperor's castles we had to guard,
    Pay compliments, and that was hard,
    It wasn't war, but playing a game,
    Our hearts weren't in it, it wasn't the same,
    We were trying not to offend anyone –
    In a word, there was no glory to be won;
    It made me impatient, I nearly went back
    To my desk at home, that had seemed so black,
    When just at that moment we heard far and wide
    That Friedland was drawing recruits to his side.

SERGEANT-MAJOR: And how long this time do you think
    you will stand?

FIRST TROOPER: Joking apart! While *he's* in command,
    I'll not think of deserting, upon my soul!
    Can there be a better place to enrol?
    Everything goes with a martial swing,
    There's style and grandeur in everything.
    The spirit that moves in this uniform
    Sweeps all before it like the storm,
    Even the veriest underling.
    Then in my step I feel a new spring,
    Stride over the citizens, fearless and bold,
    Like the general over the princes' heads.
    It's just as in the days of old,
    When it was only the sword that told;
    When there was only one crime in the land,
    To disobey the word of command!
    There's perfect freedom where no law impedes,

No questions are asked of confessions or creeds,
There's only one difference that anyone heeds:
Do you belong to the army or no?
And it's to that flag my allegiance I owe.

SERGEANT-MAJOR: That's the style, trooper! Why, now I hear
You speak like a Friedland cavalier!

FIRST TROOPER: The way he gives orders, you'd never believe
That he held his office by the Emperor's leave!
To serve the Emperor's not his concern –
What profit through him did the Emperor earn?
What has he done, with all his great power,
To keep the Empire safe and secure?
A kingdom of soldiers he wanted to found,
To raze this world and its works to the ground,
All things within his grasp to impound –

TRUMPETER: Who dares to speak such words as these!

FIRST TROOPER: What I think, I may say as I please.
We are free to speak, our General proclaims!

SERGEANT-MAJOR: I heard him say so a number of times.
Now let me see – Yes: 'Speech is free,
Action is silent, obedience blind.'
Those are his very words, you'll find.

FIRST TROOPER: His very words – well, I wouldn't know that:
But the facts of the matter are so, and that's flat.

SECOND TROOPER: His fortunes in battle will never go down,
As happens to others who take the field.
General Tilly outlived his renown,
But wherever Friedland's standards are planted
Victory's certain to be granted.
He's charmed good fortune, it cannot yield,
And all who fight beneath his banner

Are protected in a special manner:
For everyone must know full well
That Friedland keeps an imp of hell
In his pay, to protect his person.
SERGEANT-MAJOR: Yes, that he's bullet-proof is certain!
For at Lützen – and that was a bloody affair –
Under the enemy's noses he'd dare
To ride up and down, attracting their shot.
His hat looked like a pepper-pot;
Through his jerkin and boots in a dozen places
The bullets went in, you could see the traces;
Not one of them could graze his skin,
For he had an ointment from hell rubbed in.
FIRST TROOPER: I've heard some tales, but that one's tall!
It's a deerskin jacket, tough and tight,
That can't be pierced by any ball.
SERGEANT-MAJOR: It's the juice of the mandrake, that witches delight
To brew with a spell at the dead of night.
TRUMPETER: It isn't natural and right!
SERGEANT-MAJOR: And some will tell you that he can foresee
By the stars what the shape of the future will be;
But I know how that story began.
Sometimes at night a little grey man
Past all the locked doors to his room will go in;
Often the sentries cried out he was here.
And each time that that little man was seen
Some great event for certain was near.
SECOND TROOPER: Yes, he's sold his soul to the prince of hell;
That's why his troops can live so well.

SCENE 7

[*Enter a* RECRUIT, *a* CITIZEN, DRAGOONS.]

RECRUIT [*emerges from the tent with a helmet on his head and a wine-bottle in his hand*]:
Say good-bye to my father and uncles too!
I'm a soldier, and never again I'll see you!

FIRST TROOPER: Another one to join the throng!

CITIZEN: Oh, Franz, you'll be sorry before long!

RECRUIT [*sings*]:
Drum and fife,
The sound of war!
A wandering life
The whole world o'er!
I'll lead my horse
A merry course,
With sword at my side
I'll go far and wide,
Swift as an arrow,
Free as a sparrow
Through bushes and trees
Like heaven's fair breeze!
Hurray there! Friedland's the flag that I serve!

SECOND TROOPER: Well spoken! we'll see you get all you deserve!
[*They make him welcome.*]

CITIZEN: Let him go! His parents are decent folk.

FIRST TROOPER: We weren't found under a gypsy's cloak.

CITIZEN: But he has money and means, I tell you.
Just feel this cloth, the finest they'll sell you!

TRUMPETER: The Emperor's coat has the highest value.

CITIZEN: He'll inherit a share in a hatter's trade.

SECOND TROOPER: By his own will man's fortune is made.

CITIZEN: His grandmother's shop will be his when she dies.

FIRST TROOPER: Pah! who talks of trade when the sulphur
    flies?

CITIZEN: And an inn from his godmother's estates,
    A cellar with twenty casks of wine.

TRUMPETER: That's something for him to share with his
    mates.

SECOND TROOPER: Brother! your tent must be pitched next
    to mine.

CITIZEN: He leaves a bride in sorrow and tears.

FIRST TROOPER: Good, that shows an iron heart that's a
    stranger to fears.

CITIZEN: When his grandmother hears it, she'll pass away!

SECOND TROOPER: All the better, then he can inherit
    straightway.

SERGEANT-MAJOR [*approaches with dignity, and lays his hand
    on the* RECRUIT'*s helmet*]:

    See here! you know what you have done.

    You have made your choice, a new man you've put on,

    With this helm on your head and a sword at your waist,

    In a worthy band yourself you have placed.

    A noble spirit you must be airing –

FIRST TROOPER: Especially with money you mustn't be
    sparing.

SERGEANT-MAJOR: Upon the good ship Fortunah

    About to set your course you are;

    The whole wide world is yours, my son,

    But nothing ventured, nothing won.

    These foolish townsfolk will always drag

    Round and round on the spot, like the tanner's nag;

    Only the soldier can prove his worth,

    For war is the password now on earth.

    Look at *me* now! Here in my coat

    I carry the Emperor's stick – just note!

All forms of government and rule
Start with the stick – it's their very first tool;
The sceptre in the king's own hand
Is only a stick, be it never so grand;
Once you're a corporal, you stand
On the ladder that leads to power and might;
Yes, even you can reach such a height.

FIRST TROOPER: Provided you can read and write.

SERGEANT-MAJOR: I'll give you an example straightway,
I heard it myself the other day.
The commander of the dragoon brigade,
Butler by name, was a comrade of mine
Thirty years ago, at Cologne on the Rhine.
Major-general now he's been made.
It's because he didn't stay in the shade;
All the world with his exploits has rung –
My services remained unsung.
Yes, and Friedland himself, our commander-in-chief,
Who's powerful now beyond belief,
Was a simple nobleman once, and no more,
But he put his trust in the goddess of war,
And now to such greatness and power he has grown
That he's the next man to the Emperor's throne!
Who knows if he'll ever meet his match – [Slyly]
But don't count your chickens before they hatch.

FIRST TROOPER: Yes, he started with little, and now he's so
great.
At Altdorf, when he wore a student's gown
His name was soon known all over the town,
For – if such a thing it's permitted to state,
He nearly broke his servant's crown.
The gentlemen in Nuremberg city
Wanted to lock him up, without pity;
They'd built a fine new prison cell,
For the honour of christening it they'd picked him.

But what did he do? He was sly, you can tell,
He sent in his poodle as the first victim.
They call it the kennel to this very day.
He's a fine one to think of that, I'd say!
And of all his mighty deeds, that trick
Is the one to remember him I'd always pick.

[*The girl has come to serve them; the* SECOND TROOPER
flirts with her.]

DRAGOON [*intervening*]: Stop that, comrade, and let her go.

SECOND TROOPER: Whose business is it, I'd like to know!

DRAGOON: Then let me tell you, that girl is mine!

FIRST TROOPER: A girl for himself alone! That's fine!
Master dragoon, are you out of your senses?

SECOND TROOPER: The camp's no place for such pretences.
A pretty face isn't just for one,
It's for all to share, like the light of the sun! [*Kisses her.*]

DRAGOON [*tearing her away*]: I tell you again, I'll not stand it!
Have done!

FIRST TROOPER: Here come the bandsmen, forget your
offences!

SECOND TROOPER: If you want a fight, that's all right by me!

SERGEANT-MAJOR: Peace, peace, you fellows! A kiss is free.

SCENE 8

[*A band of Bohemian miners enters and plays a waltz,
first slowly and then quicker and quicker. The* FIRST
TROOPER *dances with the* SERVING-GIRL, *the*
CANTEEN-WOMAN *with the* RECRUIT; *the* GIRL
runs away, the TROOPER *runs after her and finds himself
embracing the* CAPUCHIN FRIAR, *who has just
appeared on the scene.*]

CAPUCHIN: Hip, hip, hooray and fiddle-de-dee!

A merry scene. Is there room for me?
Is this an army of Christian men?
Are we Turks or Antibaptists, then?
Is the Sabbath Day turned into a rout,
As if God Almighty had the gout
In his fingers, and to strike was unwilling?
Is this the time for belly-filling?
The time for merriment and idle swilling?
Quid hic statis otiosi?
Why do you stand thus idly by?
On the Danube, the fury of war is let fly,
The bulwark of Bavaria laid low,
Regensburg in the clutches of the foe,
And here in Bohemia the army lies curled,
Stroking its belly, with no concern for the world.
Would rather wet its whistle than prime its pistol,
Cares rather for whoring than for warring,
On wine, women and food its thoughts only turn,
It would rather roast oxen than Oxenstiern.
In sackcloth and ashes all Christendom grieves,
What does the soldier do? He thieves.
It is a time of weeping and woe,
In heaven signs and portents show,
And from the clouds, as red as blood,
Hangs the war-mantle of the Lord God.
Out of the window of heaven, mark!
He thrusts the comet, his rod, as a warning;
The whole world is a house of mourning,
On a sea of blood floats the Church's ark,
And the Holy Roman Empire – I declare,
The *Hollow* Empire is the name it should bear;
The River Rhine is a river of pain,
Every abbey is stripped and shabby,
The dioceses are ravaged with diseases,
The convents are dens of convicts,

The naves and cloisters full of knaves and shysters,
And the blessed lands of Germany
Filled far and wide with misery –
And what is the cause of so much distress?
I will tell you: your sins and your wickedness,
The godless life, the pagan disgrace
Soldier and officer alike embrace.
Sin's like a magnet, held in the hand;
It draws iron after it into the land.
Where evil has led, there sorrow appears,
Just as an onion draws bitter tears;
After M and N there follows Oh!
That's the A B C, you know.
Ubi erit victoriae spes,
Si offenditur Deus? Can victory be ours
If at mass you never show your face,
But lie about in the tavern for hours?
The woman in the gospel found
The piece of silver on the ground;
Saul found his father's asses again,
Joseph his brothers, eleven fine men.
But anyone who in this army would seek
The fear of God and virtue meek
And modesty, would find little reward,
Though a hundred lanterns their beams outpoured!
To the preacher in the wilderness,
As we read in the Gospel story, no less,
Even the soldiers came and listened,
Confessed their sins and had themselves christened,
And asked, *Quid faciemus nos?*
What shall we do that God may receive us?
Et ait illis, and he said,
Neminem concutiatis,
Do no violence, break no man's head,
Neque calumniam faciatis,

Accuse no man falsely with intent,
Contenti estote, be content,
Stipendiis vestris, with your wages,
And shun all vices and libertinages.
Know that it is written: the name
Of the Lord thy God thou shalt not take in vain!
And where can there be heard more blaspheming
Than this camp with Friedland's soldiers teeming?
If for every oath and curse
That you with impious tongues rehearse
The bells should be rung in the churches around,
There'd soon be no bellringers more to be found.
If for each sacrilegious word
That on your filthy lips is heard
You were to lose just a single hair,
In a single night you'd be bald and bare,
Though thick as Absalom's locks they grew!
Joshua was a soldier too,
David Goliath overthrew,
And is it written anywhere to see
That they were given to profanity?
It should be no harder, at least to my mind,
To utter a prayer than a 'God strike me blind!'
But what the heart in abundance possesses
The mouth too readily confesses.
It is also written: thou shalt not steal.
Yes, the letter of that law you obey,
For you take everything openly away;
From your clutching claws, your grasping greed,
Your knavish tricks, your cunning and speed
The gold's not safe in the chest, I vow,
The calf's not safe inside the cow,
You'll take the eggs and the chicken too now!
What saith the preacher? *Estote contenti*,
Be content with your rations, for they are plenty.

But how shall the servants be commended,
When this evil from above is descended!
As it is down here, it's the same upstairs;
Who knows to whom *he* says his prayers!

FIRST TROOPER: Now look here, priest! Us troops you may slander,
    But don't speak like that about our commander.

CAPUCHIN: *Ne custodias gregem meam!*
    Another Ahab, a Jeroboam,
    Who from the true faith leads his men
    And bids them bow to idols vain!

TRUMPETER *and* RECRUIT: Let us not hear such words again!

CAPUCHIN: A fire-eating braggart, a swaggerer bold,
    Who swears that he'll conquer every stronghold;
    Boasted with godless profanities
    That Stralsund city must be his
    Though it were chained to the firmament;
    But it was in vain his powder was spent.

TRUMPETER: Can no one stop his mouth at all?

CAPUCHIN: A black magician, a new King Saul,
    A Jehu, a Holofernes defying,
    Like Peter his lord and master denying,
    That's why he can't bear the crowing of cocks –

BOTH TROOPERS: Priest, this will be the end of you!

CAPUCHIN: Another King Herod, a cunning fox –

TRUMPETER *and* BOTH TROOPERS [*crowding in on him*]:
    Silence! We'll beat you black and blue.

CROATS [*intervening*]:
    Stay there, padre, have no fear,
    Tell us your story, we want to hear.

CAPUCHIN [*louder and louder*]:
    A Nebuchadnezzar with pride swollen thick,
    A father of sins and a heretic,
    And he calls himself Prince *Wallenstein.*
    A *stony wall*, a *stain* on us *all*,

A blot, a plot of hellish design,
And I say there will be no peace indeed
Until from this Friedland this land is freed!

[*During these last words, uttered at the top of his voice, he has gradually made his retreat, the* CROATS *protecting him from the other soldiers.*]

SCENE 9

[*All from the preceding scene except the* CAPUCHIN.]

FIRST TROOPER [*to the* SERGEANT-MAJOR]:
  Tell me! What did he mean by that, do you know,
  That the General couldn't bear to hear the cock crow?
  Was it just some scandal to make us doubt him?
SERGEANT-MAJOR: No, it's true, there's something strange
    about him,
  Since the day he was born, it's always been found
  That his ears were alive to the slightest sound,
  To hear a cat mewing will give him fits,
  And the crow of a cock drives him out of his wits.
FIRST TROOPER: In that the lion himself he resembles!
SERGEANT-MAJOR: To make a sound every guardsman
    trembles,
  About his presence like mice they must creep,
  So as not to disturb him – his thoughts are too deep.
VOICES [*in the tent. Commotion*]:
  The villain, the robber! Seize him, seize!
VOICE OF THE PEASANT: Help, have mercy on me!
OTHER VOICES: Peace!
FIRST TROOPER: The devil take me, there's a fight!
SECOND TROOPER: Don't leave me out!
    [*They run into the tent.*]

CANTEEN-WOMAN [*coming out*]: The parasite!

TRUMPETER: Mistress, what's all the fuss about?

CANTEEN-WOMAN: The vagabond! The thief! The lout!
What a thing to happen in my place!
I'll lose my good name through such a disgrace.

SERGEANT-MAJOR: What is it, my dear?

CANTEEN-WOMAN: What would you have thought?
A cheating peasant they've just caught,
A pair of loaded dice he had.

TRUMPETER: Here they come bringing him, with his lad.

SCENE 10

[*Soldiers drag on the* PEASANT.]

FIRST TROOPER: Let's have him strung up!

SHARPSHOOTERS *and* DRAGOONS: To the marshal's tent!

SERGEANT-MAJOR: There's a new order dealing with this
kind of thing.

CANTEEN-WOMAN: Within the hour I'll see him swing!

SERGEANT-MAJOR: An evil trade earns an evil wage.

FIRST ARQUEBUSIER [*to the other*]:
It comes of desperation and rage.
If you ruin his livelihood, it's my belief
You'll turn any honest man into a thief.

TRUMPETER: What? What? Do I hear you take his part?
The dog! Has the devil got into your heart?

FIRST ARQUEBUSIER: Even a peasant's a man of a sort.

FIRST TROOPER: [*to the* TRUMPETER]:
Take no notice! They're Tiefenbach's folk,
Tailors and glovers – as soldiers, a joke!
They were garrisoned at Brieg before,
They don't know much of the customs of war.

SCENE II

[*Enter* CUIRASSIERS.]

FIRST CUIRASSIER: Peace, there! What did that peasant do?

FIRST SHARPSHOOTER: He was cheating at dice, we caught
    him red-handed.

FIRST CUIRASSIER: Who was it that he was cheating? You?

FIRST SHARPSHOOTER: Yes, every last penny I had he'd
    landed!

FIRST CUIRASSIER: What? Are you one of Friedland's men,
  And can value yourself at such a mean price
  That you gamble your fortune with peasants at dice?
  Let him go, and not show himself again.

    [*The* PEASANT *escapes, the others draw closer together.*]

FIRST ARQUEBUSIER: There you are: quickly and with
    determination,
  That's the way to deal with the population.
  Who was he? No Bohemian, for a fact.

CANTEEN-WOMAN: He's a Walloon. A man to respect!
  One of the Pappenheim cuirassiers.

FIRST DRAGOON [*joining the group*]:
  Young Piccolomini their fortune steers.
  The men themselves chose him to be
  Their colonel, by their own decree,
  When Pappenheim fell on Lützen field.

FIRST ARQUEBUSIER: Do they presume such power to
    wield?

FIRST DRAGOON: That regiment's something apart from the
    pack.
  In every battle they led the attack.
  They dispense their own justice, without direction,
  And Friedland holds them in special affection.

FIRST CUIRASSIER [*to the other*]:
  Can it be true? Who brought the news back?
SECOND CUIRASSIER: I heard it from the colonel's own
    lips.
FIRST CUIRASSIER: The devil! Are we dogs to their whips?
FIRST TROOPER: See there, how with venom they burn!
SECOND TROOPER: What is it, comrades, is it our concern?
FIRST CUIRASSIER: It is, and no cause for merriment.
    [SOLDIERS *gather round.*]
  To the Netherlands we are to be sent;
  Cuirassiers, sharpshooters and troopers beside,
  Eight thousand men must mount and ride.
CANTEEN-WOMAN: What? What? Again to be on our way?
  I came here from Flanders but yesterday!
SECOND CUIRASSIER [*to the* DRAGOONS]:
  You men of Butler's too must report.
FIRST CUIRASSIER: And we Walloons especially.
CANTEEN-WOMAN: Why, those are the best of the com-
    pany!
FIRST CUIRASSIER: It's himself from Milan that we're to
    escort.
FIRST TROOPER: The Infant! Can it be true, what you say?
SECOND TROOPER: The priest! There'll be the devil to pay!
FIRST CUIRASSIER: Are we to be taken from Friedland's
    side,
  Who keeps the soldier in state and style,
  And take the field with the Spaniard vile,
  The skinflint whom we all hate and deride?
  No, we'll not do it! We'll desert, I swear.
TRUMPETER: Damnation! what business should we have
    there?
  We're pledged to the Emperor, we all know that,
  Not to the Spaniard with his red hat.
SECOND TROOPER: Only Friedland's word could make

Us lend the Emperor our hand;
If it wasn't for Wallenstein's own sake
We'd never be serving Ferdinand.

FIRST DRAGOON: It was Friedland himself that raised this
    force,
His fortune alone shall guide our course.

SERGEANT-MAJOR: Let me tell you, listen a bit,
You haven't got to the bottom of it.
I know, I can see further ahead,
A wicked trap for us all has been laid.

FIRST TROOPER: Silence for the order of the day!

SERGEANT-MAJOR: Cousin Gussie, before I get under way,
Bring a glass of Melnecker for me to drink,
Then I will tell you all what *I* think.

CANTEEN-WOMAN [*pouring him a glass*]:
Here, sergeant-major! You give me a fright.
Surely there's no trap in sight!

SERGEANT-MAJOR: Now, gentlemen, it's all well and
    good,
Each thinks of one thing at a time, as he should;
But, as the General is accustomed to say,
We should keep the whole under our survey.
We all call ourselves Friedland's troops.
The citizen quarters us, in our flocks,
Provides for us, cooks us our roasts and our soups.
The peasant must give up his nag and his ox
And harness them up in our baggage train,
And it will do him no good to complain.
If a lance-corporal with a handful of men
Turns up in a village out on the land,
He's the authority there and then,
The place is his to rule and command.
I'll be hanged if they've any love for our race!
They'd as soon meet the devil face to face

As catch a sight of our jackets of buff.
Blazes! Then why don't they throw us out? They're enough
To outnumber us, if they came in their hordes,
And they have their cudgels, as we have our swords.
Why is it then that we can laugh at them so?
Because we strike fear when together we go!

FIRST TROOPER: Yes, yes! in the mass, there's the secret of power!
Friedland has known that well, since the days
Eight or nine years ago, when he set out to raise
Such a force that the Emperor's foes should cower.
To begin with, they only asked twelve thousand men;
Such a number, he said, I can't feed *them*.
But sixty thousand I'll raise by and by,
I know *they* won't go hungry and die.
And so we serve under Wallenstein's name.

SERGEANT-MAJOR: Let's suppose, for example, that some-one came
And of my fingers, out of spite,
Chopped off the little one here on the right.
Is it only a single finger I've lost?
The devil it is! The whole hand it's cost!
It's only a stump, no use at all.
Yes, and these eight thousand horse they'd haul
From here to Flanders, beyond recall,
Are the army's little finger, you see?
Will you let them go, and say, never mind,
We are only less by the fifth degree?
No, the whole is gone! you must be resigned!
The peasants will soon get too big for their boots,
The fear and respect will be gone from the brutes,
The clerks in Vienna will do as it suits,
They will give us our orders and move us along,
And once again it will be the old song.

Yes, and how long do you think it will last
Before our general's time is past?
There's hardly a man at court is his friend –
And that, mark my words! will be the end.
Who will there be to see that we're paid,
And the contracts are kept that with us have been made?
Who is there who has the strength and the skill,
The sharpness of mind and the firmness of will,
To form and to bind together as one
These bands from all countries under the sun?
You from the dragoons, for example, declare,
Have you a fatherland? Tell us where!

FIRST DRAGOON: Beyond the water, Hibernia fair!

SERGEANT-MAJOR [*to the two* CUIRASSIERS]:
You're from Wallonia, that I know;
You from Italy, for your accent says so.

FIRST CUIRASSIER: Who am I? No one has ever told me;
While I was still a child they stole me.

SERGEANT-MAJOR: Nor are you from these parts either, I'd
say?

FIRST ARQUEBUSIER: No, I'm from Buchau on Federsee.

SERGEANT-MAJOR: And you, neighbour?

SECOND ARQUEBUSIER: From Switzerland.

SERGEANT-MAJOR [*to the* SECOND TROOPER]:
You, trooper, how shall we identify?

SECOND TROOPER: In Wismar my father's house used to
stand.

SERGEANT-MAJOR [*pointing to the* TRUMPETER]:
And we are from Eger, he and I.
Well now! and who is there could have told
That we have collected and drifted forth
From the south and from the north?
Are we not all cast in the very same mould?
Do we not close our ranks to the foe
So that not a chink or cranny may show?

When the word is spoken, who has not seen
How we all move in harmony, like a machine?
Who is it has forged us so tightly together
That none can distinguish the one from the other?
Why, no man other than Wallenstein!

FIRST TROOPER: To be honest, I've never seen any sign
That we were as perfectly matched as you say;
I've always chosen to go my own way.

FIRST CUIRASSIER: What the sergeant-major says is true.
They'd gladly bid the military adieu;
They want the soldier overthrown,
So that they themselves can rule alone.
It's all a conspiracy, I tell you, a plot!

CANTEEN-WOMAN: A conspiracy? good heavens, I hope
not!
They won't be able to pay their debts!

SERGEANT-MAJOR: Of course not! they'll be bankrupt, the
lot!
There'll be many a general and captain regrets
The money from his own purse he's spent
To make a show with his regiment.
They spent far more than they could earn,
Thought it would bring them a power in return.
And they will be ruined, one and all,
If the head that leads them, the Duke, should fall.

CANTEEN-WOMAN: Oh, God save me! That won't be
funny!
Half of the army owes me money.
Count Isolani always pays up late,
And there's two hundred guilders still on his slate!

FIRST CUIRASSIER: What can we do, my comrades-in-arms?
Only one thing will save us, if anything can:
United we need fear no alarms,
We must all stand together as one man.
Let their ordinances resound,

Here in Bohemia we'll hold our ground,
We will not obey them, we will not move,
It's his honour the soldier must fight to prove!

SECOND TROOPER: We'll not give in, and go where they'd take us!
If they want to try, let them come and make us!

FIRST ARQUEBUSIER: Friends, think for a moment and understand,
It is the Emperor's will and command.

TRUMPETER: What should we care for the Emperor's word?

FIRST ARQUEBUSIER: Don't say again what I've just heard!

TRUMPETER: You may not like it, but it's a fact.

FIRST TROOPER: Yes, yes, for all that I've ever known,
We take our orders from Friedland alone.

SERGEANT-MAJOR: We do, it was laid down in his contract.
He has the power absolute
To make war or peace, as it may suit;
He can confiscate money or property,
Can execute, or show clemency,
He can promote, or grant a commission,
All matters of honour are at his disposition:
The Emperor himself gave him this as his right.

FIRST ARQUEBUSIER: The Duke is a man of wisdom and might;
But he is no more, when all's said and done,
Than the Emperor's servant, like anyone.

SERGEANT-MAJOR: No! not like one of the common run.
He is a Prince immediate,
As good as Bavaria, for all his state.
Didn't I see with my own eyes,
When I was mounting guard at Brandeis,
How the Emperor bid him, where he stood,
Cover his head, like a prince of the blood?

FIRST ARQUEBUSIER: That was on account of the Mecklenburg lands

That the Emperor had mortgaged into his hands.

FIRST TROOPER [*to the* SERGEANT-MAJOR]:
What? When the Emperor himself was there?
That's a privilege very grand and rare!

SERGEANT-MAJOR [*putting his hand into his pocket*]:
If my word doesn't count for much,
Here's something you can see and touch.
  [*Pulling out a coin.*] Whose image is this?

CANTEEN-WOMAN: Show us! Let's see!
Why, it's a Wallensteiner, and there's his text!

SERGEANT-MAJOR: There you are, then! What more proof
  can there be?
Is he not a prince, as good as the next?
Hasn't he his own coinage like Ferdinand?
His own people and his own land?
Men call him Your Highness, and bow to him deep.
His own soldiers he must be able to keep.

FIRST ARQUEBUSIER: No one would deny him his place,
But it's the Emperor we must all obey,
And from the Emperor we get our pay.

TRUMPETER: And that, my friend, I deny to your face!
It's from the Emperor we get *no* pay!
For the past ten months, again and again,
We've been promised our wages, but all in vain!

FIRST ARQUEBUSIER: No matter! It's in good hands,
  everyone knows.

FIRST CUIRASSIER: Peace there, friends! Would you come
  to blows?
There's no dispute, we are all in accord
That the Emperor is our supreme lord.
But just for that very reason, and since
We would seek honour in serving our prince,
We are not going to be herded along
By the priests and toadies and all their throng,
And it's good for the general, it can't be denied,

If his soldiers carry themselves with pride.
Who but the troops that call themselves his
Make him the mighty power that he is?
Makes and keeps *his* the word, in sum,
That is heard throughout all Christendom?
Let them bear the burden in his place
That also enjoy the fruits of his grace,
That sit in his golden rooms at table.
Our only share of his glory and fable
Is the struggle and toil, the pain and the smart,
And the pride in ourselves that we bear in our heart!

SECOND TROOPER: All the great tyrants and emperors ever
Did it that way, and that was clever.
All other men they harried and rent,
But the soldier lacked nothing for his content.

FIRST CUIRASSIER: The soldier must feel his worth and his
price.
The man who can't live with style and swing
Had better find other tunes to sing.
If my life I'm to gamble and sacrifice,
Then something of more worth I must see,
Or let myself be slaughtered and shorn
Like a Croat – and look on myself with scorn.

BOTH TROOPERS: Yes, honour is more than life to me!

FIRST CUIRASSIER: The sword's not a ploughshare or a
spade,
For tilling the fields it was never made.
For us there grows no corn nor grass,
On the face of the earth the soldier must pass
Homeless, in a fleeting swarm,
With no hearth of his own to keep him warm.
Beyond the bright cities he must roam,
Beyond the cheerful village green,
The vintage and the harvest home
May only from afar be seen.

The soldier has no worldly possession,
Nothing but pride in his profession.
A man must have something to call his own,
Or the seeds of murder and pillage are sown.

FIRST ARQUEBUSIER: It's a life of misery, God knows!

FIRST CUIRASSIER: And yet there is no other I'd choose.
Look, I have travelled far and wide,
All the ways of man I have seen and tried.
I have served the Spanish monarchy,
The Venetian republic, the kingdom of Naples,
But fortune never favoured me.
I have seen all these lands and their peoples,
The merchant and the gentleman,
The craftsman and the clergyman,
But in none of their comfortable coats would I feel
So well as in this my jacket of steel.

FIRST ARQUEBUSIER: No! I couldn't say that, I must confess.

FIRST CUIRASSIER: If any man will seek worldly success,
Let him stir, and join the press;
If honour and rank within the state,
Let him bow beneath their golden weight.
If his father's blessing he would hear,
See children and grandchildren gathered near,
Let him peacefully follow an honest trade.
But I – my spirit is not so made,
I would live and would die as free as the air,
Rob no man and leave no man my heir,
And from the rabble turn my eye
As boldly on my horse I fly.

FIRST TROOPER: Bravo, bravo! and so say I.

FIRST ARQUEBUSIER: It's a merry life, it can't be gainsaid,
To gallop over another man's head.

FIRST CUIRASSIER: Comrade, we live in perilous times,
The sword with the balance no longer rhymes.
But as it is so, let no man rebuke me

That it was to the sword that I betook me.
I can bear like a man the hazard of war,
But give up my freedom? Nevermore!
FIRST ARQUEBUSIER: But it's on us soldiers the blame must
 be placed
That the peasantry is so disgraced.
The war, the miseries and fears
Must have lasted close on sixteen years.
FIRST CUIRASSIER: We cannot all praise God at once, good
 brother.
What pleases one man will not suit another.
One man loves the sun, and one shades his eye;
This man will have wet, the other will have dry.
Where you see but miseries and fears,
Life's broad daylight to me appears.
If peasant and townsman must bear the cost,
I swear I am sorry for what they have lost;
But I can do nothing to bring it back.
It's the same when we charge to the attack;
The horses snort and gallop away,
And if anyone's lying in the way,
Be it my brother, my very own son,
Though the strings of my heart by his screams were undone,
Over his body I must ride,
I cannot gently bear him aside.
FIRST TROOPER: Who can stop to ask if another has died?
FIRST CUIRASSIER: And since it has now turned out so,
That the soldier fortune's favour may know,
Let us seize it and hold it fast
For as long as we may, for it cannot last!
One day, without warning, peace will descend,
And then these things will be at an end;
The soldier unbridles, and, lo and behold!
The peasant yokes up as in days of old.
We still stand together in this land,

We still hold the reins of power in our hand.
But if we let them separate us,
We'll be at the mercy of them that hate us.

FIRST TROOPER: No, never shall that moment come!
We'll stand together, all as one!

SECOND TROOPER: Yes, let's agree on what to do!

FIRST ARQUEBUSIER [*taking out a leather purse, to the* CANTEEN-WOMAN]:
Tell me, my dear, what do I owe you?

CANTEEN-WOMAN: Oh, nothing to speak of! a copper or two.
[*They reckon up.*]

TRUMPETER: The back of you we're glad to see,
You only spoil the company.
[*The* ARQUEBUSIERS *leave.*]

FIRST CUIRASSIER: It's a pity about them, they're not so bad.

FIRST TROOPER: With the spirit of a soap-boiler's lad?

SECOND TROOPER: Now we are left to our own affairs,
Let's hear how you'll stop this plan of theirs.

TRUMPETER: We'll not go! and there the matter ends.

FIRST CUIRASSIER: But keep your discipline, my friends!
Each one of you, go to your own corps.
Explain to your comrades what it is for,
So that they understand what you say.
And we must not go too far away.
For the Walloons, I'll guarantee
That every one of them thinks like me.

SERGEANT-MAJOR: Terzky's regiments, mounted and foot,
Are all agreed, and resolute.

SECOND CUIRASSIER [*placing himself beside the other*]:
The Lombard goes where the Walloon is sent.

FIRST TROOPER: Freedom's the trooper's element.

SECOND TROOPER: Freedom goes only with power, say I;
With Wallenstein I'll live and die.

FIRST SHARPSHOOTER: The Lorrainese will swim with the
  flood,
Where spirits are merry and life is good.

DRAGOON: The Irishman follows fortune's star.

SECOND SHARPSHOOTER: The Tyrolean, his lord from afar.

FIRST CUIRASSIER: Then let every regiment
  Draw up a solemn document
  Declaring we will stay together,
  And that we never will be forced,
  Neither by cunning be divorced,
  From Friedland, who's the soldier's father.
  This paper then we humbly lay
  Before Piccolomini – the son, that's to say;
  He understands about matters like these,
  And Friedland will do anything him to please.
  He's highly thought of too, so they tell me,
  By his imperial majesty.

SECOND TROOPER: That's it! Agreed! This shall be our call:
  Piccolomini speaks for us all!

TRUMPETER, DRAGOONS, FIRST TROOPER, SECOND CUIR-
  ASSIER, SHARPSHOOTERS [*all together*]:
  Piccolomini speaks for us all!
    [*They make as if to leave.*]

SERGEANT-MAJOR: Comrades, a glass before you go!
  [*Drinks.*]
  Here's to Piccolomini – may his honour grow!

CANTEEN-WOMAN [*bringing a bottle*]:
  Have this on the house, if it won't offend you!
  Gentlemen, may success attend you!

CUIRASSIERS: The profession of arms: long may it live!

TROOPERS: The profession of farms: long may they give!

DRAGOONS *and* SHARPSHOOTERS: The army: may it never
  perish!

TRUMPETER *and* SERGEANT-MAJOR: May Friedland as its
  leader flourish!

SECOND CUIRASSIER [*sings*]:

Comrades, to horse, to horse and away!
To freedom and battlefield!
In battle a man still has his say,
And his heart shall never yield.
There on no other let him depend,
For he must stand alone at the end.

[*During this verse, the soldiers in the background have
gathered around to form a chorus.*]

CHORUS:

There on no other let him depend,
For he must stand alone at the end.

DRAGOON:

Freedom no more in the world we see,
There is only master and slave,
'Tis falsehood reigns and trickery,
Every man is a coward and knave.
The soldier alone, of the whole human race,
Is free, for he can look death in the face.

CHORUS:

The soldier alone, of the whole human race,
Is free, for he can look death in the face.

FIRST TROOPER:

The fears of life he casts aside,
Not for him the care and the fret,
To meet his fate he can merrily ride,
For one day it must surely be met.
And if that be tomorrow, then let us today
Drink our fill of time's precious drops while we may.

CHORUS:

And if that be tomorrow, then let us today
Drink our fill of time's precious drops while we may.

[*Their glasses have been filled again; they clink glasses and
drink.*]

SERGEANT-MAJOR:

    His destiny falls from heaven in his lap,
    Without need of labour and toil;
    The serf digs and strains, and thinks he may hap
    On treasure beneath the soil.
    He digs and he shovels, the poor foolish knave,
    All the days of his life, till he's dug his own grave.

CHORUS:

    He digs and he shovels, the poor foolish knave,
    All the days of his life, till he's dug his own grave.

FIRST TROOPER:

    The cavalryman on his swift-flying beast,
    Is a guest whose arrival men fear.
    When the candles are lit for the wedding-feast,
    Uninvited, at once he is near!
    No gifts does he bring, nor sit long to admire,
    He captures by storm the prize of desire.

CHORUS:

    No gifts does he bring, nor sit long to admire,
    He captures by storm the prize of desire.

SECOND CUIRASSIER:

    Why must the girl make such grief and moan?
    Let him go, it is no use to weep!
    He has no place he may call his own,
    True love he never can keep.
    Destiny swift drives him on without cease,
    Nowhere on earth may he know rest and peace.

CHORUS:

    Destiny swift drives him on without cease,
    Nowhere on earth may he know rest and peace.

FIRST TROOPER [*takes his two neighbours by the hand; the
    others do the same, and all who have spoken form a large half-
    circle*]:

    So merrily, comrades! come, bridle your steeds,

Let your breasts rise and swell for the fight!
Let us follow where youth's rushing torrent leads,
Come, away! while the spirit is bright.
For if your own life you're not willing to stake,
That life will never be yours to make.

CHORUS:

For if your own life you're not willing to stake,
That life will never be yours to make.

[*Before the* CHORUS *has quite finished, the curtain falls.*]

THE PICCOLOMINI

IN FIVE ACTS

CHARACTERS

WALLENSTEIN, Duke of Friedland, Imperial commander-in-chief in the Thirty Years' War

OCTAVIO PICCOLOMINI, lieutenant-general

MAX PICCOLOMINI, his son, colonel of a regiment of cuirassiers

COUNT TERZKY, Wallenstein's brother-in-law, commander of several regiments

ILLO, field-marshal, confidant of Wallenstein

ISOLANI, general commanding the Croatian troops

BUTLER, commander of a regiment of dragoons

TIEFENBACH
MARADAS
GÖTZ } generals under Wallenstein
COLALTO

NEUMANN, captain of horse, Terzky's adjutant

QUESTENBERG, Imperial War Commissioner, emissary of the Emperor

BATTISTA SENI, an astrologer

DUCHESS OF FRIEDLAND, Wallenstein's wife

THEKLA, Princess of Friedland, their daughter

COUNTESS TERZKY, the Duchess's sister

A CORNET

COUNT TERZKY'S CELLARER

PAGES AND SERVANTS to Friedland

SERVANTS AND MUSICIANS to Terzky

NUMEROUS GENERALS AND COLONELS

ACT ONE

*A large old Gothic room in the Town Hall of Pilsen,
decorated with banners and other warlike trophies.*

SCENE I

[ILLO *with* BUTLER, ISOLANI.]

ILLO: Count Isolani – better late than never!
  Your lengthy journey is excuse enough.
ISOLANI: And it is not with empty hands we come!
  The word was passed to us at Donauwörth
  A Swedish baggage-train was on its way
  With provender, six hundred wagons full.
  My good Croatians made quick work of that,
  We have it with us.
ILLO: Just what we are needing,
  To entertain our guests assembled here.
BUTLER: I see it's lively here already.
ISOLANI: Yes,
  Even the churches are packed full of soldiers.
  [*Looking around*] Here in the town hall too, I see, you
    have
  Set up yourselves in style – well, well! The soldier
  Makes shift to help himself as best he may!
ILLO: Colonels-in-chief of thirty regiments
  Already are assembled in this place,
  Terzky you'll see is here, and Tiefenbach,
  Colalto, Götz, Maradas, Henderson,
  Both son and father Piccolomini –

Many old comrades you will greet again.
Gallas is not here yet, nor Altringer.
BUTLER: Wait not for Gallas.
ILLO [*taken aback*]:   What? Can you have heard –
ISOLANI [*interrupting*]:
Max Piccolomini here? Oh! Lead me to him!
Still I can see him – ten years must have passed –
When we were fighting Mansfeld there at Dessau,
Setting his horse to leap down from the bridge
And charging through the Elbe's onrushing flood
To help his father, who was sorely pressed.
Then he had scarce a hair upon his chin,
Now, I am told, the hero is complete.
ILLO: You shall see him today. He comes to bring
The Princess Friedland and her mother to us,
This morning from Carinthia they are here.
BUTLER: His wife and daughter too the Prince has summoned?
He summons many here.
ISOLANI: So much the better.
I thought that we should only hear of marches,
Of batteries, attacks, and suchlike things;
But look! The Duke has taken care to find
Some fairer object for our eyes as well.
ILLO [*who has been standing musing, to* BUTLER, *drawing him aside a little*]:
How do you know that Gallas will not come?
BUTLER [*meaningfully*]:
Because he tried to keep *me* back with him.
ILLO [*warmly*]:
And you stood fast by us? O noble Butler!
BUTLER [*grasping his hand*]:
After the obligation that the Prince
So recently laid on me –
ILLO: Yes, Major-General! My congratulations!

ISOLANI: Yes, on the regiment, is not that so, the Prince
  Presented to him? And the same, I hear,
  In which he rose up from a common trooper?
  Why, every man in the whole corps will be
  Spurred on by such example, when he sees
  An old and trusty soldier make his way.

BUTLER: I do
  Not know if I may yet accept your greetings
  – The Emperor must still confirm the gift.

ISOLANI: Come, take it, take it, come! The hand that
    raised
  You up has strength yet to maintain you,
  Come Emperor, come ministers.

ILLO: If all
  Of us would have such scruples!
  The Emperor gives us nothing – from the Duke
  Comes everything we hope for, all we have.

ISOLANI [to ILLO]:
  Why, brother! Did I tell you this? The Prince
  Has said he'll satisfy my creditors,
  Will manage my affairs from this day on,
  And make an honest man of me at last.
  And think of it! This is the third time now
  This regal spirit has delivered me
  From ruin and restored me to my honour.

ILLO: If he could only, as he gladly would,
  He'd give the lands and peoples to his soldiers.
  But in Vienna there they check his arm,
  Do everything they can to clip his wings!
  Here now! just look at all the new demands
  They've sent this Questenberg to make!

BUTLER: I too
  Have heard of what the Emperor is now
  Demanding of him – but I hope
  The Duke will not give way on any point.

ILLO: He will not yield his right, but if he yields
  – His place!

BUTLER [*startled*]:
                    What have you heard? Sir, you alarm me!

ISOLANI [*at the same time*]:
  It would be ruin for us all!

ILLO: Peace, now!
  Here comes our man, and walking at his side
  Lieutenant-General Piccolomini.

BUTLER [*shaking his head dubiously*]: I fear,
  Before we leave this place, our fortunes change.

SCENE 2

[*Enter* OCTAVIO PICCOLOMINI *and* QUESTENBERG.]

OCTAVIO [*still at a distance*]:
  What? More guests do I see? Admit, my friend,
  It took this war, and all its bitter tears,
  To bring so many heroes crowned with fame
  Together in the circuit of one camp.

QUESTENBERG: Let no man come to one of Friedland's
    camps,
  If he of war would only ill believe.
  Almost I had forgotten all its torments,
  When order's noble spirit here I saw,
  Through which, while all-destroying, war itself
  Is yet preserved, maintains its majesty.

OCTAVIO: And now! See here a noble pair, most worthy
  To close these heroes' ranks: Count Isolan
  And Colonel Butler. Now, I think we see
  With our own eyes the whole estate of war.
  [*Introducing* BUTLER *and* ISOLANI]

Here you see strength, my friend, and swiftness here.

QUESTENBERG [*to* OCTAVIO]:

And here between them, wisdom and experience.

OCTAVIO [*presenting* QUESTENBERG *to them*]:

Counsellor and State Secretary Questenberg,
The bearer of Imperial commands,
Master and generous patron of the soldier,
We honour in his most distinguished guest.
   [*Silence.*]

ILLO [*approaching* QUESTENBERG]:

I think it is not, Minister, the first time
That you have graced us with your noble presence.

QUESTENBERG: Under these banners I have stood before.

ILLO: And *where* you stood beneath them, you remember?
At Znaym in the Moravian lands, where on
The Emperor's behalf you came to beg
The Duke that he would take supreme command.

QUESTENBERG: To *beg* him, General? I did not think
My orders, nor my zeal, had gone so far.

ILLO: Why, then, to force him, if you like it. *I*
Remember very well – Count Tilly had
Been beaten on the Lech – Bavaria
Lay open to the foe, nothing could stop him
From thrusting to the heart of Austria.
Then *you* appeared, and Werdenberg came too,
Before our lord, besieging him with pleas,
And threatening the Emperor's disfavour,
Unless the Prince took pity on his woes.

ISOLANI [*joining them*]:

Yes, Minister! I understand full well
Why with the task in which you come today
You do not willingly recall the other!

QUESTENBERG: Why should I not? For I can see between
   them
No contradiction! Then, Bohemia must

Be saved from foes, today it is my duty
To save her from her friends and her protectors.

ILLO: A pretty office! After we have spilt
Our blood to wrest Bohemia from the Saxon,
In gratitude you drive us from the land!

QUESTENBERG: Unless it should not be but to exchange
Old misery for new, this wretched land
Must now be freed from scourge of friend or foe.

ILLO: Pah! It has been a fruitful year, the peasant
Can give again.

QUESTENBERG: Why, now, if you are speaking
Of pastures, and of flocks and herds, Field-Marshal –

ISOLANI: War feeds on war. If peasants cannot live,
All the more soldiers will the Emperor gain!

QUESTENBERG: And all the fewer subjects he will have!

ISOLANI: Bah! Are we not his subjects, every one?

QUESTENBERG: But with a difference, Count! For there are
some
Who fill his chests with useful industry,
While others know not but to scoop them clean.
The sword has made the Emperor a pauper;
It is the plough must make him strong again.

BUTLER: The Emperor were no pauper, were there not
So many – leeches battening on the land.

ISOLANI: Nor can it yet have come to that. I see [planting
himself in front of QUESTENBERG and inspecting his clothes]
There is still gold in plenty yet uncoined.

QUESTENBERG: Praise be to God! There is a little still
Kept back, sir – from the clutches of the Croats.

ILLO: Look here, sir! Slavata and Martinitz,
Those two on whom the Emperor, in despite
Of good Bohemians, showers gifts and honours –
Who glut themselves with spoils of citizens expelled –
Who wax and grow while all about them rots,
Who reap alone amidst the general famine –

With regal ostentation mock the woes
Of all the land – let *them* and others like them
Pay for the war, the bearer of destruction,
That they and they alone brought on their country!

BUTLER: And all those parasites, who keep their feet
Tucked cosily beneath the Emperor's table,
Snapping with greed for every tasty morsel,
They would dole out the soldier's rations, while
He lies before the foe, and skimp his bread!

ISOLANI: I shall remember all my life, how when
I went to Vienna, seven years ago,
To raise new horses for our regiments,
They dragged me from one antechamber to
Another, made me wait among the rows
Of hangers-on, for hours on end, as if
I only came to beg a crust in mercy.
At last – they sent a Capuchin to me;
I thought it was to shrive me of my sins!
But no! that was the man with whom I must
Do business for our mounts!
And then I had to go back empty-handed.
It took the Prince three days to find for me
What thirty could not get me in Vienna.

QUESTENBERG: Yes, yes! The bills for that came on to us,
I know that there is money owing still.

ILLO: War is a rough and violent handicraft.
You cannot take the gentle road, you cannot
Afford too many scruples. Who would wait
Till in Vienna they had found the least
Of four-and-twenty evils, would wait long!
– Straight to your goal, and boldly, that is better!
Let break what may! – The common run of men
Know only how to patch and mend their lives,
And bear a brute necessity they loathe
More willingly than face a bitter choice.

QUESTENBERG: Yes, that is true! Our choice our prince
   makes for us.

ILLO: A true prince is a father to his soldiers,
   We see how much the Emperor cares for us.

QUESTENBERG: For all estates of men his heart's the same,
   He cannot yield the one up to the other.

ISOLANI: And so he casts us to the ravening beasts,
   That he may keep his precious sheep at peace.

QUESTENBERG [*scornfully*]:
   Count! The comparison is yours – not mine.

ILLO: But if we were what to the Court we seem,
   Then it was dangerous to give us freedom.

QUESTENBERG [*gravely*]:
   This freedom was not given, taken rather,
   So it is needful now it should be bridled.

ILLO: You'll find you mount upon a fiery steed.

QUESTENBERG: It will be gentle with a better rider.

ILLO: It bears no man but only him that tamed it.

QUESTENBERG: If it is tamed, it will obey a child.

ILLO: That child, I know, you've found for it already.

QUESTENBERG: Seek but to know your duty, not his name.

BUTLER [*who has been standing on one side with* PICCOLOMINI
    until now, though obviously keenly following the conversation,
    approaching nearer]:
   The Emperor, Master President, has in Germany
   A mighty army; in this kingdom here
   Are quartered thirty thousand, as I think,
   Another sixteen thousand in Silesia;
   Ten regiments are stationed on the Weser,
   On Rhine and Main; six more in Swabia,
   Twelve in Bavaria stand against the Swedes.
   And still I do not count the garrisons
   That guard the fortresses along the border.
   These men obey the orders, every one,
   Of Friedland's captains. All those who command

Have learnt their trade, have drawn their nourishment
From one alone, one heart beats in them all.
Strangers and foreigners on German soil,
Their calling is their only house and home.
They are not moved by love of fatherland,
For thousands, like myself, were born far distant;
Nor of the Emperor, half of them and more
Came to us as deserters from the foe,
As glad to fight beneath the double eagle
As underneath the lilies and the lion.
And yet all these, one man can lead upon
A single rein, one single love and fear
Can bind them as one people fast to him.
And as the spark of lightning, swift and sure,
Runs its appointed course along the iron,
So his command runs from the furthest sentry
Who hears the Baltic pound the sandy dunes
Or scans the fruitful valleys of the Tyrol,
To him who mounts his guard upon the square
Before the palace of the Emperor!

QUESTENBERG: In short the meaning of these fulsome words!

BUTLER: That the respect, the trust and the affection,
That bind us in obedience to Friedland,
Cannot be switched, without a further thought,
Upon some other, sent us from Vienna.
We hold it still in loyal memory
How the command was laid in Friedland's hands.
Was it, in truth, imperial majesty
That brought the army to him, ready made,
Sought but a leader for its fighting hosts?
– There was no army. It was not created
Till Friedland came, no, he did not receive it,
He brought it to the Emperor! It was not
The Emperor who gave us Wallenstein
To be our general. No, it was not so!

But Wallenstein who made the Emperor
Our master, and who binds us, he alone,
To serve beneath these flags.

OCTAVIO [*intervening between them*]:

He only would remind you, counsellor,
That you are in a camp of warriors here –
His boldness and his freedom make the soldier;
Could he be brave in action, might he not
Be brave with words? The two go hand in hand –
The boldness of this worthy officer [*indicating* BUTLER],
Which now was but mistaken in its aim,
That day in Prague, when only boldness could
Subdue the mutiny that raged, held for
The Emperor his capital!

    [*Distant martial music is heard.*]

ILLO: Hark there!

The sentinels salute – it is the signal
That the Princess is here within the walls!

OCTAVIO [*to* QUESTENBERG]:

Max too, my son, will be returned. He went
To be her escort from Carinthia.

ISOLANI [*to* ILLO]:

Shall we not go together to receive them?

ILLO: Surely! Come, Colonel Butler, go with us!

    [*To* OCTAVIO] Remember, before noon we meet again –
This gentleman too – before the Prince himself.

SCENE 3

[Exeunt all but OCTAVIO *and* QUESTENBERG.]

QUESTENBERG [*showing astonishment*]:
  Lieutenant-General, what is this I hear?
  What thoughts, what brazenness without restraint!
  – If this should be the spirit of the mass –
OCTAVIO: Three-quarters of the army you have heard.
QUESTENBERG: Alas for us! Where is another army
  To keep watch over this! I fear the thoughts
  Of this man Illo may be wilder yet
  Than what he spoke. This Butler too
  Cannot conceal the ill-will that he bears us.
OCTAVIO: It is no more than hurt and wounded pride;
  No, Butler I will not give up; I know
  The spell that will subject this evil demon.
QUESTENBERG [*pacing up and down in astonishment*]:
  No! this is worse, my friend! no, worse by far
  Than in Vienna we did ever dream.
  We saw these doings with our courtiers' eyes,
  Still blinded by the throne's imperial blaze;
  The general himself we had not seen,
  All-powerful, encamped amidst his troops.
  Here all is otherwise!
  Here is no Emperor more. The Prince is Emperor!
  What now I saw, as through the camp I walked
  Beside you, was as poison to my hopes.
OCTAVIO: You see now for yourself what dangerous task
  It is that you have brought me from the Court,
  How ill appears the part that I must play.
  If but the general should once suspect it,
  My freedom would be forfeit and my life,

    And his accursed enterprise would but
    Be hastened.
QUESTENBERG: Where was prudent foresight then,
    When we could trust this madman with our swords
    And lay such might and power in such a hand!
    Too strong for this but ill-defended heart
    Was such temptation! Must it not indeed
    Have been a danger to a better man!
    He will refuse, I tell you truly,
    The Imperial order he will disobey.
    He can and will. Unpunished, his defiance
    Will shame our helplessness for all to see.
OCTAVIO: And do you think it was for nothing that
    He brought his wife and daughter here to join him,
    Now, at this moment, when we arm for war?
    To take beyond the Emperor's lands these two
    Last pledges of his loyalty, shows plain,
    Open rebellion must be near at hand.
QUESTENBERG: Alas for us! How shall we stand the storm,
    That gathers threatening on every side?
    The enemies of Empire at our borders,
    Masters already of the Danube, still
    Their power increasing day by day, throughout
    The land alarums and revolt,
    Peasants in arms – all the estates conspired –
    And here the army, that we look to help us,
    Seduced, undisciplined, in disarray,
    Forsworn the State, forsworn its Emperor.
    Dizzily led by him that's dizzier yet,
    A fearful instrument, in blind obedience
    Surrendered to the boldest criminal –
OCTAVIO: My friend, let us not all too soon despair!
    Men's words are always braver than their deeds,
    And many a one who now in reckless zeal
    Seems resolute to take the fatal step,

Will unforeseen find that he has a heart,
When once the crime's true name rings out aloud.
And more! Defenceless we may seem; but no.
Count Altringer and Gallas, I must tell you,
Have kept their sturdy band at duty's call,
Their strength grows day by day. – He cannot take
Us by surprise, for as you know, I have
Him set about with spies on every hand;
One step – and straightway I shall be informed
Of it – in truth, he tells me it himself.

QUESTENBERG: It is past comprehension he should not
remark
The enemy at his side.

OCTAVIO: Yet do not think
That I with lies and smooth-tongued trickery
Have wormed my way into his grace and favour,
Or keep his confidence with flattery.
Though prudence should command it, and the duty
I owe the Empire and the Emperor,
That my true heart remain concealed from him,
I have not shown a false to seek his favour!

QUESTENBERG: It is the manifest design of Heaven.

OCTAVIO: What it can be, I do not know, that draws
And binds him fast to me and to my son.
Friends we have always been, comrades-in-arms;
Custom and the adventures we have shared,
Early united us. – And yet I think
I know the day when all at once it seemed
His heart was opened to me and his trust.
It was the morning of the fight at Lützen –
I had an evil dream that made me seek him,
To make him change the horse he rode to battle.
Far from the soldiers' tents, beneath a tree
I found him sleeping. When I had aroused
Him, and revealed to him my doubts and fears;

He gazed at me in wonderment, then fell
About my neck and seemed to be more touched
Than such a petty service could deserve.
Since that same day his trust in me has grown
In the like measure as mine fades in him.

QUESTENBERG: Your son is fully in your confidence?

OCTAVIO: No!

QUESTENBERG: What? Should you not even seek to warn
  him,
In what malignant clutches he may fall?

OCTAVIO: His innocence must be his guardian angel.
Deceit is stranger to his candid soul,
His ignorance of this alone will save
His frankness, that will keep the Duke at ease.

QUESTENBERG [anxiously]:
Respected friend! I have a great regard
For Colonel Piccolomini – and yet –
Consider –

OCTAVIO: It must be risked. But silence! Here he comes.

SCENE 4

[Enter MAX PICCOLOMINI.]

MAX: Why, there he is himself. Father, be welcome!
  [He embraces him. Turning round, he sees QUESTENBERG
  and steps back, coldly.]
But you have business? Let me not disturb you.

OCTAVIO: What, Max? Do you not know our guest? See
  who it is!
Attention an old friend may duly claim,
Respect demands the envoy of your Emperor.

MAX [*curtly*]:
  Von Questenberg! Welcome, if it is good
  That brings you to headquarters.

QUESTENBERG [*has taken him by the hand*]: Do not take
  Your hand away, Count Piccolomini,
  I grasp it not on my account alone,
  It is no common greeting that I bring.
  [*Taking both of them by the hand*] Octavio – Max Piccolomini!
  Names fraught with prophecy and tidings fair!
  Never will fortune turn from Austria,
  While two such stars as these, so bright to watch
  And bless, shine forth above her armies!

MAX: Minister, you forget yourself, I think,
  I know you are not sent to us to praise,
  Your mission is to scold and to rebuke,
  Let me seek no advantage of another!

OCTAVIO [*to* MAX]:
  He comes to us from Court, and there the Duke
  Is looked upon less favourably than here.

MAX: What new complaints about him will they make?
  That he alone decides in matters such
  As he alone can understand? In truth!
  Rightly he does, and so it shall remain.
  Once and for all, he is not made to bow
  And humbly suit him to another's will;
  His nature will not suffer it, he cannot.
  His soul, by nature fashioned to command,
  In a commander's place now seemly sits.
  And well for us that it is so! There are
  But few who know to rule themselves, to use
  Their minds with cunning skill – And well for men,
  If one be found, to be the gathering-point
  For many thousands, and their rock; to stand
  Firm as a mighty column, where in turn

Others may cling in confidence and joy.
Just such a man is Wallenstein, and if
The Court had rather see another – such
A man the Army needs.

QUESTENBERG: The army! Yes!

MAX: And it is joy to see how he inspires
And stirs and all about him wakes to life,
How each man's strength speaks out, how each man's
     gifts
He feels himself more keenly in his presence!
From every man he draws the secret strength
That lies in him, and brings it to its peak,
Lets every man remain that which he is,
Looks but to see that it shall always find
Its proper place; and so it is he knows
To gather to himself the powers of all.

QUESTENBERG: Who would deny he knows the hearts of
     men,
Knows how to use them! But in ruling them
He quite forgets that he should serve as well,
As if he had been born to ruler's state.

MAX: And was he not? With all a ruler's strength
He was, and stronger yet, as if by force
To execute himself great nature's plan,
And conquer ruler's seat for ruler's might!

QUESTENBERG: Then it were on his magnanimity
We must depend, if we should still be heard!

MAX: A man so rare demands our trust in rare degree,
Make way, and for himself he'll set his goal.

QUESTENBERG: So we have seen.

MAX: Yes! So it is! Are they
Not frightened all, to gaze into the depths!
Only in shallows can such men be happy.

OCTAVIO [to QUESTENBERG]:
My friend, content yourself, and wait awhile!

You'll not conclude this argument!

MAX: You summon up the spirit in your need,
    And turn in terror when he comes to you.
    You'd have the rare, the noblest enterprise
    Seem everyday. But on the battlefield,
    The moment presses – there, a man commands
    In person, sees with his own eyes. He needs,
    The general, the stamp of nature's greatness;
    So let him follow in his life the pulse
    Of nature. Let him hear the oracle
    That speaks within him, in his living soul –
    Not wait to ask of dusty papers, books
    And mouldering ordinance what he should do.

OCTAVIO: My son! Let us not look with scorn upon
    These ancient ordinances, narrow though they seem.
    For they are precious, priceless: checks and weights
    That man oppressed can bind to hem the will
    And tyrant whim of those who might oppress him;
    For tyrant's will is always to be feared. –
    The paths of order, crooked though they seem,
    Lead surely to their goal. Straight goes the lightning,
    Straight goes the cannon-shot in fearsome flight,
    Speeds headlong forward by the shortest path,
    And crushes all aside, to crush again.
    My son! The road that man in life must tread,
    On which prosperity awaits, this road will run
    Along the rivers, crooked like the valleys,
    Circling the cornfield and the vineyard's slopes,
    Respecting what is one man's, what another's,
    More slowly, but more surely, to its end.

QUESTENBERG: O, hear the words your father speaks – O hark
    To him, a hero who is yet a man.

OCTAVIO: I hear in you the child of this wild camp,
    Fifteen long years of war have been your schooling.
    – Peace you have never seen! There are, my son,

Yet higher, worthier goals than those of war;
War is not all men seek. In war itself
The swift and mighty deeds of martial power,
The miracles that for a moment blind,
Are not the works that in their train will bring
Contentment, permanence, stability.
Quickly in haste the soldier builds himself
His flimsy canvas city, in a moment
All is astir with comings and with goings,
Markets spring up, the roads and rivers bear
Their loads of freight, and trade and commerce thrive.
But suddenly one morning, then we see
The tents are struck, the horde is moving on,
And dead, as if they were a graveyard, lie
The ploughland and the battered fields of corn,
And in that year no harvest will be seen.

MAX: Oh, father! Let the Emperor make peace!
The laurel's bloodied crown I'd give with joy
For the first violet that blooms in March,
Rejuvenated earth's sweet-smelling pledge.

OCTAVIO: What is it? Why are you so strangely moved?

MAX: Peace I have never seen? Yes, father, I
Have seen sweet peace – have I not come this day,
This very day, from where the way I took
Led me through lands where war has never been,
– Oh, father! – no, this life has joys of which
We may but dream awhile. We only sail
About this smiling life's deserted coasts,
Like wandering pirates in their narrow ship,
Living wild lives upon the sea's wild waves,
Of continents knowing but bays and creeks
Where they may venture on their plundering raids.
What precious treasures in its inner valleys
The land conceals – oh no! oh no! of that
We have seen nothing on our desperate voyage.

OCTAVIO [*with increasing attention*]:
  And has this journey shown such things to you?
MAX: Never before in life was I at leisure.
  Tell me, what is the goal and prize of toil,
  The sweat and misery that stole my youth,
  A desert left my heart, my spirit starved
  Of nourishment, raw and uncivilized?
  For all the din and turmoil of this camp,
  The neigh of horses and the trumpets' blare,
  The task upon the appointed hour's stroke,
  The bark of orders and the drill at arms –
  Has nothing to assuage a yearning heart.
  There is no soul in all these empty things –
  There is another joy and happiness.
OCTAVIO: Much did you learn, my son, in this brief journey!
MAX: Oh fair the day! when at the last the soldier
  Comes home again to life, to human kind,
  In joyful train the banners are unfurled,
  And homeward wends the gentle march of peace;
  When every man shall deck his hat and helm
  With buds of may, last plunder of the field!
  The cities' gates fly open of themselves,
  There is no need of shells to burst their locks;
  The people climb the ramparts all about
  In peaceful throng, to greet the merry air;
  From all the towers, brightly peal the bells
  To close the day of blood with happy vespers.
  From cities and from villages pour forth
  The people's cheerful hosts, that gaily check
  With busy joy the army's slow advance.
  See where so happy to have seen this day
  The greybeard greets his son returning home!
  A stranger as he opens his own door,
  So long unseen; then with broad spreading boughs
  The tree receives him back, as he returns,

That when he left a pliant sapling swayed;
With modest maiden's steps she comes to meet him,
Whom last he saw a child at nurse's breast.
Happy the man to whom that day a door
Shall open, gentle arms enfold and greet him!

QUESTENBERG [*with emotion*]:

Oh! that it is of such far, far-off days
And not tomorrow or today you speak!

MAX [*turning fiercely upon him*]:

Whose fault is that but yours, you in Vienna?
Yes, freely I confess it, Questenberg!
When now I saw you standing here, I felt
The anger clutching at my heart within –
You it is, you, stand in the way of peace!
It is the warrior who must force it on you.
You make the Prince's life a burden, make
His every step a trouble, paint him black.
And why? Because for Europe's greater good
He cares far more than for an acre here,
An acre there that Austria gains or loses. –
You make of him a rebel, and – dear God! –
What else, because he treats the Saxons fairly,
Seeks to secure the enemy's good will,
Which is the only way that leads to peace;
For if not war in war already ceases,
Where then shall peace be found? Go, leave me, go –
Because I honour what is good, I hate you –
And here I swear it, I will shed my blood
For him, for Wallenstein, yes, drop by drop,
Until my heart is drained, before I see
You triumph at his fall! [*Exit.*]

SCENE 5

[QUESTENBERG, OCTAVIO PICCOLOMINI.]

QUESTENBERG [*urgently, impatiently*]:
  Alas, can it be so, my friend, and shall
  We let him thus deluded go, not call
  Him back straightway, that here and now his eyes
  Be opened?
OCTAVIO [*rousing himself from profound thought*]:
           It is mine that he has opened,
  And what I see, I do not like!
QUESTENBERG: What is it, friend?
OCTAVIO: Curses upon this journey!
QUESTENBERG: What is it? Why?
OCTAVIO: Come, come, my friend! I must
  Myself straightway trace his unhappy course,
  Behold with my own eyes – Come, come, I pray –
    [*Attempting to lead him off.*]
QUESTENBERG: Where would you take me, then?
OCTAVIO: To her!
QUESTENBERG: To her?
OCTAVIO: No – to the Duke! Come! Oh, I fear the worst.
  I see the net that they have cast for him,
  My son will not come back to me the same.
QUESTENBERG: Why, will you not explain –
OCTAVIO: And could I not
  Foresee all this? Not hold him from this journey?
  Why was I silent? – You were in the right,
  I should have warned him – now it is too late.
QUESTENBERG: What is too late? Consider now, my friend,
  These are but riddles that you speak to me.

OCTAVIO [*with greater composure*]:
  We'll go to see the Duke. Come then. The hour
  Is fast approaching too, that he appointed
  To give us audience. Come! –
  Accursed! accursed again, I say, this journey!
  [*As he leads* QUESTENBERG *off, the curtain falls.*]

ACT TWO

A reception room in the Duke of Friedland's suite.

SCENE I

[SERVANTS *bring chairs and spread rugs. Immediately
following them comes* SENI, *the astrologer, dressed like
an Italian doctor, in black and somewhat fantastically. He
comes into the centre of the room and points to the four
quarters of the heavens with a white stick which he holds
in his hand.*]

SERVANT [*going round with a censer*]:
  Quickly, and let's be done! I hear the guard
  Presenting arms. They will be here straightway!
SECOND SERVANT: But tell me then, why was the oriel
    room,
  The crimson one, not used, that is so bright?
FIRST SERVANT: Well, ask the doctor there, and you'll be
    told
  That room's unlucky.
SECOND SERVANT: What? An old wives' tale!
  Just to make work for folk. A room's a room.
  How can the place be of the least importance?

SENI [*with gravity*]:
Son! nothing in this world is unimportant.
Yet first and foremost, most significant
In all our life's affairs is place and time.

THIRD SERVANT: Nathaniel, you must not argue with him!
Even our master has to do his will.

SENI [*counting the chairs*]:
Eleven! Evil number. Set twelve chairs.
Twelve signs the zodiac has, and Five and Seven,
The holy numbers, make together twelve.

SECOND SERVANT: What's to be said against eleven? Tell
me!

SENI: Eleven's sin. Eleven oversteps
The ten commandments.

SECOND SERVANT: Oh? And why is five
A holy number? What of that?

SENI: Five is
The soul of man. For just as man of good
And evil is a blend, so five's the first
Of numbers that is mixed from odd and even.

FIRST SERVANT: The fool!

THIRD SERVANT: Oh, let him be! I like to hear him talk,
His words can make you think a thing or two!

SECOND SERVANT: Away! They're coming! Through the
side door here.
[*They hurry away.* SENI *follows them, slowly.*]

SCENE 2

[*Enter* WALLENSTEIN *and the* DUCHESS.]

WALLENSTEIN: Well, Duchess? On your way you passed
    Vienna,
  Had audience of the Queen of Hungary?
DUCHESS: The Empress too, and both their majesties
  Admitted us in turn to kiss their hands.
WALLENSTEIN: How did they take it that my wife and
    daughter
  Were summoned to the field these wintry days?
DUCHESS: I did as you had told me, said to them
  That for our daughter you had made a match
  And wished the man who was to be her husband
  Should see her now, before the next campaigns.
WALLENSTEIN: On whom did they suppose my choice had
    fallen?
DUCHESS: They hoped indeed, it might not be a stranger,
  And not a Lutheran that you would choose.
WALLENSTEIN: What are your hopes, Elizabeth?
DUCHESS: You know my will was ever one with yours.
WALLENSTEIN [*after a pause*]:
  So – And how else then did the Court receive you?
  [*The* DUCHESS *remains silent, with downcast eyes.*]
  Keep nothing from me. Tell me how it was.
DUCHESS: Oh! husband, no – it is no longer as
  Of old – a change has come upon their hearts.
WALLENSTEIN: What? Did they not respect you as before?
DUCHESS: Respect they did. Seemly and dignified
  Was their demeanour – but alas! instead
  Of that most fair and gracious condescension,
  A stiff and formal gaze they turned on me,

And if they showed me tenderness and favour,
Then it was pity rather than good-will.
No, no! the princely consort of Duke Albrecht,
Count Harrach's noble daughter, should not thus –
Not thus have been received, nor treated so!

WALLENSTEIN: No doubt my latest measures were rebuked.

DUCHESS: Oh, if they had been! I have long been used
To make excuses for you, pacify
With soothing speech their spirits roused to anger –
No one rebuked you, none, but all were veiled
In such a solemn and oppressive silence.
Oh, no! this is no mere misunderstanding,
This is no passing mood of jealousy –
Some great misfortune and irreparable
Has happened. – Always in the days gone by
The Queen of Hungary would call me her
Dear cousin, would embrace me when we parted –

WALLENSTEIN: And this time, she did not?

DUCHESS [*drying her tears, after a pause*]:

                                She did embrace me,
But only when we had already taken leave, and when
Our steps were turned already to the door, she came
In haste, as if she had forgotten, pressed
Me to her breast, in token more of grief
Than generous affection.

WALLENSTEIN [*seizing her hand*]: Calm yourself!
And what of Eggenberg, of Liechtenstein,
And others of our friends?

DUCHESS [*shaking her head*]: I did not see them.

WALLENSTEIN: Nor him, the Count Ambassador of Spain,
Who used to be so zealous on my part?

DUCHESS: He had no words to speak on your behalf.

WALLENSTEIN: So, if those suns will shine for us no more,
Henceforth we must be warmed by our own fires.

DUCHESS: And could it? my dear Duke, oh could it be

The truth they whisper at the court, speak out
In all the land, what Father Lamormain
With nods and hints –
WALLENSTEIN [*quickly*]: What? Lamormain? What says he?
DUCHESS: That you are charged with wantonly exceeding
The powers given you, with wilfully
Refusing to obey the Emperor's orders.
The Spaniards and Bavaria's proud Duke,
He said, were your accusers.
A thunderstorm was gathering above
Your head, more blackly threatening than that
Which laid you low before, at Regensburg.
And they were talking – no, I cannot bear
To speak the word he spoke – I cannot –
WALLENSTEIN [*urgently*]:   What, then?
DUCHESS: Of yet again – [*She hesitates.*]
WALLENSTEIN: Again –
DUCHESS: And ignominiously –
Dismissing you.
WALLENSTEIN: They were?
     [*He paces up and down the room in agitation.*]
                                   Oh! they will force me, drive me,
Compel me yet, against my will, to do it.
DUCHESS [*clinging to him in supplication*]:
Oh! if there is still time, my husband – if
Humility, submissiveness may yet
Prevent it – husband, oh I beg, submit –
Conquer your too proud heart and make it yield –
To him who is your Emperor and master.
Oh! do not let this creeping malice still
Succeed in blackening your best intentions,
Stand forth and be victorious with the truth,
And put the lying slanderers to shame.
You know we have so few to call our friends,
Our fortune's rise so swift has laid us bare

To jealousy and hatred – what are we,
If we no longer know Imperial favour!

SCENE 3

[*Enter* COUNTESS TERZKY, *leading the* PRINCESS
THEKLA *by the hand.*]

COUNTESS: What, sister? Talking of affairs already,
And, as I see, of none that bode us well,
Even before his child comes to rejoice him?
This moment yield of right to happiness.
Here, Friedland! father, see! this is your daughter!
   [THEKLA *approaches shyly and bends as if to kiss his hand;
   he takes her in his arms and stands for a while looking at her.*]
WALLENSTEIN: Yes! Fair indeed my hopes have come to
   blossom.
As pledge of fairer fortune I receive her.
DUCHESS: She was a tender child still when you left us,
To raise the mighty army for the Emperor,
And when from Pomerania you returned,
The campaign over, she was in a convent,
Where she remained until this day.
WALLENSTEIN: While we
Here in the field have striven to make her great.
To conquer for her all that earth may yield,
Within quiet convent walls, good mother nature
Has played her part, her heavenly gifts bestowed
Most freely on this lovely child, and now
She sends her forth to glorious destiny
And to the consummation of my hopes.
DUCHESS [*to* THEKLA]:
I doubt, my child, that you could recognize

Your father still? Scarce eight years old you were,
When last your eyes did rest upon his face.

THEKLA: Yes, mother, at a glance I did – my father
  Has not grown old – and as his image dwells in me,
  So stands he now in manhood's flower before me.

WALLENSTEIN [*to the* DUCHESS]:
  The pretty child! What charming words, and full
  Of understanding! See, I grudged the fate
  That I should have no son who should inherit
  The glory of my name and of my fortune,
  And should pass on my life, so quickly spent,
  To other princes in a lineage proud.
  Wrongly I did so! Here now, on this head
  In maiden blossom, I will lay the wreath
  That I have earned in busy warrior's life;
  I shall not count it wasted, if one day
  Upon this brow so fair my hand may place it,
  Transformed into a queenly diadem.

SCENE 4

[*Enter* MAX PICCOLOMINI, *and soon afterwards* TERZKY.]

COUNTESS: Here is the paladin who guarded us.

WALLENSTEIN: Be welcome, Max. You always were to me
  The bringer of some most especial joy;
  And now, like that fair star that heralds day,
  You bring my life's own sun to shine on me.

MAX: My General –

WALLENSTEIN: Till now it was the Emperor
  Who through my hand rewarded you. Today
  You earn a happy father's gratitude,
  And Friedland must himself discharge the debt.

MAX: My Prince, you are too quick to recompense.
   Ashamed I come, yes, even sorrowing;
   For scarcely have I yet returned, delivered
   Mother and daughter safe into your arms,
   When from your stables, richly harnessed, comes
   A coach and four fine horses as a gift
   To pay me for the trouble I have taken.
   Yes, yes, to pay me back. A trouble only,
   An office to perform, it was! Not what
   I thought, a privilege, for which I came
   Too hastily to thank you, from the bottom of
   My heart – no, it was not intended so,
   That this my task should be my greatest joy!

     [*Enter* TERZKY, *bringing the* DUKE *dispatches, which he
     quickly opens.*]

COUNTESS [*to* MAX]:
   Is it your trouble he repays? His happiness
   He only would reward. If it is meet
   That you should thank so graciously, then it
   Is fitting that my brother too should show
   Such magnanimity as may become a prince.

THEKLA: Then even I must come to doubt his love,
   For did he not adorn me with his hand,
   Before a father's heart I had yet heard!

MAX: He must be always giving, making glad!

     [*Seizing the Duchess's hand, with growing ardour*]

   Do I not owe him everything – oh, what
   Does not the precious name of Friedland mean to me!
   For all my life I shall remain in thrall
   To that great name – for me therein shall bloom
   All joy, all fortune, all my fairest hopes –
   As in a magic circle, destiny
   Holds me a prisoner within that name.

COUNTESS [*who has been observing the* DUKE *closely, notices
    that in reading the dispatches he has taken on a brooding look*]:

My brother would be left alone. Come with me.

WALLENSTEIN [*turns sharply, then regains his composure and
        addresses himself to the* DUCHESS *with an expression of
        cheerfulness*]:

Once more, Princess, I welcome you among us.
You are the mistress of this court – you, Max,
Will this once more discharge your former office,
While we attend the business of our master.

    [MAX *offers the* DUCHESS *his arm,* COUNTESS TERZKY
    conducts the PRINCESS. *Exeunt.*]

TERZKY [*calling after him*]:

Do not forget you must attend the council !

SCENE 5

[WALLENSTEIN, TERZKY.]

WALLENSTEIN [*brooding, to himself*]:

It was the truth she saw – for it confirms
Entirely what we have from other hands –
Yes, they have made their minds up in Vienna,
And found the man who shall succeed me here:
The King of Hungary, young Ferdinand,
The Emperor's boy; he is their saviour now,
Their rising star ! They think that we are done with
Already, and that they can parcel out
Our goods between them, as if we were dead.
Why then, there is no time to lose !

    [*Turning, he observes* TERZKY *and hands him one of the
    dispatches.*]

Altringer begs to be excused, you see,
And Gallas too. – I do not like it.

TERZKY: If
  You still delay, then one by one they'll leave you.

WALLENSTEIN: Altringer holds the passes in the Tyrol,
  I must send word to him that he must not
  Allow the Spaniard through them from Milan.
  – Now! Sesina, our go-between, I see,
  Has newly given signs of life again.
  What does he bring us from Count Thurn?

TERZKY: The Count
  Reports, he met the Swedish Chancellor
  At Halberstadt, where now they hold their councils,
  But he had said that he was tired of this,
  And would have nothing more to do with you.

WALLENSTEIN: And why?

TERZKY: Because you never spoke in earnest,
  You only meant to play the Swedes a trick,
  Ally yourself with Saxony against them,
  At last with money buy them off and send
  Them packing.

WALLENSTEIN: So! What, does he think I should
  Give German provinces to him as booty,
  That we no longer should be masters of
  Our own fair land? We must be rid of them!
  Off with them, off! We will not have such neighbours.

TERZKY: Oh, let them have their piece of land, it's not
  From yours they'll take it! What can it mean to you,
  When you have won the fame, who pays for it?

WALLENSTEIN: Off, off with them – you do not under-
  stand.
  Never shall it be said of me I carved
  Up Germany, and sold her to a stranger,
  Just to be sure I had my own share too.
  The Empire shall revere me as its saviour;
  Myself conducting as befits a Prince

Of Empire, I shall take any place among them.
I shall allow no foreign power to gain
A foothold in the Empire, least of all
These Goths, these hungry, frozen savages
Who cast their greedy eyes so jealously
Upon the fruitful lands of Germany.
They shall be there to help me in my plans,
But there shall be no pickings for them, no!

TERZKY: But will you not then deal more fairly with
The Saxons? Soon they will have lost their patience,
Following all your crooked ways –
Why these disguises, why these masks? Come, speak!
Your friends despair and lose their faith in you. –
Arnim and Oxenstierna, neither knows
What meaning he shall give your hesitations.
At last it's me they'll call the liar, all
Has gone through me. I've nothing in your hand.

WALLENSTEIN: You know that I put nothing down in
writing.

TERZKY: But how can any know you are in earnest,
Unless deeds follow words? Admit yourself,
All your negotiations with the foe
Might just as well have had no other purpose,
Could all have happened to no other end,
Than make a fool of him!

WALLENSTEIN [after a pause, in which he looks fixedly at
TERZKY]:
How do you know I do not mean in truth
To make a fool of him? Might I not mean
To make you all look foolish? Do you know me?
I do not think I ever let you see
The secrets of my heart – The Emperor,
Indeed, has done me wrong! Yes, if I wished,
I could repay him ill for ill most sorely.
It is my pleasure to know the power I have;

But whether I shall ever use it, that, I think,
You know no better than another man.

TERZKY: So you have always played your game with us!

SCENE 6

[*Enter* ILLO.]

WALLENSTEIN: What news out there? Are all in readiness?

ILLO: You'll find them all disposed as you would wish.
They know what now the Emperor demands,
They rage!

WALLENSTEIN: And what says Isolani to it?

ILLO: Body and soul are yours, since you have set
Him up again before the gaming-table.

WALLENSTEIN: Colalto too? And are you quite assured
Of Deodati and of Tiefenbach?

ILLO: What Piccolomini does, they will do too.

WALLENSTEIN: And so you think that I can stake on them?

ILLO: – If you are sure of Piccolomini.

WALLENSTEIN: As of myself, the father and the son.

TERZKY: And yet I wish you would not trust so much
That cunning fox, Octavio.

WALLENSTEIN: Would you
Teach me to know my men? Sixteen campaigns
It is I've fought at old Octavio's side.
– And then – why, I have cast his horoscope;
We two were born beneath the self-same stars –
And so, in short – [*mysteriously*]
                                    It is a private matter.
If you can swear to me for all the rest –

ILLO: One voice alone among them can be heard:
You shall not abdicate from your command.

They talk of sending you a deputation.

WALLENSTEIN: If *I* am to make promises to *them*,
   They must make promise too to *me*.

ILLO: Of course.

WALLENSTEIN: Give me their word, their oath, their
      written pledge,
   To serve me only and without condition.

ILLO: Why not?

TERZKY: Without condition? Emperor
   And Austria make claims upon their service
   That must come first.

WALLENSTEIN [*shaking his head*]: I say without condition
   They must be mine. I'll hear of no prior claims!

ILLO: I have a plan. Is it not true, Count Terzky,
   That you are dining us this evening?

TERZKY: Yes,
   I have invited all the generals.

ILLO [*to* WALLENSTEIN]: Tell me, will you allow me a free
      hand?
   I'll make the generals pledge their word to you,
   Just as you wish.

WALLENSTEIN: Get me their signatures;
   How you will get them, let that be your own affair.

ILLO: And when you see it there in black and white,
   That all the generals assembled here
   Blindly submit themselves to you – why, then
   Will you at last in earnest try your fortune
   With bold, unflinching deeds?

WALLENSTEIN: Get me their promise!

ILLO: Think what it is you do! You cannot meet
   The Emperor's demands, you cannot let
   The army be disbanded, cannot let
   Your regiments go to join the Spaniard, if
   You would not bid your power be gone for ever.
   But think of this as well! You cannot spurn

The Emperor's order and his grave command,
You cannot make excuses, temporize,
If you would not break formally with Court.
Resolve! Will you with action resolute
Strike the first blow? Or hesitate until
The fatal moment comes?

WALLENSTEIN: Is that not fitting,
Before we take a fatal step?

ILLO: Oh! know the hour before it has escaped you!
So rarely comes the moment in our lives,
That is so weighty and so great. For one
Decision to be made, so many threads
Must meet in fortunate coincidence –
And only scattered, one by one, we see
The lines of fate, the opportunities,
Which, gathered tightly in one point of life
And bound together, form the fruitful knot.
See how decisively, how fatefully
All draws about you now! The army's chiefs,
The best, most excellent of men, assembled
Around yourself, their princely leader, here,
Awaiting but the sign from you – oh, do
Not let them go their several ways again!
Never again in all the course of war
Will you be able to unite them thus.
It is the flood that lifts the heavy ship
That's beached – And every single man will find
His spirit growing in this gathered tide.
You have them now, you have them! Soon the war
Will scatter them once more, some here, some there –
The common spirit will be lost in petty cares,
In private interests. He who today,
When borne on by the tide, forgets himself,
Will soon be sober when he's left alone,
Will feel his impotence, and quickly set

His course once more upon the old, well-worn,
Familiar paths of duty, only seek
To come back whole to friendly roof and shelter.

WALLENSTEIN: The time is not yet come.

TERZKY: So you say always.
When will the time be come?

WALLENSTEIN: The day I say.

ILLO: Oh! you will sit and wait upon the stars
Until the time on earth is past! Believe me,
The stars of destiny are in your heart,
Faith in yourself, and firm resolve, these are
Your Venus, and the one unlucky star
That harms you is your own irresolution.

WALLENSTEIN: You know no better than you speak. How
often
Have I explained it to you! Jupiter,
Bright-shining god, was set when you were born;
These secrets are beyond your understanding.
In earth to burrow is your place, blind like
That subterranean god who lit your way
Into this life with grey and leaden beams.
Common and earthly things you may perceive,
May shrewdly see the links that lie at hand;
In this I trust you and believe your words.
But what in mystery is woven, what
Great secrets grown and shaped in Nature's depths –
The spirit ladder, from this world of dust
Ascending by a thousand rungs to reach
The stars, and trod by countless heavenly powers
Pursuing up and down their busy ways –
The circles within circles, that draw close
And closer yet upon the focal sun –
These things the unclouded eye alone can see
Of Jupiter's fair children, born in light.

[*He paces the length of the room, then stands still and continues.*]

The heavenly constellations do not make
But day and night, summer and spring – it is
Not only to the sower they give sign
Of sowing-time and harvest. Deeds of men as well
Are sown by fate, in future's darkness broadcast,
In trust and hope to destiny surrendered.
He who would reap must seek to learn the times,
To read and choose the star-appointed hour,
To seek with diligence through heaven's mansions,
Lest that the enemy of growth and ripeness
Should lie in ambush in some secret quarter.
– So give me time. Meanwhile, look to your tasks.
I cannot say as yet what I will do.
But I will not submit to them. Not I!
And they shall not dismiss me. No, on that
You may rely.

SERVANT [*entering*]: The generals.

WALLENSTEIN: Let them come.

TERZKY: Would you have all the chiefs be here in person?

WALLENSTEIN: There is no need. Both Piccolomini,
Maradas, Butler, Forgatsch, Deodati,
Caraffa, Isolani – these should come.

  [*Exit* TERZKY *with the servant.*]

Have you set careful watch on Questenberg?
Did he not speak to anyone in secret?

ILLO: He has been closely watched. He was alone
But for Octavio.

SCENE 7

[*Enter to them* QUESTENBERG, *both the* PICCOLO-
MINI, BUTLER, ISOLANI, MARADAS *and three
other generals. At a sign from the commander-in-chief,*
QUESTENBERG *takes his place immediately opposite
him, the others follow according to rank. There is a
moment's silence.*]

WALLENSTEIN: So, I have heard the burden of your errand,
　Von Questenberg, and weighed it carefully,
　Made my decision, which will not be altered.
　But it is only right that my commanders
　Should hear from your own lips the Emperor's will –
　And so I ask that you declare your mission
　Before these noble heads assembled here.

QUESTENBERG: I am prepared, but beg you to remember
　Imperial authority and state
　Speak with my tongue, not boldness of my own.

WALLENSTEIN: No introductions.

QUESTENBERG: 　　　　　　　　When his majesty
　The Emperor upon his sturdy troops
　Conferred a head renowned and skilled in war
　In person of the noble Duke of Friedland,
　He did so in the happy trust that soon
　War's fortunes would be favourably turned.
　At first it seemed his wish would be fulfilled.
　Bohemia was cleansed of Saxon armies,
　The Swedes' victorious tide was stemmed – these lands
　Could once again draw breath revivified,
　When Friedland drew the enemy's full force
　From all the scattered streams of Germany,
　Summoned to meet him in one single place

The Rhinegrave, Bernard, Banner, Oxenstiern,
And even that great king invincible,
At last within the sight of Nuremberg
To fight the bloody and decisive battle.

WALLENSTEIN: To business, if you please.

QUESTENBERG: Spirits renewed
At once proclaimed the new commander's hand.
No longer fury fought with fury blind,
In clear-cut lines of battle now we saw
How constancy could stand the attack of boldness
And skilful art exhaust insensate valour.
In vain they try to lure him out to fight,
Deep and more deeply still he digs his camp,
As if to found a house to last for ever.
Despairing at the last the king attacks,
Drags headlong to the butcher's block his men,
Already in his corpse-filled camp of plague
And ravages of hunger slowly dying.
Now through the outworks of the camp, where death
In thousand muzzles lies in wait, the man
Whom none could stop attempts to storm his way.
That was an onslaught and a counter-stroke!
Fortunate eye has never seen its like.
At last the king in tatters leads his men
Home from the battlefield, and not a foot
Of ground his fearful sacrifice had gained.

WALLENSTEIN: You need not read the chronicle to me
Of horrors we have seen with our own eyes.

QUESTENBERG: My office and my mission is complaint,
In praise my heart would gladly speak its word.
The King of Sweden lost at Nuremberg
His glory – and on Lützen's plains, his life.
But who was not amazed to see the Duke
Of Friedland now, as if he had been vanquished,
Flee to Bohemia, quit the battlefield,

While young heroic Weimar, unimpeded,
Thrust forward to the heartland of Franconia,
Swept all before him till he reached the Danube,
And in a trice stood before Regensburg,
A terror to all pious Catholics!
Then did Bavaria's well-deserving prince
Cry out for speedy aid in his distress,
The Emperor sends seven mounted men
To lay his plea before the Duke of Friedland
And begs, where as a lord he might command.
In vain! For in this moment Friedland hears
Only the ancient voice of grudge and hate,
Lets fall the common cause, to satisfy
His vengeance on an ancient enemy.
And thus falls Regensburg!

WALLENSTEIN: What days are these he is recalling, Max?
My memory is failing me.

MAX: He means
When we were in Silesia.

WALLENSTEIN: Indeed!
But tell me, what should we be doing there?

MAX: Clearing the land of Saxons and of Swedes.

WALLENSTEIN: Good! Why, his description made me quite
forget
The war we fought –
[To QUESTENBERG]   Continue, if you please!

QUESTENBERG: Perhaps there by the Oder was regained
What on the Danube shamefully surrendered.
Deeds great beyond the telling we expected
To see and hear upon the stage of war,
Where Friedland's very person took the field,
And Gustav's rival rode to meet a – Thurn,
An Arnim, or such men as these, and truly,
The parties here came close enough together;
– To sit down at one table, friends and guests!

Germany groaned beneath the yoke of war,
But in the camp of Wallenstein was peace.

WALLENSTEIN: Many a bloody fight is fought for nothing,
Because young generals need their victories.
It is the proven general's advantage
That he no longer needs to fight to show
The world he knows the way to win a battle.
I could have no desire to summon fortune
To help me prove myself against an Arnim;
But Germany would thank my moderation
If I had had the fortune to dissolve
The fateful bond of Saxony and Sweden!

QUESTENBERG: That fortune failed you, though, and so once
   more
The bloody game of war began. At last
The prince's ancient fame seemed justified.
On Steinau's field the Swedish army lays
Its weapons down, without a blow defeated –
And here, with others, Heaven's justice put
Into the hands of vengeance Matthew Thurn,
That ancient trouble-maker, torch of war.
– But he had fallen into generous hands:
Instead of punishment he found reward,
And laden with rich presents did the Prince
Release his Emperor's arch-enemy.

WALLENSTEIN [laughing]:
I know, I know – already in Vienna
You had hired out the balconies and windows,
To see him pass by on the hangman's cart –
I might have thrown a victory away,
But never will the Viennese forgive
That I could rob them of a spectacle!

QUESTENBERG: Silesia was relieved; Bavaria's
Distress once more now calls upon the Duke.
And he indeed sets out – at steady pace,

The *longest* road he takes across Bohemia;
But yet before he sees the foe, he turns
In haste, encamps for winter, and oppresses
Imperial lands with the Imperial army!

WALLENSTEIN: The army's state was pitiful, it lacked
All needs, all comforts – winter was drawing on.
Does not the Emperor know his troops are men?
Does he not know that we are subject too
To cold and wet and every mortal need?
Accursed is the soldier's fate! Wherever
He comes, men flee from him – and when he goes,
They curse him! All he seeks he has to take,
Nothing is given him; to take by force
From all men is a task all men must hate.
Here stand my generals. Caraffa, speak!
Count Deodati! Butler! Speak, and tell him
How long the men have gone without their pay!

BUTLER: A year it is already.

WALLENSTEIN: Shall a man
Who *takes* the Emperor's shilling not *receive* it?

QUESTENBERG: A very different tune it was the Duke
Of Friedland sang eight years ago or nine.

WALLENSTEIN: Yes, yes, I know it is my fault, myself
I spoilt the Emperor thus. Nine years ago,
I raised him, in the Danish war, a power
Of forty or of fifty thousand men
That cost him not a farthing of his own
Sweet money – Through the Saxon provinces
War's fury raged, and bore the terror of his name
Before it to the skerries of the Belt.
That was a time indeed! In all the Imperial lands
No name was held in honour as was mine,
And Albrecht Wallenstein he called
The third amongst the jewels of his crown!
But in the Diet there in Regensburg,

It came into the open, all could see
Whose pockets I had emptied for my work.
And now, what thanks were mine, that I had taken,
As loyal servant of my prince, the curse
Of all the peoples on me – made the princes
Pay for this war that only him made great?
What? I was sacrificed to their complaints,
I was dismissed.

QUESTENBERG: I think your grace must know
How little was the freedom he enjoyed
At that unhappy Diet.

WALLENSTEIN: Death and devils!
I *had* what could have given him that freedom!
– No, sir! Since it rewarded me so badly
To serve the throne at the expense of Empire,
Better of Empire I have learnt to think.
I have my baton of the Emperor,
But wield it as the Empire's general,
For all men's benefit and the common good,
No longer for the aggrandizement of *one*!
But now to business. What would you have of me?

QUESTENBERG: Firstly it is his majesty's desire
The army quit Bohemia at once.

WALLENSTEIN: What, at this time of year? And may I ask
Where we should go?

QUESTENBERG: To seek the enemy.
His Majesty desires that Regensburg
By Easter shall be cleansed of enemy troops,
That the cathedral shall no longer hear
Lutheran sermons – that vile heresy
Shall not pollute the Church's festival.

WALLENSTEIN: Tell me, can this be done, my generals?

ILLO: It is impossible.

BUTLER: Cannot be done.

QUESTENBERG: The Emperor has commanded Colonel Suys

At once to make advance into Bavaria.

WALLENSTEIN: And Suys, what has he done?

QUESTENBERG: His duty, sir.
Advanced.

WALLENSTEIN: Advanced! And I, his general,
Had ordered him, expressly, that he should
Not quit the post I gave him! What, is this
All my authority is worth? This the obedience
That I am shown, the discipline that makes
War possible? You here, my generals,
Shall judge! What has an officer deserved,
Who breaks his oath and contravenes his orders?

ILLO: He dies!

WALLENSTEIN [as the others hesitate and are silent, raising his
  voice]: Count Piccolomini, what has he
Deserved?

MAX [after a long pause]: The letter of the law demands – he
  dies!

ISOLANI: He dies!

BUTLER: He dies, according to the law of war!
  [QUESTENBERG stands up. WALLENSTEIN follows suit, and
  all rise to their feet.]

WALLENSTEIN: To death the law condemns him thus – not
  I!
And if I pardon him, it is because
I honour, duty-bound, my Emperor's word.

QUESTENBERG: If thus it stands, my breath is wasted here.

WALLENSTEIN: I took command upon my own conditions;
The first of them was that no mortal soul,
No, not the Emperor himself, should have
A voice but I in what concerns the army.
If I am held to answer with my head
And honour for the outcome, then I must
Be master absolute. What was it made
Gustavus seem invincible on earth?

Why, this: that in his army he was king!
A king, I tell you, though, that *is* a king,
Was never beaten yet but by his equal. –
Say on, though. Is the best not yet to come?

QUESTENBERG: The Cardinal-Infant will leave Milan
In springtime and will lead a Spanish army
Through Germany into the Netherlands.
So that he may with safety make his way,
Our monarch bids you from the army send
Eight mounted regiments to be his escort.

WALLENSTEIN: I see, I see – Eight regiments! Yes, yes!
A cunning plan, good Father Lamormain!
Were it not schemed with such accursed cunning
I might have thought a fool made such request.
Eight thousand horse! Yes, yes, I see what lies
Behind it.

QUESTENBERG: I assure you there is nothing
To see. Prudence, necessity command it.

WALLENSTEIN: What, sir ambassador? Should I not notice
   that
Your masters tire of seeing it is I
Who wield the sword, the power, in my hand?
That greedily they seize upon this pretext,
Invoke the Spanish name to trim my forces,
To bring into the Empire a new power,
That will not be subject to me? I am
Too mighty still for you to cast me off
So simply. My commission runs that all
Imperial armies shall obey my word,
Where, far and wide, the German tongue is spoken.
But Spanish troops, and Spanish princes, who
As guests invited wander through the Empire,
Of them there is no mention. Quietly, then,
And roundabout you seek to sap my powers,
Thwart my commission, do without my service,

Till you can make short shrift with me at last.
— Why all these crooked ways, sir minister?
Speak out! It irks the Emperor to deal
With me. He would be glad if I would go.
I will do him this favour, *that* I had
Decided, sir, before you showed your face.

   [*There is a stir amongst the generals, which continues to grow*.]

Yet I feel sorry for my colonels here,
I do not see how they will get the money back
They have advanced, the pay that they have earned.
Under a new command new men will rise,
And earlier merit fade and be forgotten.
Many a foreigner serves within these ranks,
And if he was an honest man and bold
I did not seek to know his ancestry
Or catechize him much about his faith.
Those things will change as well in days to come!
Well — it is no concern of mine. [*Sits down*.]

MAX: May God
  Preserve us from this pass! The army will
  Rise up and mutiny in dreadful ferment, —
  The Emperor's name is mocked, it cannot be.

ISOLANI: It cannot be, for all would fall in ruins.

WALLENSTEIN: Yes, faithful Isolani, all will fall
  In ruins, that we so patiently have built.
  And yet, another general will be found,
  And yet, another army will come flocking
  To serve the Emperor, when they beat the drum.

MAX [*hurrying eagerly from one to the other, seeking to pacify them*]:
  Hear me, my general! Hear me, Colonels all!
  Prince, let us urge you, take no quick decision,
  Before we have all met in council, made
  Representation to you — Come, my friends!

I hope that everything may be restored!

TERZKY: Come! In the anteroom we'll find the rest. [*Exeunt.*]

BUTLER [*to* QUESTENBERG]: If to hear good advice you have
    an ear,
Then in the next few hours you will not show
Yourself in public, for your golden keys
May not protect you from unkindly hands.
    [*Loud disturbance offstage.*]

WALLENSTEIN: Butler's advice is good. Octavio,
I charge you with our guest's security!
I trust you will be well, von Questenberg!
    [*As the latter attempts to speak*]
No, no, say nothing of these hateful matters!
It was your duty that you did. I know
The man must be distinguished from his office.
    [*As* QUESTENBERG *is about to leave with* OCTAVIO,
    GÖTZ, TIEFENBACH, *and* COLALTO *come rushing on,*
    followed by several more commanders.]

GÖTZ: Where is the man who says our General –

TIEFENBACH [*at the same time*]:
What is it we must hear, you surely will –

COLALTO [*at the same time*]:
With you we seek to live, with you to die.

WALLENSTEIN [*with dignity, indicating* ILLO]:
Field-Marshal Illo knows what is my will. [*Exit.*]

ACT THREE

A Room.

SCENE I

[ILLO *and* TERZKY.]

TERZKY: Say now! What is the plan you have this evening
  To win the colonels over at the banquet?
ILLO: Look here! We will compose a document,
  In which we swear the Duke our absolute
  Devotion, to be his with life and soul,
  To shed our blood for him to the last drop;
  Though never more than be consistent with
  The oath we owe the Emperor. Now see!
  This oath specifically we except
  In a proviso, thus to save our conscience.
  Now then! The document we've thus composed
  We lay before them to approve before
  The banquet, none will take exception – Now!
  After the dinner, when their wine-dulled wits
  Have shut their eyes and left their hearts unguarded,
  We send another piece of paper round,
  With no proviso, for their signatures!
TERZKY: What? Do you think that they will hold themselves
  Obliged to keep an oath that we have tricked
  Them into swearing by deceit and cunning?
ILLO: In any case, we have them. Let them cry
  That they've been tricked, as loudly as they care;
  At court their signatures will be believed
  More than their plaints and their asseverations.

Traitors they are and traitors they'll remain,
They'll make a virtue of necessity!

TERZKY: Well, I care not, if only something happens,
If only we can set things on the move!

ILLO: And then as well – it does not so much matter
How far we can persuade the generals;
Enough, if we can only show the chief
That they *are* his – for if *he* will but act
In earnest, as if they were his already,
Then he *will* have them, carry them along.

TERZKY: Often I cannot think how I should read him.
He lends the enemy his ear, he makes
Me write to Thurn and Arnim, he will speak
So boldly out before that Sesina,
Will talk to us for hours of all his plans,
And if I think I have him – all at once
Out of my grasp he slips, and I must think
That he will never take a step in earnest;
He only seeks to keep his present place.

ILLO: What, he abandon all his plans of old?
I tell you, waking, sleeping, he can think
Of nothing else, for this alone he scans
The planets day by day –

TERZKY: Yes, do you know
That in the coming night he and the doctor
Will shut themselves in the observatory
And make their astrological predictions?
For this, I hear, will be a night of high
Importance, long-awaited, great events
Take place in heaven.

ILLO: If only they would happen here below!
The generals are zealous at this moment,
Can be persuaded to do anything
Rather than lose their chief. Do you not see?
We have occasion, ready-made, at hand,

To bind them in a league against the Court.
The name is innocent enough, we say
Only that we would keep him at our head.
But you well know, in hot pursuit of ends
We soon lose sight of where we had begun.
I think I can arrange it that the Prince
Shall find them willing – shall *believe* them willing
To venture all. The opportunity
Will tempt him on. For once the step is taken,
That they will not forgive him in Vienna,
Then the compulsion of events will lead
Him on and ever onward. It is choice
Alone is hard for him; necessity
Restores his strength, brings clarity again.

TERZKY: And that is all the enemy awaits
To lead his troops to us.

ILLO: Come! We must see
This work set on in motion further now
In these few days than it has come in years – And let
It once be started well below, then you
Will see the stars will give their blessing too!
Come with me to the colonels. We must strike
While yet the iron is hot.

TERZKY: Will you go to them, Illo.
I have to speak with Countess Terzky here.
Neither have we been idle – so, if one
Rope breaks, another is already spun.

ILLO: I saw your wife was smiling cunningly.
What is it, then?

TERZKY: A secret. Hush! She comes.

    [*Exit* ILLO.]

SCENE 2

[*Enter* COUNTESS TERZKY *from a side-chamber, then a* SERVANT *and after him* ILLO.]

TERZKY: Will she be here? I cannot keep him back.
COUNTESS: Straightway. Do you but send him in.
TERZKY: Indeed I do not know if we shall earn
　　His thanks for this. Upon this point, you know
　　He never has revealed his mind to us.
　　You have persuaded me and you must know
　　How far you dare to go.
COUNTESS:　　　　　　　On my head be it!
　　[*Aside*] What need is there of words? No, we two, brother,
　　We understand each other – Or do I
　　Guess wrongly why he called his daughter here,
　　Chose *him* of all to be his daughter's escort?
　　Let others be deceived by all this talk
　　Of a betrothal to an unknown bridegroom;
　　Not I! I understand your purposes. –
　　But it would not be fitting you should have
　　A hand in such affairs. They must be left
　　To me and to my skills. So be it! You
　　Shall not be disappointed in your sister!
　　　[*Enter a* SERVANT.]
SERVANT: The Generals! [*Exit.*]
TERZKY [*to the* COUNTESS]: Do you but take good care
　　To warm his brain, put thoughts into his head –
　　That when he comes to dinner, he will not
　　Be hesitant in signing.
COUNTESS: Go and attend your guests, and send him here!
TERZKY: For it is all-important he should sign.

COUNTESS: Your guests are waiting. Go!
   [*Re-enter* ILLO.]
ILLO: Where are you, Terzky?
   The hall is full, and all await your coming.
TERZKY: Yes, yes! –
   [*To the* COUNTESS] And let him not remain too long –
   His father otherwise might well suspect –
COUNTESS: You need not fear!
   [*Exeunt* TERZKY *and* ILLO.]

SCENE 3

[*Enter* MAX PICCOLOMINI.]

MAX [*peeping shyly in*]:   Dear cousin Terzky! Dare I?
   [*He advances to the centre of the room and looks anxiously around.*]
   She is not here! Where is she?
COUNTESS: Look well in
   The corner, see if she is hiding there
   Behind the screen –
MAX: Why, see, there are her gloves!
   [*He reaches quickly for them, but the* COUNTESS *picks them up.*]
   Oh, aunt, you are unkind! You will not say –
   You take your pleasure in tormenting me!
COUNTESS: Such thanks for all my pains!
MAX: Oh, if you knew
   My feelings. Ever since we have returned –
   To watch myself, to weigh each word, each look –
   I am not so accustomed!
COUNTESS: You will find
   Yourself accustomed, friend, to many things!

Upon this test of your submissiveness
I must insist, only on this condition
Can I consent to be your go-between.

MAX: But where, where is she? Why does she not come?

COUNTESS: You must leave matters in my hands alone.
What better ally could you have than me?
No one must know, not even your own father,
He least of all!

MAX: There is no need. No face
Do I see here to whom I would entrust
The secret wish that moves my raptured soul.
– O good aunt Terzky! Is then everything
Here changed, or I alone? I seem to find
Myself as among strangers. Not a trace
I find of all my former joys and wishes.
Where have they fled? I was not used to feel
Such lack of pleasure in the world I knew.
How shallow now it all appears, how petty!
My comrades' company I cannot bear,
My father even, him I cannot speak to,
Service and arms, they seem such empty toys.
So must a blessed spirit surely feel,
Who from the mansions of eternal joy
Returned to childish pastimes and pursuits,
Returned to ancient friendships and affections,
And to the common lot of mortal men.

COUNTESS: Yet I must ask that you will deign to cast
A further glance upon this petty world,
Where even now weighty events are moving.

MAX: Something about me is afoot, I see it
In all the unaccustomed stir and bustle;
When it is ripe, no doubt I'll hear of it.
Where do you think that I have been, good aunt?
But I'll not mock! I felt shut in amid
The camp's commotion, my acquaintances

Tortured me with their importuning, with
Their empty jests, their words so void of meaning.
I felt so close, I had to flee away,
To look for silence to assuage my heart,
A pure asylum for my happiness.
No, countess, do not smile! I went to church –
There is a convent here called Heaven's Gate;
There I went in, and found myself alone.
Above the altar hung the Virgin Mother;
A simple image, but it was the friend
That I was seeking in this very moment.
How often have I seen Her in Her glory
And splendour, seen Her worshippers adore Her –
It had not touched me; now at once I knew
The meaning of devotion and of love.

COUNTESS: Enjoy your happiness. Forget the world
About you. Friends shall watch and act for you.
But you must follow then, when you are shown
The way that leads you to your happy fortune.

MAX: But why is she not here? – O golden days
Upon our journey, when each morning's sun
Brought us together, night alone did part us!
No sands to run, no clock to strike the hour;
It seemed, such was my bliss, that time stood still,
Forgot to run its everlasting course.
Heaven already far is left behind me
When we must count the hours as they pass by!
No happy man must wait upon the clock.

COUNTESS: When did you first disclose your heart to her?

MAX: I did not dare a word until this morning.

COUNTESS: Three weeks, and not a word until today?

MAX: It happened in the hunting-lodge, between
This place and Nepomuk, where you had joined us,
The final resting-place upon our journey.
We stood there in a window-bay and cast

Our silent gaze upon the barren fields,
While the dragoons the Duke had sent to be
Our escort formed their ranks before our eyes.
Heavy the dread of parting lay upon me,
And at the last, I dared this trembling word:
Lady, this sight reminds me that today
My happiness and I must part. For you
New friends are waiting, in a few brief hours
Your father greets you; I shall be a stranger,
Lost from you in the crowd. – 'Speak to my aunt,
The Countess Terzky!' quickly she cut short
My words, her voice was trembling, and I saw
A blush of crimson stain her cheeks so fair;
Slowly her downcast eyes rise from the ground
To meet my own – I can control myself
No longer –

> [PRINCESS THEKLA *appears in the doorway and remains
> standing there, observed by the* COUNTESS *but not by*
> PICCOLOMINI.]

         – boldly seize her in my arms,
My lips touch hers – and then we hear a noise
In the next room, and part – it was yourself.
What happened more, you know.

COUNTESS [*after a pause, with a stealthy glance in* THEKLA'S
     direction]:
Are you so modest, then, or do you have
So little curiosity you do
Not ask me what *my* secret is?

MAX: Your secret?

COUNTESS: Why, yes! How, when I came into the room
So soon behind you, how I found my niece,
What, in that very moment of her heart's
Surprise, she –

MAX: What?

SCENE 4

[THEKLA *hurries forward to join them.*]

THEKLA: You need not trouble, aunt!
  Better that he should hear from me myself!
MAX: My lady!
  What were these things you made me say, aunt Terzky!
THEKLA: Has he been here for long?
COUNTESS: Indeed he has, and he must soon be gone.
  Where have you been this time?
THEKLA: My mother wept again. I see she grieves –
  And cannot help it that I am so happy!
MAX [*gazing rapt at her*]:
  Now I am bold to look at you again.
  Today I could not, for the precious stones
  That shone about you hid my love from me.
THEKLA: Your eye then looked alone, and not your heart.
MAX: Oh! When I came and saw you there this morning
  Amidst your own, and in your father's arms,
  Myself a stranger in their gathering –
  How fiercely in that moment I did long
  To fling my arms about his neck, to call
  Him father! But his eye was stern, and bid
  Me hold in check the flood of my emotion,
  And I was frightened by those diamonds
  That hung about you like a chain of stars.
  And why must he, as soon as he receives you,
  Cast on you such a spell, bedeck his angel
  As for a sacrifice, this happy heart
  Load with the dismal burden of his rank?
  Love unashamed to love may make its suit,
  No lesser than a king approach such glory.

THEKLA: Speak of this pantomime no more! You see
How soon the burden has been cast aside.
[*To the* COUNTESS] He is unhappy. Why should he be so?
You, aunt, have done this, cast his spirits down!
Why, he was quite another on our journey!
So calm and bright! So full of cheer! I wish
I always saw you so and never else!

MAX: You found yourself, within your father's arms,
In a new world, that brings its homage to you.

THEKLA: So much delights me, I cannot deny,
The stage of war, so bright with many colours,
That all around reflects a much-loved image,
And shows me that in life and truth appears
What I had thought must be a happy dream.

MAX: To me, it turns to dreams my present joy.
Upon an island in ethereal heights
I have been living in these days gone by;
Now it has sunk to rest upon the earth,
And now this bridge that leads me back into
My former life would part me from my heaven.

THEKLA: Serenely we may gaze upon life's play,
When in our hearts we bear a certain treasure,
And after I have gazed my fill, more gladly
Shall I return to that more fair possession! –
   [*Breaking off, and adopting a more playful tone*]
What novelties, what things unheard-of, have
I not beheld in this brief present time!
And yet not one of them can be compared
To the strange secret that this castle holds.

COUNTESS [*pondering*]:
What might this be? I think I know my way
Through every darkest corner of this house.

THEKLA [*smiling*]:
The way that leads to it is watched by spirits:
Two griffins mount their guard before its door.

COUNTESS [*laughing*]:
  Ah, yes! the astrologic tower! But could
  It be, this shrine so jealously defended
  Opened its doors to you but scarce arrived?
THEKLA: A little, aged man with long white hair
  And kindly face, whose favour I had gained
  Straightway, unlocked the doors and bade me enter.
MAX: Seni it is, the Duke's astrologer.
THEKLA: He questioned me so many things, when I
  Was born, which month and on which day it was,
  Whether by day or in the hours of night –
COUNTESS: That was to help him cast your horoscope.
THEKLA: He looked into my hand as well, and shook
  His head as if in doubt, and I believe
  The lines did not seem favourable to him.
COUNTESS: But once inside that room, what did you see?
  I never looked in there but fleetingly.
THEKLA: So strange a feeling came upon me, as
  I entered quickly from the day's bright glare.
  For suddenly dark night enveloped me,
  By strange illumination dimly lit.
  Around me in a semicircle stood
  The images of six or seven kings,
  Their sceptres in their hands, and on each head
  A star, and all the light within the tower
  Seemed only to proceed from those their stars.
  These were the seven planets, so my guide
  Explained to me, they ruled our destinies,
  And so it was as kings they were portrayed.
  The outermost, a dark and grim old man
  Whose star was dull and yellowish, was Saturn;
  He with the ruddy light, that opposite
  Him stood in warlike armour, that was Mars,
  And neither of them bringer of good fortune.
  But at his side a lady fair there stood,

Gentle the star that shimmered on her brow,
And that was Venus, harbinger of joy.
Upon the left stood winged Mercury;
And in the very centre silver-bright
A man serene, and with a kingly brow,
And that was Jupiter, my father's star,
And sun and moon on either hand beside him.

MAX: Oh! I will not reproach him for his faith
In spirits, and the power of the stars.
It is not only human pride that fills
The air with spirits and with secret forces,
A loving heart must also find the world
Of everyday too narrow, and a meaning
Far deeper lies in childhood's fairy-tales
Than in the truth that life would have us learn.
Only the realm of wonders so serene
Gives answer to the transports of our heart,
Opening wide its everlasting mansions,
And stretching forth a thousand fruitful branches,
Wherein the giddy spirit rocks in bliss.
The realm of fable is the home of love,
That gladly dwells with fairies, talismans,
Trusts willingly in gods, itself divine.
They are no more, the ancient race of fable,
The beauteous ones, our lands they have deserted;
And yet our heart must speak, the ancient longing
Brings back the ancient names that are its language,
And through the starry skies they wander now,
That once did friendly walk with us in life.
There from above they greet and smile on lovers
And still today all greatness we receive
From Jupiter, from Venus every grace.

THEKLA: Is this astrology, then gladly will
I make confession of this happy faith.
It is a soothing and a gracious thought

That far above us in the heights of heaven
Love's garland, at the moment we were born,
Was woven for us from the glittering stars.

COUNTESS: Not roses only, thorns heaven also bears,
Let us but hope they do not tear your garland.
What Venus, bearer of good fortune, joined,
Mars, the unlucky star, can quickly sever.

MAX: His gloomy rule will soon be at an end!
Blessings upon the Prince's earnest zeal,
He'll bind the olive in the laurel wreath
And set the joyful world at peace once more.
Then his great heart will know no further wish,
His deeds sufficiently assure his fame,
To his estates he will retire and stay,
To live but for himself and for his own.
At Gitschin and at Reichenberg and Friedland
Broad smiling lands are his, and houses fair;
To the Giant Mountains' very foot extend
His forests, and the woods his huntsmen roam.
His great ambition to create and build
He can pursue unhindered, every art
And everything that's glorious and noble
Encourage with his princely patronage –
Can cultivate the fields, observe the stars –
And if his strength and valour will not rest,
Then he may battle with the elements,
May turn aside the river, blast the rocks,
Make smooth the roads the merchant's foot may tread.
The histories of war will then be told
As tales to while away the winter evenings –

COUNTESS: And yet, good cousin, if I may advise you,
Do not put up your sword before its time!
For such a bride as this, is she not worthy
That you should woo her with your skill in battle?

MAX: Oh! could she but be won by force of arms!

COUNTESS: But what was that? Did you not hear? I thought
I heard loud argument and noise at table. [*Exit.*]

SCENE 5

[THEKLA *and* MAX PICCOLOMINI.]

THEKLA [*as soon as the* COUNTESS *has left them, quickly and
    secretively to* PICCOLOMINI]:
    Do not believe them. They are false.

MAX: Could they –

THEKLA: Trust no one here but me. I saw at once,
    They have some purpose.

MAX: Purpose! What could that be?
    What could it help them to encourage us –

THEKLA: I do not know. But be assured they do
    Not mean to make us happy, to unite us.

MAX: Why do we need these Terzkys? Have we not
    Your mother? Kind and gracious as she is,
    Surely she must deserve our confidence.

THEKLA: She loves you and esteems you above all,
    But never would she have the courage to
    Withhold such secret from my father's ear!
    So for the sake of her own peace we must
    Not tell her this.

MAX: But why then everywhere
    This secrecy? You know what I will do?
    I will go straight and kneel before your father,
    He shall decide my fortune, he is frank
    And undeceiving, hates their crooked ways.
    He is so good and noble –

THEKLA: That are you!

MAX: You have not known him till today. But I

Have lived for ten years now in sight of him.
Why, would it be the first time he had done
A strange, unhoped-for thing? It is his way
To overwhelm us like a god, he must
Amaze us always and transport our souls.
Who knows but he this minute only waits
To hear myself, to hear yourself confess it,
To make us one – You do not speak. You look
At me in doubt? What can you hold against your father?

THEKLA: I? Nothing – Only that he seems too busy
To have the time and leisure to be thinking
Of us and of our happiness.
[*Tenderly taking his hand*]   Trust me!
Let us not put our faith too much in others.
We must be grateful to these Terzkys for
The favours that they show us, but confide
In them no more than they deserve, and for
The rest – rely upon our hearts alone.

MAX: Oh! Shall we ever in this world be happy!

THEKLA: Are we not happy? Are you not mine? Am I
Not yours? Within my soul there dwells
A noble courage love bestows on me –
I should not be so open, should conceal
My heart from you, so custom would demand.
But where would truth be found in all this place
If you could not receive it from my lips?
See, we have found each other, hold each other
Tightly embraced, for ever. Oh, believe me!
This is far more than they had ever wished.
So let us guard it like a stolen prize
And keep it sacred in our heart of hearts.
It came upon us as a gift from heaven,
Let us give thanks for it to heaven alone!
For heaven may work a miracle.

SCENE 6

[*Enter* COUNTESS TERZKY.]

COUNTESS [*in haste*]:
  My husband sends for you. It is high time
  To come to table –
    [*As they take no notice, she separates them.*]
                      Part!
THEKLA: Oh! must this be?
  It is but scarce a moment.
COUNTESS: It seems time flies for you, my princely niece.
MAX: There is no hurry, cousin.
COUNTESS: Come! you're missed;
  The Duke her father twice has asked for you.
THEKLA: My father! Oh!
COUNTESS: So now you see, my niece.
THEKLA: Why must he always join their company?
  It is not right for him; they may be men
  Of worth and of repute, but he is still
  Too young, he is no company for them.
COUNTESS: So you would rather keep him for yourself?
THEKLA [*with animation*]:
  That is my mind exactly, you have guessed it!
  Let him stay here, yes, tell the gentlemen –
COUNTESS: Niece, have you lost your wits entirely? –
    Count!
  You know what the conditions were –
MAX: Lady, I must obey. Good-bye –
    [*As* THEKLA *turns quickly away from him.*]
                      What is it?
THEKLA [*without looking at him*]:
  Why, nothing. Go.

MAX: How can I, when I see
   You angry –
   [*He approaches her; their eyes meet, she stands still for a moment in silence, then throws herself upon his breast; he presses her tightly to him.*]

COUNTESS: Come! If anyone should see!
   I hear a noise – strange voices drawing near.
   [MAX *tears himself from her embrace and goes out, the* COUNTESS *accompanying him.* THEKLA *at first lets her eyes follow him, then paces the room in agitation before standing still lost in thought. She picks up a guitar which is lying on the table, and after playing a melancholy prelude, begins to sing.*]

SCENE 7

THEKLA [*plays and sings*]:
         The clouds rush by, the oak-trees roar,
         The maiden wanders upon the shore,
         The waves so heavily, heavily break,
         The maiden sings in the night so bleak,
         Her eyes dim with weeping, alone.

         The world so empty, so dead my heart's fire,
         No more can there be to delight my desire,
         Thou holy one, call back thy child to thy breast,
         I have tasted earth's joys, and now I would rest,
         For life, ah! and love I have known.

SCENE 8

[*Re-enter* COUNTESS TERZKY.]

COUNTESS: Niece, what was this? Fie, must you throw
    yourself
At him? It would befit you, I had thought,
To set a higher price upon yourself.

THEKLA [*standing up*]:
  What do you mean, aunt?

COUNTESS: You should not forget,
  Niece, who you are, and who he is. Why, I
  Believe you have not thought of it!

THEKLA: Of what?

COUNTESS: That you are daughter of the Prince of Friedland.

THEKLA: Why, then, what of it?

COUNTESS: What? A pretty question!

THEKLA: What we have but become, he is by birth.
  He is of ancient Lombard family,
  His mother a princess.

COUNTESS: I think you dream!
  Indeed! Are we to go and humbly beg
  Him favour Europe's richest heiress with
  His hand?

THEKLA: I think there is no need of that.

COUNTESS: Yes, one is well advised to take no risks.

THEKLA: His father loves him, Count Octavio
  Will not object –

COUNTESS: *His* father! *His*! And *yours*, my niece?

THEKLA: Why, yes, indeed! I think you fear *his* father,
  Because from *him* you have concealed it so.

COUNTESS [*looking searchingly at her*]:
  Niece, you are playing false.

THEKLA: Oh, aunt, be kind,
Do not be angry with me!
COUNTESS: Do you think
That you have won your game already?
Do not rejoice too soon!
THEKLA: Be kind, I beg!
COUNTESS: We are not yet so far in this!
THEKLA: No, no!
COUNTESS: Do you believe that he has spent a life
Of such importance in the toils of war,
Denied himself all quiet and happiness,
Exposed his noble head to pain and care,
Only to make a happy pair of you?
To bring you from your convent, finally,
To lead you home in triumph to the man
Your fancy lights on! That he could have had
Much cheaper! No, he did not sow this seed
For you to pluck its flower with childish hand
And wear it at your breast in ornament
So lightly!
THEKLA: That which he did not plant for me could yet
Bear of itself for me its fairest fruit.
And if my good and kindly destiny
Seeks in the fearful shadow of his being
To nourish and bring forth my life's own joy –
COUNTESS: You see these matters like a love-sick girl.
Look here about. Consider where you are –
It is no pleasure-seat that you have entered,
No wedding-ornaments bedeck the walls
Or crown the heads of guests. Here you will see
No gleam but that of arms. Or did you think
That all these thousands had been here assembled
To be the guard of honour at your wedding?
You see your father's brow is veiled in thought,
Your mother weeping; in the balance lies

Our house's fate, its mighty destiny!
Leave now the childish feelings of a girl,
The petty wishes, far behind you! Prove
That you are daughter to this peerless man!
A woman may not claim to own herself,
To others' fate she is too firmly bound;
But she does best, who of her own free will
Can make that other hers, can bear it in
Her heart, give it her love and her devotion.

THEKLA: Those were the words repeated in the convent.
I had no wishes, knew myself but as
His daughter, daughter of that mighty man,
The echo of his life, that reached me too,
Gave me no other feeling but that I
Was destined to submit to him alone.

COUNTESS: That is your fate. Accept it willingly.
I and your mother set you our example.

THEKLA: Now fate has shown me him to whom I must
Submit, and I will follow him with joy.

COUNTESS: It is your heart, dear child, and not your fate.

THEKLA: Our own heart's prompting is the voice of fate.
I can be his alone. It is his gift
To me, this fair new life that now I live.
He has a right to what he has created.
For what was I, before his love inspired me?
Nor will I of myself think less than does
My love. He cannot be so petty who
Possesses such a treasure. And I feel
New strength my happiness has given me.
Gravely my soul sees life lie grave before it.
That I may claim to own myself, I know now.
I am acquainted with the strength of will,
Indomitable, here in my own breast,
And for the highest I can stake my all.

COUNTESS: And you would set yourself against your father,

If he has made a different choice for you?
You think you can compel him? Know, my child,
His name is Friedland.

THEKLA: It is my name too,
And he shall find I am indeed his daughter.

COUNTESS: His emperor, his monarch cannot force him,
And you, his child, would battle with his will?

THEKLA: What no man dares, his daughter dares to do.

COUNTESS: Why now, indeed! This he will not expect,
When every obstacle was overcome,
To find his very daughter's own self-will
Offer fresh opposition! Child! my child!
You have as yet but seen your father's smile,
You have not seen his eye aflame with anger.
What, will you dare to raise your trembling voice
In contradiction, when you stand before him?
Indeed, when you are by yourself, you may compose
Fine speeches, think yourself an orator,
Arm dove-like spirits with a tiger's strength.
But try! Do you but step into his presence,
His eye upon you fixed, and say your no!
You will dissolve before him, as the flower
Will wilt and droop before the fiery sunbeam.
– Dear child, I do not seek to frighten you!
You will not take that fatal step, I hope –
Nor do I know what is his will. Perhaps
His purposes accord with your desire.
But never, never can it be his will
That you, proud daughter of his fairest fortune,
Behave like any common love-sick girl,
And throw yourself before the man who, if
Such high reward is meant for him, shall pay
The highest price that love alone can bear! [Exit.]

SCENE 9

THEKLA [*alone*]:
   I thank you for this warning! Certain
   It makes my evil intimations now.
   So it is true? No one we have to call
   Our friend and no one here to trust – we have
   Ourselves alone. Fierce struggles lie before us.
   O love, O power divine, give us your strength!
   It is the truth she speaks! No happy signs
   Attend our hearts' alliance with their light.
   This is no place where hope was ever found.
   Here but the dismal clang of war resounds,
   And even love itself must tread the stage
   As clad in steel, in combat to the death.
   A spirit dark upon our house does brood,
   And destiny would strike us from its roll.
   It comes to drive me from my quietude,
   A tender magic must bewitch my soul.
   It calls, enchants me with its godlike form,
   Closer it comes, and holds me in its sway,
   Bearing me onward with its mighty storm
   To the abyss, I cannot bid it stay.
      [*Distant music is heard from the dinner-tables.*]
   When dynasties go to their fiery end,
   Then heaven shall pile its thunderclouds on high,
   From skies serene the lightning blasts descend,
   The subterranean flames assault the sky,
   In fury blind, the very god of joy
   With his own hand the blazing house destroy!

ACT FOUR

Scene: A large hall, brightly lit for a feast. In the middle, towards the back of the stage, a richly decorated table, at which are sitting eight generals, including OCTAVIO PICCOLOMINI, TERZKY *and* MARADAS. *To right and left, further back, are two more tables, each with six dinner-guests sitting at it. Downstage, the buttery table, leaving the whole front of the stage free for the* PAGES *and* SERVANTS *waiting on the guests. All is in lively motion;* MUSICIANS *from Terzky's regiment are passing over the stage between the tables. Before they have completely disappeared from the scene, enter* MAX PICCOLOMINI; *coming to meet him* TERZKY *with a document,* ISOLANI *with a drinking-goblet.*

SCENE I

[TERZKY, ISOLANI, MAX PICCOLOMINI.]

ISOLANI: Brother, by all that's dear! Where have you been?
   Come, find your place, and quickly! Terzky has
   Been broaching all his mother's finest wines,
   It's like the palace feast at Heidelberg.
   The best has gone already. Over there
   They're sharing prince's bonnets out between them;
   Slavata's, Eggenberg's and Liechtenstein's,
   Sternberg's estates are going for the asking,
   And all the great Bohemian fiefs; if you
   Are quick, you'll find there's something left for you.
   Hurry! Sit down!

COLALTO *and* GÖTZ [*call out from the second table*]:
                    Count Piccolomini!
TERZKY: Yes, you shall have him! Straightway! – Read this
    oath
  We have composed, and see if you approve it.
  Each man that's here has read it in his turn,
  And everyone will put his name to it.
MAX [*reads*]: '*Ingratis servire nefas.*'
ISOLANI: That sounds like Latin. Brother, can you tell
  Us what it means?
TERZKY: No man that is a man serves thankless masters.
MAX: 'Whereas our most puissant commander, the noble and
  excellent Prince of Friedland, on account of many griev-
  ances endured, having been minded to quit the Emperor's
  service, has nonetheless allowed himself to be persuaded by
  our unanimous pleas, to remain still with the army and not
  to leave us without our assent; so we all together likewise,
  and each one of us for himself, shall be held obliged, as by
  the oath of our bodies, to remain true and loyal to him in
  return, in no wise to part from him, and to venture for him
  all that is our own, to the last drop of our blood, in so far as
  shall be *permitted by the oath we have sworn the Emperor.*

  [*The last words are repeated by* ISOLANI.]
  Likewise do we declare, if any man of us, this treaty not-
  withstanding, shall separate himself from the common
  cause, that that man shall be considered a traitor and a
  renegade, and that we shall be held bound to take revenge
  upon him, life and limb and upon his worldly goods. To
  which our signatures this day bear witness.'
TERZKY: Tell us, will you consent to sign this paper?
ISOLANI: Why should he not! No officer, no man
  Of honour can refuse – hey, pen and ink there!
TERZKY: Wait, until after dinner.
ISOLANI [*dragging* MAX *with him*]: Come then, come!
    [*Both go to table.*]

SCENE 2

[TERZKY, NEUMANN.]

TERZKY [*signals to* NEUMANN, *who is waiting at the buttery table, and comes forward with him*]:
Have you the copy, Neumann? Here! Drawn up,
So that it may be taken for the other?
NEUMANN: I copied it exactly, line for line,
Only the phrase about the oath left out,
Just as your excellence commanded me.
TERZKY: Good. Put it there, and this one straight into
The fire! The purpose of it has been served.

[NEUMANN *puts the copy on the table and returns to the buttery table*.]

SCENE 3

[*Enter* ILLO *from a room adjoining at the back.*]
ILLO: How is it with young Piccolomini?
TERZKY: Good, I believe. He said no word against it.
ILLO: He is the only one I do not trust,
He and his father – Keep a watch on both!
TERZKY: How does your table look, my friend? I hope
You keep your guests well-warmed.
ILLO: They are
Most cordial. I think they will be ours.
And as I told you it would be – Already
They say they're not content to save the Duke's
Position and his honour. Since they are
Assembled, so says Montecuculi,

They should be marching on Vienna, there
To make the Emperor agree their terms! Believe me,
But for these Piccolomini alone,
We could have spared the trouble of our ruse.
TERZKY: Quiet! What can Butler want?

SCENE 4

[BUTLER *joins them from the second table.*]

BUTLER: I'll not disturb you.
  I understand you very well, Field-Marshal.
  Wish you good fortune – and, for my own part, –
    [*Confidentially*] You may be sure of me.
ILLO [*with animation*]:   May count on you?
BUTLER: With or without proviso! I care not!
  You understand? The Prince can put my loyalty
  To any test he likes – so you may tell him.
  I am the Emperor's officer, as long
  As he remains the Emperor's general;
  And I am Friedland's slave, as soon as he
  Is pleased to own no master but himself.
TERZKY: You make a good exchange. It is no miser,
  No Ferdinand to whom you swear your oath.
BUTLER [*gravely*]:
  My loyalty is not for sale, Count Terzky,
  It was no good idea, six months ago,
  To seek to buy what now I freely offer.
  I bring with me my regiment to serve
  The Duke, and I do not believe that others
  Will fail to follow where I give the lead.
ILLO: Who does not know that Colonel Butler is
  The paragon whom all our troops admire!

BUTLER: Indeed, Field-Marshal? Why, then, I do not
　　Regret my loyalty these forty years,
　　If my good name, preserved with such good care,
　　Now I am sixty, buys such sweet revenge! –
　　Let not my words dismay you, gentlemen,
　　You will not be concerned *how* you have won me,
　　And scarcely will yourselves expect, I think,
　　That tricks of crookedness will mar my judgement –
　　Scarcely believe hot blood or fickle temper
　　Or such slight cause could tempt a grey-haired man
　　To quit the path of honour, trod so long.
　　Come, come! I am for that no less resolved,
　　Knowing so clearly what it is I forfeit.
ILLO: Speak, tell us plainly what we are to think!
BUTLER: That I am your good friend! My hand on it,
　　With everything I have I am your man.
　　Not troops alone, the Prince needs money too.
　　Some fortune I have gained in serving him,
　　I'll lend it him, and if he should outlive me,
　　He is my heir, so I have long decided.
　　I stand alone here in the world, I do
　　Not know the feeling that can bind a man
　　Close to a wife, to children that he loves;
　　My name will die with me and be no more.
ILLO: Your money it is not we need – a heart
　　Like yours is worth its weight in gold and treasures.
BUTLER: I came, a simple squire, to Prague from Ireland
　　And buried there the knight I came to serve;
　　From humble duties in the stable rose
　　By skill in war to rank and eminence,
　　A lucky plaything of capricious fate.
　　Wallenstein too is wilful Fortune's child;
　　I love to see a path that's like my own.
ILLO: All mighty souls are to each other kin.
BUTLER: It is a great and a momentous hour,

The bold it favours and the resolute.
City and castle pass from hand to hand,
Change owners with no more ado than coin.
The sons of ancient lines are lost to view,
New names arise, new coats-of-arms are seen;
Unwelcome on the soil of Germany
Bold strangers from the north would stay and settle.
The Prince of Weimar arms himself with might
To found beside the Main a new dominion;
Mansfeld and Halberstadt, if they had lived
A few years more, could well have won themselves
Estates and realms upon the battlefield.
And who amongst all these can match with Friedland?
There's nothing is so lofty but the strong
Will claim the right to scale it with his ladder.

TERZKY: Why, this is spoken like a man!

BUTLER: Will you
Make sure of the Italians and Spaniards;
The Scotsman Leslie you may leave to me.
Come now, to table, come!

TERZKY: Where is the cellarer?
Bring up more wine! Let's see the best you have!
Today decides, and things stand well with us!

   [*Exeunt, each for his table.*]

SCENE 5

[CELLARER *and* NEUMANN *come forward.* SERVANTS
pass to and fro.]

CELLARER: Such noble wines! If only my old mistress,
His mother, saw such riotous behaviour,
I think she'd turn within her very grave!

Yes, yes, sir officer! This noble house
Is falling – see, they know no moderation!
And now the Duke's his lordship's brother-in-law;
Alliances like this bring us no blessings!

NEUMANN: Fie, in God's name! Your fortune's yet to bloom.

CELLARER: Yóu think so? I could say a thing or two!

SERVANT [entering]:
More burgundy! they cry at the fourth table.

CELLARER: Lieutenant, that makes seventy bottles now.

SERVANT: That German, Tiefenbach, is sitting there,
You see! [Exit.]

CELLARER [continues, to NEUMANN]:
            They aim too high. They want to set themselves
Beside Electors, act the part of kings,
And where the Prince dares set his foot, the Count
My gracious master will not stay behind!
[To the servants] Why do you stand there listening? I'll teach
    you!
See to the tables, see to the bottles! There!
Count Palffy has an empty glass before him!

SECOND SERVANT [entering]:
They want the goblet, master cellarer,
The golden cup with the Bohemian arms,
You know the one they mean, the master said.

CELLARER: The one that master William made himself,
To celebrate King Frederick's coronation?
The finest prize that we brought home from Prague?

SECOND SERVANT: Yes, that's the one! They want to pass it
    round.

CELLARER [shaking his head, taking out the goblet and rinsing it]:
More gossip to be carried to Vienna!

NEUMANN: Show me! That goblet is a masterpiece!
Such heavy gold; and here, in high relief,
Skilful designs are formed upon its surface.
There on the first escutcheon, let me see!

A haughty amazon upon a charger
Leaps over bishops' croziers and mitres,
Bearing a hat aloft upon a staff,
A banner too, emblazoned with a chalice.
Now, can you tell me what this all may mean?

CELLARER: The lady you see sitting there on horseback,
Is the elective freedom of Bohemia's crown.
You see this represented by the hat,
And by the fiery steed she rides upon.
The hat's the noblest ornament a man
May wear, for he who may not keep his hat
Upon his head before an Emperor
Or king is not a man at liberty.

NEUMANN: What is the chalice there upon the banner?

CELLARER: The liberty of the Bohemian church,
Such as it was in our forefathers' times.
For in the Hussite wars, our fathers won
That precious right the Pope keeps jealously,
For he will grant the chalice to no layman.
The chalice is our greatest privilege,
Our rarest jewel, for which Bohemia's sons
Have shed their blood in many fearful battles.

NEUMANN: The scroll above it, what does that convey?

CELLARER: It is Bohemia's Letter of Majesty,
That we compelled from Emperor Rudolf's hand,
A document to us beyond all price,
That guarantees the new faith like the old
Its public worship and its peal of bells.
But now, since Ferdinand has come to rule us,
All that is at an end, and since the battle
At the White Hill, where Frederick lost his crown,
Our faith has lost its pulpits and its altars,
Our brothers turn their backs upon their homeland,
And Emperor Ferdinand tore up the Letter
Of Majesty himself, with his own hands.

NEUMANN: You know all this! Why, master cellarer,
   You have your country's history by heart!
CELLARER: My ancestors were Taborites, lieutenant,
   And served with Prokop and with Zizka too.
   Peace be upon their bones! The cause was good
   They fought for – Come and take this to the table!
NEUMANN: Let me first see the other scutcheon there.
   Why, see, there are the Emperor's ministers.
   Martinitz and Slavata, being thrown
   Head over heels out of Prague castle window!
   Yes, look! there stands Count Thurn and gives the order.
   [*Exit* SERVANT *with the goblet.*]
CELLARER: O do not speak to me of that – it was
   The twenty-third of May, the year of grace
   One thousand and six hundred and eighteen.
   It seems to me as if it were today,
   And from that ill-starred day began the woes,
   The torment of our land, and sixteen years
   Have passed since there was peace on earth –
A VOICE [*calls out at the second table*]:
   The Prince of Weimar!
VOICES [*at the third and fourth tables*]:
                  Long life to Duke Bernard!
   [*Music.*]
FIRST SERVANT: Hark, what a tumult!
SECOND SERVANT [*enters, running*]: Did you hear? They drink
   The health of Weimar!
THIRD SERVANT: Austria's foe!
FIRST SERVANT: The Lutheran!
SECOND SERVANT: Just now, when Deodati called for them
   To drink the Emperor's health, they all were silent!
CELLARER: It is the wine. A servant, if he knows
   His duty, will not listen to such things.
THIRD SERVANT [*aside, to* FOURTH SERVANT]:
   Keep your ears open, Johann, we must tell

Father Quiroga all the things we hear;
He'll give us dispensation from our sins!

FOURTH SERVANT: That's why I find myself so many errands
That take me by the place where Illo sits;
If you but heard the words that pass his lips!

[*They go to the tables.*]

CELLARER [*to* NEUMANN]:
Who is the gentleman in black, there with
The cross, who has so much to tell Count Palffy?

NEUMANN: Another of those ones they trust too much,
A Spaniard, Don Maradas is his name.

CELLARER: I tell you there is nothing to the Spaniards,
These Southerners are all no good.

NEUMANN: What, now?
You must not say so, master cellarer!
The greatest generals are some of them,
The very ones the Duke regards so highly.

[TERZKY *comes and fetches the paper. There is a stir at the
tables.*]

CELLARER [*to the* SERVANTS]:
The lieutenant-general has stood up. Look out there!
They're leaving table. Go and take their chairs!

[*The* SERVANTS *hurry upstage, as a number of the guests
come forward.*]

SCENE 6

[OCTAVIO PICCOLOMINI *and* MARADAS, *in conversation, advance to the very front of the stage, at one side
of the proscenium. Enter at the other side* MAX
PICCOLOMINI, *alone, lost in thought and taking no
notice of the other proceedings. In the space between them,
but a few paces upstage,* BUTLER, ISOLANI, GÖTZ,
TIEFENBACH, COLALTO, *and soon after* TERZKY.]

ISOLANI [*as the company advances downstage*]:
   Good night! Good night, Colalto – lieutenant-general,
   Good night! Or should I rather say good morning!
GÖTZ [*to* TIEFENBACH]:
   Brother, your health! Until the next time!
TIEFENBACH: That was a feast fit for a king!
GÖTZ: The Countess
   Knows how to do such things. Her husband's mother –
   God rest her soul – she taught her. That was a lady!
ISOLANI [*making to leave*]: Lights, lights, I say!
TERZKY [*bringing the paper to* ISOLANI]:
   Brother, I beg two minutes more. Here is
   A paper that must still be signed.
ISOLANI: I'll sign
   What you desire, but do not make me read it.
TERZKY: I'll spare you that. It is the oath that you
   Have seen already. Here, a stroke or two!
      [*As* ISOLANI *passes the paper to* OCTAVIO]
   Just as you come! No rank or precedence!
      [OCTAVIO *glances over the paper with apparent indifference.*
      TERZKY *watches him from a distance.*]
GÖTZ [*to* TERZKY]: Permit me, count, to take my leave of
      you.
TERZKY: You must not hurry so – A nightcap –
                        [*To the* SERVANTS] Hey!
GÖTZ: I've had enough.
TERZKY: A game or so.
GÖTZ: Excuse me!
TIEFENBACH [*sitting down*]:
   Forgive me, gentlemen, I must sit down.
TERZKY: Why, master of the ordnance, as you wish!
TIEFENBACH: My head is clear, my stomach in good order,
   Only my legs decline to do their duty.
ISOLANI [*indicating his corpulence*]:
   I think that you have over-burdened them.

[OCTAVIO *has signed and hands the paper to* TERZKY, *who passes it to* ISOLANI; *he goes to the table to sign.*]

TIEFENBACH: It's from the war in Pomerania,
We had to take the field in ice and snow,
I'll not get over it in all my days.

GÖTZ: The Swedes! They cared not what the season was.

[TERZKY *passes the paper to* DON MARADAS, *who goes to the table to sign.*]

OCTAVIO [*approaching* BUTLER]:
You do not seem to like these Bacchic revels,
Colonel, as I have noticed, and I think
That you would rather hear the din
Of battle than of merriment and feasting.

BUTLER: I must admit, it is not to my taste.

OCTAVIO [*confidingly, approaching closer*]:
Nor is it to my own, I can assure you,
And I am glad, most worthy Colonel Butler,
That we should think alike upon this matter.
No more than half-a-dozen of one's friends,
A small, round table, and a glass or two
Of good Tokay, a frank and open heart,
Sensible talk – yes, that is how I like it!

BUTLER: Yes, if it can be so, I'll gladly join.

[*The paper is passed to* BUTLER, *who goes to the table to sign. The proscenium is left empty, with only the* TWO PICCOLO-MINI *standing at either side.*]

OCTAVIO [*after observing his son silently from a distance for some time, approaching him a little*]:
We have had long to wait for you, my friend.

MAX [*turning quickly, embarrassed*]:
I – urgent business kept me back elsewhere.

OCTAVIO: And you are hardly with us even now?

MAX: You know such tumult always makes me silent.

OCTAVIO [*drawing closer to him*]:
I may not know what kept you back so long? [*Slyly*]

– But Terzky knows it!

MAX: What does Terzky know?

OCTAVIO [*meaningfully*]:
He was the only one that did not miss you.

ISOLANI [*who has been observing them from a distance, joining them*]:
Right, father! Fall upon his baggage-train!
Break up his camp! This is no way to treat us!

TERZKY [*coming with the paper*]:
Are there no more? Has everybody signed?

OCTAVIO: Yes, everyone.

TERZKY [*calling out*]: Here! Who is still to sign?

BUTLER [*to* TERZKY]:
Count them! There should be thirty names exactly.

TERZKY: Here is a cross.

TIEFENBACH: The cross is mine.

ISOLANI [*to* TERZKY]:
He cannot write his name, but makes a cross;
Christian and Jew will all accept his mark.

OCTAVIO [*hurriedly, to* MAX]:
Come, colonel, it is late. We'll go together.

TERZKY: I only see one Piccolomini.

ISOLANI [*pointing at* MAX]:
Look, there's the missing one, the guest of stone,
Who has deserted us the whole night through!

SCENE 7

[*Enter* ILLO *from the further room, holding the golden goblet in his hand and in great excitement. After him* GÖTZ *and* BUTLER, *who are trying to hold him back.*]

ILLO: What do you want? Let go!

GÖTZ *and* BUTLER: Illo! Stop drinking!

ILLO [*going up to* OCTAVIO *and embracing him, drinking*]:
    Octavio! Your health, sir! Let us drown
    Resentment in a draught of brotherhood!
    I know you never liked me – and God knows,
    Nor did I you! But let what's past be past
    And done with! I esteem you very highly,
       [*Kissing him repeatedly*]
    I am your truest friend, and hear you all!
    If any of you calls him foxy traitor,
    He'll have to deal with me!
TERZKY [*aside*]:   Are you insane?
    Illo, remember where you are!
ILLO [*stoutly*]:
    What is the matter? We are all good friends!
       [*Beaming at all those around with a self-satisfied expression*]
    There are no villains here, I'm glad to see.
TERZKY [*to* BUTLER, *urgently*]:
    Take him away with you, I beg you, Butler.
       [BUTLER *takes him off to the buttery table.*]
ISOLANI [*to* MAX, *who has been staring fixedly but absent-
    mindedly at the paper*]:
    Well, brother, have you studied it enough?
MAX [*as if waking from a dream*]:
    What must I do?
TERZKY *and* ISOLANI [*together*]: Just sign your name
    below.
       [OCTAVIO *is seen to be watching him with tense anxiety.*]
MAX [*giving back the paper*]:
    No, wait until tomorrow. It is business,
    I have no mind today. Bring it tomorrow.
TERZKY: Consider, though –
ISOLANI: Quick! Sign your name! What next!
    He is the youngest head of all those here,
    Does he believe that he alone is wiser
    Than all the rest together? Look! Your father

Has signed it too, and so has everyone!

TERZKY [*to* OCTAVIO]:

Can you not use your influence to persuade him?

OCTAVIO: My son has come of age.

ILLO [*has put the goblet down on the serving table*]: What are you
  saying?

TERZKY: He has refused to sign the declaration.

MAX: I say that it can wait until tomorrow.

ILLO: It cannot wait. We all have signed the paper,
  And you, you too, *must* give your signature.

MAX: Illo, sleep well.

ILLO: No! You shall not escape!
  The Prince must know for sure who are his friends.
  [*All the guests gather round the two of them.*]

MAX: My feelings for the Prince he knows full well,
  You know them all, what need of these charades?

ILLO: There's gratitude, this is the Duke's reward,
  For always favouring these southerners!

TERZKY [*in the greatest embarrassment, to the commanders who
    are gathering closer round*]:

  It is the wine! I beg you, take no notice!

ISOLANI [*laughing*]:

  Wine blurts out secrets, it does not invent them!

ILLO: The man that is not *for* me is against me!
  Their tender consciences! If they had not
  Found some back door, included some proviso –

TERZKY [*interrupting quickly*]:

  His senses have quite left him, do not listen!

ILLO [*shouting more loudly*]:

  Included some proviso to excuse them!
  Proviso! Why, to hell with their proviso –

MAX [*taking notice, and looking at the paper again*]:

  What can it be that is so dangerous?
  You make me curious to look again!

TERZKY [*aside to* ILLO]:

What are you doing, Illo? You will ruin us!

TIEFENBACH [to COLALTO]:

I thought it sounded different before.

GÖTZ: Yes, before dinner.

ISOLANI: What do I care for that?

Where others set their names, I can do likewise.

TIEFENBACH: There was a reservation, I remember,

And a proviso of the Emperor's service.

BUTLER [to one of the commanders]:

Shame on you, sirs! Think what it is at issue!

The question is, whether we are to keep

The General or let him go from us?

We cannot be so nice or so exact.

ISOLANI [to one of the generals]:

What, did the Prince take refuge in provisos,

When he presented you your regiment?

TERZKY [to GÖTZ]:

You the supplies, that brought you a return

Of nigh a thousand pistoles in a year?

ILLO: Scoundrels yourselves, to make us play the villain!

Who's not content, speak out, and here stand I!

TIEFENBACH: Now, now! We only spoke.

MAX [returns the paper, after reading it]: Tomorrow, then!

ILLO [stammering with rage and no longer able to control himself, holding out to him in one hand the paper, in the other his sword]:

Sign – Judas!

ISOLANI: Illo, shame!

OCTAVIO, TERZKY, BUTLER [together]:

                              Up with your sword!

MAX [seizing him quickly by the arm and taking away his weapon; to TERZKY]: Put him to bed!

[Exit. Some of the commanders take hold of ILLO, who is uttering curses and abuse. As the company breaks up, the curtain falls.]

ACT FIVE

Scene: A room in PICCOLOMINI's *apartments. It is night.*

SCENE I

[OCTAVIO PICCOLOMINI. SERVANT *holding a light. Shortly afterwards,* MAX PICCOLOMINI.]

OCTAVIO: Show in my son to me, as soon as he
Is here – What is the time?
SERVANT: Almost the morning.
OCTAVIO: Put down your light – We shall not want to go
To bed tonight, but you may go and sleep.
　　[*Exit* SERVANT. OCTAVIO *paces the room in thought.
　　Enter* MAX PICCOLOMINI, *whom he does not immediately
　　notice, and who observes him in silence for a few moments.*]
MAX: Octavio, are you angry? God be with me,
That hateful quarrel was no fault of mine.
– Of course, I saw that you had signed the paper;
What you approved, I could have well
Agreed to – but it seemed – you know – I can
Not follow others' lights in such a matter,
Only my own.
OCTAVIO [*goes up to him and embraces him*]:
　　　　　　　　Follow your own light still,
My son ! It has conducted you more surely
Thus far than the example of your father.
MAX: Explain yourself more clearly.
OCTAVIO: I will do so.
After the things that we have seen tonight,

No secret may remain between us two.
   [*They both sit down.*]
Max, tell me what you think, then, of that oath
They put before us for our signature?

MAX: It seemed a harmless thing enough to me,
Although I do not love these formal phrases.

OCTAVIO: There was no other reason you withheld
The signature that they demanded of you?

MAX: No – it was *business*, and I was distracted –
The thing itself did not appear so urgent –

OCTAVIO: Be frank now, Max. Did you have no
    suspicion –

MAX: Suspicion, why, of what? No, not the least.

OCTAVIO: Now thank your guardian angel, Piccolomini!
Innocent yet, he held you from the brink.

MAX: I do not understand.

OCTAVIO: I will explain.
To monstrous villainy you were to lend
Your name, abjure your duty and your oath
Of loyalty with one stroke of the pen.

MAX [*standing up*]: Octavio!

OCTAVIO: Sit still, my friend, for there
Is much that you have yet to hear; for years
In wondrous ignorance you have been living.
The blackest of intrigues has spun itself
Before your eyes, the very power of hell
Veils with its clouds the daylight of your senses –
I can no longer hold my peace, I must
Remove the bandage from your eyes –

MAX: But first,
Before you speak, consider! If surmise
Is all you have to tell me – and I fear
It can be little more – then spare me! As
My mind is now disposed, I cannot hear it.

OCTAVIO: However grave your cause to flee this light,

More urgent mine to bring it to your eyes.
Till now I could entrust you to your heart,
To your own judgement and your innocence.
But when I see them spread their fatal nets
To snare that very heart – the secret which
  [*Staring pointedly at him*]
You keep from me makes me disclose my own.
  [MAX *attempts to answer, but cannot speak, and casts his eyes*
  down in confusion.]

OCTAVIO [*after a pause*]:
Know then! They have betrayed you – they are playing
A shameful game with you and with us all.
The Duke pretends that he is of a mind
To leave the army; and this very hour
Their plans are laid to steal the army from
The Emperor and to lead it to our foes!

MAX: I know that tale the priests tell, but I did
Not think that I should hear it from *your* lips.

OCTAVIO: The lips from which you hear it at this moment
Assure you that it is no tale of priests.

MAX: What madness they would credit to the Duke!
How could he think of luring thirty thousand
Well-tried and trusted troops and honest soldiers,
More than a thousand noblemen among them,
To quit their oath, their honour and their duty,
And join together in a monstrous crime?

OCTAVIO: Nothing so shameful and contemptible
Is what he seeks; no, his ambition bears
A name more innocent by far than that.
He only seeks to bring the Empire peace,
And as the Emperor detests *this* peace,
So he will – *force* him to agree to it!
All parties shall be satisfied, and he,
As recompense for all his troubles, keep
Bohemia – which he occupies already.

MAX: Has he deserved of us, Octavio,
That we, that *we* should think so basely of him?
OCTAVIO: It is not thoughts that we are speaking of,
But facts, and proof incontrovertible.
I think you know, my son, how low our stock
At court has fallen – but you can hardly guess
At the intrigues, at all the lying schemes
That were devised to stir up mutiny
Here in the camp. Broken is every bond
That binds the captain to his Emperor,
The common soldier to the civil order.
Lawless and mindless of their duty, they
Confront the state it is their task to guard,
And threaten they will turn their swords against it.
Now we have come to such a pass, the Emperor
At his own army trembles, fears the daggers
Of traitors in his capital – his palace;
Yes! would enjoin his tender princes flee,
Not from the Swedes, not from the Lutherans,
No! but before his own imperial troops.
MAX: No more! I tremble at your words in fear.
I know men quake before imagined terrors,
But such delusions bring us ill in truth.
OCTAVIO: No, it is no delusion. Civil strife,
The most unnatural of wars, will flare,
Unless we hasten now to damp the spark.
The colonels' loyalty is sold already,
The subalterns are on the brink, and with them
Whole regiments, whole garrisons may fall;
Strongholds are in the hands of foreigners,
Schafgotsch, a man whom none should trust, commands
The whole Silesian army, Terzky has
Five regiments of cavalry and foot,
Illo and Kinsky, Isolan and Butler
Have been entrusted with the best-heeled troops.

MAX: And so have we.

OCTAVIO: Because they think they have us,
  Think they can win us with their promises.
  I am to have the principalities
  Of Glatz and Sagan, and full well I see
  The bait that they have set for you.

MAX: No, no!
  I tell you, no!

OCTAVIO: Oh, will you use your eyes!
  Why do you think that we were ordered here
  To Pilsen? That our counsels might be taken?
  Did Friedland ever need to hear our counsel?
  We are called here to sell ourselves to him,
  And if we will not – to remain here hostage.
  That is the reason Gallas did not come,
  And you would not behold your father here,
  Were it not higher duty bid him stay.

MAX: He makes no secret of it, on his own account
  We have been summoned here – does not deny
  He needs our power to maintain himself.
  He did so much for us; it is our duty
  To do our share for him!

OCTAVIO: And do you know
  What is this share that now we are to do?
  Illo betrayed it in his drunken rage.
  Will you not think what you have heard and seen?
  Does not the forged petition, the proviso,
  The all-important phrase left out, betray
  That to no good we should commit ourselves?

MAX: This evening's business with that piece of paper,
  I think was nothing more than a base trick
  Of Illo's. Politicians like this man
  Will always take such matters to extremes.
  They see the Duke is fallen out of favour
  At court, and think they serve his interest

By widening the breach beyond repair.
The Duke, believe me, knows no word of it.
OCTAVIO: It grieves me that I must destroy your faith
In him, that seems to you so well-deserved.
But here I cannot spare you – you must take
Swift and decisive measures, you must act.
– I cannot but confess to you – that all
That I confided to you, that to you
Seems so incredible, I learnt from his
Own lips – the Prince's.
MAX [*in violent agitation*]: No, it cannot be!
OCTAVIO: Himself in confidence he told me – what
Indeed I had long since found out elsewhere;
He purposed to go over to the Swedes,
And at the head of the united armies
Compel the Emperor –
MAX: He is impatient,
The Court's behaviour had provoked his temper;
So in a hasty moment, very well!
He may have uttered words he did not mean.
OCTAVIO: Cold-bloodedly enough did he admit
This plan to me; and thinking my amazement
Betokened fear, in confidence he showed me
Dispatches from the Swedes and from the Saxons,
That gave him hope of definite assistance.
MAX: This cannot be! can *not* be! *cannot* be!
Do you not see it cannot be! You must
Have shown him the abhorrence that you felt,
He must have listened to you, or – or you –
Would not be standing here alive beside me!
OCTAVIO: Of course I did express my reservations,
Advised him, warned him earnestly against it;
But my abhorrence, my true inner feelings
I kept concealed from him.
MAX: And you could be

So false? No, this is not the manner of
My father! I did not believe your words,
When you spoke ill of *him* to me; still less
Can I, when now it is yourself you slander.

OCTAVIO: It was not I that sought his confidence.

MAX: His trust in you demanded honesty.

OCTAVIO: To hear the truth from me he was not worthy.

MAX: Unworthier still of you was such deceit.

OCTAVIO: My son! It is not always possible
In life to be as pure as little children,
As we are bidden by the voice within us.
In constant battle with despite and malice
Even the upright spirit stays not true –
This namely is the curse of evil deeds,
That they will never cease to breed and bring forth evil.
I split no hairs, I only do my duty,
I carry out my Emperor's commands.
Better indeed if we could always follow
The promptings of our heart, but we must then
Give up all hope in many a worthy purpose.
Our place, my son, is here to serve the Emperor.
Our hearts may say about it what they will.

MAX: It seems today that I am not to grasp
Your meaning, not to understand your words.
You say the Prince *frankly* revealed his heart to you
In *evil* purpose, and you say that *you*
In a *good* purpose could *deceive* the Prince!
No more, I beg you – you will not defraud
Me of my friend – let me not lose my father!

OCTAVIO [*suppressing his emotion*]:
You do not yet know all, my son. There is
Still more I must reveal.

    [*After a pause.*]   The Duke of Friedland
Has made his preparations. In his stars
He puts his trust. All unawares he thinks

To come on us – already he believes
The golden circlet lies within his grasp.
He is mistaken – we have acted too.
He grasps his secret evil destiny.

MAX: Oh, father, not too quickly! I implore you,
By all that's good, do not be over-hasty!

OCTAVIO: As soft and silent as he crept his wicked ways,
So soft and cunning vengeance creeps upon his trail,
Already waits unseen and dark behind his back,
But one step more, and shuddering the two are met.
– You saw that I had Questenberg with me;
As yet you only know his public errand –
A secret message too he brought with him,
For me alone.

MAX: And may I know it?

OCTAVIO: Max!
With these few words I lay the Empire's fate
And your own father's life into your hands.
Your heart feels stronger love for Wallenstein,
For since you were a boy, a mighty bond
Of trust and reverence has drawn you to him –
You cherish the desire – let me but speak
What still you are unwilling to confide –
The hope you cherish, closer to him yet
To find your place.

MAX: Father –

OCTAVIO: I trust your heart,
Can I be certain of your strength of mind?
Will you be able still to look him in
The face unflinching, when I have confided
To you the compass of his destiny?

MAX: Only if you confide in me his guilt!

[OCTAVIO *takes a paper from a drawer and hands it to him.*]

MAX: What's this? An open letter from the Emperor!

OCTAVIO: Read it.

MAX [*after glancing at it*]:

   The Prince condemned, declared an outlaw!

OCTAVIO: So, is it.

MAX: Oh, it is too much, unhappy error!

OCTAVIO: Read on! Compose yourself.

MAX [*after reading further, looking at his father in astonishment*]:

                         What? You? You are—

OCTAVIO: But for the moment, and until the King

   Of Hungary can come to take command,

   I am to oversee the army—

MAX: And do you think that you can wrest it from him?

   Do not believe it—Father! father! father!

   Unhappy is the office you are given.

   This paper here—how are you to enforce it?

   Disarm the mighty man amidst his troops,

   Surrounded by his men in all their thousands?

   You will be lost—you, all of us destroyed!

OCTAVIO: The risk I have to run I know full well.

   The Almighty holds me in his hand; he will

   Put forth his shield to guard the pious house

   Of Austria and destroy the work of darkness.

   There will be men enough and brave to rally

   Around the Emperor and the cause of good.

   Those who are loyal are warned, the others watched,

   I only wait for his first move, straightway—

MAX: On mere suspicion will you act so swiftly?

OCTAVIO: Let no man think the Emperor a tyrant!

   The will he would not punish, but the deed.

   The Prince still holds the thread of his own fate—

   Let him but stay, and leave this crime undone,

   And quietly his command will be withdrawn,

   And for his Emperor's son he will make way.

   An honourable exile in his castles

   Will rather seem reward than punishment.

   But let him take one single open step—

MAX: And what will you call such a step? He will
 Not take a wicked one. – But you could put
 (You have!) a foul construction on the purest.
OCTAVIO: However criminal his purposes,
 The steps the Prince has taken publicly
 Till now admit a fair interpretation.
 It is not my intent to use this paper
 Until he acts to prove beyond all doubt
 His treason and declare his guilt himself.
MAX: And who shall be the judge of that?
OCTAVIO: – You shall.
MAX: Oh! then this paper never will be needed!
 I have your word for it, you will not act
 Until you have convinced myself, no less.
OCTAVIO: Can it be true? Still, after all you know,
 You can believe him innocent?
MAX [with animation]:
 Your judgement may speak false, but not my heart.
  [He continues in a more restrained manner]
 This spirit is no common one to grasp.
 As to the stars he links his destiny,
 So too like them he goes his secret way,
 Mysterious, beyond men's comprehension.
 Believe me, he is wronged. Those matters all
 Will be resolved. In splendour we shall see
 Him step forth pure, above these black suspicions.
OCTAVIO: I shall be waiting.

SCENE 2

[Enter to them a SERVANT, *subsequently a* COURIER.]

OCTAVIO: What news?

SERVANT: A courier waits before your door.

OCTAVIO: At such an hour? Who is it, and from where?

SERVANT: He would not tell me.

OCTAVIO: Send him to us, and speak no word of this.

    [Exit SERVANT, *enter* CORNET.]

  So Cornet, it is you? You come from Gallas?

  Here, your dispatch.

CORNET: I have no written message.

  The general would not take the risk.

OCTAVIO: What is it?

CORNET: He bids me tell you – Am I free to speak?

OCTAVIO: My son knows all.

CORNET: We have him.

OCTAVIO: Whom do you mean?

CORNET: Why, Sesina, their go-between!

OCTAVIO [*quickly*]: Is yours?

CORNET: Two days ago, in the Bohemian forest,

  Our Captain Mohrbrand caught him, early in

  The morning, on the road to Regensburg,

  Bearing dispatches with him for the Swedes.

OCTAVIO: And the dispatches –

CORNET: General Gallas sent them on

  Straight to Vienna with the prisoner.

OCTAVIO: At last! at last! This is the best of news!

  That man is precious to us, as the vessel

  That carries things of moment – How much was there?

CORNET: Six or so packets with Count Terzky's arms.

OCTAVIO: None in the Prince's hand?

CORNET: I do not think so.

OCTAVIO: And Sesina?

CORNET: Took fright, you may be sure,
When he was told his way led to Vienna.
But then Count Altringer assured his safety,
If only he would freely tell them all.

OCTAVIO: Is Altringer there with your master? Was
He not in Linz, and sick?

CORNET: He has been with
The general three days in Frauenberg.
Already they have sixty companies
Assembled, hand-picked men, and bid you know
That they are ready to receive your orders.

OCTAVIO: So much can happen in the space of days!
When do you leave?

CORNET: I wait on your command.

OCTAVIO: Stay till this evening.

CORNET: Sir! [Going.]

OCTAVIO: Did no one see you?

CORNET: No one. The Capuchins admitted me
As usual, through the convent's wicket-gate.

OCTAVIO: Go, rest yourself, and keep yourself concealed.
I shall have letters for you before nightfall.
This business nears its turning-point at last;
Before the day that now so fatefully
Tinges the eastern sky has run its course,
The die is cast, on which so much must turn.

   [Exit CORNET.]

SCENE 3

[*The* TWO PICCOLOMINI.]

OCTAVIO: What now, my son? Soon we shall see the light,
  For all – I know it – went through Sesina.
MAX [*who has stood throughout the whole preceding scene in a
      violent inner struggle; decisively*]:
  A shorter way to clarity I seek.
  Farewell!
OCTAVIO: Where? Stay!
MAX: The Prince!
OCTAVIO [*startled*]:   What do you say?
MAX [*returning*]:
  If you believed that I would play a part
  In such a game as this, then you deceived
  Yourself in me. My way lies straight ahead.
  I cannot make my tongue speak truth while in
  My heart is falsehood, – cannot watch, and let
  Another trust me as his friend, and stifle
  My conscience with the thought that it is *he*
  Who runs the risk my lips may yet betray him.
  What men believe I am, that I must be.
  – I go to find the Duke. This very day
  I shall demand he clears his name before
  The world, and with a plain, straightforward step
  Breaks through the net your guile has set to snare him.
OCTAVIO: You would do this?
MAX: I will. You need not doubt it.
OCTAVIO: Yes, I have been mistaken in my son.
  I thought that I had raised you wise and prudent,
  Thought you would bless the hands that drew you back,
  Saved you from the abyss – and now I find

You are a fool, dazzled by two fair eyes,
Blinded and helpless in a fog of passion,
Not even to be cured by light of day.
Go then, and ask him! Go! Be rash enough
To give your father's and your Emperor's
Secret away to him. Compel me so
To break with him before the time is ripe!
And now, when till today a miracle
Of Heaven's contrivance has preserved my secret,
Has lulled to sleep the sharp eyes of suspicion,
Let me be witness how my very son,
With heedless, headlong, and insensate haste,
Destroys the work of patient statesmanship!

MAX: Of statesmanship! Oh, curses on that name!
Yes, you will drive him with your statesmanship,
To take that step – yes, you could even now,
Since you would *have* him guilty, *make* him so.
Oh! this can only end in ill – and let
It be decided how it may, I fear
I see draw on the turning-point of woe.
For when he is laid low, this king of men,
A world will topple with him in his fall,
And like a ship, that on the open sea
Has suddenly caught fire, and bursting wide
Her planks, hurls forth her crew and all that sailed
In her, between the ocean and the sky,
So he will bring us all, who are bound fast
To him and to his fate, to ruin with him.
Act as you will! But me you must allow
To live my life as it seems right to me.
Between myself and him all must be pure;
Before this day is done, I must have news,
If it is friend or father I must lose.

    [*As he turns to go, the curtain falls.*]

WALLENSTEIN'S DEATH

A TRAGEDY IN FIVE ACTS

CHARACTERS

WALLENSTEIN
OCTAVIO PICCOLOMINI
MAX PICCOLOMINI
TERZKY
ILLO
ISOLANI
BUTLER
CAPTAIN NEUMANN
AN ADJUTANT
COLONEL WRANGEL, the Swedish envoy
GORDON, Commandant of Eger
MAJOR GERALDINE
DEVEREUX   ⎫
MACDONALD ⎭ captains in Wallenstein's army
A SWEDISH CAPTAIN
A DEPUTATION OF CUIRASSIERS
THE BURGOMASTER OF EGER
SENI
THE DUCHESS OF FRIEDLAND
COUNTESS TERZKY
THEKLA
NEUBRUNN, lady-in-waiting   ⎫
VON ROSENBERG, equerry   ⎭ to Princess Thekla
DRAGOONS
SERVANTS, PAGES, etc.

The scene of the first three acts is Pilsen, that of the last two Eger.

ACT ONE

A room appointed for astrological observations, with globes, charts, quadrants and other astronomical instruments. A curtain is drawn back to reveal a rotunda containing statues representing the seven planets, each in its own niche, strangely illuminated. SENI *is observing the stars,* WALLENSTEIN *is standing in front of a large blackboard with the positions of the planets drawn on it.*

SCENE I

[WALLENSTEIN, SENI.]

WALLENSTEIN: Seni, it is enough for now. Come down.
  The dawn is breaking, Mars in the ascendant.
  It is no longer good for us to work.
  Come! We know all we need.
SENI: Your highness, let
  Me look once more at Venus. She is rising.
  There in the east she glitters like a sun.
WALLENSTEIN: Yes, she is drawing to her perigee,
  Exerting all her force on us below.
    [*Looking at the drawing on the board*]
  Fortunate aspect! So at last we see
  These mighty three momentously conjoined.
  The bringers of good fortune, Jupiter
  And Venus, now embrace the old malignant,
  The spiteful Mars, between them, and compel
  The bearer of ill-luck to serve my cause.
  For long since has he been my enemy,

And now oblique, now perpendicular,
Now in the quartile, now in opposition,
Has cast his ruddy beams against my stars
And brought the blessings that they bore to nothing.
Now they have conquered him, the ancient foe,
Bring him to me, their prisoner in heaven.

SENI: And neither luminary in the least obscured
By any hostile power! Saturn declining,
Impotent, powerless to harm our cause.

WALLENSTEIN: No longer Saturn rules, who masters all
The secret generation of earth's womb,
All that men's darker spirits brood upon
And everything that shuns the light of day.
This is no time for doubts and ponderings,
For Jupiter the bright proclaims his reign,
And summons forth the work conceived in darkness
With mighty word into the light. – Now we
Must act, and quickly, now, before the signs
Of fortune's favour take their flight again,
For ever-changing is the face of heaven.
[*There is a knocking at the door.*]
Someone is knocking. See who's there.

TERZKY [*offstage*]: Come, open!

WALLENSTEIN: Terzky!
What can there be so urgent? We are busy!

TERZKY [*offstage*]:
Whatever it may be, I beg you leave it,
This matter cannot wait.

WALLENSTEIN: Let him in, Seni.
[*While* SENI *goes to open the door for* TERZKY, WALLEN-
STEIN *draws the curtain before the statues.*]

SCENE 2

[WALLENSTEIN, COUNT TERZKY.]

TERZKY [*entering*]:
    You know? He is their prisoner, Count Gallas
    Handed him over to the Emperor!
WALLENSTEIN: Who is their prisoner? Who is handed over?
TERZKY: Why, he who knows our every secret, knows
    Of all our dealings with the Swedes and Saxons,
    He through whose hands the whole affair has passed –
WALLENSTEIN [*starting back*]:
    Not Sesina? Say no, I beg you, no!
TERZKY: Heading to meet the Swedes in Regensburg
    He was when Gallas' soldiers captured him,
    Who had been trailing him for many days.
    And all my documents for Kinsky, Thurn,
    For Oxenstiern and Arnim he had with him.
    All that is in their hands, now they can see
    With their own eyes all that we have been doing.

SCENE 3

[*Enter* ILLO.]

ILLO [*to* TERZKY]: He knows?
TERZKY: He knows.
ILLO [*to* WALLENSTEIN]:   Now do you still believe
    That you can make peace with the Emperor,
    Win back his confidence? And even if
    You should renounce the plans that you have made,

What you *have* planned, they know. You must go forward,
For now you can no more go back.

TERZKY: They can bring documents in evidence
Against us, in hands incontestible –

WALLENSTEIN: Nothing in mine, I swear it; there you lie!

ILLO: Indeed! And do you think that what this man,
Your brother-in-law, has done on your behalf
Will not be charged by them to your account?
The Swedes are to accept his word for yours,
But not your enemies there in Vienna!

TERZKY: Nothing put down in writing – but consider
Just what it was you *said* to Sesina!
And will he hold his tongue? If he can save his skin
By telling them your secret, will he keep it?

ILLO: No, you had never thought of that! And now
They know how far you have already gone,
Say then, what next? You can no longer keep
The office you have held, but you are lost
If you resign, beyond all hope of rescue.

WALLENSTEIN: The army is my surety. The army
Will not leave me. Whatever they may know,
The power is mine, and that they have to stomach,
– And if I can find bail for my good faith,
They must accept it and be satisfied.

ILLO: The army, that is yours; now, at this moment, it
Is yours; but yet beware the creeping, silent
Powers of time. Today, tomorrow still
The favour of the troops protects you from
All hostile force; but wait a little while,
Secretly, slowly, they will undermine
Your high renown, on which you base your hopes;
Steal your supporters from you, one by one,
Till when the earthquake's shock is felt at last,
The feeble edifice comes crashing down!

WALLENSTEIN: Unlucky chance!

ILLO: Oh, I will rather call it fortunate,
  If only it affects you as it should,
  Urges you now to act – The Swedish colonel –

WALLENSTEIN: He has arrived? And do you know his
    errand?

ILLO: He will not say to anyone but you.

WALLENSTEIN: Unlucky, oh unlucky chance – no, no!
  Sesina knows too much; he'll not keep silent!

TERZKY: He is a rebel and a renegade,
  A price is on his head; if he can save it
  At your expense, why should he hesitate?
  And if they question him upon the rack,
  Will he have strength, the coward, to resist?

WALLENSTEIN [*lost in thought*]:
  No, I shall not win back their confidence,
  Let me do anything I will, I am
  And shall remain a traitor in their eyes.
  And were I even to return, and tread
  The path of duty, – it will be no use –

ILLO: It will mean ruin. Not your loyalty,
  Your weakness they will say has made you do it.

WALLENSTEIN [*pacing up and down in great agitation*]:
  What? Must it then be carried out in earnest,
  Because I toyed too freely with the thought?
  Curses on playing with the devil! –

ILLO: If all of this was but a game, believe me,
  In deadly earnest you must pay for it!

WALLENSTEIN: And if it must be carried out, then now,
  While still the power is mine, it must be done –

ILLO: If possible, before the Viennese
  Have time to think, and to anticipate you –

WALLENSTEIN [*looking at the signatures*]:
  I have the generals' pledge in writing, here –
  Max Piccolomini's name is missing. Why?

TERZKY: There was – he thought –

ILLO: A foolish, vain conceit!
  Between yourself and him there was no need.
WALLENSTEIN: He was quite right, there is no need –
  The regiments will not be sent to Flanders;
  They have composed their own petition to me
  And openly refuse to follow orders.
  The first step to rebellion is taken.
ILLO: Believe me, you will find it easier,
  To make them join the Swedes than join the Spaniard!
WALLENSTEIN: Let me first hear this Swede, and what he
    has
  To say to me.
ILLO [quickly]: Will you not call him, Terzky?
  He is already here.
WALLENSTEIN: No, wait a little.
  I was surprised – It came on me so quickly –
  I am not so accustomed to blind chance
  Sweeping me onward in its dark design.
ILLO: Hear what he has to say, and then consider. [Exeunt.]

SCENE 4

[WALLENSTEIN, alone.]

WALLENSTEIN: What? I, no longer act as I might choose?
  No longer turn back if I wanted? Must
  The deed be *done* because I *thought* of it,
  Did not dismiss temptation, let my heart
  Draw sustenance from this fair dream, assembled
  The means by which it *could* perhaps come true,
  Merely kept open doors where I might enter?
  Great God in Heaven! It was never meant
  In earnest, I had never so resolved.

I took my pleasure in the thought alone;
The freedom and the power were my delight.
Was it so wrong to cherish and enjoy
Those royal hopes, though they might be illusion?
Was not my will within my breast still free,
Did I not see the better way beside me,
Always ensuring me a safe retreat?
Where is it all at once I find myself?
All paths cut off behind me, and a wall
Arises, piled on high, of my own building,
A barrier to all return!

[*He stands still, deep in thought.*]

Guilty I must appear, and, let me try
My utmost! cannot shake this burden off;
Life's ambiguity is my accuser.
Even the pious deed of pure intent
Suspicious enmity will twist and poison.
Were I the traitor that they take me for,
Zealous I should have been to keep appearance,
To draw the veil of secrecy around me,
To give no chance for calumny. But sure
Of innocence and of unsullied will,
I gave free rein to fancy and to passion –
My words were bold, because my deeds were not.
Now all these things that undesigned have happened
They will combine into a great design,
And words that anger and unthinking courage
Brought to my lips out of my heart's abundance,
They with false art will weave into a plan
And from it draw a fearful accusation,
To which I cannot speak. And thus have I
Ensnared myself with my own fatal net,
And cannot breach it but by act of force.

[*Standing still again.*]

How unlike this! when courage, ranging free,

To that same deed of boldness drove, that now
My life's necessity so harshly orders!
A grim and deadly earnest is this moment.
Not without chill does man put forth his hand
To draw the hidden lots of destiny.
Within my breast my deed was still my own;
But once surrendered from the fastness of
The heart, the mother's womb in which it grew,
Cast forth upon the alien seas of life,
It is entrusted to deceitful powers
That no man's art can summon to his call.

[*He paces up and down the room in agitation, then again
stands still in thought.*]

And what is it you seek? Have you confessed
It even to yourself? You would shake down
Established power, sure upon its throne,
Possessions, rights, that centuries of use
And sacred custom firmly have established,
Securely rooted with a thousand fibres
In pious faith and childlike loyalty.
This is no equal match of strength with strength,
That I fear not. I fight with any foe
That I can see, and look into his eye,
His courage rousing courage too in me.
Invisible the enemy I fear,
Who stands against me in the hearts of men,
Through cowards' fear alone fearsome to me –
Not that which shows itself in life and vigour
Is threatening and fearful, but the common
Dross that is always left from yesterday,
That ever was and ever will be so,
Tomorrow always as it was today!
It is of such a dross that man is made,
Accustomed habit is the nurse that fed him.
Woe betide him, who lays his finger on

His precious ancient lumber, cherished heirlooms!
The march of years has power to sanctify;
Whatever's grey with age, men will call holy.
Once in possession, you are in the right;
The mass will hold it sacred and preserve you.
[To a PAGE who enters] The Swedish colonel? Well, let him
    come in.
    [Exit PAGE. WALLENSTEIN has fixed his gaze pensively
    upon the door.]
Still it is pure, this threshold – still! No crime
Has sullied it as yet – How narrow is
The boundary that parts two ways of life!

SCENE 5

[Enter WRANGEL.]

WALLENSTEIN [after fixing him with a penetrating gaze]:
    Your name is Wrangel?
WRANGEL: Gustav Wrangel, colonel
    In the Blue Regiment of Södermannland.
WALLENSTEIN: It was a Wrangel who served me so ill
    Before Stralsund, and by his brave resistance
    Kept me from capturing that sea-girt city.
WRANGEL: Thanks to the elements with which you fought,
    Not to my work, your grace! The Belt defended
    The city's freedom with its mighty storm,
    Lest land and sea should come to serve one man.
WALLENSTEIN: You wrested from my head the admiral's
    hat.
WRANGEL: Today I come to set a crown upon it.
WALLENSTEIN [motions him to sit down, and does so himself]:
    Your papers. Have you full authority?

WRANGEL [*hesitantly*]:
  So many doubts remain to be resolved –
WALLENSTEIN [*after reading*]:
  A letter to the point. It is a shrewd
  And wily master, Wrangel, that you serve.
  Your Chancellor declares that it is but
  The late king's own intent he carries out
  In helping me to the Bohemian crown.
WRANGEL: It is the truth. The king (God rest his soul!)
  Had always for your grace's subtle brain
  And military gifts a high regard,
  And always said, the man with brains to rule
  Alone *should* rule, and bear the name of king.
WALLENSTEIN: He had the right to say it!
    [*Taking his hand, confidentially*]
  In good faith, Colonel Wrangel – I was always
  A loyal Swede at heart – why, that you must
  Have learnt at Nuremberg and in Silesia.
  Often I had you in my power and let
  You time and time again slip from my grasp.
  That they will not forgive me in Vienna,
  And that now drives me to this step – And since
  Our interests must now go hand in hand,
  So let us also take each other in
  Full confidence.
WRANGEL: That confidence will come,
  But not before each has assurances.
WALLENSTEIN: I see your Chancellor does not yet trust me.
  Yes, I admit – the game is not entirely
  To my advantage. No, your master thinks,
  If I can play the Emperor a trick
  Like this, then I could play it just as well
  Upon his enemy, and might not one
  More readily be pardoned than the other?
  Is that not your opinion, Colonel Wrangel?

WRANGEL: I have a mission only, no opinions.

WALLENSTEIN: The Emperor has driven me to take
  The fatal step. I can no longer be his servant.
  In self-defence, I must for my own safety
  Do what my conscience cannot but condemn.

WRANGEL: No man would do this thing unless he must.
  [*After a pause*] What motives may have swayed your grace
    to act
  Against the Emperor in such a way,
  Is not our place to judge or to interpret.
  We Swedes are fighting for a righteous cause
  With righteous swords and with our conscience clear.
  Conditions now, it seems, are in our favour,
  We must seize every opportunity,
  Take every chance that offers, without scruple;
  And if all this is as it would appear –

WALLENSTEIN: What is it then you doubt? Is it my will?
  My power? I gave your Chancellor my promise,
  If he would give me sixteen thousand men,
  To bring another eighteen thousand of
  The Emperor's troops –

WRANGEL: Your grace is much renowned,
  A mighty prince of war, as all men know,
  A second Pyrrhus and a new Attila!
  Still with astonishment it is recalled
  How years ago, against all supposition,
  You summoned up an army as from nothing.
  And yet –

WALLENSTEIN: And yet –

WRANGEL: His excellency thinks
  It might well be an easier task to raise
  A force of sixty thousand men from nothing,
  Than to persuade the sixtieth part – [*He pauses.*]

WALLENSTEIN: What then?
  Come, speak!

WRANGEL: To break their oath of loyalty.

WALLENSTEIN: He thinks so? Spoken like a Swede, and like
   A Protestant. You Lutherans fight for
   Your Bible, and do battle for your cause;
   Your *heart* is with the banner that you follow. –
   Should one of *you* cross to the foe, then he
   Has broken faith not with one lord but two.
   With us there is no question of such things.

WRANGEL: By God in Heaven! Can you people have
   No home, no hearth, no church to claim allegiance?

WALLENSTEIN: Listen and I will tell you. Yes, indeed,
   The Austrian has his own fatherland,
   Loves it and has good cause to love it too.
   This army, though, that calls itself Imperial,
   Encamped here in Bohemia, it has none;
   This is the scum of every nation, is
   The dross of foreign lands, the outcasts who
   Have nothing but the sun that shines on all.
   And this Bohemia, for which we struggle,
   Has no heart for its master, whom it owes
   To battle's fortune, not to its own choice.
   It groans beneath the tyranny of faith,
   Power has subdued it, but not pacified.
   It is aglow with longing to avenge
   The horrors that were done upon its soil.
   How can the son forget he saw his father
   Driven with packs of hounds into the mass?
   A people treated so is terrible,
   Whether it rise, or suffer yet in silence.

WRANGEL: But the nobility, the officers?
   Such a desertion, such a crime, your highness,
   Has not its fellow in all history.

WALLENSTEIN: In any circumstances, they are mine.
   You need not take my word: trust your own eyes.

[*He gives him the declaration.* WRANGEL *reads it through and then lays it on the table, without saying a word.*]
Well? Do you see?

WRANGEL: I see, but scarcely grasp it.
Your highness! I will drop my mask – indeed!
I have authority to act in this.
The Rhinegrave stands but four days' march away
With fifteen thousand men, only awaiting
The order to join forces with your army.
I give that order, when we are agreed.

WALLENSTEIN: What are your Chancellor's demands?

WRANGEL [*hesitantly*]:
Twelve regiments it is, of Swedish troops.
My head must answer for it. Everything
Might yet be trickery –

WALLENSTEIN [*starting up*]: Sir Swede!

WRANGEL [*continues calmly*]:   And so I must
Insist the Duke of Friedland formally,
Irrevocably break with Ferdinand,
Or we can trust no Swedish troops to him.

WALLENSTEIN: Come, out with your demands, what are
     they? Speak.

WRANGEL: That you disarm the Spanish regiments
Loyal to the Emperor, that you take Prague
And hand it over, with the border fortress
Of Eger, to the Swedes.

WALLENSTEIN: You ask for much!
Prague! Eger, well; but Prague? It cannot be.
I will afford you any pledge within
The bounds of reason that you ask of me.
But Prague – Bohemia – I can guard myself.

WRANGEL: We do not doubt it. We are not concerned
To see it guarded merely. We would not
Have lost our money and our men for nothing.

WALLENSTEIN: Indeed not.

WRANGEL: So, till we are recompensed,
Prague is our surety.

WALLENSTEIN: Do you not trust us?

WRANGEL [*standing up*]:
We must take care in dealing with the Germans.
Across the Baltic we were summoned here;
We saved the Empire from destruction, sealed
The sacred doctrine of the Gospel and
The freedom of religion with our blood.
But now already men no longer feel
The benefaction but the burden only, look
Askance upon the strangers in the Empire
And would be glad to send us packing with
A purse of money to our forests. No!
It was not for the price of Judas, not
For chinking gold and silver that we left
Our king a corpse upon the battlefield.
The blood so many noble Swedes have shed
Is not to be repaid with gold and silver!
Nor are we satisfied with laurel wreaths
To deck our flags when we set sail for home.
We would stay citizens upon this soil
Our king in falling conquered for himself.

WALLENSTEIN: Help me hold down the common enemy,
And that fair border land is surely yours.

WRANGEL: And when the common enemy is conquered,
Who will preserve the bond of this new friendship?
We know, your highness – even though the Swedes
Are not supposed to hear – that you are dealing
In secret with the Saxons. Who will be
Our surety that we are not to be
The sufferers by these agreements which
You find it needful to keep hid from us?

WALLENSTEIN: Indeed, your chancellor had picked his man,

He could have found no tougher one to send me!
  [*Standing up.*]
Think of some better bargain, Gustav Wrangel.
Prague, never.

WRANGEL: My authority ends here.

WALLENSTEIN: Give up my capital to you! Why, rather
Rejoin my Emperor!

WRANGEL: If there is time.

WALLENSTEIN: That I am free to do, today and always.

WRANGEL: Until some days ago, perhaps. Not now.
Since Sesina was captured – no, not now.
  [*As* WALLENSTEIN, *taken aback, makes no reply*]
Prince! We believe that you are in good faith;
Since *yesterday* – we have been sure. And now
This paper pledges us the troops, no more
Stands in the way of our full confidence.
No quarrels over Prague. Our chancellor
Will only take the Old Town, and your highness
May keep the Hradschin and the Littleside.
But Eger first and foremost must be ours,
Before there can be talk of our alliance.

WALLENSTEIN: I must trust you, but you will not trust me?
I will consider what you have proposed.

WRANGEL: Do not be long about it, I must ask you.
More than a year our meetings have drawn out;
Should this one too be fruitless, then our chancellor
Regards the whole affair as broken off.

WALLENSTEIN: You press too hard. A step like this must be
Well weighed.

WRANGEL: Before you even think of it,
Your highness! For success demands swift action. [*Exit.*]

SCENE 6

[Re-enter ILLO *and* TERZKY.*]*

ILLO: Well, is it right?

TERZKY:　　　　　　　Are you agreed?

ILLO:　　　　　　　　　　　That Swede
　Looked well content. Yes, you must be agreed.

WALLENSTEIN: Listen! Nothing has happened yet, and – no,
　I think I will not, after all.

TERZKY:　　　　　　　What do you mean?

WALLENSTEIN: Live by the grace and favour of those
　　　Swedes?
　Their condescension? I could not endure it.

ILLO: What, do you come in flight, craving their aid?
　You bring far more to them than you receive.

WALLENSTEIN: Think of the history of that royal Bourbon,
　Who sold himself to France's enemy
　And struck his fatherland and his own people.
　Curses were his reward, and men's revulsion
　Took its revenge on such unnatural crime.

ILLO: Is that *your* case?

WALLENSTEIN:　　　　I tell you, loyalty
　Is closest kin by blood to every man,
　Born to be its avenger he must feel.
　Sectarian strife, the rage of hostile parties,
　Old enmities and jealousies make peace;
　All forces raging to destroy each other
　Are reconciled, make common cause to hunt
　The wild beast down, humanity's own foe,
　That ravening breaks down the sheltered fold
　Where man resides in safety – for his own
　Sharp wits alone are not enough to guard him.

Only upon his brow did nature give
Him eyes to see, and pious loyalty
Must watch his flank, where he is left exposed.

TERZKY: Think of yourself no worse than does your foe,
Who in this deed gives you his hand with joy.
Charles did not entertain such squeamish thoughts,
The ancestor of this imperial house.
He took that Bourbon in with open arms;
It is advantage rules the world's affairs.

SCENE 7

[*Enter* COUNTESS TERZKY.]

WALLENSTEIN: Who summoned you? This is no woman's
    work.
COUNTESS: I come to offer my congratulations.
  – But have I come too soon? I hope not so!
WALLENSTEIN: Terzky, you are her lord. Bid her be gone.
COUNTESS: I gave Bohemia a king before.
WALLENSTEIN: He showed it.
COUNTESS [*to the others*]: Well, what is it, then? Speak out!
TERZKY: The Duke will not.
COUNTESS: Will not do what he must?
ILLO: It is your turn. Try, I can do no more,
When I must hear of loyalty and conscience.
COUNTESS: What? When your goal still lay so far before you,
  Endless the road stretched forth into the distance,
  Then you were bold and resolute – and now,
  When dreams at last could be reality,
  Achievement is so close at hand, success
  Assured, now you begin to have your doubts?

Only in scheming you are bold, a coward
In action? Good! Show that your foes were right,
For this is what they have expected of you.
Yes, your intentions they believe; be sure
That they have letters signed and sealed to prove them!
But none believes that you will ever act,
Or surely they would fear you and respect you!
Can it be possible? You have come so far,
They know the worst, they charge you with
The deed already, sure as it were done,
Will you draw back, when you could pluck the fruit?
The plan is nothing but a common crime,
The action, an immortal enterprise;
And let it but succeed, it will be pardoned,
For in success or failure God gives judgement.

    [*Enter a* SERVANT.]

SERVANT: Sir, Colonel Piccolomini.

COUNTESS [*quickly*]:   — Must wait.

WALLENSTEIN: I cannot see him now. Another time.

SERVANT: He only asks to see you for two minutes
   On urgent business —

WALLENSTEIN: Who knows what this might be? Yes, I will
   see him.

COUNTESS [*laughs*]: Urgent for him, but it can wait for you.

WALLENSTEIN: What is it?

COUNTESS: I will tell you, later on.
   Now you must think what answer to give Wrangel.

    [*Exit* SERVANT.]

WALLENSTEIN: If there were still a choice – if I could still
   Find some more peaceful way – still I will choose
   It even now, and shun the fatal step.

COUNTESS: If that is all you seek, then such a way
   Lies open yet. Send Wrangel on his way.
   Forget your ancient hopes, cast off entirely
   The life that you have led, and be resolved

To start afresh. For even virtue has
Its heroes, just as well as fame and fortune.
Go to Vienna, to the Emperor,
Without delay, take a full chest of money,
Say you would merely test his servants' loyalty,
And trick the Swede, to show him for a fool.

ILLO: Too late for that, as well. They know too much.
He would but lay his neck upon the headsman's block.

COUNTESS: I have no fear of that. They have no proof
In law, and will not seek to act the tyrant.
The Duke will be allowed to go in peace.
Yes, I can see how it will be. The King
Of Hungary will come, and so of course
It will be natural the Duke should leave;
It will not call for any explanation.
The King will make the troops swear their allegiance,
And everything will be maintained in order.
But then one morning, see! the Duke is gone.
Then at his castles, life begins to stir,
There he will hunt and build and keep his stables,
Hold court in splendour, hand out golden keys,
Dispense his hospitality in banquets,
In short, be a great king – in miniature!
And since he wisely thus contents himself,
No longer seeks to be of real importance,
They let him seem what he desires; a prince
Until his days are ended he will seem.
Why then! The Duke is just another one
Of those new men, who rose up overnight upon
The tide of war, a creature of court favour,
That makes a prince as soon as make a baron.

WALLENSTEIN [stands up, in violent agitation]:
Show me a way out of this fearful press,
You powers that aid me! Show me one that I
Can find it in myself to follow – never

Can I content myself with words alone,
Or like those paragons of virtue, use
My will and noble thoughts to keep me warm!
Nor say to fortune, when it turns its back
On me, so grandly, 'Go! I do not need you!'
If I can no more act, then I am nothing;
No sacrifice or danger will I fear
If I can shun that fatal, final step;
But rather than be lost in nothingness,
I, who began so mighty, and so small,
Rather than have the world confound me with
Those wretched creatures of a single day,
Let generations now and yet to come
Pronounce my name with loathing, and let *Friedland* be
The password for all deeds of shame!

COUNTESS: What is there so unnatural in this?
I cannot see it, tell me – oh! do not
Let superstition and its night-borne ghosts
Become the masters of your day-bright spirit!
You are accused of treason; whether rightly
Or wrongly, that is not the question now;
But you are lost, unless you swiftly use the power
That you possess – What! is there any creature,
However peaceable, that will not fight
For life with all the strength of life it has?
What boldness will not self-defence excuse?

WALLENSTEIN: This Ferdinand was once so gracious to me;
He loved me, held me in esteem, I stood
The closest to his heart. There was no prince
He honoured more. And now, to end like this?

COUNTESS: So gratefully you think of these small favours,
And for an insult have no memory?
Must I recall what recompense you earned
At Regensburg for all your loyalty?
You had offended all the princes;

To make him great, had taken on yourself
The hatred and the curse of all the world,
You had no friend, not one in Germany,
Because you served your Emperor alone.
And so in him alone you trusted when
At Regensburg the storms of enmity
Were gathering about your head – and then
He left you – let you fall! Yes, to appease
Bavaria's pride, he let you fall a victim!
And do not say your dignity restored
Makes good that first, that terrible injustice.
It was not their good will, it was the law
Of harsh necessity that brought you back
The place they would so gladly have denied you.

WALLENSTEIN: No, not to their good will, that is the truth,
Nor his affection do I owe this office.
If I abuse it, I abuse no trust.

COUNTESS: Affection! Trust! They needed you – no more!
Necessity, that tarries for no man,
That is not served with names or empty ciphers,
That will have action, not the sign alone,
Always seeks out the greatest and the best
To place him at the rudder, even if
It had to pick him from the mob – necessity
Gave you your place, and put you in this office.
For long, until they can no more, these men
Will be content with servile, venal souls
And with the wire-drawn puppets of their art.
But when at last the fatal die is thrown,
The hollow mask no longer serves, they fall
Into the mighty hands of nature, of
The spirit that obeys none but itself,
Knows of no treaties, and will deal with them
Not on their terms, but on its own alone.

WALLENSTEIN: True! They have always seen me as I am,

Could not but know the bargain they were making,
For never did I think it worth my while
To hide from them my bold, free-ranging spirit.

COUNTESS: Rather – you always showed them they should
    fear you.
Not you, who have remained true to yourself,
But they are in the wrong, who were afraid
Of you and yet put power in your hands.
A man of character is always right
If but consistent with himself, there is
No wrong for him except in contradiction.
Were you another, when eight years ago
You scoured the German lands with fire and sword,
Wielding your scourge upon the provinces,
Scorning all custom and Imperial order,
Imposing but the fearful law of might,
And casting down all territorial rights,
Only to spread abroad your sultan's power?
That was the time for them to break your will
And pride, to bind you to the paths of order!
What profited the Emperor, that pleased him;
And silently he set upon those crimes
The seal of his approval. What was right,
Then when you did it *for* him, is it now
Become at once so wicked, when *against*
Him it is turned?

WALLENSTEIN [*standing up*]:
I had not seen it in this way – Yes! So
It is indeed. This Emperor used my arm
To perpetrate throughout the Empire deeds
Which order never should have countenanced;
Even the princely mantle that I wear
I owe to services that were but crimes.

COUNTESS: Admit then, that between yourself and him
    There never can be talk of right and duty,

Only of power, and opportunity!
The moment has arrived, when you should draw
The sum conclusion of your life's account;
The signs of victory stand about your head,
The planets nod good fortune from above,
And cry: the time is come! Is it in vain
That all your days you have so closely told
The courses of the stars? Wielded the compass
And quadrant? painted on these walls the vault
Of heaven and the zodiac, and gathered
About you with their silent, bodeful signs
The seven lords of destiny?
Was it an idle game that you were playing?
Shall all this preparation lead to nothing,
Is there no marrow in this empty art,
That it means nothing to you, cannot sway
You in this very moment of decision?

WALLENSTEIN [*has been pacing up and down during this last
    speech, his mind in violent turmoil; suddenly he stops still, and
    interrupts the* COUNTESS]:

Call Wrangel here, and have three messengers
Saddle straightway.

ILLO: At last, praise be to God!
    [*He hurries away.*]

WALLENSTEIN: It is his evil genius, and mine,
Punishing him through me, the tool of his ambition,
And I expect that vengeance is already
Whetting its blade to pierce my breast as well.
Let not the man who sows the dragon's teeth
Hope for a joyful harvest. Every crime
Carries its own avenging angel with it,
The evil hopes that swell within its bosom.

He can no longer trust me, – so I can
No more turn back. Let happen then what must.

Fate always wins, for our own heart within us
Imperiously furthers its design.
[*To* TERZKY] Bring Wrangel to me in the inner room.
I will address the messengers myself.
Send for Octavio!
    [*To the* COUNTESS, *whose face shows an expression of triumph*]
                Do not rejoice!
For jealous are the powers of destiny,
Triumph too soon and we their wrath shall see.
The seeds of action in their hands we sow;
Good luck or ill the end alone will show.
    [*As he turns to go, the curtain falls.*]

ACT TWO

A Room.

SCENE I

[WALLENSTEIN, OCTAVIO PICCOLOMINI. *Soon afterwards,* MAX PICCOLOMINI.]

WALLENSTEIN: He sends me word from Linz that he is sick,
  But I have heard for sure, he can be found
  At Frauenberg, in hiding with Count Gallas.
  Arrest them both and send them here to me.
  The Spanish regiments you will take over,
  Draw out your preparations without end,
  And if they press you to advance against me,
  You will say yes, and stay just where you are.
  I know that it is doing you a service
  To keep you standing idle in this game.

You would keep up appearance while you may,
Extreme and drastic steps are not for you,
And that is why I choose this part for you to play;
This time by doing nothing you will serve
Me best – If meanwhile fortune should declare
Itself for me, you know what you must do.

   [*Enter* MAX PICCOLOMINI.]

Now, father, go. You must away this evening.
Take my own horses. This young man shall stay
With me – Let your good-byes be brief!
I do not doubt that we shall meet again,
All safe and well.

OCTAVIO [*to his son*]: A word, before I go. [*Exit.*]

SCENE 2

[WALLENSTEIN, MAX PICCOLOMINI.]

MAX [*approaching him*]: My general –

WALLENSTEIN: I am that no longer,
  If you still call yourself the Emperor's servant.

MAX: So it is settled, you will leave the army?

WALLENSTEIN: I serve the Emperor no longer.

MAX: And you will leave the army?

WALLENSTEIN: Rather do
  I hope to bind it closer, firmer to me.

   [*Sitting down.*]

Yes, Max. I did not wish to tell you sooner,
Before the hour of action should have struck.
Youth's happy instincts easily will seize
On what is right, and it is joy to us
To use and exercise our powers of judgement,
When simple is the task that stands before them.

But when we have to pick the lesser of
Two certain evils, when our heart cannot
Survive unscathed amidst the clash of duties,
Then it is blessing to have no free choice,
Necessity itself appears a favour.
– Now is that moment. Cast no backward glances.
They can no longer help you. Look ahead!
And pass no judgement, but prepare to act!
– The powers at Court are set upon my downfall,
And so I am resolved I will forestall them.
– We will ally our forces with the Swedes.
They are fine fellows, and good friends of ours.

> [*He pauses, awaiting* PICCOLOMINI's *answer.*]

– I see I have surprised you. Do not answer.
You shall have time to recompose yourself.

> [*He rises and moves upstage.* MAX *stands motionless for a long time, plunged into the most violent grief; as soon as he stirs,* WALLENSTEIN *comes back to face him.*]

MAX: My general! Today you make me free.
Until this moment, I was spared the pains
Of finding my own way and my direction.
I followed you, unquestioning. I need
But look to you, and knew the path of right.
For the first time today you cast me back
Upon myself; compel me, by your words,
To make the choice between my heart and you.

WALLENSTEIN: Until today your destiny was kind,
You could fulfil your duty as in play,
Satisfy every fair and natural impulse,
And always act with undivided heart.
It can be so no more. In enmity
The paths divide. Duty with duty clashes.
You must take sides, for war is breaking out
Between your friend and Emperor.

MAX: What, war?

War is a terror, like the scourge of heaven,
Yet it is good, our heaven-sent destiny.
Is this war good, that you would wage upon
The Emperor with his imperial army?
O God in Heaven, what is this change? How can
I speak such words to you, who always shone
Before me like my lodestar, fixed and bright
To guide me and to be my rule of life?
Oh! what a rift you open in my heart!
The native impulse of my old respect,
The sacred custom of obedience
That I have paid your name, must I deny?
No! do not turn your countenance upon me!
It always seemed to me a face divine
Cannot so soon lose its authority;
My senses still are bound in thrall to you,
Although my bleeding soul tears itself free!

WALLENSTEIN: Max, listen to me.

MAX: Do not, do not do it!
Oh, see, these pure and noble features still
Know nothing of this deed of infamy.
Only your fancy saw its fleeting shadow,
And innocence will not be driven out
From your majestic and imperious presence.
Cast that black shadow out, your enemy,
And it was nothing but an evil dream,
Such as may warn the surest virtue. Men
May know such moments when they stand in doubt,
Their happy instincts though must be victorious.
No, no, you will not end like that, or all
Such might and natural greatness in men's eyes
Would be dishonoured, and the vulgar proved
Aright, when they deny all noble freedom
And put their trust in impotence alone.

WALLENSTEIN: I know the world will judge me harshly for it.

All you can say to me, I told myself.
Who would not shun, while he can yet avoid it,
The fatal step! But here there is no choice,
I must use force, or suffer it myself –
So matters stand. I have no other course.

MAX: So be it! Keep yourself in power by force,
Resist the Emperor's authority.
If it must be, stir up open rebellion,
I will not praise it, but I can forgive,
Will stand by you, though I do not approve.
But – do not be a traitor! Now the word
Is spoken. Anything, but not a traitor!
That is no mere excess, not a mistake
Courage can make that oversteps its strength.
Oh, that is quite another thing – is black,
As black as Hell itself!

WALLENSTEIN [*frowning darkly, but moderating his speech*]:
The tongue of youth is quick to utter words
Of fearful weight, that cut as sharp as knives,
And from its hot and reckless fancy takes
The measure of all things, not from themselves.
Straightway it judges shameful or sublime,
Evil or good – and every vain conceit
Imagination piles on these dark names,
Youth sees in life and in reality.
The world is narrow, wide the mind of man.
Our thoughts make easy neighbours for each other,
But roughly jostling, things crowd close in space;
Where one sits fast, another must make room,
And who would not be driven out must drive;
Strife is the rule, and strength alone will conquer.
– Yes, he who goes through life without desires,
Denies himself all purpose, he can dwell
Like salamander in the fire unscathed,
And stay still pure in the pure element.

But nature made me of a coarser stuff,
And my desires will hold me fast to earth.
The evil spirit rules this earth, and not
The good. The gifts that heaven sends down to us
Are only common goods, that all may share;
Their brightness gladdens, but makes no man rich,
And in their realm are no possessions won.
The precious stone, the gold that all men prize,
They must be wrested from the fickle powers
That hold their evil sway beneath the light.
Not without sacrifice their grace is won,
And there is no man living on this earth
Who served them yet, and kept his soul unspotted.

MAX [*urgently*]:
Oh, fear them! Yes, oh, fear these fickle powers!
They will *not* keep their word, these lying spirits,
Deceiving, luring you to the abyss.
Be warned by me, and do not trust them! Turn
Back to the path of duty, for you *can*!
Yes, send me to Vienna, and let *me*,
Me, reconcile you to the Emperor.
He does not know you truly, but I do,
He shall see you with my unsullied eyes,
And I will bring you back his trust again.

WALLENSTEIN: It is too late. You have not heard what
    happened.

MAX: And if it is too late – if it has come to this,
    That only crime can save you from your fall,
    Then fall! Fall as you stood, with dignity.
    Surrender your command, and leave the field
    In glory, as you can – and innocence!
    You have lived much for others, now at last
    Live for yourself, and I will go with you,
    My destiny and yours shall not be parted –

WALLENSTEIN: It is too late. While you stand here and waste

Your words, my messengers already leave
The milestones one by one behind them as they fly
To Prague and Eger, bearing my command.
– Submit. We do what we are bound to do.
So let us act our part with dignity
And firm unshaken step. – Is what I do
Worse than that Caesar did, whose name is still
Renowned above all other in this world?
He turned and marched on Rome the very legions
That Rome had given him for her defence.
If he threw down his sword, he had been lost,
As I should be, if I were to disarm.
I feel his spirit's trace within me too.
Grant me his fortune, I will bear the rest.

[MAX, *who has been standing in an agony of indecision,
hurries off.* WALLENSTEIN *watches him in surprise and
dismay as he goes, and remains standing deep in thought.*]

SCENE 3

[*Enter* TERZKY, *soon afterwards* ILLO.]

TERZKY: Was that Max Piccolomini who left you?
WALLENSTEIN: Where is that Wrangel?
TERZKY: Wrangel? Gone.
WALLENSTEIN: So soon?
TERZKY: It was as if the earth had swallowed him.
    I looked for him, just after he was with you,
    We still had things to say, but – he was gone,
    And none could tell me anything about him.
    I do believe it was the fiend himself,
    No man can disappear like that, so quickly.
        [*Enter* ILLO.]

ILLO: You will not send that fox! Can it be true?

TERZKY: What, old Octavio? What are you thinking?

WALLENSTEIN: Yes, he will go to Frauenberg, to lead
  The Spanish and Italian regiments.

TERZKY: No, God preserve us, you will not do that!

ILLO: Trust him with men and arms, that plays you false?
  Let him out of your sight, the very moment
  That must decide the outcome of our fate?

TERZKY: You cannot do it. Not for all the world!

WALLENSTEIN: How strange you people are.

ILLO: Oh! just this once
  Believe our warning. Do not let him go.

WALLENSTEIN: And why should I not trust him, now, this
    once,
  When I have always trusted him? What is there
  To rob me of my good opinion of him?
  Upon your fancy, not my own, I am
  To change my judgement, old and well-confirmed?
  Do not think me a woman. I have trusted
  Him *till* today, and so *today* I trust him.

TERZKY: Must it be he? Can you not send another?

WALLENSTEIN: It must be he, for I have sought him out.
  This is *his* office, so I choose him for it.

ILLO: He's an Italian, and so you choose him.

WALLENSTEIN: I know you never liked the pair of them,
  Because I value, love them, rank them higher
  Than you and others, just as they deserve,
  You cannot bear to see them. What have I
  And my affairs to do with your resentment?
  Your hating them makes them no worse for me.
  Love or despise each other as you will,
  I make no claim to change a man's affections;
  I know how I must rank each one of you.

ILLO: He shall not go – and if I have to smash the wheels
  Beneath his carriage!

WALLENSTEIN: Illo, calm yourself!

TERZKY: That Questenberg, when he was here in camp,
  He always had his head together with him.

WALLENSTEIN: It was with my full knowledge and consent.

TERZKY: And that dispatches come to him in secret
  From Gallas, I know too.

WALLENSTEIN: That is not so.

ILLO: Oh, you are blind, though you have eyes to see!

WALLENSTEIN: Believe me, you will not destroy my faith
  For it is based upon profoundest science.
  If he is false, then so is all my art,
  For let me tell you, I have fate's own pledge
  That he of all my friends is truest to me.

ILLO: And have you one that *that* pledge is not false?

WALLENSTEIN: Know there are moments in the life of man
  When he stands closer than at other times
  To the directing spirit of the world,
  And may put question to his destiny.
  It was at such an instant, when, the night
  Before the action that we fought at Lützen,
  I leant against a tree, alone, in thought,
  And gazed out on the plain. The camp-fires burned
  With dismal glow to pierce the swirling mists,
  The muffled clang of weapons and the cry
  Of sentinels alone disturbed the silence.
  Then in that moment all my life, both past
  And future, sped before my inward eye,
  And on the coming morning's fate my spirit
  In ranging dreams hung all that was to come.
  So to myself I said, 'So many men
  Obey your word! Your stars alone they follow,
  Upon your head stake all they have and in
  Your fortune's ship sail on life's seas with you.
  And yet the day will come when once again
  All these will scatter at the nod of fate,

And with you but a loyal few remain.
Who is it, I would know, of all the men
Within this camp will stay most loyal to me?
Destiny, give a sign! Let it be he
Who when the morning breaks first comes to me
To greet me with a sign of his affection.'
Then on the battlefield I saw myself
In my mind's eye. The press was thick. A shot
Bore down my horse, I fell, and over me
Unheeding rolled the surge of men and horses,
And panting like a dying man I lay,
Shattered beneath the pounding of their hooves.
Then suddenly I felt a helping arm,
It was Octavio's – straightway I awoke,
The day had dawned, and there – Octavio stood.
'Brother,' he said, 'I beg you, do not ride
Your dappled horse today, but rather take
This sturdy mount that I have picked for you.
Do this for me. I had a warning dream.'
That horse's speed it was that saved me from
Banner's dragoons that were pursuing me.
My cousin rode the dappled horse that day,
And man and mount I never saw again.

ILLO: That was but chance.

WALLENSTEIN [*meaning fully*]: There is no chance, I say;
What seems to us but blind coincidence,
That from the deepest springs of all is sprung.
I have it signed and sealed that *he* is my
Good angel, and I'll hear no more of it! [*Going.*]

TERZKY: My comfort is that Max stays here as hostage.

ILLO: And he shall never leave this place alive.

WALLENSTEIN [*stopping and turning back*]:
Are you not just like women, who repeat
Time and again their first and only word,
When one has reasoned with them, hour by hour?

– The thoughts and deeds of men, I tell you this,
Do not roll blindly like the waves of ocean.
The inner world, the microcosm, is
The deep eternal fountain of their motion.
They grow inevitable, like the fruit
Upon the tree, beyond all fickle chance;
When I have probed a man, and found his root,
I know his will and actions, at a glance. [*Exeunt.*]

SCENE 4

PICCOLOMINI's *rooms.*

[OCTAVIO PICCOLOMINI *in travelling clothes. An* ADJUTANT.]

OCTAVIO: Is the detachment there?
ADJUTANT: Waiting below.
OCTAVIO: And they are men you can depend upon?
   Tell me the regiment from which you took them.
ADJUTANT: From Tiefenbach's.
OCTAVIO: That regiment is loyal.
   Let them wait calmly in the further courtyard,
   Not show themselves, unless you hear the bell;
   Then close all doors and keep the strictest watch,
   And anyone you find must be arrested.
     [*Exit* ADJUTANT.]
   I hope indeed we shall not need these measures,
   For I believe my schemes will be successful;
   But better too much caution than too little.
   The stakes are high; we serve the Emperor.

SCENE 5

[Enter ISOLANI.]

ISOLANI: Well, here I am. Are not the others coming?
OCTAVIO *[secretively]*:
　A word with you before, Count Isolani.
ISOLANI *[likewise]*:
　What, is it starting? Has the Duke a plan?
　You can trust me. Come, put me to the test.
OCTAVIO: That I may well.
ISOLANI:　　　　　　　　Brother, I am not one
　Of those who bravely boast with words
　But when it comes to action, run away.
　The Duke has been a friend to me indeed,
　God knows! I owe him everything I have.
　My loyalty is certain.
OCTAVIO:　　　　　We shall see.
ISOLANI: But take good care. Not everyone thinks so.
　There are still many who are for the Court
　And say their signatures, the other night,
　Were stolen from them and cannot be binding.
OCTAVIO: Indeed? Tell me their names who say such things.
ISOLANI: Why, devil take them, all the Germans say so,
　And Esterhazy, Kaunitz, Deodati.
　They all say now the Court must be obeyed.
OCTAVIO: Good! I am pleased.
ISOLANI:　　　　　　　　Pleased?
OCTAVIO:　　　　　　　　　　　That the Emperor
　Still has such loyal friends and trusty servants.
ISOLANI: You need not jest. They are not bad, these fellows.
OCTAVIO: Indeed not. God forbid that I should jest!
　In earnest, I am pleased to see the cause

Of right so strong.

ISOLANI: The devil! What is this?
What, are you not – ? Why did you send for me?

OCTAVIO [*with dignity*]:
Because I want to hear, quite plainly, whether
The Emperor may call you friend or foe.

ISOLANI [*defiantly*]:
That is no question that I care to answer
Except to him who has the right to ask it.

OCTAVIO: Whether I have, this paper may inform you.

ISOLANI: Wha – what? That is the Emperor's hand and seal.
[*Reads*] 'Wherefore all officers who hold command
Within Our army shall obey the word
Of Our beloved and most loyal servant,
Lieutenant-General Piccolomini,
As if it were Our own' – Hm! Well! Indeed!
I – offer my congratulations, general.

OCTAVIO: You will submit to this command?

ISOLANI: I? – But
You take me by surprise – I hope I may
Be granted time to think of this –

OCTAVIO: Two minutes.

ISOLANI: But God in Heaven, this matter is –

OCTAVIO: Quite simple.
Merely declare if you intend to be
Your master's faithful servant, or a traitor.

ISOLANI: A traitor? In God's name, who speaks of treason?

OCTAVIO: It is afoot. The Prince would play the traitor,
And lead the army to our enemy.
Come, speak. Will you desert the Emperor?
Sell yourself to the enemy? Say! Will you?

ISOLANI: What do you mean? Desert his majesty
The Emperor? What, I? Did I say that?
And when?

OCTAVIO: You have not said it yet. Not yet.

I wait to find out whether you will say it.

ISOLANI: Why, now, it is most kind of you to swear
To me yourself that I said no such thing.

OCTAVIO: So you will stay no longer with the Prince?

ISOLANI: If he's a traitor – treason breaks all ties.

OCTAVIO: And are resolved that you will fight against him?

ISOLANI: He did me good – but if he is a villain,
God damn his soul! His claim on me is void.

OCTAVIO: It pleases me to see you act so wisely.
Tonight in secrecy you must depart
With all the lighter troops; it must appear
The order has been given by the Duke.
Frauenberg is the place where we assemble,
And there Count Gallas gives you further orders.

ISOLANI: It shall be done. But speak a word, and tell
The Emperor how willing you have found me.

OCTAVIO: I shall commend you.

[*Exit* ISOLANI. *Enter a* SERVANT.]

                                Colonel Butler? Good!

[*Re-enter* ISOLANI.]

ISOLANI: Forgive me that I was so rough, old friend.
By God, how could I know that I had such
Important company?

OCTAVIO: Good, never mind.

ISOLANI: My blood runs sometimes hot, I know, and if
Perhaps some thoughtless words about the Court
Escaped me, when I had a drop of wine,
Believe me, it was not meant ill. [*Exit.*]

OCTAVIO: You need
Not fear on that account! – Our first success.
Grant we have such good fortune with the others!

SCENE 6

[*Enter* BUTLER.]

BUTLER: I am at your command, Lieutenant-General.

OCTAVIO: Be welcome, as a valued friend and guest.

BUTLER: The honour is too great.

[*They both sit down.*]

OCTAVIO: You have not answered the affection
  Which yesterday I showed towards yourself.
  Perhaps you thought it just a form of words.
  That wish proceeded from my heart, I was
  In earnest with you, for the time has come
  For all good men to make a common cause.

BUTLER: Only like-minded men can be allied.

OCTAVIO: To me, all good men must be of like mind.
  The only deeds I count in judging men
  Are those their character brings calmly forth;
  For blind misunderstanding often drives
  The best of men by force from his true path.
  You came by Frauenberg. Did not Count Gallas
  Say anything to you? He is my friend.

BUTLER: The words were wasted that he spoke to me.

OCTAVIO: That I am sad to hear, for he was right,
  And my advice to you would be the same.

BUTLER: Then save yourself the trouble, and spare me,
  If thus it is I earn your good opinion.

OCTAVIO: The time is precious, let us speak out frankly.
  You know how matters stand. The Duke is planning
  An act of treason, I can tell you more,
  He has committed it; alliance with
  The enemy was made some hours ago.
  To Prague and Eger messengers are riding,

Tomorrow he would lead us to the foe.
But he deceives himself, for prudence watches,
The Emperor still has his faithful friends,
Invisible but mighty is their league.
This proclamation renders him an outlaw,
Sets free the army from its oath to him,
And calls upon all men of noble mind
Under my leadership to be united.
Choose whether you will fight for good with us
Or with him share the lot of evil men?

BUTLER [*rising*]: His destiny is mine.

OCTAVIO: Is that your last
Resolve?

BUTLER: It is.

OCTAVIO: Consider, Colonel Butler.
There is still time. Here in my loyal breast
That rashly-spoken word will stay forgotten.
Go back on it, and find a better cause
To fight for. You have taken up a bad one.

BUTLER: What else would you command, Lieutenant-
General?

OCTAVIO: Consider your white hairs. Go back on it!

BUTLER: Good-bye.

OCTAVIO: What? Would you draw your trusty sword
In such a fight as this? Would you see turned
To curses all the thanks that you have earned
In serving Austria these forty years?

BUTLER [*laughing bitterly*]:
Thanks from the house of Austria!

OCTAVIO [*lets him go to the door, then calls out to him*]:
Butler!

BUTLER: Your pleasure?

OCTAVIO: Count Butler, should I say?

BUTLER: Count! What is this?

OCTAVIO: You should have been a count.

BUTLER [*starting violently*]: Why, death and devils!

OCTAVIO [*coldly*]:
You sought the title, but you were refused.

BUTLER: You shall not make a mock of me unpunished.
Draw!

OCTAVIO: Put up your sword. Tell me what happened. I
will not
Deny you satisfaction, afterwards.

BUTLER: Let all the world know of my foolish weakness,
Even if never I forgive myself!
– Yes, I too have my pride, Lieutenant-General.
I never could endure the scorn of men.
It was a pain to me that birth and title
Could count for more than merit in the army.
Why should I rank less highly than my fellows?
And so, in that unlucky hour I let
Myself be led to take that step. – A folly,
That yet did not deserve such harsh reward!
They could refuse. But did they have to barb
Dismissal with such scorn and such contempt,
To crush an old man and a faithful servant
Beneath the weight of bitter words and insults,
So cruelly mind him of his base descent,
That in a moment's weakness he forgot!
But nature gave the worm itself a sting,
Although vainglorious might may crush its head –

OCTAVIO: Someone had slandered you. Do you suspect
The enemy who served you in this way?

BUTLER: Let it be who it may! A cowardly scoundrel
It must have been, some courtier, a Spaniard,
Some fine young fellow of an ancient line
Whose light I clouded, yes, some envious villain
Offended by my hard-won dignity.

OCTAVIO: But tell me, did the Duke approve your step?

BUTLER: He urged me on to take it, exercised

His influence for me, like a true friend.

OCTAVIO: Indeed? Are you so sure?

BUTLER: I read his letter.

OCTAVIO [*meaningfully*]:
   I too – but differently it read to me.
      [BUTLER *is taken aback.*]
   By chance, I have this letter here upon me,
   And can convince you through your own two eyes.
      [*Gives him the letter.*]

BUTLER: Ha! what is this?

OCTAVIO: I fear, good Colonel Butler,
   You were the victim of a shameful trick.
   The Duke, you said, urged you to take that step? –
   But in this letter he speaks scornfully
   Of you, urges the minister to punish
   Such rash presumption, as he calls it.
      [BUTLER *has read the letter. His knees tremble, he reaches for
      a chair and sits down.*]
   No enemy pursues you with his malice.
   The Duke alone it is you have to thank
   For your humiliation; it is clear,
   He sought to lure you from your Emperor,
   Hoping to gain through your desire for vengeance
   What your long-proven loyalty had shown
   That he could not expect on calm reflection:
   To make you his blind instrument, to use
   You as the means to his perfidious purpose.
   And he succeeded. All too well he managed
   To turn your footsteps from the paths of right,
   Upon which you have trod for forty years.

BUTLER [*with trembling voice*]:
   Can his imperial majesty forgive me?

OCTAVIO: He will do more. He will make good the insult
   That such a worthy man bore undeserved,
   And freely of his own accord confirms

The gifts the Duke with evil purpose made.
The regiment that you command is yours.

[BUTLER *attempts to stand up, but sinks back on to his chair.
His mind is in violent agitation; he attempts to speak but
cannot. Finally, he takes his sword from his belt and hands it to*
PICCOLOMINI.]

OCTAVIO: What do you want? Be calm.

BUTLER: Take this!

OCTAVIO: Why? Think!

BUTLER: Take it! I am not fit to bear this sword.

OCTAVIO: Receive it back again, here from my hand,
And wield it nobly in the cause of right.

BUTLER: I would betray this gracious Emperor!

OCTAVIO: You can repay him. Quickly leave the Duke.

BUTLER: I, leave him!

OCTAVIO: What? Can you be hesitant?

BUTLER [*in a terrible outburst*]:
Leave him? No more than that? He shall not live!

OCTAVIO: Come with me now to Frauenberg, to join
Our loyal friends with Altringer and Gallas.
Many another I have summoned back
To duty, and tonight they flee from Pilsen.

BUTLER [*who has been pacing up and down in great agitation,
turning to* OCTAVIO *with an expression of determination*]:
Count Piccolomini! May he who broke
His oath of loyalty still speak of honour?

OCTAVIO: He may, when he so earnestly repents it.

BUTLER: Then on my honour, leave me here.

OCTAVIO: What would you?

BUTLER: Let me and all my regiment stay here.

OCTAVIO: I trust you. Tell me, though, what you are
planning?

BUTLER: The deed will show. Ask me no further now.
Trust me! You can! By God, it is not his
Good angel you consign him to! – Farewell. [*Exit.*]

[*Enter a* SERVANT *with a note.*]

SERVANT: A stranger gave me this, and went away.
   His highness' horses stand below already. [*Exit.*]

OCTAVIO [*reading*]:
   'Leave this place soon. Your faithful Isolani.'
   – Oh! would this town already lay behind me!
   So near to harbour, could we still be wrecked?
   Away! away! It is no longer safe
   For me to stay here. But where is my son?

SCENE 7

[*Enter* MAX PICCOLOMINI *in a state of wild agitation, with rolling eyes and unsteady gait. He appears not to notice his father, who stands at a distance watching him with sympathy. He paces through the room with long strides, then stops again and finally flings himself into a chair, his eyes staring straight in front of him.*]

OCTAVIO [*drawing nearer*]:
   I must be gone, my son.
   [*As he receives no reply, he takes* MAX *by the hand.*]
                              My son, farewell!

MAX: Farewell!

OCTAVIO: But you will follow soon?

MAX [*without looking at him*]:   I, you?
   Your ways are crooked, mine they cannot be.
   [OCTAVIO *lets go of his hand, and starts back.*]
   Oh! if you only had been straight and true,
   It never would have come to this, no, never!
   This fearful thing he never would have done,

Good in his counsels still would have prevailed,
The wicked never caught him in their snares!
Why must you creep so slyly, furtively
Upon your errands, like a common thief?
Accursed falsehood! Mother of all evil!
Bringer of sorrow, you will be our ruin!
Honesty, truthfulness, the rock on which
The world is based, had served us all. Oh, father!
I can find no excuse for you, I cannot.
The Duke betrayed my trust, most fearfully,
But this that you have done is little better.

OCTAVIO: My son, my son! Oh, I forgive your grief.

MAX [*standing up and looking at him with an expression of
        doubt*]:

What, father? Is it possible? Could it
Be your design, to drive this thing so far?
His fall will raise you up. Octavio,
I do not like to see it.

OCTAVIO: God in Heaven!

MAX: Alas! No longer do I know myself;
How could my open soul admit suspicion?
My trust, my faith, my hopes, all are destroyed,
For everything I valued was a lie.
No, no! Not everything! I still have her,
And she is pure and truthful as the heavens.
Deceit is everywhere and treachery,
Poison and death, treason and perjury,
Our love the one pure spot that yet remains
Still undefiled in all humanity.

OCTAVIO: Max! Quickly, come with me, it will be better.

MAX: What? And before I say farewell to her,
For the last time? No, never!

OCTAVIO: Spare yourself
The pain of parting, since it must be so.
Come, follow! come, my son! [*Attempting to drag him off.*]

MAX: As true as God lives, no!

OCTAVIO [*more urgently*]:
Come with me, I command you as your father.

MAX: Command what flesh and blood may do. I stay.

OCTAVIO: Max! Follow me! Come, in the Emperor's name!

MAX: No Emperor gives orders to my heart.
What, would you rob me of the last possession
That in misfortune I am left, her pity?
Must cruel fate so cruelly take its course?
That which I cannot alter, must it be
Ignobly done, must I a coward flee,
In secret like a villain steal away?
No, she must see my suffering, my pain,
Hear the lament of my dismembered soul,
And shed her tears on my account – Oh! men
Are cruel, but she is like an angel;
From raging grief and hideous despair
My soul she will deliver, ease this pain
Of death with gentle comfort and lament.

OCTAVIO: You cannot tear yourself away, you will not.
Oh come, my son, and save your noble virtue!

MAX: Waste no more words, you speak to me in vain;
My heart I follow, that alone I trust.

OCTAVIO [*trembling, losing his composure*]:
Max! Max! If this should be – this fearful thing,
If you – my son – my flesh and blood – should sell
Yourself – I cannot bear the thought! – to *him*,
Should set this mark of shame upon our house,
Then shall the world behold a deed of horror,
A father's blood upon the dripping sword
His own son wielded in the hideous fight.

MAX: Oh! if you had but had more worthy thoughts
Of man, more worthy would your deeds have been.
Accursed doubt! Ill-fated, black suspicion!
Nothing remains unmoved and firm against it,

And everything must quake where faith is lacking.

OCTAVIO: And if I trust your heart, will it remain
Within your power to follow it unshaken?

MAX: You could not quell the promptings of my heart,
Be sure the Duke will have no greater might.

OCTAVIO: Oh! Max, I shall not see your face again!

MAX: Unworthy of you, you shall never see me.

OCTAVIO: I go to Frauenberg, but you shall keep
The Pappenheimers here; Lorraine, Toscana
And Tiefenbach stay too, they will protect you.
They love you and are faithful to their oath,
And they will rather bravely fight and die
Than quit their leader and desert their honour.

MAX: Depend on me, I shall lay down my life
In fighting here, or lead them free from Pilsen.

OCTAVIO [making to leave]:
My son, farewell!

MAX: Farewell!

OCTAVIO: What? Shall there be
No loving glance, no handshake as we part?
Bloody the war to which we both must go,
Uncertain, hidden from us in its outcome.
It was not thus we used to take our leave.
Can it be true? Have I a son no longer?

[MAX falls into his arms; they hold each other in a long, silent
embrace, then part and leave the stage on opposite sides.]

ACT THREE

A hall in the Duchess of Friedland's apartments.

SCENE I

[COUNTESS TERZKY, THEKLA, FRÄULEIN NEU-
BRUNN. *Both the latter engaged in sewing.*]

COUNTESS: Nothing you have to ask me, Thekla? Nothing?
  I have been waiting long to hear you speak.
  How can you bear it, in so many hours
  Not even to pronounce your lover's name?
  What? Or perhaps you do not even need me,
  Have found already other ways to meet?
  Come now, my niece, and tell me. Have you seen him?
THEKLA: Today and yesterday I have not seen him.
COUNTESS: Nor even heard from him? Be frank with me.
THEKLA: No word.
COUNTESS: And you can be so calm!
THEKLA: I am.
COUNTESS: Leave us, Neubrunn.
    [*Exit* FRÄULEIN NEUBRUNN.]

SCENE 2

[COUNTESS, THEKLA.]

COUNTESS: I do not like to see
  Him keep so silent, now the least of all.

THEKLA: Now least of all?

COUNTESS: When he knows everything!
  Now is the time he should declare himself.

THEKLA: I do not understand you, speak more plainly.

COUNTESS: That was my reason when I bid her go.
  Thekla, you are a child no more. Your heart
  Has come of age, you are in love, and courage,
  As you have shown, to your love is no stranger.
  You show the spirit of your father's blood
  More than your mother's. Therefore I can say
  To you what she could never bear.

THEKLA: I beg you, spare me all your preparations.
  Be what it may, speak out with it! It can
  Be scarce more fearful than this introduction.
  Say what you have to tell me, and be brief.

COUNTESS: You must not be afraid –

THEKLA: Speak out, I beg you!

COUNTESS: It is within your power to do your father
  A precious service –

THEKLA: In my power! What can –

COUNTESS: Max Piccolomini loves you. You can
  Bind him, with bonds unyielding, to your father.

THEKLA: What need of me? Is he not bound already?

COUNTESS: He was.

THEKLA: And why should he no longer be,
  Not always be?

COUNTESS: He loves the Emperor too.

THEKLA: No more than duty and his honour bid him.

COUNTESS: It is his love of which we would have proof,
  Not of his honour – what, duty and honour!
  Those names face many ways, have many meanings,
  You must interpret them for him, his love
  Must show him where his honour lies.

THEKLA: But how?

COUNTESS: He must renounce the Emperor or you.

THEKLA: He will be glad to stay beside my father
  In his retirement. You have heard him say
  How much he longs to lay his weapons down.

COUNTESS: It is not meant that he should lay them down,
  But draw them for your father.

THEKLA: Gladly will
  He shed his blood, will serve my father with
  His life, should any seek to injure him.

COUNTESS: You will not guess my meaning – listen, then.
  Your father's broken with the Emperor,
  And is about to join the enemy
  And take the army with him.

THEKLA: O my mother!

COUNTESS: We need some great example, for the troops
  To follow him. The Piccolomini
  Enjoy the army's high regard, command
  Opinion, and decide by what they do.
  The father we make sure of through the son –
  A weighty issue lies within your hand.

THEKLA: Oh, pitiful, my mother! What a deadly blow
  It is awaits you! – She will not survive it.

COUNTESS: She will accept what is inevitable,
  I know her – What is far and in the future
  Worries her heart with fear; but what is real
  And not to be withstood, she bears with patience.

THEKLA: O dismal visions of my soul – O now,
  Now it is come, the icy hand of terror,
  To grasp my hopes of joy with fearful grip.
  I knew it – straightway when I entered here,
  Within my heart an anxious intimation
  Told me the stars ill-favoured looked upon me –
  But how can I be thinking of myself –
  O mother! O my mother!

COUNTESS: Calm yourself.
  Do not give way to vain lamenting. Save

    Your father a good friend, yourself a lover,
    And all can still be well, our fortunes prosper.

THEKLA: All still be well? No, we must part for ever! –
    Oh, we must speak no word of it again!

COUNTESS: He will not go! He cannot leave your side!

THEKLA: Unhappy man!

COUNTESS: If he loves you indeed, why, then his mind
    Will quickly be resolved.

THEKLA: His mind will soon,
    Soon be resolved, you need not doubt. Resolved!
    What is there to resolve?

COUNTESS: Be calm. I think I hear
    Your mother coming.

THEKLA: Oh, how shall I bear
    To look at her?

COUNTESS: Be calm.

SCENE 3

[Enter the DUCHESS.]

DUCHESS [to the COUNTESS]: Sister, what was it?
    I heard loud voices.

COUNTESS: There was no one here.

DUCHESS: I am so fearful. Every slightest noise
    To me portends some messenger of evil.
    Can you not tell me, sister, how it stands?
    Will he do what the Emperor desires,
    And send the cardinal his horsemen? Speak!
    When he sent Questenberg away, was it
    With favourable answer?

COUNTESS: –It was not.

DUCHESS: Oh, then it is the end! I fear the worst.

They will depose him, everything will be
Just as it was at Regensburg.

COUNTESS: It will
Not be. Not this time. That you can be sure of.

[THEKLA, *in great agitation, runs to her mother and clasps her,*
weeping, in her arms.]

DUCHESS: O the untamable, unbending man!
What have I had to suffer and to bear
In the ill-starred alliance of this marriage.
For as if pinioned to a wheel of fire,
That whirls on headlong to eternity,
I lived with him a life of anxious dread,
And always to the brink of the abyss,
As if to fall, his dizzy footsteps led.
– No, do not weep, my child. Let not my grief
Seem harbinger of suffering for you,
Make fearful the condition that awaits you.
There lives no other man like Friedland; you,
My daughter, will not share your mother's fate.

THEKLA: O my dear mother, let us flee from here!
This is no place for us. Come quickly, quickly!
Each hour that comes upon us brings new terrors.

DUCHESS: Your lot will be more peaceful. – Yet we too,
I and your father, had our happy days;
Our early years I still recall with joy.
Then still he strove ahead with cheerful vigour,
A brightly-warming fire was his ambition,
Not yet this flame that rages all-consuming.
The Emperor still loved him, trusted him,
And all that he attempted brought success.
But from that fateful day at Regensburg,
That brought him tumbling from his lofty height,
A lone and wayward spirit came upon him
And black suspicion clouds his open mind.
His calm is gone, no longer can he trust

His own glad strength, or fortune's ancient favour,
But turns his heart toward those gloomy arts
That never yet brought fortune to their adepts.

COUNTESS: That is how *your* eyes see it. – But is this
How we should speak, when him we are awaiting?
You know that he will soon be here. Must he
Find *her* in this condition?

DUCHESS: Come, my child,
Come, dry your tears, and greet your father with
A cheerful face. – But see, this ribbon here
Is loose – we must bind up your hair again.
Come, wipe away these tears, that spoil your eyes
So fair – But yes, what was it I was saying?
Of course – this Piccolomini: he is
A worthy nobleman of great renown.

COUNTESS: Sister, he is indeed.

THEKLA [*to the* COUNTESS, *anxiously*]:
                                  Will you excuse
Me, aunt? [*Going.*]

COUNTESS: But why? Your father will be here.

THEKLA: I cannot see him now.

COUNTESS: But he will ask
For you, expect you here.

DUCHESS: Why is she going?

THEKLA: The sight of him is more than I can bear.

COUNTESS [*to the* DUCHESS]:
She is not feeling well.

DUCHESS [*anxiously*]:   What is the matter?

    [*Both follow* THEKLA, *and are concerned to prevent her from
    going.*]

SCENE 4

[*Enter* WALLENSTEIN *and* ILLO.]

WALLENSTEIN: Is everything still quiet in camp?

ILLO: All quiet.

WALLENSTEIN: Within the space of hours the news may
   come
  From Prague to say the capital is ours,
  And then it will be safe to drop the mask,
  To tell our forces here what we have done,
  When we may tell of its success as well.
  In matters such as this, example's all.
  Man is a creature born to imitate.
  But stand in front, and you command the herd.
  The troops in Prague, for all they have been told,
  Believe that these have sworn to us in Pilsen,
  And here in Pilsen they will give their oath,
  Because of the example Prague has set.
  – Butler, you said, has now declared himself?

ILLO: Unsummoned, of his own free will he came
  Himself to offer you his regiment.

WALLENSTEIN: Not every voice, it seems, must be believed,
  That speaks its warning message to our heart.
  Deceiving us, the prince of lies will speak
  To us in accents borrowed from the truth,
  And scatter omens that we should not heed.
  And so I must atone for silent wrong
  That I have done this brave and worthy Butler;
  For some strange feeling that I cannot master,
  I will not call it fear, comes creeping on me
  When I am in his presence, numbs my senses
  And checks the happy impulse of affection.

And this same honest man, of whom my spirit
Would warn me, is the first to pledge good fortune.
ILLO: And his revered example, do not doubt,
Will bring you all the best men in the army.
WALLENSTEIN: Go now and send me Isolani here
Without delay; I put him in my debt
Not long ago, with him I will begin.
[*Exit* ILLO. *Meanwhile the others have come downstage again.*]
WALLENSTEIN: Why, see, my dearest daughter and her
mother!
Let us for once take rest from our affairs –
Come! This was what I sought, to spend an hour
Of happiness alone here with my dear ones.
COUNTESS: Yes, it is long since we were thus together.
WALLENSTEIN [*aside, to the* COUNTESS]:
Have you prepared her? Can she bear to hear it?
COUNTESS: Not yet.
WALLENSTEIN: My daughter, come and sit beside me.
A gracious spirit dwells upon your lips,
Your mother speaks of your accomplishments
With praise, and tells me that a delicate
And sweet harmonious voice is yours, that charms
The soul. Just such a voice as this it is
I need to drive the evil demon from me,
That beats his dusky wings about my head.
DUCHESS: Where is your zither, Thekla? Come and take it,
And let your father hear a sample of
Your art.
THEKLA: O mother, O my mother! God in Heaven!
DUCHESS: Come, Thekla, give this pleasure to your father.
THEKLA: I cannot, mother –
COUNTESS: What is this, my niece!
THEKLA [*to the* COUNTESS]:
Spare me, I beg you – Sing – now, when my soul
With fear and dread is laden – sing to him –

When he will send my mother to her grave!

DUCHESS: What, Thekla, why these fancies? Will you not
Do what your loving father asks of you?

COUNTESS: Here is the zither.

THEKLA: O great heavens – how can I –
[*She takes the instrument with trembling hands, her soul
wrestling violently within her, and at the moment when she
should begin to sing shudders convulsively, throws down the
instrument and hurries off.*]

DUCHESS: My child – she is not well!

WALLENSTEIN: What is the matter? Is she often thus?

COUNTESS: Since she herself betrays it, why, then I
Will not be silent longer.

WALLENSTEIN: What?

COUNTESS: She loves him.

WALLENSTEIN: She loves him! Whom?

COUNTESS: Young Piccolomini.
Have you not noticed it? Sister, nor you?

DUCHESS: Oh, was it this that pressed upon her heart?
My child, God bless you! No, you need
Not feel ashamed of such a choice.

COUNTESS: This journey –
If it was not what you intended, you
Must blame yourself. You should have picked another
To be her escort!

WALLENSTEIN: Does he know?

COUNTESS: He hopes to call her his.

WALLENSTEIN: He hopes to call
Her his, indeed – what, is he mad, the boy?

COUNTESS: Now let her hear it for herself!

WALLENSTEIN: He thinks
To carry off the Princess Friedland? Well! I like
His spirit! Such a thought does not disgrace him.

COUNTESS: Because you always showed him so much favour,
So –

WALLENSTEIN: At the last he thinks to be my heir.
  Why, yes, I value him and hold him dear,
  But what does that concern my daughter's hand?
  Is it one's daughters, is it one's own children
  One gives away as marks of favour?
DUCHESS: The noble manner of his mind and breeding –
WALLENSTEIN: Assure him of my heart, not of my daughter.
DUCHESS: His rank and family –
WALLENSTEIN: His family!
  He is a subject, and my son-in-law
  I look to find on one of Europe's thrones.
DUCHESS: Your grace, I beg, let us not strive to fly
  Too high, or else too great will be our fall.
WALLENSTEIN: Was it for this I gave so much to climb
  These heights, to tower above the heads of all
  The common run of men, to play a part
  Of greatness, only at the last to end
  It with a common match? – Was this the reason –
  [*He suddenly stops, composing himself.*]
  She is the only thing that will remain
  Of me on earth; and I will see a crown
  Upon her head – or I will live no more.
  What? Everything – yes, everything, I'll stake
  To make *her* great – yes, at this minute, while
  We speak –
  [*Checking himself.*]
             And am I now, like any fond
  Soft-hearted father of a lowly rank,
  To give my blessing to their match of love?
  And at this very moment, when I set
  The crowning garland on my finished work –
  No, long have I been saving up this jewel,
  This last, most precious coin in all my treasure,
  I swear that I do not intend to part
  With her for less than a king's royal sceptre –

DUCHESS: Oh husband, husband! You must always build
   Into the clouds, you build and build and do
   Not stop to ask whether such narrow base
   Can bear the giddy towers of your work.

WALLENSTEIN [*to the* COUNTESS]:
   Have you revealed to her where I propose
   To send her?

COUNTESS: No, not yet. Tell her yourself.

DUCHESS: Are we not going to Carinthia?

WALLENSTEIN: No.

DUCHESS: What? Nor to another of your castles?

WALLENSTEIN: There you would not be safe.

DUCHESS: Not safe, in lands
   The Emperor rules, and under his protection?

WALLENSTEIN: He will no longer shelter Friedland's wife.

DUCHESS: O gracious God, has it then come to this?

WALLENSTEIN: In Holland you will find protection.

DUCHESS: What?
   You will not send me to the Protestants?

WALLENSTEIN: The Duke of Lauenburg will see you safe
   Delivered there.

DUCHESS: The Duke of Lauenburg?
   The friend of Sweden and the Emperor's foe?

WALLENSTEIN: The Emperor's foes are foes of mine no
      longer.

DUCHESS [*staring in terror at the* DUKE *and the* COUNTESS]:
   Then it is true? It is? You are deposed?
   Have been dismissed from your command? O God
   In Heaven above!

COUNTESS [*on one side to the* DUKE]: Let her believe it so.
   You see that she could not endure the truth.

SCENE 5

[*Enter* TERZKY.]

COUNTESS: Terzky! What can it be? What look of terror,
    As if he had beheld a ghost!
TERZKY [*taking* WALLENSTEIN *aside, secretively*]:
    Is it at your command the Croats ride?
WALLENSTEIN: I know of nothing.
TERZKY: Then we are betrayed!
WALLENSTEIN: What?
TERZKY: They are gone, last night, the rifles too,
    No one in all the villages around.
WALLENSTEIN: And Isolani?
TERZKY: You dispatched yourself.
WALLENSTEIN: I?
TERZKY: Did you not? Did not dispatch him? Nor
    Count Deodati? Both of them have vanished.

SCENE 6

[*Enter* ILLO.]

ILLO: Has Terzky told you –
TERZKY: He knows all.
ILLO: And that Maradas, Esterhazy, Götz,
    Colalto, Kaunitz have deserted?
TERZKY: Devils!
WALLENSTEIN [*with a gesture*]:
    Be silent!

COUNTESS [*who has been anxiously watching from a distance,
     coming to join them*]:
             Terzky! In God's name, what is it?
WALLENSTEIN [*about to go*]:
     Nothing! Come, let us go.
TERZKY [*following him*]:   Nothing, Theresa.
COUNTESS [*holding him back*]:
     Nothing? Can I not see that all the blood
     Of life from both your ghost-white cheeks has drained,
     That my own brother can but feign composure?
          [*Enter a* PAGE.]
PAGE: An adjutant is asking for Count Terzky.
          [*Exit.* TERZKY *follows him.*]
WALLENSTEIN: Hear what he has to say –
                         [*to* ILLO] They could not go
     So quietly without mutiny – who keeps
     The watch upon the gateways?
ILLO: Tiefenbach's.
WALLENSTEIN: Have Tiefenbach's relieved immediately,
     And send up Terzky's grenadiers. – But listen!
     Have you no news of Butler?
ILLO: Butler I met.
     He will be here himself. He will stay loyal.
          [*Exit* ILLO. WALLENSTEIN *makes to follow him.*]
COUNTESS: No, do not let him leave you, sister! Stop him –
     But some misfortune –
DUCHESS: God in Heaven! What is it?
          [*Clinging to him.*]
WALLENSTEIN [*disengaging himself from her*]:
     Be calm, and let me be! Dear wife, and sister!
     This is a camp of war! It must be so,
     Sunshine and storms swiftly succeed each other,
     To guide these heady spirits is not easy,
     And never is the leader's head at peace.

If I must stay, then leave me! For the moans
Of women match but ill the deeds of men.

   [As he is about to go, re-enter TERZKY.]

TERZKY: Stay here, and you will see it from this window.

WALLENSTEIN [*to the* COUNTESS]:

Go, sister.

COUNTESS: Never!

WALLENSTEIN: Then I will.

TERZKY [*leads her aside, gesturing meaningfully in the direction of
   the* DUCHESS]:

               Theresa!

DUCHESS: Come, sister, it is his command.

   [*Exeunt.*]

SCENE 7

[WALLENSTEIN, TERZKY.]

WALLENSTEIN: What is it?

TERZKY: There is a running and a gathering
Amongst the troops. No one can tell the cause.
In secrecy and with mysterious stillness,
Each corps assembles underneath its standards,
Tiefenbach's men look grimly on all comers,
And only the Walloons remain apart
In their own camp, allow no strangers near,
And keep their countenance, as is their custom.

WALLENSTEIN: Is Piccolomini amongst the men?

TERZKY: We looked, but he is nowhere to be found.

WALLENSTEIN: What did that adjutant report to you?

TERZKY: It was my regiments that had dispatched him.
They swear anew their oath to you, await
With martial joy the summons to the fight.

WALLENSTEIN: But how did this disturbance reach the camp?
  It was agreed we would not tell the army
  Till fortune had declared for us at Prague.

TERZKY: Oh, if you had believed me! Yesterday
  We both besought you not to let that fox,
  Octavio, slink from within these gates,
  You gave him horses for his flight yourself –

WALLENSTEIN: The old, old song! Once and for all, I say,
  This foolish calumny I'll hear no more!

TERZKY: You trusted Isolani too, remember,
  And now he is the first to have deserted.

WALLENSTEIN: It was but yesterday I raised him up.
  Let him be gone! I never looked for thanks.

TERZKY: So are they all, the one just like the next.

WALLENSTEIN: And does he do me wrong to leave me thus?
  He follows still the god that all his life
  He's worshipped at the gaming table. Not
  With me, but with my fortune he has broken.
  What was I then to him, or he to me?
  No, I am nothing but the ship on which
  He stowed his hopes, and boldly sailed the seas;
  But when he sees it close upon the rocks
  He saves his goods as quickly as he can.
  Like bird from nesting-branch he flies from me;
  No human bond between us two is broken.
  He would deserve to find himself betrayed,
  Who in that thoughtless breast would find a heart.
  On his smooth brow the images of life
  With but a quickly-fading stroke are drawn;
  Nothing disturbs his bosom's silent depths,
  His cheerful senses stir to easy life,
  But he is cold within, and has no soul.

TERZKY: And yet I should be happier to trust
  Smooth brows than others that are deeply lined.

SCENE 8

[Enter ILLO, furious.]

ILLO: Treason and mutiny!

TERZKY: Ha! now what more?

ILLO: Tiefenbach's men, when I commanded them
To stand down guard – the scoundrels and deserters!

TERZKY: Well, then?

WALLENSTEIN: What did they – ?

ILLO: They would not obey.

TERZKY: Then shoot them down! Oh, will you give the
order!

WALLENSTEIN: Patience! Did they give reason for refusing?

ILLO: They say that they obey no other than
Lieutenant-General Piccolomini.

WALLENSTEIN: What – what was that?

ILLO: That those were his instructions,
Confirmed in writing in the Emperor's hand.

TERZKY: The Emperor's hand – prince, do you hear!

ILLO: The colonels
Fled yesterday upon his instigation.

TERZKY: You hear!

ILLO: Caraffa, Montecuculi
And six more generals have disappeared
As well, that he persuaded to go with him.
They say that he has long been carrying
His papers from the Emperor, and took
His final briefing now from Questenberg.

[WALLENSTEIN sinks on to a chair and covers his face.]

TERZKY: Oh, if you only had believed me!

SCENE 9

[*Enter* COUNTESS TERZKY.]

COUNTESS: I cannot bear this dread – no longer bear it.
 Say in the name of God what is the matter.
ILLO: The regiments are all deserting.
 Count Piccolomini is proved a traitor.
COUNTESS: O my suspicions! [*Rushes from the room.*]
TERZKY: Had *I* been believed!
 Now do you see the lies the stars have told you!
WALLENSTEIN [*standing up*]:
 The stars can tell no lies, but this refutes
 The stars, and thwarts the course of destiny.
 My arts are honest, but this perjured heart
 Stains heaven's own truthful face with lies and falsehood.
 Truth is the base of truthful prophecy;
 Where nature bursts from her appointed bounds,
 All art must err. Was it but superstition
 That made me shun to cast dishonour on
 A fellow-man by nursing base suspicion,
 I will not be ashamed of such a weakness!
 Religion's urge all animals obey,
 The savage will not drink together with
 The sacrifice whose breast his sword must pierce.
 Octavio, this was no hero's deed!
 This was no victory of prudent wisdom,
 Your evil heart has scored a shameful triumph
 Over my own so simple and so straight.
 There was no shield to meet your blow, you struck
 With murderous stroke my unprotected breast.
 Against such weapons I am but a child.

SCENE 10

[Enter BUTLER.*]*

TERZKY: Ah, Butler! Here is still a friend at last!

WALLENSTEIN *[going to meet him with outstretched arms and embracing him warmly]*:

Come to my heart, my old comrade-in-arms!
The warmth of sun in spring is not so sweet
As friendly face in such an hour as this.

BUTLER: My general – I come now –

WALLENSTEIN *[leaning on his shoulder]*: Have you heard?

He has betrayed me to the Emperor.
What do you say to that? For thirty years
We lived and bore the toils of war together.
We two have slept together in one bed,
Drunk from one glass, and shared one bite of bread;
I leant upon his shoulder, as I now
Upon your loyal shoulder bear my weight;
And in the very moment when in love
And trust my breast is beating at his own,
He takes advantage of me, thrusts his knife
With slow and stealthy cunning in my heart!
    [Hiding his face against BUTLER's *breast.]*

BUTLER: Forget the traitor. Say, what will you do?

WALLENSTEIN: Yes, yes, well spoken. Leave me, then! I am
Still rich in loyal friends, is it not so?
Destiny loves me still, for even now,
As his deceitful cunning was unmasked,
A faithful heart was sent to me as well.
No more of him. Think not the loss of him
Is painful; painful only is his falsehood.
For prized and precious they were both to me.

And Max, – I think he loved me truthfully,
Did not deceive me, no, not he – Enough,
Enough of them! Swift we must take our counsels –
The messenger Count Kinsky will be sending
From Prague may reach us any moment now.
Whatever he may bring, we must not let
The mutineers take hold of him. So, quickly,
Send one we can depend upon to meet him
And bring him to me by a secret path.

[ILLO *makes to leave.*]

BUTLER [*holding him back*]: My general, who is it you expect?

WALLENSTEIN: The messenger who comes to bring me news
Of what success we had at Prague.

BUTLER: Hm!

WALLENSTEIN: What?

BUTLER: You do not know?

WALLENSTEIN: What then?

BUTLER: Who brought this noise
Into the camp?

WALLENSTEIN: No, speak!

BUTLER: That messenger –

WALLENSTEIN [*expectantly*]:
Well?

BUTLER: He has come.

TERZKY *and* ILLO: Has come?

WALLENSTEIN: My messenger?

BUTLER: Some hours ago.

WALLENSTEIN: And I have not been told?

BUTLER: They intercepted him.

ILLO [*stamping his foot*]:   Be damned!

BUTLER: His letters
Were opened, and the whole camp now has seen them –

WALLENSTEIN [*in tense anticipation*]:
You know what they contain?

BUTLER [*hesitantly*]:   You must not ask.

TERZKY: Oh, Illo! Woe to us! it is the end!

WALLENSTEIN: Keep nothing from me. I can hear the
worst.

Prague then is lost? It is? Confess it freely.

BUTLER: Yes, Prague is lost; and all the regiments
At Budweis, Tabor, Braunau, Königingrätz,
At Brünn and Znaym have all deserted you,
Sworn to the Emperor anew – yourself
And Kinsky, Terzky, Illo, are proscribed.

[TERZKY *and* ILLO *show fear and rage.* WALLENSTEIN
remains standing firm and composed.]

WALLENSTEIN [*after a pause*]:
It is decided, well and good; and fears
And doubts may torture other breasts than mine;
How swiftly once again my spirit clears!
It must be night for Friedland's stars to shine.
With hesitant resolve, uncertainly
I drew my sword, when still my choice was free;
Necessity now speaks, all doubts take flight,
Now for my head and for my life I fight.

[*Exit, the others following.*]

SCENE II

[*Enter* COUNTESS TERZKY *from the side-chamber.*]

COUNTESS: No! I can bear no more – Where are they? All
Have fled. They leave me here alone – alone
With all my fear and dread – I have to wear
A false composure in my sister's presence,
A face of calm, and lock within my breast
The torments that I feel – I cannot bear it!
– If it should fail, if he should have to go

With empty hands, a beggar, to the Swedes,
Not in his princely state, a treasured ally,
Bringing his mighty army – no! if we
Should have to wander like the Palsgrave through the lands,
A shameful monument of greatness humbled –
I will not see that day! and even if
Himself he could abide to sink so low,
I could not bear to see him fallen thus.

SCENE 12

[*Enter the* DUCHESS *and* THEKLA.]

THEKLA [*seeking to hold the* DUCHESS *back*]:
  My dearest mother, will you not stay here!
DUCHESS: No, there is some more fearful secret yet
  That is withheld from me – Why does my sister
  Avoid my presence? Why so full of dread
  Do I behold her, you so full of terror?
  What is the meaning of these silent gestures
  That you exchange so furtively in secret?
THEKLA: Nothing, dear mother!
DUCHESS: Sister, I will know!
COUNTESS: Why then, what use to make a secret of it!
  Can it be hidden? She must now or later
  Hear everything and bear it as she may.
  This is no time to yield to weakness now,
  Courage we need, a spirit resolute,
  And strength must be no stranger to our breasts.
  Better her fate should be decided in
  A single word – You are deceived, my sister.
  You think the Duke has been dismissed – the Duke
  Is not dismissed – he has –

THEKLA [*going towards the* COUNTESS]: Oh, would you kill her?

COUNTESS: The Duke – his highness –

THEKLA [*putting her arms round her mother*]: Oh, be brave, my
   mother!

COUNTESS: His highness has rebelled and made attempt
   To join the enemy, the army has
   Deserted him, and all has been in vain.

   [*During these words, the* DUCHESS *totters and falls insensible
   in her daughter's arms.*]

Scene: *A large hall in the Duke of Friedland's quarters.*

SCENE 13

[WALLENSTEIN, *in armour.*]

WALLENSTEIN: This you have done, Octavio – once more
   I find myself alone, almost as on
   The day I left the Regensburg assembly.
   Then I had nothing but myself – but what
   One man can weigh, you have already found.
   My leafy branches you have hacked away,
   A naked trunk I stand! But here within
   My inmost marrow springs the vital power
   That put forth shoots, and gave a world its birth.
   Already once before I was your army,
   Myself alone. Before the might of Sweden
   Your armies one by one melted away.
   Tilly, your paladin, fell beside the Lech;
   Into Bavaria, like a swollen torrent
   Gustavus poured his might, and in Vienna
   The Emperor lay trembling in his palace.

Soldiers could not be found, for it is fortune
That draws the mass of men – then eyes were turned
To me, your help in hour of need; the Emperor
Humbled his pride to make apology:
I was to rise and speak the mighty word
And fill the empty camps with men once more.
I did. The drum was beaten, and my name
Ran like a war-god through the world. The plough,
The workshop are abandoned, all come flocking
Beneath the flag of hope they knew of old –
– And still I feel myself the same as ever!
The spirit shapes the body for its dwelling,
And Friedland soon will fill his camp about him.
Yes, lead your men in thousands bold to meet me,
Often they tasted victory beneath me,
But not against me – Part the head and limbs,
And you will see in which the soul was dwelling.
    [*Enter* ILLO *and* TERZKY.]
Courage, my friends! We are not yet laid low.
Five regiments of Terzky's are still ours,
And Butler's gallant troops – tomorrow comes
A force of sixteen thousand Swedes to join us.
No stronger did I ride nine years ago
To conquer Germany for the Emperor.

SCENE 14

[*Enter* NEUMANN, *who takes* TERZKY *on one side and speaks to him.*]

TERZKY [*to* NEUMANN]:
  What do you want?
WALLENSTEIN: Who's there?

TERZKY: Ten cuirassiers
  Of Pappenheim's are asking, in the name
  Of their whole regiment, to see you.
WALLENSTEIN [*quickly to* NEUMANN]: Send them in.
    [*Exit* NEUMANN.]
  I think it may be useful. You will see,
  They are still doubtful, we can win them still.

SCENE 15

[*Enter ten* CUIRASSIERS, *led by a* LANCE-CORPORAL.
They form up at the word of command before the DUKE
and present arms.]

WALLENSTEIN [*to the* CORPORAL, *after looking closely at them
  for a while*]:
  I know you well. You come from Bruges in Flanders,
  Your name is Mercy.
LANCE-CORPORAL: Henry Mercy, sir.
WALLENSTEIN: Once on the march you were surrounded by
  The Hessians, and fought your way to freedom,
  Less than two hundred men against a thousand.
LANCE-CORPORAL: That is the truth, my general.
WALLENSTEIN: And what
  Was your reward?
LANCE-CORPORAL: I had the honour, sir,
  For which I asked, of serving with this corps.
WALLENSTEIN [*turning to another of them*]:
  And you came forward, when that day upon
  The Altenberg I called for volunteers
  To go and take the Swedish battery.
SECOND CUIRASSIER: I did, my general.
WALLENSTEIN: I forget no man

With whom I ever spoke a single word.
Say what you have to say.
LANCE-CORPORAL [*giving orders*]: Squad, shoulder arms!
WALLENSTEIN [*turning to a third*]:
Your name is Risbeck, and Cologne your home.
THIRD CUIRASSIER: Risbeck, and from Cologne.
WALLENSTEIN: And you it was who took the Swedish
    colonel
Duval a prisoner at Nuremberg.
THIRD CUIRASSIER: Not I, my general.
WALLENSTEIN: Of course! It was
    Your elder brother did it – and you had
    A younger brother too, what came of him?
THIRD CUIRASSIER: He is at Olmütz with the Emperor's
        troops.
WALLENSTEIN [*to the* LANCE-CORPORAL]:
    Speak then.
LANCE-CORPORAL: A letter from
    The Emperor has come into our hands,
    Which –
WALLENSTEIN [*interrupting him*]: Who selected you?
LANCE-CORPORAL: Each company
    Picked its own man by lot.
WALLENSTEIN: To business, then.
LANCE-CORPORAL: A letter from
    The Emperor has come into our hands,
    Which orders us to cease obeying you,
    Because you are a traitor and our foe.
WALLENSTEIN: And what did you decide to do?
LANCE-CORPORAL: Our comrades
    At Braunau, Budweis, Prague and Olmütz have
    Complied already, and the Tiefenbach,
    Toscana regiments have followed suit
    – But we do not believe you are a traitor
    And thus our foe, we think it is a lie

And some invention of the Spaniards.
[*Forthrightly*] Yourself must tell us what is your intent,
For you have always spoken true to us,
Our faith and trust we gladly place in you,
No stranger's word shall come between ourselves,
The good commander and his goodly troops.

WALLENSTEIN: I see my Pappenheimers have not changed!

LANCE-CORPORAL: And this is what your regiment would
    say:
If all you purpose is to keep in hand
The marshal's baton that you hold of right,
Entrusted to you by the Emperor,
Remaining Austria's faithful general,
Then we will stand beside you and protect you
And guard your lawful rights against all men –
And if the other regiments, each one,
Desert you, we alone will keep our oath,
Be true to you, lay down our lives for you.
For this we hold our solemn duty, rather
To suffer death than to abandon you.
But if this letter of the Emperor's
Is true, and if indeed you would break faith
And lead us over to the enemy –
God grant it is not so! But if it is,
We too will leave you and obey that letter.

WALLENSTEIN: Listen, my lads –

LANCE-CORPORAL: Come, waste no words, but tell
Us yes or no, and that will be enough.

WALLENSTEIN: Listen. I know that you are thinking men
Who do not follow blindly with the herd.
And therefore, as you know, I always marked
You out with special honour from the rest;
For when the general scans with flying glance
The field, the standards only he can see,
He does not tell the face of every man,

Blind are the eyes that flash their harsh command,
And man to man can count for nothing here –
You know that this was not my way with you;
But as yourselves in war's rough work you showed
That you remained composed, as from your brows
I saw the light of human reason shining,
So I have treated you as men, and free,
And granted you the right of your own voice –

LANCE-CORPORAL: Yes, you have always nobly dealt with
     us,
My general, have honoured with your trust
And favoured us above all regiments.
And you can see we are not following
The mass, but we would loyally stand by you.
Say but a word, a word from you suffices,
That it is not your plan to turn a traitor,
To lead your army to the enemy.

WALLENSTEIN: I turn a traitor? I have *been* betrayed!
The Emperor has sacrificed me to
My enemies, and I must fall, unless
My own brave troops will stand by me and save me.
In you I put my trust, and make your hearts
My fortress! See, this very bosom is
Their target, and this grizzled head! Yes, this
Is Spanish gratitude, this our reward
For deadly battle before Nuremberg,
On Lützen's plain! For this it was we hurled
Ourselves upon the spears with naked breasts,
For this we made the hard unyielding stone,
The ice-bound earth our pillow; not a river was
Too swift for us, no forest was too dense.
We followed Mansfeld and we never flagged
In all the twists and turnings of his flight;
Our life was but one long unresting march,
And like the howling wind that knows no home

We swept across the war-torn face of earth.
And now, when we have done our work of arms,
That hard, ungrateful, and accursed task,
Have borne upon untiring faithful shoulders
The burden of the war, this royal youth
Would lightly carry off the peace, would weave
Into his blond and boyish locks the wreath
Of laurel that belongs upon *our* brow.

LANCE-CORPORAL: That he shall not, while we can still
prevent it.
No one but you, that with renown have fought
This fearful war, shall bring it to its close.
You led us out upon the bloody field
Of death, and none but you shall lead us back
Rejoicing to the smiling fields of peace,
And share with us the fruits of all our toil –

WALLENSTEIN: What? Do you think, when you are old, at
last
You will enjoy those fruits? Do not believe it!
The ending of this strife you will not live
To see! This war will swallow up us all.
Austria wants no peace, and for that reason,
Because *I* work for peace, so I must fall.
Austria does not care if this long war
Devours the army, devastates the world;
She only seeks to grow and gain in lands.
I see that you are touched – that noble rage
Starts in bright flashes from your warlike eyes.
I would my spirit could inspire you now
To boldness, as in battle once it led you!
You want to stand by me, to use your arms
To guard my rights – and it is nobly said!
But do not think you can accomplish this,
My little army! No, in vain you will
Have sacrificed yourselves for your commander.

[*Confidentially*]

No! We must move with care, and look for friends,
If Sweden offers help, then let us seem
To take it, till, the terror of both sides,
We hold the fate of Europe in our hands,
And from our camp lead forth, before the world
Rejoicing, peace with fairest garlands crowned.

LANCE-CORPORAL: So you would only seem to side with
    Sweden?
Will not betray the Emperor, not make
Us Swedish? – for you see that that is all
That we would have you give assurance of.

WALLENSTEIN: What do I care for Sweden? I detest her,
Worse than the pit of hell, and with God's help
I hope to drive her back across the Baltic.
My cares are for the whole. I have a heart
That suffers with the pains of Germany.
You are but common men, and yet your thoughts
Are not the common sort – yes, you deserve
That I should speak with you in confidence.
See now! For fifteen years the torch of war
Has blazed, and still no pause. Germans and Swedes!
Papists and Lutherans! No man will give
The other ground! Each hand is turned against
The next! All in dispute, and none to be
Their judge! Where will it end? Who can unravel
This tangled knot, that grows upon itself
And never stops? It must be cut asunder.
I feel I am the man that fate has chosen,
And hope that with your aid I may achieve it.

SCENE 16

[*Enter* BUTLER.]

BUTLER [*in agitation*]:
  This was not well advised, my general.
WALLENSTEIN: What?
BUTLER: It cannot but be harmful to our cause.
WALLENSTEIN: What then?
BUTLER: It is a proclamation of revolt!
WALLENSTEIN: What is it?
BUTLER: Terzky's regiments are tearing down
  The eagle of the Empire from their standards,
  And setting up your badge instead!
LANCE-CORPORAL [*to the* CUIRASSIERS]: Right turn!
WALLENSTEIN: Curses upon this plan and on its author!
  [*To the* CUIRASSIERS, *who are marching off*]
  Stop, lads, and listen – this is some mistake –
  But stop, and listen – and it shall be punished!
  They will not hear.
              [*To* ILLO] Go after them, persuade them,
  And bring them back here, cost it what it may!
  [ILLO *hurries off*.]
  Oh, this will be our ruin – Butler, Butler!
  You are my evil demon, did you have
  To tell me in their presence – Everything
  Was going well – they had been half won over –
  The madmen, with their thoughtless, hasty show
  Of loyalty – O cruel trick of fate!
  The zeal of friends it is that hurls me to
  My doom, and not the hatred of my foes!

SCENE 17

[*The* DUCHESS *rushes in, followed by* THEKLA *and* COUNTESS TERZKY; *later* ILLO.]

DUCHESS: Albrecht, what have you done!

WALLENSTEIN: Now this as well!

COUNTESS: Forgive me, brother. I could not prevent it,
  Now they know everything.

DUCHESS: What have you done!

COUNTESS [*to* TERZKY]:
  Is there no hope? Can it be true that all
  Is lost?

TERZKY: It is. The Emperor holds Prague.
  The regiments have all renewed their oath.

COUNTESS: O treacherous Octavio! – And is
  Count Max still here?

TERZKY: Where should he be? He will
  Be with his father and the Emperor.
    [THEKLA *falls into her mother's arms, hiding her face upon her breast.*]

DUCHESS [*holding her in her arms*]:
  Unhappy child, and more unhappy mother!

WALLENSTEIN [*taking* TERZKY *aside*]:
  A carriage, quickly, have it ready in
  The court beyond, to take those three away.
    [*Pointing to the women*]
  Send someone – Scherfenberg is loyal to us –
  To Eger with them. We will join them there.
    [*To* ILLO, *who has returned*]
  Have you not brought them back?

ILLO: You hear the noise?
  The Pappenheimers to a man are on

Their way, demanding that you set their colonel,
Young Max, at liberty again, for they maintain
That he is in the castle, held by force,
And if you will not let him go, then they
Will show you they can use their swords to free him.
[*All stand amazed.*]

TERZKY: What can this message mean?

WALLENSTEIN: Did I not say so?
O my prophetic heart! He is still here!
No, he has not betrayed me, could not find
It in him – never did I doubt him.

COUNTESS: O if he is still here, then all is well,
I know then what will bind him here for ever!
[*Putting her arms round* THEKLA.]

TERZKY: It cannot be. But think of it! His father
Has gone, betrayed us to the Emperor,
How can he dare to stay?

ILLO [*to* WALLENSTEIN]: I saw them take
The coach-and-four you gave him recently
Across the square, an hour or two ago.

COUNTESS: Then he will not be far off!

THEKLA [*with her gaze riveted on the door, cries out with anima-*
tion]:   Here he is!

SCENE 18

[*Enter* MAX PICCOLOMINI.]

MAX [*coming into the centre of the room*]:
Yes, I am here! I can endure no longer
To creep with silent tread about this house,
To lie in ambush like a thief to snatch
The favourable moment – no, this dread,

This waiting is beyond my strength!

[*He approaches* THEKLA, *who has thrown herself into her mother's arms.*]

O blessed angel, do not look away!
Confess before them all. You need not fear them.
Let all who will, hear that we love each other.
What need is there to hide it? Secrets are
For happy lovers; but misfortune needs
No veil to cover it, when hope is none,
Beneath a thousand suns it can go free!

[*He notices the* COUNTESS *looking at* THEKLA *with an expression of triumph.*]

No, cousin Terzky! Do not look at me
In hope and joy! I have not come to stay.
I come to say farewell, for it is past.
I must, I must desert you, Thekla – must!
And yet I cannot take with me your hatred.
Only a single glance of pity grant me,
Say that you do not hate me. Say it, Thekla.

[*Seizing her hand, with great emotion*]

O God! O God! I cannot leave this place.
I cannot – cannot let this hand from mine.
Say, Thekla, say that you have pity on me,
That you believe I can do nothing other.

[THEKLA, *avoiding his gaze, indicates with her hand her father's presence;* MAX *turns to face the* DUKE, *seeing him now for the first time.*]

You here? It was not you whom I was seeking.
My eyes should not have looked on you again.
With her alone I have to speak. This heart,
This heart alone shall speak me innocent,
And nothing more in all this world concerns me.

WALLENSTEIN: You think that I am such a fool, to let you go,
And act a scene of magnanimity?

Your father played a scoundrel's trick on me,
You now to me are nothing but his son, it shall
Not be for nothing you are in my power.
You need not think that I will honour our old friendship
That he abused so shamefully. The time
Of love and tender gentleness is gone,
Revenge and hatred come to take their turn.
I can forget I am a man, as he does.

MAX: According to your power, you may use me.
But yet you know that I shall not defy
Your rage, nor fear it. What it is that keeps
Me here, you know! [*Seizing* THEKLA *by the hand*]
See! – Everything I would have owed to you,
So gladly have received my happiness
From your paternal hand. You have destroyed
That happiness; you do not care. You blindly trample
The lives of all about you in the dust;
The god *you* serve is not a god of mercy.
Like the blind element that mindless rolls,
The fearful power that makes no pact with men,
The savage promptings of your heart you follow.
Woe to all those that trust in you, and build
On you the fragile shelter of their fortune,
Deceived by you with welcoming display!
Swift, unforeseen, and at the dead of night
In treacherous abyss the fires ferment,
To spew their pent-up force upon the haunts
Of men, engulfing them in hideous fury.

WALLENSTEIN: It is your father's heart that you depict.
Just as you say, so is it in his breast,
Within the entrails of that black deceiver.
Oh, arts of hell have tricked me. The infernal
Regions sent me the worst of lying spirits,
The most accomplished at his work, and placed
Him as my friend beside me. Who can stand

Against the might of hell! The basilisk
I cherished in my bosom, nurtured him
With blood of my own heart, and greedily
He drank and fattened at my loving breast.
I would not hear a breath of ill against him,
I left the gates of prudence standing wide
And threw the key of circumspection from me –
Far in the starry skies my eyes were seeking,
In space beyond the earth, my enemy,
And in my heart of hearts I held him close!
If ever I had been to Ferdinand
All that Octavio was to me – then never
Would I have warred on him – I could not do it.
He was but my dread lord, and not my friend,
Between us there was war already, when
He laid the marshal's baton in my hands,
For cunning and suspicion war for ever,
And only faith and trust can live at peace.
O, he that poisons faith, he strangles in
Its mother's womb the unborn generation.

MAX: I will not seek to justify my father;
Alas for me, I cannot!
Unhappy, fateful deeds have come to pass,
One wicked action follows on the other
Like close-forged links within a hideous chain.
But how came we, we who have done no wrong,
Within this circle of ill-fated crime?
With whom did we break faith? Why must the guilt
And wickedness our fathers share entwine
Us like a serpent pair in loathsome knot?
Why the unyielding hatred of our fathers
Sunder us too, and rend our bond of love?
   [He embraces THEKLA in violent grief.]

WALLENSTEIN [has fixed his gaze on him, silently, and now
   draws near to him]:

Max! Stay with me. Do not go from me, Max!
Remember, in our winter camp at Prague
When you were brought to me, a tender lad
Unused to German winters, and your hand
Was stiff with holding up your heavy standard,
But like a man you would not let it go;
I took you up, and covered you with my own cloak,
I was your nurse myself. I did not scorn
To do those humble services, I cared
For you with womanly solicitude,
Until once more upon my heart you warmed
And felt with joy your youthful life returning.
When have my feelings altered since that day?
I have made many thousands wealthy men,
Rewarded them with honours, given them
Estates of land – but you alone I *loved*,
Gave you my heart, gave you my very self.
They were all strangers to me, you the child
Of my own house – Max! You cannot desert me!
It cannot be, no, I will not believe
That Max, my Max could leave me.

MAX: God in Heaven!

WALLENSTEIN: I bore you up, have been your life's support
Since you were but a child – What has your father
Done for you that I have not done, and more?
A net of love I spun and wound about you,
Break from it if you can – to me you are
Bound fast by every tender bond of spirit,
By every tie of natural affection
That men are joined by and that they hold sacred.
Go then, desert me, serve your Emperor,
And earn yourself a dainty chain of gold,
A golden fleece indeed as your reward,
For thinking nothing of your friend, the father of
Your youth, the holiest of human feelings.

MAX [*in a turmoil of conflict*]:
  O God in Heaven! What can I do but this?
  My oath – my duty –
WALLENSTEIN: Duty to whom? Who are you?
  If I should wrong the Emperor, then I
  Do wrong, not you. Can you command yourself,
  Or call yourself your own, stand free to face
  The world, as I do, so that you alone
  Could claim to be the author of your deeds?
  I am your root, I am your Emperor,
  To me do you belong, to hear me and
  Obey – that is your honour and your law.
  And if the star on which you live and dwell
  Should quit its path, and hurl itself in flames
  Upon some nearby world and set it burning,
  You cannot choose to follow or to stay,
  Its hurtling force will tear you onwards with it,
  Together with its ring and all its moons.
  Light is the guilt you bear in this dispute;
  The world will not condemn, but rather praise you,
  That you could rank your friend above all else.

SCENE 19

[*Enter* NEUMANN.]

WALLENSTEIN: What is it?
NEUMANN: The Pappenheimers have dismounted, and
  Advance on foot, with sword in hand, determined
  To storm the castle and release the Count.
WALLENSTEIN [*to* TERZKY]:
  Draw up the chains, and have the guns in place,
  They shall have chain-shot for their welcoming.
  [*Exit* TERZKY.]

To give me orders with the sword! Go, Neumann,
And say that I command them to withdraw
Upon the instant, and in proper order, silently
To wait upon my pleasure.

[*Exit* NEUMANN. ILLO *has gone to the window.*]

COUNTESS: Let him go,
I beg you, let him go!

ILLO [*at the window*]:   Death and damnation!

WALLENSTEIN: What is it?

ILLO: They have climbed the town hall, cleared
The roof, are bringing cannon, aiming at
The castle –

MAX: Madmen!

ILLO: Now they are preparing
To fire at us –

DUCHESS *and* COUNTESS: Great God!

MAX [*to* WALLENSTEIN]:   Let me go down
And talk with them –

WALLENSTEIN: You shall not move one step!

MAX [*pointing to* THEKLA *and the* DUCHESS]:
Think of their lives, and yours!

WALLENSTEIN: What is it, Terzky?

SCENE 20

[*Re-enter* TERZKY.]

TERZKY: A message from our loyal regiments.
They can no longer check and stay their courage,
They ask you for permission to attack.
The Prague and Mill Gates they command already,
And if you would but give the word, then they

Could fall upon the enemy from the rear,
Confine him in the town, and easily
Be master of him in the narrow streets.

ILLO: Come, give the word! Let not their zeal grow cold.
All Butler's men are faithful to us too,
We have superior numbers and can crush them,
And stop the whole rebellion here in Pilsen.

WALLENSTEIN: What, shall this town become a battlefield,
And shall fraternal strife with eyes of fire
Here be unleashed, and rage within its streets?
What, shall we leave the issue of this day
To savage frenzy, deaf to any leader?
There is no room to fight, but only butcher;
The fury of their anger, once unloosed,
No master's voice can bid them check again.
But very well! Long have I thought of this,
If it must be, let it be swift and bloody.
    [*Turning to* MAX]
What then? Have you a mind to try this match?
You are at liberty to go. Take up
Your post against me. Lead them into battle.
You are not ignorant of war, for you
Have learnt from me, I need not be ashamed
Of such an enemy as you, and you
Will have no finer day than this to pay
Me for your lessons.

COUNTESS: Has it come to this?
O cousin, can you bear to do this thing?

MAX: The regiments entrusted to my orders
I will deliver to the Emperor
As I have promised loyally, or die.
My duty asks no more of me. I will
Not fight with you, unless I cannot help it;
Your head is sacred to me, though my foe's.
    [*Two shots are fired.* ILLO *and* TERZKY *hurry to the window.*]

WALLENSTEIN: What's that?

TERZKY: He's fallen.

WALLENSTEIN: Fallen? Who?

ILLO: It was the Tiefenbachs that fired the shot.

WALLENSTEIN: At whom?

ILLO: At Neumann, whom you sent just now –

WALLENSTEIN [*starting up*]:

  Death and damnation! Let me go –

TERZKY: And face their fury?

COUNTESS *and* DUCHESS: No, in Heaven's name!

ILLO: Not now, my general.

COUNTESS: Stop him!

WALLENSTEIN: Leave me!

MAX: No,

  No, do not go, not now. This bloody deed
  Has put them in a rage, they will regret –

WALLENSTEIN: Away! I have delayed too long already.
  That, they could have the insolence to do
  Because they had not seen my face – they shall
  Behold my face, my voice their ears shall hear –
  Are they not mine, these troops? And am not I
  Their general, the commander they must fear?
  Let's see if they no longer know this face
  That was their sun amidst the dark of battle.
  Weapons will not be needed. I will show
  Myself upon the balcony before
  These rebels, and their spirits, you will see,
  Unruly now, will quickly find their way
  Back to the channel of obedience.

    [*Exit, followed by* ILLO, TERZKY *and* BUTLER.]

SCENE 21

[COUNTESS TERZKY, DUCHESS, MAX *and* THEKLA.]

COUNTESS [*to the* DUCHESS]:
When they see him – sister, there is still hope.
DUCHESS: Hope! I have none.
MAX [*who during the last scene had stood apart in visible agitation,
   approaches them*]:

                              No! This I can no longer bear.
I came here fixed and resolute of soul,
Believing I did right beyond reproach,
And now must stand here hateful in the eyes
Of those I love, inhuman and accursed,
Reviled by all who are so dear to me,
Unworthy stand and look on their distress,
When I can make them happy with a word –
My heart rebels within me, warring voices
Arise within my breast, in me is night.
I do not know how rightly I should choose.
Oh, yes, it was the truth you spoke, my father,
Too great the trust I placed in my own heart,
I stand in doubt, do not know what to do.
COUNTESS: You do not know? And will your heart not tell
   you?
Then let *me* tell you, sir!
Your father has betrayed us – how it shrieks
To highest Heaven! – conspired against the Duke
Our prince, brought shame upon us, and from this
It must be plain what you, his son, must do:
Make full amends for his disgraceful treason,
Example set of loyalty and faith,
So that the name of Piccolomini

Shall not be cursed and shamed for ever in
The house of Wallenstein.

MAX: Where shall I find
A voice of truth to follow? Passion drives
Us all, our own desires deceive us. Would
That some bright angel might descend to me,
To show me right, to draw with its pure hand
From the pure source of light the truth unsullied!

[*As his eyes fall upon* THEKLA]

But what? Do I still seek this angel? Can
There be another?

[*He goes up to her and embraces her.*]

                              Here, upon this heart,
So holy, pure, infallible, I will
Rely, your love shall be my oracle,
Which blesses none but him already blessed,
And turns away from him accursed with guilt.
Speak, can you love me still, if I stay here?
Say that you can, and I will be your man.

COUNTESS [*urgently*]: Think well –

MAX [*interrupting her*]: No, do not think. Say what you feel.

COUNTESS: Think of your father –

MAX [*interrupting her*]:   No, not Friedland's daughter,
Yourself, my own dear love, shall answer me!
It is not our concern to win a crown,
Of that a prudent spirit well might think.
It is your friend's own peace, it is the joy
Of heroes' gallant hearts, a thousand strong,
Who in their deeds will follow his example.
Am I to break faith with the Emperor?
Am I to send into Octavio's camp
The bullet that could bear my father's death?
For when the bullet leaves the gun behind,
It is no more a lifeless thing, but quick,
And bears a spirit; Furies seize upon it,

Those goddesses who wreak revenge on crime,
And guide its baleful path with all their cunning.

THEKLA: O Max—

MAX [*interrupting her*]: No, do not speak too hastily.
I know you. Such a noble heart as yours
Might well think what was hardest, duty. Let
Us not seek greatness, but humanity.
Think now of all the Duke has done for me;
Think too of how my father has repaid him.
Oh, but the free and gracious impulses
Of hospitality, and loyalty to friend,
Give to the heart a sacred, pious duty,
And nature will exact a grim revenge
On the barbarian who would defile them.
Lay all this in the balance too, then speak
And let your heart decide it.

THEKLA: Oh, but yours
Has long decided. Do what you first felt
Was right—

COUNTESS: Unhappy creature!

THEKLA: How could that
Be good, that instantly this tender heart
Did not proclaim, and light upon the first?
Go, leave us, do your duty. I should love
You always. For whatever you had chosen,
It would have been a noble act and worthy
Of you—but never shall repentance cloud
The radiant peace and beauty of your soul.

MAX: So I must leave you, part from you for ever!

THEKLA: True to yourself, you will be true to me.
Fate parts us, but our hearts remain united.
A bloody hatred sunders for all time
The house of Friedland and of Piccolomini,
But we do not belong to our own house.
—And now away, away! Let your good cause

Be severed quickly from our luckless fate.
The curse of Heaven lies upon our head,
And it is doomed to be destroyed. Me too
My father's guilt will drag down to the depths
With him. But do not grieve for me. My lot
Will be decided soon.

> [MAX *seizes her in his arms, with great emotion. Offstage is heard a loud, wild and prolonged shouting of* Vivat Ferdinandus!, *accompanied by martial instruments.* MAX *and* THEKLA *remain embraced, without moving.*]

SCENE 22

[*Enter* TERZKY.]

COUNTESS [*turning to meet him*]:
  What's that? What was the meaning of that shouting?
TERZKY: That all is finished, everything is lost.
COUNTESS: What, and they paid no heed when he appeared?
TERZKY: None. It was all in vain.
COUNTESS: They shouted Vivat.
TERZKY: The Emperor.
COUNTESS: Oh, traitors to their duty!
TERZKY: They would not listen to a single word.
  When he began to speak, they cut him off
  And drowned his voice with martial instruments.
  – But here he is.

SCENE 23

[*Enter* WALLENSTEIN, *accompanied by* ILLO *and*
BUTLER; *later* CUIRASSIERS.]

WALLENSTEIN [*entering*]:
  Terzky!
TERZKY: Your highness?
WALLENSTEIN: Let our regiments
  Stand by in readiness to march today,
  For we are leaving Pilsen by this evening.
    [*Exit* TERZKY.]
  Butler!
BUTLER: My general?
WALLENSTEIN: The commandant of Eger
  Is your compatriot and friend. Send him
  A message, quickly, that he must prepare
  For our reception in the fort tomorrow –
  And you will follow with your regiment.
BUTLER: It shall be done, my general.
WALLENSTEIN [*parting* MAX *and* THEKLA, *who have remained
    all the while in a close embrace*]:   Part!
MAX: O God!
    [CUIRASSIERS *with drawn swords enter the hall and gather in
    the background. Some brisk passages from the Pappenheim
    March are heard, as if to summon* MAX.]
WALLENSTEIN [*to the* CUIRASSIERS]:
  Look, here he is. He is at liberty.
    [*He turns away and stands so that* MAX *can neither approach
    him nor come nearer to* THEKLA.]
MAX: You hate me, and in anger drive me from you.
  The bond of love shall thus be torn apart,
  Not gently loosed, and you will make this rent,

That is so painful, yet more painful still.
You know that I have not yet learnt to live
Without you – to the wilderness I go
Alone, and everything that I hold dear
Stays here behind – Oh, do not turn your eyes
Away from me! Once more let me behold
The face I love and honour for all time.
Do not reject me –

    [*He tries to take* WALLENSTEIN's *hand.* WALLENSTEIN
    draws it back. He turns to the COUNTESS.]
                          Will no other eyes
Look pityingly on me – Dear cousin Terzky –

    [*She turns away; he addresses the* DUCHESS.]
Most honoured lady –

DUCHESS: Leave us, count, and go
Where duty calls you. One day, you may be
A loyal friend to us, an angel by
The Emperor's throne.

MAX: *You* give me hope at last,
You will not see me cast into despair.
Oh, do not trick me with an empty show,
My misery is sure, but praised be Heaven,
That shows me how to make an end of it.

    [*The martial music begins again. The hall becomes fuller and
    fuller with armed men.* MAX *sees* BUTLER *standing beside
    him.*]
You too here, Colonel Butler? And you will
Not follow? – Very well! Show your new master
A truer spirit than your old. Come! Promise,
Give me your hand on it, that you will guard
His life, and shield it from all injury.

    [BUTLER *refuses his hand.*]
The Emperor's proscription makes his princely head
The goal of any venal murderer
Who with such bloody deed would earn his wage;

A friend he needs to watch with zealous care,
The loyal eyes of love – and those I see
About him as I go –

[*With dubious glances at* ILLO *and* BUTLER.]

ILLO: Look for the traitors
In your own father's camp, and Gallas's.
Here there is only one remaining. Go,
Relieve us of his hateful sight. Be gone.

[MAX *tries once more to approach* THEKLA. WALLENSTEIN
*prevents him. He stands in painful indecision. Meanwhile the
hall grows fuller and fuller, and from below the trumpets
sound ever more urgently and at shorter intervals.*]

MAX: Sound, sound! Oh, would that they were Swedish
    trumpets,
Summoning straightway to the field of death,
And every sword of those that I see drawn
About me here was plunged into my breast!
Why have you come? Is it to drag me off
From here – oh, do not drive me to despair!
Do not! One day, you might regret!

[*The hall is completely filled with armed men.*]

Yet more – one weight is added to another,
To drag me down with their united mass.
Think what you do! It is not wise you choose
One who has lost all hope in life to lead you.
You tear me from the joy that I must lose,
The goddess of revenge I vow shall speed you!
To choose your own destruction you are free,
Let none fear death who takes the field with me!

[*As he turns upstage, there is a quick movement among the*
CUIRASSIERS; *they surround him and accompany his exit with
a wild tumult.* WALLENSTEIN *remains motionless.* THEKLA
falls into her mother's arms. The curtain falls.]

ACT FOUR

The Burgomaster's house at Eger.

SCENE I

BUTLER [*who has just arrived*]:
He's here. His destiny has brought him in,
Behind him the portcullis gate has fallen,
And as the bridge that bore him was let down
And with a swaying motion rose again,
All way of rescue is cut off from him.
Here, Friedland, and no further! says the goddess
Of fate. As from Bohemia's soil arose
The shooting star of your admired career,
To blaze its brilliant path across the heavens,
Here on Bohemia's borders it must fall.
Fool! to the ancient flag you would be false,
And yet you trust your ancient, kindly fortune?
To carry war into the Emperor's lands,
To overthrow the gods of hearth and home,
You rise and arm yourself with impious hand.
Beware! The evil spirit of revenge
Impels you – let not vengeance be your ruin!

SCENE 2

[*Enter* GORDON.]

GORDON: Ah, is it you? How I have longed to hear you.
The Duke a traitor! God, can this be so?

A fugitive! His princely head proscribed!
I beg you, General, tell me everything
That happened there in Pilsen, spare me nothing.

BUTLER: You have received the letter that I sent
Ahead to you by special messenger?

GORDON: And loyally have done as you commanded,
Opened the fortress to him without question,
For I am ordered by Imperial letter
To offer blind obedience to your word.
And yet, forgive me! when I saw the Prince
Himself, my doubts began to stir again.
For truly! it was not like one proscribed
The Duke of Friedland made his entry here.
Upon his brow there shone as ever bright
The ruler's majesty, that bids obey,
And calm, as in the days when all was well,
He heard me give account of my commission.
Ill-fortune and bad faith breed flattery,
And fallen pride will often bend the knee
To lesser men, and seek to win their favour;
But with restraint and dignity the Prince
Weighed every word of praise, as any master
Commends the servant who has done his duty.

BUTLER: Just as I wrote to you, so it has happened.
The Prince has sold the army to the Swede
Our foe, and would surrender Prague and Eger.
On hearing word of this, the regiments
Have left him to his fate, all barring five
Of Terzky's, that have come here with him now.
He is proclaimed a traitor to the Empire,
And every loyal servant is commanded
To give him up, be it alive or dead.

GORDON: A traitor to the Emperor – our lord!
A man so nobly gifted! What is greatness!
I often said that it must come to ill:

His greatness and his power will prove a snare,
And all the shadowy might that moves in darkness.
For man will grasp and grow, you may not trust
Him to restrain himself alone. His bounds
Will not be fixed but by the word of law
And by the paths of custom, deeply trenched.
And yet unnatural and strange it seemed,
The power of war this man held in his hands;
It made him rival to the Emperor,
His spirit in its pride forgot to bow.
O, what a man! for there is not another,
As I believe, to stand where he could fall.

BUTLER: Spare your laments until he needs your pity,
For now he still has power to make him feared.
The Swedes are on the march, approaching Eger,
And soon, unless we stop them with swift action,
Their forces will unite. That must not happen!
The Prince must not set foot at liberty
Outside these walls, for I have staked my life
And honour he shall be my captive here,
And your assistance I must count upon.

GORDON: Oh, would that I had never seen this day!
His very hand conferred this office on me,
And he it was entrusted me this castle,
That now I must transform into his prison.
We mere subordinates can have no will;
The free, the powerful alone obey
The fairest feeling that man calls his own.
We are but myrmidons who serve the law
In all its cruelty; obedience is
The only virtue we may call our own.

BUTLER: Do not regret the closer confines of
Your power. Great freedom leads to greater error.
Safe is the narrow path that duty treads.

GORDON: And do you say that all have left him, then?

He made the fortune of so many thousands,
For kingly was his spirit, ever open
His hand in plenteous generosity –
   [*With a sidelong glance at* BUTLER]
Many a man he raised up from the dust,
Exalted him in rank and dignity,
And has not gained himself a single friend,
Not one, who will stand by him in his need!

BUTLER: Yet here is one he scarcely will have hoped for.

GORDON: I have enjoyed no favours from his hand.
   I almost doubt that ever in his greatness
   He once recalled a friend of bygone youth –
   My office kept me far from him, his eye
   Lost sight of me within this castle's walls,
   Where I, beyond his princely favour's reach,
   Kept my heart's freedom in its quiet retreat.
   For when he placed this fortress in my charge,
   He knew his duty still, and I do not
   Betray his trust, if faithfully I guard
   What to my faith was long ago confided.

BUTLER: Speak then, will you not act on his proscription,
   Lend me your aid to take him prisoner?

GORDON [*after a pause of silent reflection, sadly*]:
   If it is so – if it is as you say –
   If he has left the Emperor, his master,
   Has sold the army, sought to open up
   The Empire's strongholds to her foes – yes, then
   There can be no escape – But it is hard
   That of all men the lot should fall on me
   To be the instrument of his destruction.
   For we were pages at the court in Burgau
   Together, though I was the older one.

BUTLER: I know.

GORDON: It must be thirty years ago. Already
   The youth of twenty strove with fearless courage,

Grave was his spirit, far beyond his years,
Bent only upon greatness, like a man's.
With silent mind he moved amongst our number,
His own society; the childish pleasures
Of other boys could hold no joy for him;
But often he would suddenly be seized,
And wondrous, from the secrets of his breast,
A ray of thought would beam, a shaft of wisdom,
And we would gaze upon each other, wondering
If madness, or a god had spoken from him.

BUTLER: Yes, that was where he fell two storeys' height,
When in a window-bay he fell asleep,
And picked himself up quite unharmed again.
And from that day they say there could be seen
The signs of madness in his mind and bearing.

GORDON: More grave and pensive he became, indeed,
And turned a Catholic. His wondrous rescue
Worked wondrous change in him. He felt that now
He bore a favour and a charm of freedom,
And bold as one who knows he cannot stumble
He danced upon the swaying rope of life.
Then destiny led our two paths apart,
Far, far apart! He trod the way of greatness
With swift and gallant step, giddy I watched;
Count he became and Prince and Duke, Dictator,
And now all is too small for him, he would
Reach out his hand to grasp a kingly crown –
And plunges to unfathomable doom!

BUTLER: Enough now. Here he is.

SCENE 3

[*Enter* WALLENSTEIN *in conversation with the* BURGOMASTER OF EGER.]

WALLENSTEIN: You used to be a free Imperial city?
  I see the eagle in your coat of arms.
  But only half an eagle – why?
BURGOMASTER: We *were* free,
  But then, two hundred years ago, the town
  Was mortgaged to the Bohemian crown. And so
  We only bear the eagle's upper half.
  The lower half is cancelled, till the day
  The Empire pays the mortgage.
WALLENSTEIN: You deserve
  Your freedom. Keep the peace, and do not listen
  To any agitators. How much tax
  Is levied?
BURGOMASTER [*shrugs his shoulders*]:
          Almost more than we can raise.
  We must maintain the garrison as well.
WALLENSTEIN: I promise you shall be relieved. Come, tell me,
  You still have Protestants within your walls?
  [*The* BURGOMASTER *is taken aback.*]
  Yes, yes. I know. There are still many hidden
  Here in this city – yes! Why not confess
  That you yourself – ?
  [*Fixing his gaze upon him. The* BURGOMASTER *starts in fear.*]
          You need not fear. I hate
  The Jesuits – I would expel them from
  The Empire, if I had my way. What, Bible
  Or breviary – it is one to me –

And I have proved it to the world – In Glogau
I built the Lutherans a church myself.
Listen now, burgomaster – what's your name?

BURGOMASTER: Pachelbel is my name, your highness.

WALLENSTEIN: Listen – but tell no other what I say
To you, in confidence.

[*Putting his hand on his shoulder, with a certain gravity of manner*]

                                    The time has come
When this shall be fulfilled, good burgomaster!
The mighty shall be humbled, and the lowly
Shall be uplifted – this for you alone!
The twofold rule of Spain is coming to
Its end, the order of the world shall be
Renewed – You saw three moons in heaven
Not long ago?

BURGOMASTER: With horror, yes, I saw them.

WALLENSTEIN: Two of them changed their shape and hue, like swords
Covered in blood. Only the third of them,
The middle one, kept its true shape and brightness.

BURGOMASTER: We thought that it must mean the Turks –

WALLENSTEIN: The Turks?
Two empires shall be swallowed up in blood
In East and West, I tell you this shall be,
One creed remain – the Lutheran alone.

[*He notices the other two.*]

There was a heavy firing to our left
This evening, as we made our way to Eger.
Could it be heard here in the citadel?

GORDON: It could indeed, my general. The wind
Carried the sound directly from the south.

BUTLER: It seemed to come from Neustadt or from Weiden.

WALLENSTEIN: That is the route the Swedes are taking here.
What is your garrison?

GORDON: A hundred and
Four score are fit to serve, the rest are wounded.

WALLENSTEIN: And down in Jochimsthal?

GORDON: I sent two hundred
Arquebusiers to guard the forward post
Against the Swedes.

WALLENSTEIN: Let me commend your prudence.
I saw them building on the outworks here
As well, when we arrived.

GORDON: Because the Rhinegrave
Had come so close to threaten our defences,
I had two bastions quickly put in order.

WALLENSTEIN: You serve your Emperor with zeal, I see.
Lieutenant-Colonel, I am pleased with you.
[To BUTLER] The post in Jochimsthal will be vacated
And all the rest that stand towards the foe.
[To GORDON] Commandant, in your loyal hands I leave
My wife, my sister and my only child.
For here is not my place to stay; I wait
For letters only, and expect to leave
The fort straightway with all the regiments.

SCENE 4

[Enter TERZKY.]

TERZKY: Good news, good news I bring, and welcome
    tidings!

WALLENSTEIN: Come, let us hear!

TERZKY: A battle has been fought
At Neustadt, and the Swedes have won the day.

WALLENSTEIN: What do you say? Where did you hear this
    message?

TERZKY: A peasant came with it from Tirschenreit.
  He said it had begun just after sunset,
  Imperial detachments up from Tachau
  Had forced their way into the Swedish camp,
  Two hours the firing had gone on unbroken,
  A thousand of the Emperor's men were killed,
  Their colonel too, – he could not tell me more.

WALLENSTEIN: How could Imperial troops have come to
    Neustadt?
  If it was Altringer, he must have wings,
  Yesterday he was fourteen leagues away;
  Gallas is mustering at Frauenberg,
  His men are not yet ready. Could it be
  That Suys had ventured on so far ahead?
  It cannot be.
        [ILLO appears.]
TERZKY: Well, we shall hear it soon,
  For here comes Illo, joyful and in haste.

SCENE 5

[Enter ILLO.]

ILLO [to WALLENSTEIN]: A rider is below to speak with you.
TERZKY: The victory! Speak, is the news confirmed?
WALLENSTEIN: What does he say? Where is he from?
ILLO: The Rhinegrave,
  And I will tell you what he has to say.
  The Swedes are only twenty miles from here;
  At Neustadt young Max Piccolomini
  Hurled himself at them with his cavalry,
  There was a fearful slaughter on the spot,
  But numbers won the victory at last,

And all the Pappenheimers, Max as well,
Their leader, killed; not one man left alive.

WALLENSTEIN: Where is the messenger? Come, take me to
   him.
   [*He is about to leave. At this moment* FRÄULEIN NEUBRUNN
   *rushes into the room, followed by a number of servants, who
   run through the hall.*]
NEUBRUNN: Help!
ILLO *and* TERZKY: What is it?
NEUBRUNN: The lady!
WALLENSTEIN *and* TERZKY: Knows it?
NEUBRUNN: She will die!
   [*She hurries away.* WALLENSTEIN *and* TERZKY *with* ILLO
   pursue her.]

SCENE 6

[BUTLER, GORDON.]

GORDON [*in amazement*]:
   Explain. What was the meaning of this scene?
BUTLER: Why, she has lost the man she loved;
   It was young Piccolomini that was killed.
GORDON: Unhappy lady!
BUTLER: What that Illo said, you heard.
   The Swedes are coming, they have won.
GORDON: I heard it.
BUTLER: They have twelve regiments, and five more stand
   Here close at hand to give the Duke protection.
   We only have one regiment of mine,
   The garrison is not two hundred strong.
GORDON: It is the truth.
BUTLER: It is not possible

With so few men to guard a prisoner of state.

GORDON: I must agree.

BUTLER: Their numbers would in no time have disarmed
Our paltry band, released him.

GORDON: So I fear.

BUTLER [*after a pause*]:
Listen! I am the surety for this,
And for his head I answer with my own.
My word must not be broken, come what may,
And if we cannot keep our man alive,
Then – dead we can be sure of him.

GORDON: What are you saying? God of justice! You –?

BUTLER: He cannot live.

GORDON: And you could be the man – ?

BUTLER: Yourself or I. No day dawns more for him.

GORDON: And you will murder him?

BUTLER: That is my plan.

GORDON: The man who trusted you!

BUTLER: His evil fate!

GORDON: Your general's sacred person!

BUTLER: That he *was*!

GORDON: Oh, what he was, no crime can so degrade!
Without a judgement?

BUTLER: Execution serves.

GORDON: That would be murder, never could be justice,
Even the guiltiest must still be heard.

BUTLER: His guilt is clear, the Emperor has judged him,
It is his will, we carry out his word.

GORDON: Why haste to carry out a word of blood?
Men may take back a word – but not a life.

BUTLER: Swift must our service be, to please a king.

GORDON: No man of worth will rush to serve as hangman.

BUTLER: No brave one pale to do a deed of courage.

GORDON: His life a brave man dares, but not his conscience.

BUTLER: What? Shall he freely go, to light the flames

Of war to rage unquenchable again?

GORDON: Make him your prisoner, but do not kill him,
Prevent with bloody stroke a deed of mercy!

BUTLER: Had not the Emperor's army been defeated,
Then living I should gladly have preserved him.

GORDON: Why did I open up the fortress to him?

BUTLER: No, not this place, his destiny has killed him.

GORDON: I should have died a soldier on these walls
To save this castle for the Emperor.

BUTLER: A thousand gallant men were killed today!

GORDON: In duty's cause – a glorious, noble death,
Murder is black, and flees from nature's curse.

BUTLER [*producing a paper*]:
Here is the proclamation that commands us
To seize this man. It is directed to
Yourself, just as to me. What will you do,
When through our fault he flees to join the foe?

GORDON: Oh, helpless that I am, O God!

BUTLER: Take it upon you. Bear the consequence!
Yes, come what may! I lay it in your hands.

GORDON: O God in Heaven!

BUTLER: Is there another way
To carry out the Emperor's order? Speak!
I seek his downfall, but not his destruction.

GORDON: O God! I see as clear as you do, what must be;
It is my heart beats otherwise.

BUTLER: And nor may those two, Illo and Count Terzky
Remain alive, if once the Duke must fall.

GORDON: For them I shall not grieve. They were led on
By their own evil hearts, and not the stars.
But they it was who in his breast, once calm,
Sowed seeds of evil passion and ambition,
And with accursed industry and skill
Nurtured the fatal fruit. – No, let them draw
The evil recompense of evil service!

BUTLER: Before him they shall go to meet their death.
    All is arranged. This very evening we
    Had planned to seize them while they banqueted,
    And hold them captive in the fortress here.
    This will be quicker. I will go straightway,
    And see the necessary orders given.

SCENE 7

[Enter ILLO *and* TERZKY.]

TERZKY: Now things will change! Tomorrow we shall have
    The Swedes with us, twelve thousand gallant men.
    Then for Vienna. Hey, old fellow! Why
    This gloomy face to greet such cheerful news?
ILLO: Now is our turn for laying down the law
    And taking vengeance on the shabby villains
    Who have abandoned us. The first has paid
    Already, that young Piccolomini.
    May all who wish us ill end as he did.
    The old man feels the blow a heavy one.
    His whole life long he's toiled to raise his house
    From count's to prince's rank, and there he is
    Now burying his only son and heir!
BUTLER: And yet that young man had a hero's spirit,
    The Duke himself was touched by such a loss.
ILLO: Listen, old friend. That was a thing I never
    Did like about our chief, it always grieved me
    To see him favour those Italians.
    This very day, I swear upon my life,

He'd gladly see us dead and ten times over,
If it would bring his friend to life again.

TERZKY: No more! Be silent! Leave the dead in peace!
Today we have to test our skills at drinking.
Your regiment is entertaining us.
We'll make this night a merry carnival,
Turn night to day, and with our glasses full
We shall receive the Swedes when they arrive.

ILLO: Yes, let us still enjoy ourselves today,
For I can see a busy time ahead.
This sword of mine shall not be sheathed, I swear,
Till it has drunk its fill of Austrian blood.

GORDON: For shame, what words are these you speak, Field-
Marshal?
Why do you rage against your Emperor –

BUTLER: Do not stake all on his first victory,
But think, how swiftly turns the wheel of fortune.
He is still powerful, the Emperor.

ILLO: The Emperor has troops but no commander,
For this King Ferdinand of Hungary,
He has no skill in war – Gallas? Unlucky,
He brings no army anything but ruin.
And that Octavio, the snake, though he
Can bruise your heel, and wound you secretly,
Cannot match Friedland in an open battle.

TERZKY: We cannot lose, believe me. Luck and fortune
Are with the Duke; that only Wallenstein
Brings victory to Austria, all men know.

ILLO: The Prince in no time will have gathered up
A mighty army, all will rush and stream
To fight beneath his banners, famed of old.
I see the days of old return once more,
He will be great again, the man he was –
The fools, that left him now! Then they will see

They cut their noses off to spite their face. –
For all his friends will be enriched with lands
And loyalty imperially rewarded.
But we shall be the foremost in his favour.
[*To* GORDON] You he will think of too, will take you from
This miserable hole, and let men see
Your loyalty in some more stately office.

GORDON: I am content, and do not seek to rise:
For lofty peaks have fearful chasms beneath them.

ILLO: Here there is nothing more for you to do,
The Swedes command the fortress here tomorrow.
Come along, Terzky. It is time for dinner.
What say you? Let the whole town be lit up,
In honour of the Swedes; if any man
Refuse, he is a Spaniard and a traitor.

TERZKY: No, let that be. It will displease the Duke.

ILLO: What! We are masters here, and where we rule,
Let no man stand up for the Emperor's cause.
– Gordon, good night; and for the last time, guard
This castle well, send out your sentinels,
For safety's sake the password may be changed.
Upon the stroke of ten o'clock you will
Give up the keys in person to the Duke,
Your task as commandant will then be done.
The Swedes command the fortress here tomorrow.

TERZKY [*as he goes, to* BUTLER]:
You'll join us in the castle?

BUTLER: In good time.

[*Exeunt* ILLO *and* TERZKY.]

SCENE 8

[BUTLER, GORDON.]

GORDON [*watching them go*]:
    The miserable wretches! Unsuspecting
    They fall into the fatal snare that's laid them,
    Blinded and drunken with their victory!
    I cannot grieve for them. This brazen Illo,
    This overreaching villain, who can talk
    Of gorging on his Emperor's own blood!

BUTLER: Do as he ordered you. Send out patrols,
    See that the citadel is safely guarded;
    When they are in the castle I shall seal it,
    And no one in the town will hear what happens.

GORDON [*anxiously*]:
    O do not hasten so! First say –

BUTLER: You heard
    Them say the Swedes are here tomorrow.
    This night alone is ours; the Swedes are quick,
    We will be quicker yet. – So, fare you well.

GORDON: Oh, in your looks I read but evil signs.
    Promise to me –

BUTLER: The sun has sunk to rest,
    Evening descends, heavy with destiny. –
    Those two their folly dooms. Their evil star
    Surrenders them unarmed to us, and in
    The midst of drunken revelry the flash
    Of steel shall swiftly end their empty lives.
    The Prince was always skilled in reckoning;
    All things were subject to his calculations.
    Men too, like pieces in a game of chess,
    He placed and moved according to his purpose.

He did not scruple to use others' names
And dignity and honour as his pawns,
He reckoned on and on, but at the end
His calculations are amiss; he will
Have reckoned his own life into the sum,
And like that Greek, will fall in his own circle!

GORDON: O do not think upon his errors now!
Think of his greatness, of his generous spirit,
The features of his heart that made men love him,
And all the noble deeds his life could name,
And let them like an angel crying mercy
Hold back the sword that waits to strike him down.

BUTLER: It is too late. I may not pity him,
Blood is the only thought my mind may know.

  [*Taking* GORDON *by the hand*]

Gordon! It is not hate impels me – though
I do not love the Duke and have no cause to –
It is not hate makes me his murderer.
It is his evil fate. Ill fortune drives me,
The hostile confluence of circumstance.
Man thinks that he is free to do his deeds,
But no! He is the plaything of a blind
Unheeding force, that fashions what was choice
Swiftly into a grim necessity.
What use to him, if something in my heart
Should speak on his behalf – I still must kill him.

GORDON: Oh, if your heart should warn, obey its prompting!
The heart is God's own voice, the work of man
Is all the calculation of our cunning.
What fortune can such bloody deed as this
Bring you? No good can ever come of blood!
Is it to pave for you the way to greatness?
Not so! For even though a murder please
A king, he will abhor the murderer.

BUTLER: You do not know. You must not ask. Why should

The Swedes be victors and approach so quickly?
Gladly I'd yield him to Imperial mercy,
I do not seek his blood, no, let him live!
But I must prove the honour of my word.
And he must die, or – hear, and know it then!
I am dishonoured, should the Prince escape.
GORDON: O such a man – to save him –
BUTLER [*quickly*]:   What?
GORDON: Is worth a sacrifice – Be generous!
Honour is in the heart, not men's opinion.
BUTLER [*coldly and proudly*]:
He is a great man, is the Prince, and I
A lowly creature – do you mean to say?
What does the world care, do you mean, if one
So lowly born wins honour or disgrace,
If but the prince among us may be safe.
– Each one of us names his own value. How
I choose to prize myself, is my affair.
There is no man on earth so lofty placed
That I must needs despise myself beside him.
It is man's *will* that makes him great or lowly;
As I am true to mine, so he must die.
GORDON: O I would seek to move the solid rock!
You are no man, nor born of other men.
I cannot hinder you, but may some god
Deliver him from such a fearful hand.
   [*Exeunt.*]

SCENE 9

A room in the Duchess's lodgings.

[THEKLA *in an armchair, pale, with her eyes closed. The*
DUCHESS *and* FRÄULEIN VON NEUBRUNN *are*

attending to her. WALLENSTEIN *in conversation with*
COUNTESS TERZKY.]

WALLENSTEIN: How did she hear of it so soon?
COUNTESS: It seems
  She felt a premonition of misfortune.
  The rumour of a battle, where the colonel
  Of the Imperial troops was killed, had frightened her.
  I saw it straight away. She flew to meet
  The Swedish courier, and by her questions
  Soon brought his luckless secret to the light.
  Too late we missed her, hurried to discover
  She lay already senseless in his arms.
WALLENSTEIN: So unexpected must this fearful blow
  Fall on her! My poor child! – What? Is she stirring?
  [*Turning to the* DUCHESS.]
DUCHESS: Her eyes are opening.
COUNTESS: She lives.
THEKLA [*looking about her*]:   Where am I?
WALLENSTEIN [*goes over to her and raises her up in his arms*]:
  Come to yourself now, Thekla. Be my brave daughter!
  See here your mother filled with love for you,
  And these your father's arms that bear you up.
THEKLA [*sitting upright*]:
  Where is he? Is he here no longer?
DUCHESS: Who, my daughter?
THEKLA: The man who spoke those tidings of misfortune –
DUCHESS: O do not think of it, my child! No, turn
  Your thoughts away from that unhappy scene.
WALLENSTEIN: No, let her sorrow speak! Let her lament!
  Shed tears yourselves, and mingle them with hers!
  For now she knows the meaning of great pain;
  But she will overcome it, for my Thekla
  Has from her father his unconquered heart.
THEKLA: I am not sick. I have the strength to stand.

Why is my mother weeping? Is she frightened?
I am myself again, and it is past.

[*She has stood up, and peers round the room, looking for something.*]

Where is he? He shall not be hidden from me.
I have the strength, and I will hear him speak.

DUCHESS: No, Thekla! Never shall this bearer of
Misfortune come before your eyes again.

THEKLA: My father –

WALLENSTEIN: Dearest child!

THEKLA: I am not weak,
I shall be more recovered in a while.
Grant me just one request.

WALLENSTEIN: Say what it is.

THEKLA: Permit this stranger to be called, that I
May question him alone and hear him.

DUCHESS: Never!

COUNTESS: No! That would not be good! Do not consent!

WALLENSTEIN: Why do you wish to speak with him, my
    daughter?

THEKLA: When I know everything, I shall be calmer.
I will not be deceived. My mother only seeks
To spare me pain, but I will not be spared!
The depth of horror has been told, I can
Hear no worse horrors!

COUNTESS *and* DUCHESS [*to* WALLENSTEIN]:
              No, do not allow it!

THEKLA: I was surprised and overcome by fright,
My heart betrayed me in the stranger's presence,
He was a witness to my weakness, yes,
I fainted in his arms – I am ashamed.
I must restore myself in his esteem,
And I must speak to him, most urgently,
So that the stranger does not judge me wrongly.

WALLENSTEIN: I find her in the right – and am inclined

To grant the favour she has asked me. Call him.

[*Exit* FRÄULEIN NEUBRUNN.]

DUCHESS: But I, your mother, will be at your side.

THEKLA: I should prefer to speak with him alone.
I shall be calmer thus, and more composed.

WALLENSTEIN [*to the* DUCHESS]:
Let it be so. Leave her to face the man
Alone. There is a kind of grief that man
Can only help himself to bear, a heart
That's strong will only trust in its own strength.
Her breast, and not another's, must provide
The power through which she may survive this blow.
This girl is my brave daughter; not as woman,
But like a hero I would have you use her.

[*He makes as if to go.*]

COUNTESS [*holding him back*]:
Where are you going? I heard Terzky say
That you proposed to leave this place tomorrow,
But leave us here behind.

WALLENSTEIN: Yes, you will stay,
And have some sturdy fellows to protect you.

COUNTESS: O take us with you, brother! Do not leave
Us here in gloom and loneliness to wait
Upon the issue with an anxious spirit.
Present misfortune is not hard to bear,
But doubts and fears and pain of expectation
Increase its horrors to us from afar.

WALLENSTEIN: What talk is this? Misfortune, do you say?
I have quite other hopes than these.

COUNTESS: Then take us with you. Do not leave us here
Behind you in this place of ill foreboding.
My heart is heavy in these fortress walls,
And like a vault of death they breathe on me,
I cannot say how much I hate this place.
Take us away! Come, sister, join your pleas

That he will take us with him! Help, dear niece!

WALLENSTEIN: The place's evil favours I will change:
It shall be where my dear ones are kept safe.

FRÄULEIN NEUBRUNN [returning]:
The Swedish gentleman.

WALLENSTEIN: Leave them alone. [Exit.]

DUCHESS [to THEKLA]:
See how you turn so pale! You cannot speak
To him, my dearest child. Come with your mother.

THEKLA: Let Fräulein Neubrunn stay here, close at hand.
    [Exeunt DUCHESS and COUNTESS.]

SCENE 10

[Enter the SWEDISH CAPTAIN.]

CAPTAIN [approaching respectfully]:
Princess – I must – implore you to forgive me.
My hasty, thoughtless words – How could I know –

THEKLA [with noble bearing]:
You have beheld me in my hour of pain,
Unhappy chance brought you a stranger here.
And made you suddenly my confidant.

CAPTAIN: I fear I must be hateful in your sight,
For it was I who spoke a grievous word.

THEKLA: The fault is mine. I tore it from your lips,
And yours was but the voice of my own fate.
My terror interrupted the account
You had begun. I beg you, end it now.

CAPTAIN [doubtfully]:
Princess, I fear it will recall your pain.

THEKLA: I am prepared – I mean to be prepared.
How did the fight begin? Finish your story.

CAPTAIN: We lay, not thinking we should be attacked,
In camp at Neustadt, with but slight defences,
When towards evening there arose a cloud
Of dust towards the woods, our vanguard rushed
Into the camp, and cried, The enemy!
We scarcely had the time to leap into
The saddle, when the Pappenheimers came
Full gallop through the outworks in their charge,
And soon across the ditch as well, that ran
Around the camp, they sprang in hostile frenzy.
But reckless bravery had led them on
Before their comrades, far behind them marched
The infantry, and only Pappenheim's had dared
To follow boldly where their bold commander led. –

  [THEKLA *motions. The* CAPTAIN *pauses for a moment, until*
  she gives him a sign to continue.]

Ahead and on the flanks we now attacked
Them with the force of all our cavalry,
And drove them back into the ditch, where in
Their swiftly-mustered ranks our infantry
Presented them a bristling wall of pikes.
Now neither forwards could they move, nor back,
Hemmed tight between us in a fearful press.
The Rhinegrave called out to their leader then
To yield himself in honourable surrender,
But Colonel Piccolomini –

  [THEKLA *seizes a chair to steady herself.*]
                          we knew
Him by his helmet's crest and flowing hair,
All loosened by the swiftness of his charge –
Points to the ditch, and sets, the first of all,
His noble steed to leap it, after him
The regiment – but – ah! it was too late!
His mount, pierced by a halberd, rears itself
In pain and fury, hurls its rider down,

And over him goes thundering the charge
Of horses, heedless now of rein or bridle!

[THEKLA, *who has accompanied the last speech with every
sign of mounting dread, is seized with violent trembling; as she
is about to collapse,* FRÄULEIN NEUBRUNN *hurries to her
and clasps her in her arms.*]

NEUBRUNN: My dearest lady –

CAPTAIN [*with emotion*]:   I will go away.

THEKLA: No, it is over – Tell me to the end.

CAPTAIN: But then, when they had seen their leader fall,
The troops were seized with a despairing rage.
Now no man thinks of how he may be saved,
Like savage tigers now they fight, their fierce
Resistance spurs our side to the attack,
And on the struggle goes, and will not end,
Until the last of them has met his death.

THEKLA [*with trembling voice*]:
And where – where is – You have not told me all.

CAPTAIN [*after a pause*]:
We buried him this morning. He was borne
By twelve young men of noble lineage,
With all our army following the bier.
A laurel wreath adorned his coffin, on it
The Rhinegrave laid his own victorious sword.
Nor was there lack of tears to mourn his fate,
For many in our ranks have learned to know
His generosity and noble friendship,
And all men sorrowed at his lot. The Rhinegrave
Had gladly saved his life, but he himself
Foiled the attempt; men say he sought his death.

NEUBRUNN [*with emotion to* THEKLA, *who has covered her face*]:
My dearest lady – lady, look at me!
O why did you insist on hearing it?

THEKLA: – Where is his grave?

CAPTAIN: A monastery church

At Neustadt holds his body, till the time
When word has come to reach us from his father.

THEKLA: Its name?

CAPTAIN: The convent of Saint Catherine.

THEKLA: Does it lie far from here?

CAPTAIN: Some seven leagues.

THEKLA: What is the way?

CAPTAIN: It goes through Tirschenreit
And Falkenberg and passes our positions.

THEKLA: And who commands them?

CAPTAIN: Colonel Seckendorf.

THEKLA [goes to the table and takes a ring from her jewel-box]:
You have beheld me in my hour of pain,
And shown you have a human heart – Receive
    [Giving him the ring]
This token to remind you of this moment – Go.

CAPTAIN [taken aback]: Princess –
    [THEKLA motions him silently to go, and turns away from
    him. The CAPTAIN hesitates and is about to speak.
    FRÄULEIN NEUBRUNN motions to him again. He goes.]

SCENE II

[THEKLA, NEUBRUNN.]

THEKLA [throwing her arms about Neubrunn's neck]:
Now, my good Neubrunn, show me all the love
That you have sworn to me, and prove yourself
My loyal companion and my friend in need!
We must away, this very night.

NEUBRUNN: Away, and where?

THEKLA: Where? There is but one place in all the world!
There where his coffin lies, where he is buried!

NEUBRUNN: But what would you seek there, my dearest
    lady?

THEKLA: Would I seek there? Unhappy creature! So
    You would not ask, if you had loved. There, there
    Is everything that still remains of him,
    That single spot is all the world to me.
    – O do not hold me back! Come and make ready.
    Let us but think of how to flee from here.

NEUBRUNN: And will you not bethink your father's anger?

THEKLA: I fear no man in anger from this moment.

NEUBRUNN: The scorn of all the world! Rebuke's sharp
    tongue!

THEKLA: I go to be with one who is no more.
    What, do I seek the arms – O God in Heaven!
    I only seek my lover in his tomb.

NEUBRUNN: And we alone, two weak and helpless women?

THEKLA: We will take weapons, and my arm shall guard you.

NEUBRUNN: At dead of night?

THEKLA: The night will hide our traces.

NEUBRUNN: This rough and stormy night?

THEKLA: And was *his* bed
    So soft and smooth, beneath the galloping hooves?

NEUBRUNN: O God! – and then, the enemy positions!
    They will not let us through.

THEKLA: All men are human.
    Misfortune may pass free through all the world!

NEUBRUNN: So long a journey –

THEKLA: Does the pilgrim count
    The miles that lead him to the distant shrine?

NEUBRUNN: Will it be possible to leave this town?

THEKLA: Money will open us the gates. Away!

NEUBRUNN: If we are recognized?

THEKLA: No one will know
    A hopeless fugitive for Friedland's daughter!

NEUBRUNN: Where shall we find the horses for our flight?

THEKLA: My gentleman will find them. Go and call him.

NEUBRUNN: Without his master's knowledge, will he dare?

THEKLA: Yes, he will do it. Go, do not delay!

NEUBRUNN: And oh, your mother, what is to become
  Of her when you are gone?

THEKLA [*hesitating, and gazing out with an expression of grief*]:
                         O my dear mother!

NEUBRUNN: So much already she has had to bear,
  Poor lady, must she suffer this last blow?

THEKLA: No, she may not be spared it! – Go now, go.

NEUBRUNN: Yet once more think of what it is you do.

THEKLA: All that there is to think of, I have thought.

NEUBRUNN: When we are there, what will become of you?

THEKLA: Some god will there reveal it to my soul.

NEUBRUNN: Your heart is full of restlessness, dear lady,
  This cannot be the way that leads to peace.

THEKLA: The deepest peace of all, the peace he found.
  – O hurry! go! let me hear no more words!
  A power I cannot name is drawing me
  Inexorably onwards to his grave.
  There I shall find release, upon the instant!
  The bond of grief drawn stifling round my heart
  Will there be loosed – My tears will freely flow.
  O come, we could have long been on our way.
  No peace I'll find until I have escaped
  These walls – they press as if to fall upon me –
  Away, away, dark forces urge me fly
  From here – what is this feeling in my breast!
  I see the rooms in all this castle filled
  With ghostly figures, pale and hollow-cheeked –
  There is no room for me – Yet more they come!
  Their hideous, swarming crowd will drive me out,
  Yet living, from this house!

NEUBRUNN: With dread you fill me, lady, and with terror,

Myself I feel I can stay here no longer.
I will be gone, and send for Rosenberg. [*Exit.*]

SCENE 12

THEKLA: It is his spirit calls me, and the band
Who loyally died that he might be avenged.
Accusingly they cry: Why thus hold back?
Even in death they would not part from him
Who in their lives had led them – Such a deed
From those rough hearts, and I should stay alive?
– No! not for you alone the hero's wreath
Of laurel that adorns your grave was wound.
What is this life, when starved of love's sweet breath?
An empty thing I cast upon the ground.
When I had you, when I my love had found,
My life was full of meaning: in a gleam
Of gold I saw the dawn's fresh beam!
My hopes with hours of heavenly joy were crowned.
When from the convent's shelter first I gazed
In awe upon the world, you stood beside me;
A thousand suns upon its brightness blazed,
In childhood's dream I could no longer hide me,
But like an angel you were sent to guide me
Upon my way, on life's proud summit raised.
It seemed the bliss of heaven should be my part,
My first awakened glance fell on your heart!
  [*She falls silent, pensive, then starts up with an expression of horror.*]
Then cold and grim must destiny appear,
Must seize the tender shape of him so dear
And cast him under his horses' galloping hooves –
All beauty on this earth fate thus reproves!

SCENE 13

[THEKLA. FRÄULEIN NEUBRUNN *with* ROSENBERG *the equerry*.]

NEUBRUNN: Here is the man, my lady. He will do it.

THEKLA: Will you find horses for us, Rosenberg?

ROSENBERG: Yes, I will find them.

THEKLA: Will you come with us?

ROSENBERG: To the world's end, my lady.

THEKLA: But you can

Not then go back, and join the Duke again.

ROSENBERG: My lady, I will stay with you.

THEKLA: I will

Reward you, and commend you to another
Whom you may serve. But do you know
How we may leave the castle undiscovered?

ROSENBERG: I do.

THEKLA: When can we go?

ROSENBERG: Within the hour.

Where lies our journey?

THEKLA: To – tell him, Neubrunn!

NEUBRUNN: To Neustadt.

ROSENBERG: Very well. I will make ready. [*Exit.*]

NEUBRUNN: My lady, see, here comes your mother!

THEKLA: Heaven!

SCENE 14

[Enter the DUCHESS.]

DUCHESS: The man is gone. I find you calmer now.

THEKLA: Mother, I am. – Now let me soon retire
To bed, and let Neubrunn stay here close by me.
I must have rest.

DUCHESS:　　　　Yes, Thekla, you shall have it.
And I can go at ease, if I can tell
Your father so.

THEKLA:　　　　Good night then, dearest mother!
　　[She throws her arms round the DUCHESS's *neck and
　　embraces her with great emotion.]*

DUCHESS: I think you are not yet quite calm, my daughter.
You tremble so, and I can feel your heart
Beat here against my own.

THEKLA:　　　　　　It will find rest
In sleep – Good night again, my dearest mother!
　　[As she frees herself from her mother's embrace, the curtain falls.]

ACT FIVE

Butler's rooms.

SCENE I

*[*BUTLER *and* MAJOR GERALDINE.]

BUTLER: Pick out twelve sturdy men from the dragoons,
And arm them all with pikes, for there must be

No shooting – In the dining-hall nearby
You will conceal them. When dessert is served
You will force entry and cry out, 'Who's for
The Emperor?' – I'll overturn the table –
Then you will make for those two, run them through.
The castle will be safely barred and watched,
So that the Prince shall hear no word of it.
Go now. – And did you call Captain Macdonald
And Devereux?

GERALDINE: They will be here straightway. [*Exit.*]

BUTLER: We can risk no delay. The citizens
Are on his side, I cannot understand
What madness seems to have beset this town.
The Duke in their eyes is a prince of peace
And founding father of a golden age.
Weapons have been distributed, soon there
Will be a hundred volunteers to stand
Guard over him. So we must act with speed,
For we have enemies without and in.

SCENE 2

[*Enter* CAPTAIN DEVEREUX *and* CAPTAIN MAC-
DONALD.]

MACDONALD: Present, my general.

DEVEREUX: What is the password?

BUTLER: Long live the Emperor!

THE TWO [*drawing back*]: What?

BUTLER: And Austria's house!

DEVEREUX: Is it not Friedland then, that we are sworn to?

MACDONALD: And have we not been brought here to protect
him?

BUTLER: We, guard a traitor and the Empire's foe?

DEVEREUX: But you yourself led us to follow him.

MACDONALD: And came here with him, all the way to Eger.

BUTLER: I did it to be surer of his downfall.

DEVEREUX: Aha!

MACDONALD: That's different.

BUTLER [to DEVEREUX]: Miserable creature!
Are you so quick to change your side and colours?

DEVEREUX: The devil, sir! I followed your example;
I thought: if *he* can be a scoundrel, *you* can.

MACDONALD: Ours not to think of it! That's your affair.
You are the general and give the orders,
We follow you, to hell, if it must be.

BUTLER [*reassured*]:
Good, good! We know each other.

MACDONALD: I should think so.

DEVEREUX: Soldier of fortune is our trade, we serve
The man who offers most.

MACDONALD: Aye, that's the truth.

BUTLER: But honest soldiers now you can remain.

DEVEREUX: That we would gladly do.

BUTLER: And make your fortunes.

MACDONALD: That's better still.

BUTLER: Listen.

THE TWO: We're listening.

BUTLER: It is the Emperor's will and his command,
That Friedland shall be captured, live or dead.

DEVEREUX: So it was given out.

MACDONALD: Alive or dead!

BUTLER: And he shall be rewarded handsomely
With money and with goods, that does the deed.

DEVEREUX: Yes, it sounds well. The words that come from
there
Always sound well. Yes, we know what it means!
A golden chain, or something of that kind,

A spavined horse, a parchment and so on.
– The Duke pays better.

MACDONALD: Aye, grandly he rewards!

BUTLER: But now he's finished, for his star is fallen.

MACDONALD: Is that the truth?

BUTLER: *I* tell you.

DEVEREUX: Has his luck
Deserted him?

BUTLER: Deserted him for ever.
He is as poor as we are.

MACDONALD: Poor as we?

DEVEREUX: Why then, Macdonald, it is time to leave him!

BUTLER: Leave him? That twenty thousand did already.
We must do more, my countryman! In short,
We must – kill him.

THE TWO [*starting back*]: Kill him!

BUTLER: I tell you, kill him.
– And for this task I have picked you.

THE TWO: Picked us?

BUTLER: You, Captain Devereux, Captain Macdonald.

DEVEREUX [*after a pause*]:
Choose someone else.

MACDONALD: Aye, choose somebody else.

BUTLER [*to* DEVEREUX]:
What, are you frightened, coward? You, who must
Have thirty souls at least upon your conscience –

DEVEREUX: But to lay hands upon our own commander!

MACDONALD: Whom we have sworn the oath of loyalty!

BUTLER: The oath is void, for he has broken faith.

DEVEREUX: But, Colonel, listen! No, it is too dreadful.

MACDONALD: Aye, that it is! We have a conscience too.

DEVEREUX: If only it was not the chief who gave
Us orders for so long, deserved respect.

BUTLER: Is that the reason?

DEVEREUX: Yes! Why, any other!

I'd run my own son through with my own sword,
If the imperial service should demand it.
But we are soldiers, do you see, and *murder*
Our *general*, that is a sin, a crime
We could not find confessor to absolve.
BUTLER: I am your Pope, I'll give you absolution.
Make up your minds.
DEVEREUX [*stands in hesitation*]: We cannot.
MACDONALD: No, we cannot.
BUTLER: Very well. Go, – and – send me Pestalutz.
DEVEREUX [*taken aback*]:
Send Pestalutz – him!
MACDONALD: Why should you want him?
BUTLER: If you will not, then there are plenty more –
DEVEREUX: No, no, if he *must* die, it may as well
Be us who earn the prize as any other.
Brother Macdonald, what do you say?
MACDONALD: If
He is to die, and if it must be so,
I would not grant that Pestalutz the job.
DEVEREUX [*after some thought*]:
When is it he must die?
BUTLER: This very night,
The Swedes will be before the gates tomorrow.
DEVEREUX: You'll answer for the consequences, colonel?
BUTLER: I'll answer.
DEVEREUX: And it is the Emperor's will?
Said in so many words? We've heard before
Of murders welcomed but the doers punished.
BUTLER: The proclamation says: alive or dead.
It cannot be alive, as you can see –
DEVEREUX: Then dead! Then dead! – But how are we to
reach him?
The town is full of Terzky's men.
MACDONALD: And Terzky then himself and Illo too –

BUTLER: Those two must be the first to die, of course.

DEVEREUX: What? Must they die as well?

BUTLER: And first of all.

MACDONALD: Devereux, this will be a bloody night.

DEVEREUX: And have you picked your man for that? Take
   me!

BUTLER: No, I have detailed Major Geraldine.
   Tonight there is a banquet in the castle,
   And when they are at table we shall fall
   Upon them unawares and cut them down –
   Leslie and Pestalutz will be there too.

DEVEREUX: Look, colonel! It can make no difference.
   Will you not let me change with Geraldine?

BUTLER: The lesser danger will be with the Duke.

DEVEREUX: Danger! Why, what the devil do you mean?
   It is his look and not his sword I fear.

BUTLER: How can he harm you with his look?

DEVEREUX: The devil!
   You know me, and you know I am no coward.
   But see, it is not yet a week ago
   The Duke gave twenty golden coins to help
   Buy this warm coat, that I have on today –
   And when he sees me standing with my pike
   In front of him, and sees this coat – like this –
   The devil take me! I am not a coward.

BUTLER: The Duke gave you a coat to keep you warm,
   And you, poor fool, because of that would scruple
   To take your sword and run it through his body.
   And yet the *Emperor* gave *him* a coat
   Warmer by far than this, a prince's mantle.
   What are his thanks? Rebellion and treason!

DEVEREUX: Yes, that's the truth. The devil take such thanks!
   I – I will kill him.

BUTLER: And if you would ease
   Your conscience, take your coat off while you do it,

Then you need have no doubts and hesitations.

MACDONALD: Aye! but there is one more thing to consider –

BUTLER: Consider? Why, Macdonald, what is that?

MACDONALD: What use are swords and weapons against *him*?
  He is invulnerable, he is *proof*!

BUTLER [*starting up*]:
  What can –

MACDONALD: Against all blows and bullets! He
  Is *frozen*, he is sealed with devil's arts,
  His skin cannot be pierced, I tell you so!

DEVEREUX: Yes! there was such a one in Ingolstadt,
  His body was as hard as steel, at last
  They had to club him down with musket-butts.

MACDONALD: Listen, what I will do!

DEVEREUX: Speak then!

MACDONALD: I know
  A brother in the Black Friars' convent here,
  A countryman of mine, and he shall dip
  My sword and pike in consecrated water
  And speak a word of blessing and of power.
  It is well-tried, and stronger than all magic.

BUTLER: Do that, Macdonald. But now go, I say.
  Pick from the regiment a score or thirty
  Stout fellows – make them swear to Ferdinand –
  And when eleven strikes – the first patrols
  Have gone their rounds – in silence you will lead them
  Towards the hall – I shall be close at hand.

DEVEREUX: How shall we pass the halberdiers and guards-
    men,
  Who have the watch within the inner courtyard?

BUTLER: I have found out the place's disposition.
  There is a postern gate which I will show you,
  And that is guarded by one man alone.
  My rank and office give me at all times
  Free access to the Duke. I'll go before you,

And swiftly, with my dagger in his throat
Silence the guard and clear the way for you.

DEVEREUX: And when we have come up, how shall we reach
The Prince's chamber where he sleeps, without
The servants rousing and betraying us?
For there are many in his retinue.

BUTLER: The servants all are in the right-hand wing,
For he hates noise, and occupies the left alone.

DEVEREUX: If it was only past and done, Macdonald.
The devil knows, I do not like this work.

MACDONALD: Nor I. He is too great a man by far.
We shall be called two scoundrels that have done it.

BUTLER: With honour, wealth and glory, you may laugh
At anything that men may think or say.

DEVEREUX: If only we were certain of the honour.

BUTLER: Fear not. You will have saved for Ferdinand
The crown and empire. Richly he must pay you.

DEVEREUX: He plans then to dethrone the Emperor?

BUTLER: Indeed he does! To take his crown, his life!

DEVEREUX: So he must fall beneath the hangman's hand,
If we should take him living to Vienna?

BUTLER: That fate he could in no way turn aside.

DEVEREUX: Macdonald, come! As soldiers let us send
The general to an honourable end. [*Exeunt.*]

SCENE 3

A hall, opening on to a gallery which recedes far into the distance.

[WALLENSTEIN *is sitting at a table. The* SWEDISH
CAPTAIN *is standing before him. Soon after,* COUNTESS
TERZKY.]

WALLENSTEIN: Commend me to your master. I am pleased
At his good fortune; if I do not seem

To make such show of joy as you might think
To see at this report of victory,
Believe me, it is no ill will, for from
This day our fortunes are but one. Farewell!
My thanks for all your trouble. In the morning,
When you arrive, the fortress shall be yours.

[*Exit the* SWEDISH CAPTAIN. WALLENSTEIN *sits deep in
thought, gazing fixedly in front of him, his head resting on his
hand.* COUNTESS TERZKY *enters and stands before him
unnoticed for some time; finally he makes a sudden movement,
sees her, and quickly composes himself.*]

Were you with her? What is she doing? Is she better?

COUNTESS: After their conversation she is calmer,
My sister tells me. She has gone to bed.

WALLENSTEIN: Her grief will melt and soften. She will weep.

COUNTESS: But you too, brother, I find strangely altered.
After this victory, you should be glad.
Be strong, my brother! Do not let us fall,
For you alone are light and sun to us.

WALLENSTEIN: Have no fear. It is nothing. – Where is your
husband?

COUNTESS: Gone to a banquet here, and Illo with him.

WALLENSTEIN [*stands up and paces a few steps about the room*]:
The night is dark already – Go to your room.

COUNTESS: O do not make me go, let me stay with you.

WALLENSTEIN [*has gone to the window*]:
There is a tumult in the heavens tonight,
Wind whips the vanes upon the tower, the clouds
Chase by, the sickle moon would seem to rock,
And fitful brightness flashes in the night.
– No constellation to be seen! That dull
And solitary gleam, from Cassiopeia;
Behind her there stands Jupiter – But now
The blackness of the stormy sky conceals him!

[*He stands gazing out, plunged deep in thought.*]

COUNTESS [*looking sadly at him, takes him by the hand*]:
  What is it?
WALLENSTEIN: If I could but see *him*, I should feel better.
  He is the star that shines upon my life,
  Often the sight of him brought wondrous strength.
    [*Pause.*]
COUNTESS: You will see him again.
WALLENSTEIN [*has once again fallen into a deep distraction; he
    recovers himself and turns quickly to face the* COUNTESS]:
  See him again? – O never more!
COUNTESS: What's this?
WALLENSTEIN: No, he is gone, is dust!
COUNTESS: Whom do you mean?
WALLENSTEIN: His the good fortune. He has made an end.
  There is no future more for him, now fate
  Spins no more treachery – his life lies spread
  Immaculate without a single crease,
  Without one speck of dark to mar its gleam,
  For him no hour can strike to bring misfortune.
  Beyond all fears and wishes, he belongs
  No more to planets changing and deceitful –
  O happy man! But who can tell what we
  May find the next hour brings us, blackly veiled!
COUNTESS: You speak of Piccolomini. How did he die?
  The messenger was leaving as I came here.
    [WALLENSTEIN *motions her with his hand to be silent.*]
  O do not turn your gaze upon the past!
  Let us look forward into brighter days.
  Rejoice at victory, forget its price.
  It was not just today you lost your friend;
  When he deserted, he was dead for you.
WALLENSTEIN: The sorrow of this blow will pass, I know,
  What blows can man not overcome! He learns
  To do without the meanest and the greatest,
  For time, all-powerful, must be his master.

And yet I feel what I have lost in him.
The blossom has been plucked out from my life,
And cold and colourless I see it lying.
For at my side like my own youth he stood,
Turning all harsh reality to dream,
And weaving vapours of a golden dawn
About the common clarity of things. —
Fired by the passion of his warm affection,
Life's dull and everyday creations seemed,
To my astonishment, to rise ennobled —
Whatever future goals I may achieve,
Beauty is gone, *that* I shall not recover.
For more than all good fortune is the friend
Whose love creates, whose sharing but compounds it.

COUNTESS: Do not despair of your own strength. Your heart
   Is rich enough to fire itself anew.
   The virtues that you love and praise in him
   You planted and brought forth in him yourself.

WALLENSTEIN [*going to the door*]:
   Who comes to us so late at night? — It is
   The commandant, bringing the fortress keys.
   Leave us, my sister, now, for it is midnight.

COUNTESS: I do not want to go from you tonight,
   I think I am afraid.

WALLENSTEIN: Afraid! Of what?

COUNTESS: Afraid that you might leave us in the night,
   That we might wake and find that you were gone.

WALLENSTEIN: Imaginations!

COUNTESS: Oh, my soul has been
   So long disturbed with anxious premonitions,
   And when in waking hours I fight them, then
   In dismal dreams they crowd my fearful heart.
   — Last night I saw you sitting, richly dressed,
   With your first lady, at the dinner table —

WALLENSTEIN: That dream bears omens such as I might wish,

For it was that first marriage made my fortune.

COUNTESS: And then today I dreamt I went to find
You in your room – and as I entered there,
It was your room no more, the Charterhouse
It was at Gitschin, that you founded there
And where you wish your body to be laid.

WALLENSTEIN: Your mind is running on these things, no
more.

COUNTESS: What? Do you not believe that warning voices
Can speak to us in dreams of things to come?

WALLENSTEIN: There are such voices – there can be no
doubt!
But *warning* voices I would not call those
That merely speak of the inevitable.
Just as the image of the sun is thrown
Upon the haze, before it rises, so
Great destinies send out their harbingers.
And in today, tomorrow's spirit walks.
Many a time have I reflected on
The story of King Henry and his death.
The spectre of the knife the king had long
Felt in his breast, before the murderer
Ravaillac took it in his hand. His calm
Was gone, he felt pursued within the Louvre,
Driven into the fields; like obsequies
His Queen's glad coronation seemed, he heard
With anxious and prophetic ear the steps
That hunted him throughout the streets of Paris –

COUNTESS: And does your inner voice foretell you nothing?

WALLENSTEIN: Nothing. You can be calm!

COUNTESS [*musing darkly*]:   And then, once more,
As I came hurrying after you, you ran
Away, through galleries and spacious halls,
There was no end to them – The noisy doors
Slammed tight, I followed panting, could not catch

You – suddenly I felt an icy hand
That seized me from behind – and it was you,
You kissed me, and about us both it seemed
A crimson blanket laid its flowing folds –
WALLENSTEIN: That was the crimson carpet of my room.
COUNTESS [*gazing at him*]:
   If it should come to that – if you, that stand
   Alive and breathing here with me, should ever –
     [*She falls weeping upon his breast.*]
WALLENSTEIN: The Emperor's proscription frets you.
   Words
   Can do no hurt, and hands will not be found.
COUNTESS: But if they should be, then my resolution
   Is taken – and I bear the means of comfort. [*Exit.*]

SCENE 4

[*Enter* GORDON, *then a* SERVANT.]

WALLENSTEIN: All quiet within the town?
GORDON: The town is quiet.
WALLENSTEIN: I can hear noisy music, and the castle
   Is bright with lights. Who is it making merry?
GORDON: Count Terzky and Field-Marshal Illo have
   A banquet given for them in the castle.
WALLENSTEIN [*to himself*]:
   To celebrate the victory – These fellows
   Are only happy at the supper-table.
     [*He rings. Enter a* SERVANT.]
   Undress me now, for I will go to bed.
     [*He takes the keys.*]
   So we are safe from all our enemies
   And locked in here with none but faithful friends;
   For either all is lies, or else no face

Like this [*looking at* GORDON] could be the mask of
   treachery.

   [*The* SERVANT *has removed his mantle, gorget and sash.*]
See there! What was it dropped?

SERVANT: The golden chain is broken in the middle.

WALLENSTEIN: Well, it has held for long enough. Here with
   it!

   [*Looking at the chain*]
This was the Emperor's first gift. As Archduke
He gave it me, in the Venetian war,
And I have worn it ever since, from habit.
– From superstition, if you will. It was
To be a talisman, to bind to me,
As long as I should wear it in good faith,
That fleeting fortune, which as its first sign
Of favour had bestowed it on me. – Well!
Henceforward some new fortune must be mine,
The power of this spell is finished.

   [*The* SERVANT *takes the clothes away.* WALLENSTEIN
   stands up, paces the length of the room and stops at last, pensive
   in front of GORDON.]
How times of old seem closer to me now!
I see myself at Burgau once again,
Where we were two young pages at the court.
We often had our quarrels, you meant well
And liked to preach a sermon to me now
And then, to scold me for immoderate ambition,
For my belief in daring dreams of greatness,
And told me I should seek the golden mean.
– Your wisdom has not proved itself, my friend!
For it has made you old before your time,
And were it not for me, appearing with
My greater stars to draw you out, your light
Would quietly fade and die in this dull corner.

GORDON: Your highness! Light of heart the humble fisherman

Ties up his little boat safe in the harbour,
When in the storm he sees the great ship founder.

WALLENSTEIN: So, good old fellow, is your voyage over?
Not mine. My spirit, fresh and brave as ever,
Still drives me on to ride the wave of glory,
I still name hope the goddess of my life,
My spirit is still young, and when I see
Myself and you, together, I might boast
That over *my* head with its locks of brown
The years had flown and left no mark behind.
    [*He strides powerfully across the room and stands on the far side
    opposite* GORDON.]
Is fortune fickle? It has served me well,
Lifted me from the common ranks of men
With loving hand, and borne me up
With gentle godlike strength upon life's way.
There is no dross to soil my destiny,
Nor in the furrows of my hand. Who dares
To judge my life as it were any man's?
Today indeed it seems I am sunk low,
But I shall rise again; a flowing tide
Will follow swiftly on this present ebb. –

GORDON: Let me remind you of the ancient words:
Praise not the day before the night has fallen.
I take no comfort from the length of fortune's favour,
Let comfort and sweet hope attend misfortune;
The fortunate should rather walk in fear,
For never constant are the scales of fate.

WALLENSTEIN [*smiling*]:
Yes, Gordon's voice of old I hear again.
– I know full well that things on earth can change,
The evil gods demand their toll of us;
That, heathen folk in bygone ages knew,
And so they freely chose to suffer ill,
So that the jealous god might be assuaged,

And human sacrifices bled for Typhon.
   [*After a pause, gravely and with lowered voice*]
I too have made my sacrifice – I lost
My dearest friend, and through my fault he died.
No favour of good fortune can outweigh
The sorrow of that blow – The jealousy
Of fate is satisfied, as life for life
It takes, and turns aside upon that head
Beloved and innocent the thunderbolt
That should have riven me with fatal blast.

SCENE 5

[*Enter* SENI.]

WALLENSTEIN: Is that not Seni? And beside himself!
   What brings you here to us so late, Battista?
SENI: Your highness, fear for your sake.
WALLENSTEIN: Why, what is it?
SENI: Flee before daybreak, highness. Do not trust
   Yourself to Swedish hands.
WALLENSTEIN: What are you saying?
SENI [*his voice rising*]:
   You cannot trust the Swedes!
WALLENSTEIN: What does this mean?
SENI: You must not wait until the Swedes are here!
   False friends are close at hand, and danger threatens,
   The signs are terrifying, close, close by
   You are surrounded by disaster's net.
WALLENSTEIN: You dream, Battista, fear has turned your wits.
SENI: O do not think that idle fears deceive me.
   Come, read it written clearly in the planets
   That danger waits upon you from false friends.

WALLENSTEIN: False friends have been the whole of my
misfortune.
Your words of warning should have reached me sooner,
I do not need the stars to tell me now.

SENI: O come and see! Believe your own two eyes!
A hideous sign stands in the house of Life,
An enemy close by, a fiend is lurking
Behind the brightness of your star – Be warned!
Do not go over to this pagan horde
Who make their war upon our holy Church.

WALLENSTEIN [*smiling*]:
Is *that* the tenor of your oracle?
Why, yes! I know full well you never liked
This treaty with the Swedes – Now go to bed,
Battista! These are signs I do not fear.

GORDON [*who has been deeply disturbed by these speeches, turning
to* WALLENSTEIN]:
My lord, your highness! Have I leave to speak?
A word of help may come from humble lips.

WALLENSTEIN: Speak freely!

GORDON: Your highness! If it were no idle fear,
If Providence divine should use this tongue
To work a miracle and your salvation!

WALLENSTEIN: You ramble as in fever, both of you.
How can misfortune threaten from the Swedes?
They sought alliance, it is their advantage.

GORDON: And yet, if it was just these Swedes' arrival,
Just this, that winged disaster on its way
To strike your head, so confident and sure –
    [*Falling to his knees before him*]
There is still time, your highness –

SENI [*kneeling*]:   Hear him! hear him!

WALLENSTEIN: Time, time for what? Stand up – I tell you,
stand.

GORDON [*stands up*]:

The Rhinegrave is still far away. Give order,
And I will bar this fortress' gates before him.
If he would then besiege us, let him try.
But I say this: sooner will he and all
His army perish here before these ramparts
Than will the spirit of our courage tire.
He shall discover what a band of heroes
Can do, when by a hero they are led,
Firmly resolved to make amends for ill.
The Emperor will see, and will be moved,
For gladly would his heart be reconciled,
And Friedland, turning back in penitence,
Will stand far higher in the Emperor's grace
Than he had ever stood before he fell.

WALLENSTEIN [*gazes at him in surprise and amazement and is
    silent for a while, showing a powerful inner emotion*]:
Gordon – your zeal quite carries you away,
A friend of old may take such liberties.
– Blood has been shed, good Gordon. Never can
The Emperor forgive me. If he could,
Then I myself could not accept forgiveness.
If I had known before what now has happened,
That it would rob me of my dearest friend –
Perhaps, I had done otherwise – perhaps
Had not – But what should we spare now? Too deadly earnest
It has begun, for it to come to nothing.
So let it run its course!
    [*He goes to the window.*]
See, it is night; and even in the castle
All is already quiet. – Servant, bring light!
    [*The* SERVANT, *who has entered during the preceding
    speeches and remained standing at a distance, but visibly
    moved, comes forward, with violent emotion, and throws
    himself down at the* DUKE's *feet.*]
And now you too? But yes, I know why *you*

Should wish for peace between me and the Emperor.
Poor fellow! In Carinthia he has
A plot of land, and fears that he will lose it
For being here with *me*. What, am I then
So poor I cannot recompense my servants?
Well! I will force no man. If you believe
That fortune has deserted me, then leave me.
Tonight you may undress me one last time,
And then be gone to join your Emperor –
Gordon, good night!
I hope that I shall have a long night's sleep,
For great has been the toil of these last days.
See it is not too early that they wake me!

> [*He retires, the* SERVANT *lighting the way.* SENI *follows them.* GORDON *remains standing in the darkness, following the* DUKE *with his gaze, until he has disappeared at the farthest end of the gallery; then he gives expression to his grief in gestures and leans sorrowfully against a column.*]

SCENE 6

[GORDON. BUTLER, *at first behind the scenes.*]

BUTLER: Stand and wait here, until I give the signal.
GORDON [*starting*]:
  Here, with the murderers already!
BUTLER: All
  The lights are out, and everyone asleep.
GORDON: What shall I do? Am I to try to save him?
  Shall I wake up the house, call out the guard?
BUTLER [*appearing at the back of the room*]:
  There is a light through there. That way leads to
  The Prince's bedroom.
GORDON: But should I not break
  The oath I swore the Emperor? And if he

Escapes and joins his forces to the foe,
Shall I not bring the fearful consequences
Upon my head?

BUTLER [*coming a little nearer*]: Listen! Who's there?

GORDON: Ah, better
To leave it to God's judgement. Who am I,
To take such mighty deeds upon myself?
I have not murdered him, if he should die,
But to have saved him, that would be *my* deed,
And I should have to bear the consequence.

BUTLER [*coming forward*]:
I know that voice.

GORDON: Ah, Butler!

BUTLER: It is Gordon.
What are you doing here? Did not the Duke
Release you till so late?

GORDON: Your hand is bandaged?

BUTLER: Yes, it is wounded. Like a madman did
That Illo fight, until at last we brought him to
The ground –

GORDON [*with a shudder*]: Then they are dead!

BUTLER: The deed is done.
– Is he in bed?

GORDON: Oh, Butler!

BUTLER [*urgently*]:   Is he? Speak!
What's happened cannot long remain a secret.

GORDON: He must *not* die. Not by your hand! See, heaven
Does not desire its service. It is wounded.

BUTLER: *My* hand will not be needed.

GORDON: Now the guilty
Are dead, will justice not be satisfied?
O let this be enough of sacrifice!

[SERVANT *approaches along the gallery, his finger on his lips
to command silence.*]

He sleeps! O do not murder holy sleep!

BUTLER: No, he shall die awake. [*He makes to go.*]
GORDON: His heart is still
  Attuned to earthly matters, he is not
  Yet fit to meet his Maker face to face!
BUTLER: God will have mercy! [*He makes to go.*]
GORDON [*holding him back*]:   Grant him this one night!
BUTLER: At any moment we can be betrayed.
    [*He attempts to leave.*]
GORDON [*holding him back*]:
  Grant but one hour!
BUTLER: Will you let go! What can
  So short a stay be good to him?
GORDON: O, time
  Works wonders, like a god. In one brief hour run
  So many thousand grains of sand, and swift
  As they the thoughts within men's minds may turn.
  A single hour! Your heart may yet be moved,
  His too – some news may come – or heaven may send
  Some happy turn of fortune for his rescue. –
  What may not happen in an hour!
BUTLER: You but remind me
  How precious every minute is. [*He stamps on the floor.*]

SCENE 7

[*Enter* MACDONALD *and* DEVEREUX *with halberds.
Later the* SERVANT.]

GORDON [*throwing himself between* BUTLER *and the two*]:
                                    No, monster!
  Your way to him lies over my dead body,
  For I will never live to see this horror.
BUTLER [*pushing him away*]:
  Fool, are you in your dotage?
    [*Trumpets are heard in the distance.*]

MACDONALD *and* DEVEREUX: Swedish trumpets!
  The Swedes approaching Eger! We must hurry!
GORDON: O God in Heaven!
BUTLER: Commandant, to your post!
  [GORDON *rushes off.*]
SERVANT [*hurrying in*]:
  Who's shouting here? His highness is asleep!
DEVEREUX [*in a loud and terrifying voice*]:
  My friend, now is the time to shout!
SERVANT [*screams out*]:   Help! Murder!
BUTLER: Down with him!
SERVANT [*run through by* DEVEREUX, *falls at the entrance to the*
    gallery]:   Mary and Jesus!
    [*They stride over the corpse and up the gallery. In the distance
    is heard the noise of two doors being broken down one after the
    other – muffled voices – the clash of weapons – then suddenly,
    profound silence.*]

SCENE 8

[*Enter* COUNTESS TERZKY, *with a light.*]

COUNTESS: Her room is empty, she herself is nowhere
  To be discovered, Neubrunn is gone too,
  Who was beside her – Has she run away?
  Where can she have escaped to? We must haste
  And hurry after her, set all astir!
  How will the Duke receive such fearful news
  As this! – If but my husband were returned
  From feasting! Might the Duke be still awake?
  I thought I could hear voices here and footsteps.
  Yes, I will go and listen at the door.
  But hark! Who is it, running up the stairs?

SCENE 9

[Enter GORDON, *then* BUTLER.*]*

GORDON [*rushes in, breathless*]:
    You were mistaken – it was not the Swedes.
    You are to go no further – Butler – Heaven!
    Where is he?
    [*Noticing the* COUNTESS] Countess, tell me –
COUNTESS: You're from the castle? Is my husband there?
GORDON [*in horror*]:
    Your husband – O you must not ask! Go to
    Your room – [*He is about to go.*]
COUNTESS [*holding him back*]: No, not before you tell me –
GORDON: Upon this moment's thread the world is hanging!
    Go, in the name of God – While we
    Are talking here – O God in Heaven!
                    [*Crying aloud*] Butler! Butler!
COUNTESS: But he is in the castle with my husband.
    [BUTLER *emerges from the gallery.*]
GORDON [*seeing him*]:
    You were mistaken – it was not the Swedes –
    It was the Emperor's troops, and they are here –
    The lieutenant-general sends me, he himself
    Will be here in the instant – Go no further –
BUTLER: He comes too late.
GORDON [*collapsing against the wall*]: O God, O God of mercy!
COUNTESS [*apprehensively*]:
    What is too late? Who will be here himself
    This instant? Not Octavio? In Eger?
    Betrayed, betrayed! Where is the Duke?

SCENE 10

[*Enter* SENI, *then a* PAGE, *a* LADY-IN-WAITING, *the*
BURGOMASTER. SERVANTS *run in terror across the*
stage.]

SENI [*coming from the gallery, with every sign of terror*]:
  O bloody deed, O deed of horror!
COUNTESS: What
  Has happened, Seni?
PAGE [*emerging*]:   Sight to stir all hearts to pity!
  [SERVANTS *with torches.*]
COUNTESS: What is it, in God's name?
SENI: Do you still ask?
  The Prince lies murdered there within, your husband
  Is butchered at the castle.
  [*The* COUNTESS *stands transfixed.*]
LADY-IN-WAITING [*rushing on*]:
  Help! Help, the Duchess!
BURGOMASTER [*enters, horrified*]: What is this, what cries
  Of grief awake the sleepers of this house?
GORDON: Accursed is your house, and for all time!
  Within your house's walls the Prince lies murdered.
BURGOMASTER: In God's name, no! [*Rushes off.*]
FIRST SERVANT: Flee, flee, or they will murder
  Us all!
SECOND SERVANT [*carrying silver*]:
           This way! The corridors below are full of men!
VOICES BEHIND THE SCENES: Make way! Make way for the
       Lieutenant-General!
       [*At these words the* COUNTESS *recovers from her trance,*
       regains her composure and hurries off.]
VOICES: Man all the gates, and hold the people back!

SCENE II

[*Enter* OCTAVIO PICCOLOMINI *with retinue. At the same time* DEVEREUX *and* MACDONALD *emerge from the background, with halberdiers.* WALLENSTEIN's *body is carried across the back of the stage in a red carpet.*]

OCTAVIO [*entering quickly*]:
　It cannot be! It could not happen! Butler!
　Gordon! I'll not believe it. Tell me no!

　　[GORDON, *without answering, motions behind him with his hand.* OCTAVIO *looks where he is pointing, and stands transfixed with horror.*]

DEVEREUX [*to* BUTLER]:
　Here is the Golden Fleece, the Prince's sword!

MACDONALD:　And will you have the chancery –

BUTLER [*pointing to* OCTAVIO]:　　　　　　　There stands
　The man who now alone gives orders here.

　　[DEVEREUX *and* MACDONALD *draw back respectfully; all quietly disappear, so that only* BUTLER, OCTAVIO *and* GORDON *are left on the stage.*]

OCTAVIO [*turning to* BUTLER]:
　Was this intended, Butler, when we parted?
　Merciful God! I raise my hand and swear
　That in this monstrous deed I bear no guilt.

BUTLER:　Your hands are clean, for it was mine you used
　To do it.

OCTAVIO:　Shameless villain! Must you thus
　Abuse the order that was given you,
　And with this loathsome bloody murder stain
　The sacred name of your Imperial master?

BUTLER [*unmoved*]:
　I executed the Imperial sentence.

OCTAVIO: O curse of kings, that to their every word
    Gives fearful life, and to the fleeting thought,
    That soon might be forgotten, straightway binds
    The deed that done can never be revoked!
    Must your obedience be so swift? Could you
    Not grant his mercy time to show itself?
    Time is man's angel – swiftly to append
    The deed of execution to the judgement,
    Is only meet for God immutable.

BUTLER: What is my crime, and why do you rebuke me?
    It is a good deed I have done the Empire,
    Released it from a fearsome enemy,
    And so I make my claim to be rewarded.
    The only difference between what *you*
    And *I* have done is this: you forged the bolt,
    I fired it. You sowed seeds of blood, and now
    You stand amazed, that blood has come to fruit.
    I always knew what I was doing, so
    The outcome cannot shock me or surprise me.
    Have you no other errand you would give me?
    For I am leaving straightway for Vienna,
    That I may lay my bloody sword before
    My Emperor's throne, and claim the recognition
    That swift and punctual obedience
    May rightfully demand of righteous judge. [*Exit.*]

SCENE 12

    [*Enter* COUNTESS TERZKY, *her features pale and
    contorted. Her speech is slow and feeble, without passion.*]

OCTAVIO [*going to meet her*]:
    O Countess Terzky, must it come to this?
    This is the luckless fruit of evil deeds.

COUNTESS: The issue of what *you* have done – The Duke

Is dead, my husband dead, the Duchess lies
Upon her death-bed, and my niece I know not where.
This house that once was glorious and mighty
Stands desolate, and through its open doors
The servants scurry forth to flee in terror.
I am the last to stay, I have locked up
The gates, and bring you here the keys.

OCTAVIO [*in deep grief*]:   O Countess,
My house stands too in desolation!

COUNTESS: Who
Is yet to die? Who yet must suffer outrage?
The Prince is dead, the Emperor's vengeance can
Be satisfied. But spare our faithful servants!
Let not their loyalty and love to us,
Through many years, now be accounted crime!
Fate came upon my brother with too swift
A stroke, he had no time to think of them.

OCTAVIO: No word of outrage or revenge, dear Countess!
The fearful debt is paid, the Emperor
Is reconciled, the daughter will inherit
Only her father's glory and renown.
The Empress honours your misfortune, opens
A mother's arms to you in sympathy.
And so you need not fear. Have confidence,
And throw yourself in hope and trust upon
The Emperor's mercy.

COUNTESS [*turning her gaze towards heaven*]:
                    I put my hope and trust
In a far greater Lord – where shall
His highness' body find its resting-place?
The Countess Wallenstein is laid at Gitschin,
She who first brought him his good fortune. There
In gratitude he hoped at last to sleep.
Grant him his wish, and let him lie beside her!
And let me ask you a like favour for

My husband's corpse. The Emperor now holds
Our castles, let us only be allowed
A single grave beside our ancestors.

OCTAVIO: You tremble, Countess — you turn pale — O
   heavens!
What is the meaning of these words you utter?

COUNTESS [*gathers her last strength and speaks with nobility and
   animation*]:
You must think better of me than that you believe
I should survive the ruin of our house.
We did not feel ourselves too mean to raise
Our hand and reach towards a kingly crown —
It could not be — But still our thoughts are kingly,
And we regard a free and gallant death
More highly than a life that's robbed of honour.
The poison I have —

OCTAVIO: Send for help!

COUNTESS: — It is too late.
In a few moments more, my fate will be
Accomplished. [*Exit.*]

GORDON: O this house of death and horror!

   [*A* COURIER *enters, bringing a letter.* GORDON *goes to meet
   him.*]

What do you bring? That is the Emperor's seal.

   [*He has read the address, and gives the letter to* OCTAVIO
   with an expression of reproach.]

To *Prince* Octavio Piccolomini.

   [OCTAVIO *starts in horror and looks sorrowfully up to heaven.
   The curtain falls.*]

READ MORE IN PENGUIN

In every corner of the world, on every subject under the sun, Penguin represents quality and variety – the very best in publishing today.

For complete information about books available from Penguin – including Puffins, Penguin Classics and Arkana – and how to order them, write to us at the appropriate address below. Please note that for copyright reasons the selection of books varies from country to country.

In the United Kingdom: Please write to *Dept. EP, Penguin Books Ltd, Bath Road, Harmondsworth, West Drayton, Middlesex UB7 0DA*

In the United States: Please write to *Consumer Sales, Penguin Putnam Inc., P.O. Box 12289 Dept. B, Newark, New Jersey 07101-5289*. VISA and MasterCard holders call 1-800-788-6262 to order Penguin titles

In Canada: Please write to *Penguin Books Canada Ltd, 10 Alcorn Avenue, Suite 300, Toronto, Ontario M4V 3B2*

In Australia: Please write to *Penguin Books Australia Ltd, P.O. Box 257, Ringwood, Victoria 3134*

In New Zealand: Please write to *Penguin Books (NZ) Ltd, Private Bag 102902, North Shore Mail Centre, Auckland 10*

In India: Please write to *Penguin Books India Pvt Ltd, 11 Community Centre, Panchsheel Park, New Delhi 110017*

In the Netherlands: Please write to *Penguin Books Netherlands bv, Postbus 3507, NL-1001 AH Amsterdam*

In Germany: Please write to *Penguin Books Deutschland GmbH, Metzlerstrasse 26, 60594 Frankfurt am Main*

In Spain: Please write to *Penguin Books S. A., Bravo Murillo 19, 1° B, 28015 Madrid*

In Italy: Please write to *Penguin Italia s.r.l., Via Benedetto Croce 2, 20094 Corsico, Milano*

In France: Please write to *Penguin France, Le Carré Wilson, 62 rue Benjamin Baillaud, 31500 Toulouse*

In Japan: Please write to *Penguin Books Japan Ltd, Kaneko Building, 2-3-25 Koraku, Bunkyo-Ku, Tokyo 112*

In South Africa: Please write to *Penguin Books South Africa (Pty) Ltd, Private Bag X14, Parkview, 2122 Johannesburg*

PENGUIN AUDIOBOOKS

A Quality of Writing That Speaks for Itself

Penguin Books has always led the field in quality publishing. Now you can listen at leisure to your favourite books, read to you by familiar voices from radio, stage and screen. Penguin Audiobooks are produced to an excellent standard, and abridgements are always faithful to the original texts. From thrillers to classic literature, biography to humour, with a wealth of titles in between, Penguin Audiobooks offer you quality, entertainment and the chance to rediscover the pleasure of listening.

You can order Penguin Audiobooks through Penguin Direct by telephoning (0181) 899 4036. The lines are open 24 hours every day. Ask for Penguin Direct, quoting your credit card details.

A selection of Penguin Audiobooks, published or forthcoming:

Emma by Jane Austen, read by Fiona Shaw

Pride and Prejudice by Jane Austen, read by Joanna David

Beowulf translated by Michael Alexander, read by David Rintoul

Agnes Grey by Anne Brontë, read by Juliet Stevenson

Jane Eyre by Charlotte Brontë, read by Juliet Stevenson

Wuthering Heights by Emily Brontë, read by Juliet Stevenson

The Pilgrim's Progress by John Bunyan, read by David Suchet

The Moonstone by Wilkie Collins, read by Michael Pennington, Terrence Hardiman and Carole Boyd

Nostromo by Joseph Conrad, read by Michael Pennington

Tales from the Thousand and One Nights, read by Souad Faress and Raad Rawi

Robinson Crusoe by Daniel Defoe, read by Tom Baker

David Copperfield by Charles Dickens, read by Nathaniel Parker

Little Dorrit by Charles Dickens, read by Anton Lesser

Barnaby Rudge by Charles Dickens, read by Richard Pasco

The Adventures of Sherlock Holmes volumes 1–3 by Sir Arthur Conan Doyle, read by Douglas Wilmer

PENGUIN AUDIOBOOKS

The Man in the Iron Mask by Alexandre Dumas, read by Simon Ward

Adam Bede by George Eliot, read by Paul Copley

Joseph Andrews by Henry Fielding, read by Sean Barrett

The Great Gatsby by F. Scott Fitzgerald, read by Marcus D'Amico

North and South by Elizabeth Gaskell, read by Diana Quick

The Diary of a Nobody by George Grossmith, read by Terrence Hardiman

Jude the Obscure by Thomas Hardy, read by Samuel West

The Go-Between by L. P. Hartley, read by Tony Britton

Les Misérables by Victor Hugo, read by Nigel Anthony

A Passage to India by E. M. Forster, read by Tim Pigott-Smith

The Odyssey by Homer, read by Alex Jennings

The Portrait of a Lady by Henry James, read by Claire Bloom

On the Road by Jack Kerouac, read by David Carradine

Women in Love by D. H. Lawrence, read by Michael Maloney

Nineteen Eighty-Four by George Orwell, read by Timothy West

Ivanhoe by Sir Walter Scott, read by Ciaran Hinds

Frankenstein by Mary Shelley, read by Richard Pasco

Of Mice and Men by John Steinbeck, read by Gary Sinise

Dracula by Bram Stoker, read by Richard E. Grant

Gulliver's Travels by Jonathan Swift, read by Hugh Laurie

Vanity Fair by William Makepeace Thackeray, read by Robert Hardy

War and Peace by Leo Tolstoy, read by Bill Nighy

Barchester Towers by Anthony Trollope, read by David Timson

Tao Te Ching by Lao Tzu, read by Carole Boyd and John Rowe

Ethan Frome by Edith Wharton, read by Nathan Osgood

The Picture of Dorian Gray by Oscar Wilde, read by John Moffatt

Orlando by Virginia Woolf, read by Tilda Swinton

READ MORE IN PENGUIN

A CHOICE OF CLASSICS

Honoré de Balzac	**The Black Sheep**
	César Birotteau
	The Chouans
	Cousin Bette
	Cousin Pons
	Eugénie Grandet
	A Harlot High and Low
	History of the Thirteen
	Lost Illusions
	A Murky Business
	Old Goriot
	Selected Short Storie
	Ursule Mirouët
	The Wild Ass's Skin
J. A. Brillat-Savarin	**The Physiology of Taste**
Charles Baudelaire	**Baudelaire in English**
	Selected Poems
	Selected Writings on Art and Literature
Pierre Corneille	**The Cid/Cinna/The Theatrical Illusion**
Alphonse Daudet	**Letters from My Windmill**
Denis Diderot	**Jacques the Fatalist**
	The Nun
	Rameau's Nephew/D'Alembert's Dream
	Selected Writings on Art and Literature
Alexandre Dumas	**The Count of Monte Cristo**
	The Three Musketeers
Gustave Flaubert	**Bouvard and Pécuchet**
	Flaubert in Egypt
	Madame Bovary
	Salammbo
	Selected Letters
	Sentimental Education
	The Temptation of St Antony
	Three Tales
Victor Hugo	**Les Misérables**
	Notre-Dame of Paris
Laclos	**Les Liaisons Dangereuses**

READ MORE IN PENGUIN

A CHOICE OF CLASSICS

READ MORE IN PENGUIN

A CHOICE OF CLASSICS